FUNDAMENTALS OF DEMAND PLANNING & FORECASTING

By
Chaman L. Jain
St. John's University

Graceway Publishing Company, Inc.

BOOK EDITOR
Tita Young

GRAPHIC DESIGNER
Judy Chan

Manufactured in the United States of America
Library of Congress Control Card Number: 2020905923
ISBN: 978-0-9839413-9-2
(Softcover)

1st Edition 2012
2nd Edition 2015
3rd Edition 2017
3rd Edition, 2nd Printing 2019
3rd Edition, 3rd Printing 2020

Published by:
Graceway Publishing Company, Inc.
350 Northern Boulevard
Great Neck, New York 11021 U.S.A.
+1.516.504.7576
info@ibf.org
www.ibf.org

FOREWORD

For decades, supply chain management focused only on supply planning and execution. Once a sales representative told me, "You don't plan demand, it either happens or it doesn't." This attitude was dominant among those responsible for demand planning and forecasting. Then, in the early 1990s things began to change. Globalization of the economy led to ever-changing demand patterns and volumes. Customers became increasingly more demanding and competition grew, leading to more emphasis on cost reductions and cash flow management.

These "new world" events led to firms taking a closer look at their supply chain planning processes, and most concluded they needed more emphasis on the "Fundamentals of Demand Planning and Forecasting." No longer can firms expect to achieve acceptable performance with only a supply side view of their operations. The author of this book provides a roadmap to best practices in demand planning and forecasting.

WHAT YOU DON'T KNOW

Former U.S. Secretary of Defense Donald Rumsfeld once said, "Sometimes you don't know what you don't know" when asked why the United States had not chosen a certain course of action. The same is true in supply chain management. The fundamentals and forecasting process sections of this book will help the reader gain an understanding on what is forecasting and demand planning, why we need it, and how will it help to improve the bottom-line. The placement of demand planning in the supply chain management framework and how key planning processes must be integrated to achieve desired results is also discussed in the book. Additionally, the roles and responsibilities of people, process, and technology, supplemented with real-world examples, are clearly defined. Once these fundamentals are understood, the reader will be better positioned to learn more advanced aspects of demand planning and forecasting.

BALANCING DEMAND WITH SUPPLY

While the focus of this book is demand planning and forecasting, the importance of using demand plans to drive supply decisions is also discussed. Sales and Operations Planning (S&OP) is explained in detail and case studies are used to ensure its practical application is understood. The importance of leveraging customer and supplier relationships and collaboration to improve demand numbers is discussed in detail. Alignment of the demand and forecasting process with the supply side configuration at both the tactical and operational level is well covered. With this knowledge, the forecasting and planning practitioners will be better equipped to contribute to improved supply chain and demand planning.

THE TOOLBOX

Forecasting is part art and part science. To achieve best results, those involved must know and understand the various quantitative models available and when to use them. For example, many firms apply moving average models to seasonal and trending data leading to high forecast errors and loss of confidence in the demand planning process. The book provides an in-depth knowledge of all basic forecasting models including Time Series and Cause-and-Effect approaches. Examples and case studies are used to ensure the practitioner gains insight on their practical application, and becomes capable of selecting the best model for their scenario.

In addition, the reader will learn advanced models required for complex situations where data patterns are highly complex and more sophisticated tools are required. For example, an in-depth look at multiple regression models which use independent variables like leading indicators to improve the forecast. If structured properly these models can predict upturns or downturns in business months before they take place. Non-technical, process focused discussions and examples are included for those who are interested in the concepts, but will not be forecasting. The book includes a detailed description of the modeling process itself to help the reader make the right choices. When it comes to quantitative forecasting, it is not only important to do things right, but also to do the right things.

THE ENABLERS

Once the best demand planning and forecasting process is developed, it must be implemented and performance managed. The book addresses the use of performance metrics to improve the process leading to better forecasts. The use of reports to evaluate the process and the correct approach to communicating results are also included. Above all, the author uses a unique approach to learning by introducing the concept of "Worst Practices" in the demand planning area. For example, is a business plan forecast that is only updated once a year the best period forecast? Of course, the answer is no, but many firms drive their operations with such numbers.

The forecasting software is an important enabler, but it is not the process. The discussion in the book is designed to provide a clear path to selection and use of the system. It provides details to guide the development of the firm's requirements for demand planning and forecasting. Business needs, not the vendor's software design, should drive the system selection and implementation process. The reader will learn which system architecture components are important and why. Poor selection of software and/or failure to properly configure the process and system to meet business requirements has been a major source of dissatisfaction in past implementations. The section on that will help firms to avoid or correct these mistakes.

THE FUTURE

The book also presents future trends in demand planning and forecasting. Global expansion and increasing volatility in demand are leading to more emphasis on collaboration between trading partners, using such things as real-time exception management, central data repositories, and advanced statistics. Firms that lead in implementing these tools and techniques will gain a competitive advantage over their rivals.

WHY THIS BOOK?

Demand planning and forecasting is not a luxury for a select few. Globalization, advancing technology, and increasing competition dictate that all key stakeholders in the business understand and participate as appropriate in the process. The purpose of this book is to present the "Fundamentals of Demand Planning and Forecasting" to all in the firm who want to learn how to develop accurate forecasts, communicate them to decision makers, and use the output to gain a competitive advantage. The book is a must read for all involved in operations management and supply chain planning and execution.

Alan Milliken CFPIM CSCP CPF CS&OP
Six Sigma Green Belt
Master Instructor
Senior Manager GSB/SC, Supply Chain Capability Development
BASF Group

PREFACE

This book is written with beginners in mind, particularly those who have just entered the field of demand planning and forecasting, or want to know more about it. It covers practically every aspect of demand planning and forecasting except new product forecasting, which requires a volume of its own. It is written in a simple language so that a person with little or no knowledge about the field and/or statistics can follow it. Although the book is written for beginners, persons in the field may also find it helpful. Also, it is the official publication of the Institute of Business Forecasting & Planning (IBF) for its certification program, and covers material for the preparation of both CPF and ACPF exams.

The book is the result of decades of experience in demand planning and forecasting as a researcher, practitioner, and academician. Along the way I learned a great deal from various individuals to whom I am immensely grateful. I am grateful to Alan Milliken, Master Instructor, Senior Manager GSB/ Supply Chain Capability Development, BASF Group, who taught me not only how demand planning works in the real world but also what kinds of exceptions to look for and how to deal with them. Tom Wallace, researcher, lecturer, and consultant, and Larry Lapide, a Research Affiliate at MIT, lecturer, and consultant, showed me why S&OP is important and how to implement it effectively. Richard Herrin, Director of Supply Chain Management at Axiall Corporation, has taught on which products to concentrate for best utilization of our limited forecasting resources. Michael Gilliland, Product Marketing Manager at SAS Institute, invented the tool of Forecast Value Added (FVA) to improve forecasts with minimum efforts. I owe a great debt to George C. S. Wang, an independent consultant, for providing me a deep insight into Regression and Box-Jenkins modeling. My gratitude also goes to Charles W. Chase, Jr., Chief Industry Consultant in Manufacturing & Supply Chain Global Practices at SAS Institute Inc., for helping me in understanding various concepts and practices in demand planning and forecasting. I am also thankful to numerous speakers at the forecasting conferences sponsored by the Institute of Business Forecasting and Planning (IBF) over the last 20 years who provided me a great insight into various issues of demand planning and forecasting. Above all, I am indebted to all the authors of articles published in the *Journal of Business Forecasting* over the last 35 years or so who have a great influence on my understanding of the field.

I am also grateful to those who took time from their busy schedule to review some of the chapters—Fred Andres, an Independent Consultant; Joseph C. Andraski, President & CEO, VICS; Sara Brumbaugh, President, Ceres Analytics; James Campbell, Professor, St. John's University; Thomas Chen, Professor, St. John's University; Mark Covas, Senior Director, Demand Planning, Johnson & Johnson; Craig Faulkner, S&OP Leader, W. L. Gore & Associates, Inc.; Richard

Gordon, former Director Analytics, Symphony IRI Group; John Hellriegel, Vice President of Demand Planning and Replenishment–North America, Estee Lauder; Richard Herrin, Director of Supply Chain Management, Axiall Corporation; Anish K. Jain, Managing Director, Institute of Business Forecasting and Planning; Ronald K. Ireland, a Managing Principal, Oliver Wight Americas; Martin Joseph, Managing Director, Rivershill Consultancy, Ltd.; Larry Lapide, a Research Affiliate at MIT, lecturer, and consultant; Mark Lawless, an IBF Consultant; Carlos Londono, Vice President, Global Supply Chain, O-I (Owens-Illinois, Inc.); Alan Milliken, Master Instructor, Senior Manager GSB/SC, Supply Chain Capability Development at BASF Group; Paula Natoli, Product Director, JDA Software; Jay Nearnberg, Former Global Head, Demand Planning and S&OP Excellence for the Novartis Consumer Health Division; Raja Vatti, Associate Professor, St. John's University; Robin Simon, President, SimonSez Consulting Corp. & IBF Consultant; Athanasios Vasilopoulos, Associate Professor, St. John's University; Tom Wallace, researcher, lecturer, and consultant; and George C. S. Wang, independent consultant.

There are some special people who played an important role in my life. I owe a great debt to the late Mr. Al Migliaro, my first boss, mentor, and friend, who introduced me, not only into the exciting field of business forecasting, but also showed me the power of numbers in making the right business decisions. I am also grateful to my wife, Usha R. Jain, for her moral support in completing this volume.

Finally, as Chief Editor of the IBF's flagship publication, Journal of Business Forecasting (JBF), it would be my pleasure to send you a complimentary copy of the latest issue. If interested, you can write me at the email address below.

Chaman L. Jain
Tobin College of Business
St. John's University
Jamaica, New York USA
E-mail: jainc@stjohns.edu

ABOUT THE AUTHOR

Chaman L. Jain is a Professor of Economics at St. John's University, and the editor of *Journal of Business Forecasting*. He has over 40 years of experience in demand planning and forecasting as a researcher, practitioner, and academician. His first stint with forecasting was in direct marketing; thereafter, he moved to demand planning and forecasting. He has written over 100 articles and has authored, co-authored, and edited seven books mostly in the area of demand planning and forecasting. In a consulting capacity, he has worked for a number of organizations including, Brown and Williamson, Hewlett Packard, Union Fidelity Life Insurance Company, Prince Manufacturing, CECO Doors, Taylor Made Golf, Bilgore Groves, Sweetheart Cup, Eastman Kodak, Jockey International, SABIC (Saudi Arabia), Saudi ARAMCO (Saudi Arabia), Al Nahdi Medical Co. (Saudi Arabia), DU-Emirates Integrated Telecommunications Co. (Dubai), and Symbios Consulting Group (Egypt). He is the recipient of 1994 award of "The Direct Marketing Educational Foundation" for his best paper. He has spoken on demand planning and forecasting at various conferences conducted by the Institute of Business Forecasting and Planning, Council of Supply Chain Management, John Galt Solutions, and SAS Institute.

PART I

FUNDAMENTALS

INTRODUCTION

In order to learn and understand any discipline, one needs to be well immersed in its fundamentals. Demand planning and forecasting is no exception. This part starts with what demand forecasting is, why we need it, and how it has evolved over the last two decades or so. It further explains the key fundamentals of demand planning and forecasting, which every forecaster needs to know. To have an effective demand planning process, we need to set business policies (rules) about profit objectives, pruning of products, allocation of products that are short in supply, handling of products that are difficult to forecast, customer service, etc. We also need a regular review process to monitor the performance of forecasts, inventory levels, customer service, and new products, as well as to compare forecasts with business plans. Finally, which data—shipment, demand, and POS (Point of Sale)—we use in demand planning also makes a difference. All these different aspects of demand planning and forecasting are discussed in detail in this part.

CHAPTER 1

FORECASTING: WHAT AND WHY

Demand forecasting plays a vital role in planning and execution. Every plan, whether it is of production, marketing, sales, or financial, is based on estimates of the future, which we call forecasts. If we know what happened in the past and why, we can then predict what is likely to happen in the future. With this information, we can somewhat alter the future to our own advantage.

It does not matter which industry you are in, whether your company manufactures products or offers services, whether your company is small or large, whether your forecasts turn out to be less accurate, you must have forecasts to plan. Of course, the more accurate the forecasts, the better would be the plans. Forecasts highlight opportunities and threats; tell us ahead of time which products are likely to grow and which ones may die; and which markets or channels of distribution are likely to expand and which ones may contract. Forecasts also help in establishing goals, and providing alerts about products and/or markets that require close monitoring and evaluation.

Forecasts are more useful if we get them early enough to react, instead of waiting until they would be more accurate. For Christmas, for example, retailers may need forecasts in March or April, and not later. Even a small business, like a deli shop, cannot operate without forecasts. To place an order for loaves of bread for the next day or next week, it needs a forecast now, not later, which in all honesty may very well be a wild guess. Problems facing different companies in different industries may be different, but the key issues are the same—balance supply and demand; lower inventory and stock-outs; reduce shrinkages and obsolescence; and improve customer service. Accurate and timely forecasts are critical to all these.

Forecasts play an important role in decision making, but they are just an input and not a decision. Decision makers often know much more than what is reflected in forecasts, and thus they are not a substitute for good managerial judgment.

TYPES OF FORECAST

As shown in Figure 1.1, there are two kinds of forecasting: (1) micro and (2) macro. Micro forecasting deals with company-level forecasting such as the forecasting of sales, cash flow, and shipments. Often industry-level forecasting is also considered as a part of micro forecasting. Macro forecasting, on the other hand, deals with country-level forecasting such as forecasting gross domestic product, unemployment, and inflation rate. Global forecasting also is a part of macro forecasting.

Figure 1.1 | Types of Forecasts

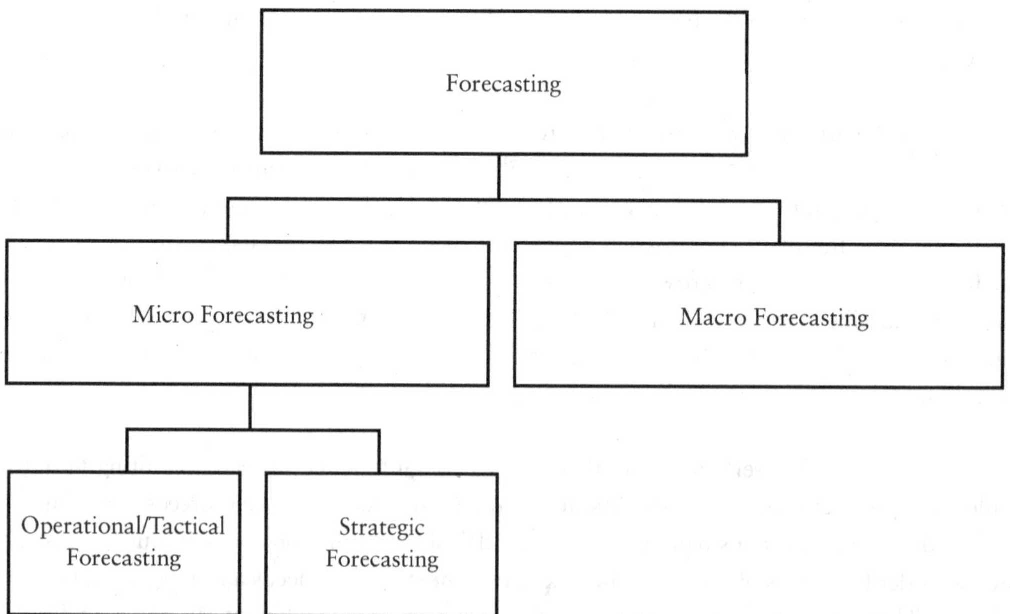

Micro forecasting can be further categorized into two: (1) Operational (also called tactical) forecasting and (2) strategic forecasting. Operational forecasting is short-term forecasting, whereas strategic forecasting is long-term forecasting, though there is no set time definition of how short is short and how long is long. This varies from company to company. Some companies regard forecasts of six months or less, operational, and over six months, strategic. Operational forecasts are mostly used for such things as production, procurement, logistic, and financial planning. Strategic forecasts, on the other hand, are mostly used for capacity planning, marketing strategy, new product planning, merger and acquisition, and allocation of resources. Industry forecasts are also a part of micro forecasting, which have more relevance for strategic planning than for operational planning.

FORECASTING: NOT ROCKET SCIENCE

Forecasting is not rocket science; a great deal of judgment goes into it. In the consensus perspective, it is an art, and in the creative sense, it is a science. Forecasts improve if errors are measured and quantified, and efforts are made to reduce them. Lack of a proper process for preparing and monitoring forecasts also contributes to errors. If we know the source of an error, we should be able find a way to reduce it. We may be using the wrong data—using shipment data for demand forecasting. Data may have a number of missing values, outliers (extreme values), and structural changes (permanent changes in the data pattern), all of which have to be taken care of before using a model. Further, each forecast is based on specific assumptions. If the assumptions are wrong, the forecasts would also be wrong. For example, we planned to spend \$10 million on advertisements but we spent only \$5 million; we planned to increase the price by 5 percent, but we increased it by 10 percent; and we planned to introduce five new products, but introduced only two. Model selection also makes a difference. Each dataset has a set pattern, and each model captures a set pattern. Error will result if the dataset and the forecasting model are not compatible. Error also results if there is no formal process in place for preparing forecasts. If forecasts are intuitively generated, it means there is no formal process. (We will discuss the role of process in forecasting, as well as how informed judgment adds to the accuracy in Part II.)

QUESTIONS FOR REVIEW

1. What is the difference between strategic and operational forecasts? Where is each one used? Give one example for each.
2. Do small businesses need forecasts? Why or why not?
3. What is the difference between micro and macro forecasting? Give one example of each.

4. Can we make a plan without a forecast? Explain.
5. Is forecasting rocket science? Explain.
6. Are industry forecasts part of micro or macro forecasting? Explain.
7. What do we mean by a forecast assumption? Can we prepare a forecast without an assumption? Explain.
8. What should be the proper role of a forecast in decision making? Explain.
9. Is global forecasting part of micro or macro forecasting? Explain.
10. How do forecasts highlight opportunities and threats? Explain.

CHAPTER 2

EVOLUTION IN FORECASTING

Forecasting has come a long way. In the Dark and Middle Ages of man's evolutionary march, prophets, seers, astrologers, and fortune-tellers were the main source of predictions. Prophets made prophecies when there would be famine, prosperity, rain, or war, because they had (or were believed to have had) a perfect vision about the future. Astrologers, seers, and fortune-tellers made predictions about business and personal lives of their patrons. Astrologers made predictions based on the movement of stars, the moon, and the sun. Fortune-tellers used and still use all the tricks of the trade. Some would tell the future by reading tea leaves and tarot cards, and others by the feel of vibration coming from a patron. All these have changed.

Now professional forecasters have assumed that role. Forecasts are based on hard facts, refined by statistical tools, and enhanced by informed judgment. Businesses no longer look at the hemline of girls' skirts to determine which way the stock market will go. The belief was if the hemline went up, so would the market. And, they no longer look at a groundhog to determine when the spring will arrive.

The business perception about forecasting has changed, and so have the processes, methodology, and technology to support it. The market dynamics have significantly changed, and so have the ways to deal with market changes. Above all, forecasting has gone through a series of name changes—from forecasting to business forecasting to sales forecasting to demand forecasting, and most recently to supply chain forecasting.

About three decades ago, companies that had a forecasting function were primarily public utility companies such as telecommunications, natural gas, and electricity. They had it because they were regulated. Rate hikes had to be justified to the Public Utility Commission with supporting forecast models. Some large companies had economists on staff, but they were mostly involved with macro forecasting. Now many companies in most industries have also created a forecasting function to improve their business plans and, consequently, their profit margin.

PERCEPTION ABOUT FORECASTING

It was not long ago when forecasting was viewed as a voodoo science. We used to hear: "We cannot forecast, only God can; so why bother." "Forecasting is only for big businesses, and not for us." "We don't need forecasting because our demand is always greater than supply." "How can a simple statistical model predict what is so complex and uncertain." "Statistical forecasts are not perfect because they are based on assumptions that are unrealistic." As such, businesses neither trusted forecasts nor used them. In 1981, I met one forecaster from a large corporation in one of the forecasting conferences and asked him how well his forecasts were used. His answer was: "I don't know. Every month I send my forecasts to various functions but I don't hear anything back from them." Business schools had forecasting courses but their emphasis was on business cycles and macro forecasting, and not on business forecasting.

Suppliers were reluctant to use Point-of-Sale (POS) data because in their mind, what mattered was not how much their customers sold to end consumers, but how much they would sell to their customers. Now, more and more suppliers recognize the importance of POS data in demand planning.

No doubt things have changed, considering where we were and where we are. More and more companies are beginning to see the need of forecasting. They are beginning to recognize how improvements in forecasts can reduce production, procurement, and logistic costs; cut down inventory, shrinkage, and obsolescence; and improve customer service. Although, at present, a number of companies have a forecasting function in place but their support from the top is still lukewarm at best. Top-management support is necessary not only for getting cooperation from other functions but also for obtaining resources to do the job. According to the 2009 survey conducted by the Institute of Business Forecasting and Planning, management of only 49 percent of the companies is highly supportive of the forecasting function.

In the academic arena, there are several business schools that now offer one or more courses on forecasting, but their emphasis is on modeling, and not on the forecasting process, which is as important, if not more so, than models. (For more detail, read Part II on Process.)

MARKET DYNAMICS

Over time market dynamics have changed, which have made the job of forecasting exceedingly difficult. Consumer behavior has changed and so have the business models to service them. The old philosophy of "stacking them high and watching them fly" no longer works. Up until the early 1980s, large manufacturing companies had a strong hold on their brands. They made what they thought would sell. If something was left over, marketing made it go away. As such, businesses focused on lowering costs by focusing on production efficiency and improving asset utilization.

Things have now dramatically changed. Consumers are now less loyal and more demanding. They have a practically zero level of tolerance. If you cannot provide what they want, someone else will. Competition has intensified. The number of products has exploded, the number of sales and distribution channels has proliferated, and the life span of products has shortened. With more and more aggressive advertisements, businesses are luring consumers away from their competitors. Globalization has further fueled the competition. Lead time has become longer as things are produced in one corner of the world and sold in another. Furthermore, larger and larger portions of sales are now coming from new products, which are difficult to forecast because of lack of history. The rise of multinational companies has further added complexity to the task of forecasting. Now forecasts have to be prepared, among other things, at regional and sub-regional levels.

Also, in the past, a number of industries, such as the fashion industry, ran mostly on the basis of make-to-order. Production started when majority of the orders was in. Core products were sold into the market months or even years ahead of actual need. In that business environment, there was no need for forecasting. Things have changed. Customers (retailers) now want to hold much less inventory and, at the same, don't have the patience to wait until products are manufactured and delivered.

FORECASTING STRATEGY

Changes in market dynamics have brought many changes in the forecasting strategy. To begin with, forecasting has become more demand driven and less supply driven. As such, companies are now focused more on what consumers are pulling (demand pull) and less on what suppliers are pushing out to customers (demand push). What matters in the end is not how much retailers are buying but how much the consumers are pulling. In the past, many manufacturers pushed their products to retailers by offering cash discounts and other incentives. These marketing programs caused retailers to stockpile inventories for future consumptions. As such, manufacturers did not need much expertise to forecast shipment to retailers. But when the market became more competitive and consumers began to demand more product choices at lower prices, retailers were forced to carry more alternatives at lower margins. This increased their cost of holding inventory. With that, they started thinking seriously about stockpiling even when the suppliers offered hefty discounts. Further, they stopped placing orders far in advance. At the same time, they started giving orders more frequently, but in less quantity. This also forced manufacturers to change their marketing strategy by shifting their marketing budget away from pushing products to retailers to directly driving consumer demand through increasing local and national advertisements.

To have more prudent inventory management, many companies with a goal to reduce inventory levels have moved toward SKU (item) rationalization—eliminating SKUs with low volume and/or low profit margins. With SKU rationalization, not only does inventory decrease but also forecasts get better for being forecasted at a higher level of aggregation. (For more detail, read Chapter 4.) Further, to reduce inventory risk and increase sales, some businesses have started updating forecasts more frequently—monthly (in some cases weekly) as opposed to quarterly and annually. They also have started monitoring forecasts more frequently so that they could respond to market changes quickly. According to the 2009 survey of the Institute of Business Forecasting and Planning, 69 percent of companies now monitor and revise forecasts once a month. Frequent revising and monitoring of forecasts enable companies to make changes to an already agreed-upon plan rather than to wait until it is too late. To reduce competition, companies are also moving toward consolidation through mergers and acquisitions.

Another new approach in forecasting strategy is lean forecasting (getting more with less forecasting resources). Companies are now paying more attention to products that are high in value and less to others. An excellent example of this is ABC classification used to distinguish products by sales frequency; products with an "A" classification are most valuable to the company, and those with "C" classification, the least. Products with "B" classification fall between the two. Some companies like Syngenta and Fiskars Brands have gone a step further by paying most attention to products that are not only high in value but also difficult to forecast. (For more detail, read Chapter 4)

PROCESS: FROM SILO TO COLLABORATION

Models are important and so is the process to prepare forecasts; after forecasts are generated, translate them into executable plans. Over the last three decades or so, the forecasting process has evolved from Silo to Consensus Forecasting to Sales & Operations Planning (S&OP) to

Collaborative Planning, Forecasting and Replenishment (CPFR®). In a silo structure, each function within an enterprise works virtually as a separate entity. Each function prepares its own forecasts, mostly based on gut-feelings, to develop its own plans. The end result was quite chaotic; different functions produced different forecast numbers. Sales had its own numbers, so did Marketing, Production, and Finance. Since no one was accountable and no one was watching the numbers, forecasts never improved. Furthermore, with multiple forecasts it was virtually impossible to align supply with demand, because each plan was based on a different set of numbers—e.g., the production plan was based on one set of numbers and the sales plan on another. This led to the development of Consensus Forecasting, where all the functions work together to arrive at a single set of forecasts. Here, the forecaster prepares statistical forecasts based on the input received from different functions, and then presents them at a consensus meeting to arrive at a consensus. In this meeting, where necessary, they collectively overlay judgment over statistical forecasts. Judgmental overlay generally improves forecasts because it accounts for information that has a bearing on forecasts but cannot be quantified and/or for information that was not available at the time forecasts were prepared.

Consensus Forecasting improved forecasts but often lacked the ability to implement the policy in a timely manner. If, for example, the expected demand exceeds the supply, the company may have to put on a second shift or outsource it. But such a decision can be made only by high-ranking executives, such as the Executive Vice President of Marketing, Executive Vice President of Supply Chain, and/or Executive Vice President of Finance, who were often not a part of the process. When the high-ranking executive(s) had a chance to go over the proposal made by the Consensus Forecasting team and was ready to take the action, it was often too late. To overcome this problem, the Sales and Operations Planning (S&OP) process was born. In this process, Demand Planners prepare demand forecasts through a consensus process and then send them to Supply Planners. Then Demand Planners and Supply Planners along with other functions meet in a Pre-Executive meeting to see if the expected demand can be met; if not, what options they have to resolve it. After that, they present their proposal at the Executive S&OP meeting, which is attended by high-ranking executives who have the power to make decisions. The committee reviews the issues and recommendations and then makes decisions. Once decisions are made, they are immediately implemented. All these activities occur in a monthly cycle. Since the S&OP process is highly structured, high-ranking executives participate in the process, and forecasts are highly scrutinized, forecasts tend to improve even further. Not only that, it brings all the functions closer. This has made people from the commercial side (Sales and Marketing) of the business and the operations side (Production, Distribution, and Purchasing) equal partners, thereby enabling them to work together as a team instead of working against each other.

Forecasts would improve even further if manufacturers (suppliers) have access to the consumption (POS) data and inventory level of their customers, as well as their business plans. This led to the development of Collaborative Planning, Forecasting and Replenishment (CPFR®). With that, forecasts as well as plans improved even further. As can be seen, all these initiatives are based on one important element: Collaboration. The Consensus Forecasting and S&OP are based on collaboration within an organization, whereas, CPFR® is based on collaboration with customers. (For more detail, read Part II on "Process.")

DATA

The effective usage of data in forecasting also has evolved over time—from shipment to demand (customer orders) to POS. Early on, manufacturers relied on shipment forecasts for their production and other plans. But shipment forecasts provide neither a true handle on customer demand (orders placed by customers) nor on consumer demand. Sometime ago, a manufacturer of steel doors was forecasting using shipment data. There were about 12 key manufacturers in the market. All of a sudden one of the manufacturers went out of business; as a result, the company started receiving many more orders, making it difficult to fulfill them on time. If an order came in that could not be fulfilled, the salesperson did not accept it, nor did it keep any record of such orders. Since the company was forecasting shipment and not demand, it took three months before it realized what was happening in the market. Had the unfulfilled orders been recorded, the company would have learned about the market change much earlier and done something to capitalize on this opportunity. The shipment forecast is a forecast of what would be shipped, and not of how many orders would be received from customers.

Realizing the problem with shipment forecasts, companies started forecasting demand, that is, how much would be demanded by customers, and used that data for developing their production and other plans. Recently, manufacturers realized even customer demand is not enough to get a true handle on market demand. What matters most is the consumer demand (demand of ultimate buyers). With the result, they started using POS data in their forecasting efforts. Since POS data are more stable than customer demand data and shipment data, forecasts based on them will be more accurate. Although there are some manufacturers that still use shipment data for forecasting, the trend toward the use of customer demand data and POS data is increasing. (For more detail, read Chapter 5.) Shipment forecasts also are needed, but their forecasts will be more accurate if they are based on customer demand data and POS data.

FORECAST MODELS

The forecasting models have also changed over time and so have their uses in business. In modeling we are seeing two major changes: One, some statistical models have been modified for forecasting purposes. For example, moving averages and exponential smoothing models did not originate as forecasting models; instead they were for smoothing the data. With some alterations, they are now used for forecasting. Not only that, exponential smoothing models have been greatly expanded over time. Volumes and volumes of books have been written on them. They are now used to capture trend and seasonality in the data, among other things. Bob Brown did the pioneering work in this area and took the simple exponential smoothing to the next level. Not only that, in 1960s and 1970s he showed how to use these models for managing inventory. Two, a number of new forecasting models have emerged over time. Box-Jenkins, a time series model, came out in 1970. The artificial Neural Networks, Cause-and-Effect models, though dating back to 1943, were not used in business until very recently. Croston is another model that came out in 1972 for preparing forecasts of data with intermittent (sporadic) demand.

The uses of models for forecasting in business also have changed, progressing from judgment-based qualitative models to fact-based quantitative models. Although currently a large number of companies still use Time Series models, where forecasts are prepared by extrapolating the past data using one technique or another, the use of Cause-and-Effect models, particularly, Regression, is growing. In Cause-and-Effect models, the relationship is developed between the cause (say, price) and the effect (say, sales), which is then used to prepare a forecast. (For more detail, read Chapters 22 & 23.)

FROM MACRO TO MICRO FORECASTING

Over time, we are also observing a shift in business practices from the use of macro to micro forecasting. For the most part, businesses believe that macro forecasts are not adding much value. In the past, business economists prepared macro forecasts and then determined their effect on business, which management felt was not helping much in its decision making.

As described earlier, micro forecasts are divided into operational and strategic forecasts. Between the two, the ones that are used in tactical planning are operational forecasts. They are used in inventory management as well as in sales, marketing, and financial planning, where they add quite a value to the business. Inventory is a big cost in many businesses. Operational forecasts help to manage inventory. The state of the economy has a role to play in business, but not in the short term (week to week or month to month) because during that time the economy does not change in a significant way. As such, it has little or no impact on operational forecasts and operational plans.

Macro forecasts play an important part in strategic planning, but between strategic and operational planning, the latter is currently getting the most attention. It is the operational forecasts that are constantly watched and manipulated to hit the strategic targets. Many companies including banks have significantly trimmed down their economic staff. The companies such as Chase Econometrics, Wharton Economic Forecasting Associates, and Data Resources, Inc., which were once the world's leading economic forecasting and consulting companies, now have merged into one (called IHS Global Insight) because of lack of demand for macro forecasts. Metropolitan Life Insurance Company, which in 1990s had an economic division with a full-time staff of 42, closed this division.

PLACEMENT OF THE FORECASTING FUNCTION

No matter where you place the forecasting function, each department has a bias that can affect the forecasts. Therefore, the best thing is to have an independent forecasting department. Looking at the survey data of the Institute of Business Forecasting and Planning over the 10-year period from 2000 to 2009, we see two major changes.

1. The percentage of companies having their forecasting function in Marketing, Sales, and Finance has declined, though very sharply in the case of Finance; whereas Supply Chain has maintained its dominant position at 36%. This is because forecasts prepared in business are primarily operational, which are mostly used in the Supply Chain. During that time, the percentage of Marketing went down from 20 percent to 12 percent; of Sales, from 18 percent to 16.0 percent; and of Finance, from 14 percent to 8 percent.

2. There is an increasing trend toward having an independent forecasting department. (For more detail, see Chapter 6.)

TECHNOLOGICAL ADVANCES

Technology has played an important role in changing the way forecasting is done, and changes have been enabled by advancements in the following areas:

1. Data storage facility
2. Data retrieval

3. Computing power
4. Business analytics
5. Forecasting software and systems

Data storage facility: The developments of data marts and data warehouses have made it possible to access large amounts of data of all kinds, both within and outside the enterprise, including sales, production, and marketing data. Previously, these were not accessible because they were either stored in far-away places or in different formats or systems. The development of data marts and data warehouses has standardized the data as well as the format in which they are maintained. Plus, it is possible to store a huge amount of data in a centralized location at a very low cost. In 2008, Walmart's data warehouse system stored roughly 2.5 petabyte (1 petabyte = 1000 terabytes) of data on sales, inventory, forecasts, markdowns, returns, etc. Further, large retail chains like Walmart have consolidated all the data at one location at a regional or corporate headquarters. This has made the data more visible; plus much easier and quicker to access.

Data retrieval: For data to be useful, the forecaster must be able to retrieve it. The innovation of EDI (Electronic Data Interchange) has made it easier to retrieve data quickly and accurately at the touch of a button. This made it possible for manufacturers to access the consumption (POS) data of their products in different markets, enabling them to know how consumers are responding to their products as well as the products of their competitors so that they can react. Companies like Walmart and Target have developed their own private exchange to transmit data to their suppliers. As such, forecasters now have access to more data/information than ever before.

Computing power: The increase in computing power has also played an important role in bringing the forecasting function to the forefront, which it did in two ways: One, it improved the data processing capability, which is vital in forecasting. This enabled forecasters to prepare forecasts of thousands of items simultaneously. Two, it made it possible to use even the most complex models in a matter of seconds and minutes, something unheard of before. Models like Box-Jenkins, Regression, and Artificial Neural Networks would not have seen the light of the day, particularly in business, had the computing processing power not advanced as far as we see today.

Business analytics: Business analytics are all about gathering market intelligence from the data. Data add value when we turn them into information, information into action, and action into competitive advantage. The advancements in computer technology and development of software in the area have made it all possible. Demand planners can now analyze data at an extremely finite level (store, location, day, etc.) to gain understanding of true patterns of consumer demand. With statistical techniques and data mining software, they can find out which products are sold more in which region, season, and channel of distribution; how sensitive demand is with respect to price; how effective promotions are; which products are purchased together; which products are bought before, and which ones are bought after an event. One Midwest grocery chain discovered that when men bought diapers on Thursdays and Saturdays, they also bought beer. Walmart has discovered that it sells more beer when hurricane is expected. This kind of information helps not only in forecasting efforts but also in developing strategies to capitalize on them.

Forecasting software and systems: The development of forecasting software and systems, which started around 1985, has made it possible to generate forecasts of thousands of products at the click of a button. Also, it has enabled forecasters to concentrate more on improving forecasts and less on collecting and managing data and then using them to prepare forecasts. The forecasting software is a stand-alone package, which generates forecasts either by the model selected by the forecaster or by the expert system built into the software. (The expert system goes through various models embedded in a forecasting software package using the historical data, selects the one that yields the lowest forecast error, and then prepares a forecast with that model.)

The forecasting system does more than forecasting. It helps in gathering input from various functions such as Sales, Marketing, and Finance to prepare forecasts. Once forecasts are prepared, the system integrates them with the planning processes including master production scheduling and distribution requirements planning, as well as sales, market, and financial planning. There are many forecasting systems in the market today that facilitate forecasting processes including Consensus Forecasting, S&OP, and CPFR®. The vendors of the Enterprise Resource Planning (ERP) system, which was originally set up to minimize costs and inventory, are now beginning to add the forecasting functionality, including an expert system, the ability to override forecasts, and automatically force down aggregate level forecasts to a granular level such as category and SKU. Today, there are companies that use forecast systems instead of forecast packages simply because they allow, among other things, greater interoperability among various planning systems and more collaboration among demand forecasters and planners.

CAREER IN FORECASTING

We are also experiencing a big change in the professional career in business forecasting. About two decades ago, people were reluctant to move into the forecasting profession. Their fear was once they moved up to the position of Forecast Manager there would be nowhere to advance because no position existed beyond that rank. Now, more and more companies recognize the value of the forecasting function. As such, they have increased significantly their forecasting staff. Furthermore, in many companies the forecasting rank has been moved up from the Manager of

Forecasting/Demand Planning to the Director of Forecasting/Demand Planning to all the way to the Vice President of Forecasting/Demand Planning.

SUGGESTED READING

1. Chimerine, Lawrence. "The Changing Role of Economist in Planning." ***Journal of Business Forecasting.*** Spring 1988, pp. 2-7.
2. Lapide, Larry. "Developments in Forecasting from Ancients Greeks to Present." ***Journal of Business Forecasting.*** Fall 1997, p. 32.

QUESTIONS FOR REVIEW

1. In the last two decades or so, what kinds of technological developments have taken place that have contributed greatly in advancing the business forecasting discipline? Explain.
2. In what way does collaboration both within and outside the organization play a part in improving forecasts and planning? Explain.
3. Why has the use of macro forecasts in business declined in recent years?
4. Describe what kinds of advancements have taken place in the last three decades or so in forecasting models, and what contributed to those developments.
5. What kind of data do businesses need to respond effectively to consumer demand, and why?
6. Does it make a difference where we place the forecasting function within an enterprise, and why?
7. How do people view forecasting as a profession, now and before?
8. To hit the strategic targets, do we align strategic goals with operational forecasts or operational forecasts with strategic goals, and why?
9. Why did companies such as Chase Econometrics, Wharton Economic Forecasting Associates, and Data Resources, Inc., which were once the leaders in providing economic forecasts and consulting services, go out of business? Explain.
10. Explain in brief:
    a. Demand pull vs. demand push
    b. Enterprise resource planning
    c. Business analytics
    d. Forecasting software vs. forecasting system

CHAPTER 3

FUNDAMENTALS OF DEMAND FORECASTING AND SUPPLY PLANNING

To understand demand forecasting and planning, you need to know some fundamentals. The more you know, the better your forecasts and plans will be. In this chapter, we discuss the most important fundamentals of forecasting and planning.

FUNDAMENTALS OF DEMAND FORECASTING

Here is a cursory review of some of the fundamentals of demand forecasting, which every forecaster and demand planner should know.

Forecasting is neither a science nor an art, but a combination of both. It is not a science because quantitative (statistical) forecasting does not capture all the elements that have a bearing on demand forecasts. There are certain elements that have a bearing on the forecasts but their information was either not available at the time or they cannot be quantified. Hurricanes, earthquakes, riots, recalls, and competitive actions—they all have an impact on forecasts, but either they are not known at the time forecasts are prepared or their impact cannot be quantified. Also, it is not unusual for a forecaster to go over the computer print-out and find certain numbers don't make sense. They are either too low or too high. Based on judgment and experience, the forecaster intuitively raises some numbers, and lowers others, which is called managing the exceptions. In addition, many companies now hold a consensus meeting where various functions get together every month, review statistical forecasts (often called baseline forecasts), and then collectively overlay judgment over them. Businesses believe that the judgmental overlays combined with statistical forecasts tend to improve the quality of forecasts. In a recent telephone survey, when 10 forecasters of large corporations (including Coca Cola, SC Johnson, Polaroid, Con Edison, and AT&T) were asked whether the judgmental overlay over statistical forecasts improves forecasts, nine of them said yes. The one who was not certain said that his company overlays judgment over forecasts but never checked for improvement. So, forecasting is an art in a creative sense, but a science when comes to modeling the historical data.

Forecasts are always wrong. No one has a crystal ball. Nor do we have a perfect vision. So, it is almost impossible to have 100-percent accurate forecasts. Once in a blue moon we may hit the mark, but that does not happen every time. The objective of forecasting is not to eliminate the error but to minimize it. This raises a question: By how much should we minimize it? The answer, of course, is as much as we can. But, there is a limit because there is a cost of doing it. This raises another question: How much error can we tolerate? There are two ways of answering it. 1) It depends on the adjustment capability, that is, how quickly can we react to an error? The quicker we can react, the larger the error we can tolerate. If the lead time is, say, three months, and customer wants the delivery in two months, then we can not tolerate a large error. So, the shorter the lead time, the larger the error we can tolerate. 2) It depends on the cost of an error. The larger the cost, the smaller the error we can tolerate. The cost of an error for fashion products, for example, may be extremely high because of their short life cycle.

It is true, the more effort we make, the more we can improve forecasts. But there is a cost of doing so. Initially, it is easier to improve forecasts and the cost of doing it would be low. But as we try to improve further and further, it becomes more difficult and more costly. How far we should go depends on the incremental cost of doing it and the benefit resulting from it.

If forecasts are 100-percent accurate, demand forecasts may be equal to shipment forecasts. Demand represents orders received, irrespective of whether or not we can fulfill them. It is also called true demand or unconstrained demand. Shipment forecasts, on the other hand, are what would be required to ship. The demand forecasts can be equal to shipment forecasts provided we have adequate capacity and encounter no disruptions in the supply chain.

Demand forecasts are better than shipment forecasts. Both are important, though demand (order) forecasts are more important than shipment forecasts because they provide better information about the changing market dynamics, thereby, making it possible to react. Also, demand forecasts are generally more accurate than shipment forecasts because logistics can move around shipment dates, but the dates of demand are somewhat fixed. In addition, shipment forecasts based on demand forecasts are generally more accurate.

As mentioned before, both these forecasts are needed, though which ones are preferred varies. Finance prefers shipment forecasts to demand forecasts because they provide a better estimate of cash flow. Sales and Marketing prefer demand forecasts to shipment forecasts because they provide better information about customer needs.

Consumer-centric demand is better than customer-centric demand. Consumer-centric demand is the demand of end-users (consumers), and customer-centric demand is the demand of customers such as distributors and retailers. Between consumer-centric demand and customer-centric demand, the former is preferred because it is more stable, and thus more predictable. Plus, what matters most to manufacturers is not how much customers are ordering but how much consumers are buying. Very often manufacturers push their products to customers by offering all kinds of incentives to meet their targets, even when there is little or no change in the consumer demand. For that reason, it is not unusual for manufacturers to experience a low sale in the first and second months of a quarter, and high in the third month. This happens because often manufacturers try to meet their quarterly targets by pushing their products to customers by offering price discounts and other incentives. However, in the end, what matters is not what manufacturers sell to customers, but what consumers buy. When manufacturers artificially push their products to customers, it is called "demand push"; what consumers buy from customers is called "demand pull."

Demand for orders shipped directly to stores is generally more stable and thus more predictable than those shipped to customers' distribution centers. Demand for orders shipped directly to stores is more stable because their orders are pretty much based on the consumer demand, which is fairly stable. Orders coming from distribution centers depend, among other things, on the ordering policy of a company. Some distribution centers may not have any specific ordering policy—they may order more at one time and less at another time.

Forecast is not a goal, not a budget, and not a plan. Forecast is not a goal, because it is what we can realistically expect. A goal is what we would like to achieve. Forecast is not a budget either. Budget is also based on expectations, which may or may not be realized. Very often people regard a budget as a forecast, which is wrong. If a budget is a forecast, then why forecast? Forecast is not a plan either, because it is based on a plan. Each forecast is based on certain assumptions, which represent a plan. We plan to spend a certain amount on advertisements, introduce a certain number of new products, and charge a certain price for a product. These are all assumptions upon which the forecast is prepared. But they do interact. If a forecast does not meet the company's plan, demand planners may decide to change the plan, that is, they may increase the promotional spending, lower the price, or introduce more products. In this respect, forecasts drive the plan.

All variables are not equally forecastable. Some are easier to forecast than others. New, fashion, and high-tech products, products that are highly promoted, products with a shorter life cycle, and products having an intermittent (sporadic or lumpy) demand are generally more difficult to forecast. Products with a shorter life cycle are difficult to forecast because they shift from one phase of a cycle to the next very quickly. For instance, in one month they may be in the initial phase where sales are increasing, though slowly; in the next month, they may be in the second phase where sales are increasing at an increasing rate; and in the third month, they may be in the phase where sales are increasing at a decreasing rate. Since products with a shorter life span shift from one phase to the next very quickly, they are difficult to forecast. On the other hand, products with a longer life cycle do not shift quickly from one phase to another, and thus have a relatively more stable demand, making them easier to forecast.

Every function has its own bias. Some functions have an over-forecasting bias, while others have an under-forecasting bias, depending on how their performance is evaluated. If salespeople's performances are evaluated by their ability to reach or exceed sales quotas and quotas are tied to forecasts, they will have a tendency to under-forecast. Lower forecasts would mean lower sales quotas, which would be easier to hit. Otherwise, they would favor over-forecasts to make sure products are in stock when orders arrive. Finance people are generally conservative by nature. However, their perspective may change when they report to Wall Street. The bias of production people also depends on how they are evaluated. If they are evaluated on the basis of inventory, they would tend to under-forecast; and if on the basis of customer service, they would tend to over-forecast.

Forecast horizon (how far ahead to forecast) depends on the lead time. If your lead time is two months, you need to make a forecast at least two months ahead, because your production plan is locked in for those periods during which no change can be made. This does not mean that you should not make forecasts in monthly buckets, nor does it mean that forecasts should not be updated monthly. It simply means that you cannot make a change in the production plan during that time. The lead time depends not only on how much time you would need to produce but also on the lead time of your suppliers. If your lead time is two months, and the lead time of your suppliers is one month, then the total lead time would be three months. This is called cycle time.

Forecast horizon also depends on the decision you want to make. For strategic planning, for example, we will need long-term forecasts, and for them, the forecast horizon will be much longer than operational forecasts.

Different functions have different forecast requirements. Production people need forecasts for production planning. For that, they may need forecasts by plant, by month, in units, and at a SKU level. The logistics people need forecasts in cases by ship date. The main concern of Finance is cash flow; thus, they need forecasts at an aggregate level, in dollars, and by month. Between demand and shipment forecasts, finance people prefer shipments because they provide a better handle on the cash flow. Salespeople, on the other hand, prefer demand forecasts by category/brand, in both dollars and units, and in monthly buckets, as well as by customer, channel of distribution, and region. Marketing people prefer demand forecasts by category/brand, in monthly buckets, by region and channel of distribution, and in dollars and units. Furthermore, they may like to have a forecast of market share of different categories/brands. Therefore, if every function gets forecasts in a format it needs and when it needs, they are more likely to be used.

Variations in demand are caused partly by businesses themselves and partly by outside forces. Businesses create volatility in demand when they use all kinds of promotions to meet their quarterly and/or annual targets. To meet a quarterly target, a company may offer a special discount in the third month of a quarter. With that, their sales in the first two months of a quarter would be low, but high in the third month. The variations in demand are also caused by outside forces such as storms, riots, and competitive actions. Although a company has no control over the variations caused by outside forces, it can control to some extent the ones caused by its own actions, thereby making the demand more stable.

When are forecasts not needed? Forecasts are not needed if the future is expected to be the same as the past, you have enough time to react, forecasts will be the same as budget, and products are always made to order. The cycle time—the time you need to purchase raw material and manufacture a product—makes a difference. If your cycle time is shorter than the customer's cycle time (time given by the customer for delivery), you can react to the customer's order without any problem. Also, you can absorb a much larger error if your cycle time is shorter. If an order for a certain product comes in and you don't have it in stock, you can quickly manufacture and ship it. In some companies, management views budget as its forecast. In that case, there is no need to forecast.

Range forecasts provide insight to risks and opportunities. The range forecast is where you get two forecast numbers—low and high. The point forecast, on the other hand, gives only one number. The risk is high if there is a big gap between the low and high forecasts. If a product is high in revenue and profit margin but long in lead time, you may like to use the high limit of a forecast to determine inventory. If, on the other hand, a product is low in revenue and profit margin but short in lead time, you may like to use the lower limit of a forecast.

FUNDAMENTALS OF SUPPLY PLANNING

There are also some fundamentals of supply planning, which every forecaster and planner should know. Although forecasts are used in every aspect of business planning, operational forecasts are mostly used in production, procurement, and logistic planning (fashionably called supply chain planning). So, our emphasis here is on operational (tactical) forecasts and supply chain planning.

Forecasts drive the supply chain. All the plans inclusive of production, procurement, and logistics are based on forecasts. The more accurate the forecasts, the more effective will be the plans. With accurate forecasts, the costs of production, procurement, and logistics will go down, inventory will decline, and customer service will improve. Production costs will go down because of fewer switchovers; procurement costs will go down because of fewer last minute purchases; and logistics costs will go down because of a drop in the expediting cost.

If production people are evaluated by the level of inventory, the expediting cost may rise. In that case, they would try to maintain low inventory, thereby causing more stock-outs. Stock-outs usually increase expediting costs. This also may increase the cost of trans-shipments by encouraging production people to move products from one warehouse to another to meet their inventory targets.

Forecasts at a granular level are generally needed for short-term planning, not for strategic planning. In strategic planning, we plan for a longer period—for the next year or the next five to ten years. So, we need forecasts of overall volume, categories, and/or market share. For short-term (tactical/operational) planning such as for production planning, we need forecasts at the most granular level—SKU level, for example.

Forecasts based on the consumer demand dampen the bullwhip effect. The bullwhip effect occurs when a small change in the downstream demand near the end consumers causes a significant change in the upstream demand closer to the manufacturer. In other words, a small change in consumer demand causes a much greater change in the inventory of each participant in the supply chain, and the change becomes bigger and bigger as we move upstream, say, from inventory of finished goods to inventory of raw material. But consumer demand is more stable than customer demand, and thus forecasts based on the former are more accurate. With accurate forecasts, there will be fewer stock-outs and, consequently, less bullwhip-effect.

Safety stock is affected by the forecast horizon. The longer the forecast horizon, the more uncertain will be the forecasts. Uncertainty leads to more safety stocks.

Production capacity and demand forecasts are independent of each other. Production capacity tells us how much we can produce with our existing capacity, whereas demand forecasts tell us how much customers will be buying. In the long run, however, demand forecasts can affect the production capacity.

The effect on inventory value of products sold on consignment depends on how it is treated. Goods sold on consignment means that the customer agrees to pay when products are sold. If the manufacturer treats consignment as on-hand inventory instead of accounts receivable, then an increase in consignment will increase the inventory. Otherwise, it will decrease it.

The larger the inventory, the better will be the customer service. Generally speaking, it is true. But inventory alone is not enough; it has to be the right inventory at the right place to meet the customers' needs.

Demand variability affects inventory. The higher the variability in demand, the more difficult it is to forecast. To account for variability, the manufacturer has to either hold more inventories or reduce their lead times.

The further down the supply chain we forecast, the more difficult it becomes. Where there are multiple levels in the supply chain— distributor, sub-distributor, wholesaler, retailer, and end-consumers—it becomes less and less transparent how much the end-consumers are buying and how much each level of the supply chain is holding inventory. With the result, it becomes more difficult to forecast.

SUGGESTED READING

1. Chase Jr., Charles W. *Demand-Driven Forecasting: A Structured Approach to Forecasting.* New York: John Wiley & Sons. 2009.

2. Jain, Chaman L. and Thomas P. Chen. "The Role of Judgment in Business Forecasting." ***Industrial Management.*** November/December 1992, pp. 1-3.
3. Jain, Chaman L. "What's the Forecast?" ***APICS—The Information Advantage.*** October 2001, pp. 47-50.

QUESTIONS FOR REVIEW

1. What is the difference between "Demand Pull" and "Demand Push" strategies? Which one is better from a business perspective?
2. What is the difference between "Consumer-Centric Demand" and "Customer-Centric Demand?" Explain.
3. What is the "Bullwhip Effect?" What kind of problem does it create in forecasting? What is the best way to handle the "Bullwhip Effect?"
4. Which forecast should a company concentrate on—shipment or demand—, and why?
5. If a forecast does not meet the management goal, should we change the forecast or plan, and why?
6. If forecasts are used to set sales quotas, what kind of forecasts would you expect from salespeople—over- or under-forecasts? Why?
7. For which planning—strategic or operational—do we need forecasts on a more granular level? Explain.
8. On a make to order, do we need to prepare forecasts if the customer's cycle time is shorter than our replenishment cycle? Explain.
9. Is a forecast a goal, budget, or plan? Explain.
10. What is the difference between strategic forecasts and operational forecasts?

CHAPTER 4

DEMAND PLANNING

Demand planning is all about effectively managing and growing demand, which requires improving forecasts, reducing costs, minimizing risks, and increasing sales and profit. Forecasting is the key to demand management. The best data to use for managing demand are sales to end-consumers (often called Point-of-Sale or POS data); the next best, of course, is customer order (or warehouse withdrawal) data. Since demand drives planning, it is often called demand-driven planning.

DEMAND MANAGEMENT

To manage demand effectively and profitably, we have to manage:

1. Volume
2. Supply and demand
3. Product portfolio
4. Product mix
5. New product introductions
6. Products that are difficult to forecast
7. Communication
8. Performance

Volume: The most important part of managing demand is managing the volume to ensure that our operational forecasts are consistent with our strategic goals. Goals may be how much sales we would like to have, how much profit we would like to generate, and/or what our market share should be. To achieve these, we need to look very closely month-to-month (or week-to-week) at expected volumes to see whether they would be sufficient to hit the strategic targets; and if not, what course of action we can take.

Since we do not have perfect knowledge how our plans are related to strategic targets, we cannot directly align our plans with strategic targets. We know that changes in plans about media spending, pricing, introduction of new products and abandonment of old ones, and the like affect sales, but their exact relationships are not known. Strategic targets may be a year or a year and a half away. If we link our plans directly to our strategic targets, we will be operating in the dark until that time comes. At that time it would be too late to do anything about it. Therefore, the best strategy is to work through operational targets/plans. Here is a step-by-step procedure:

Step 1: Working with Brand (Marketing and Sales) and Finance as well as using the best judgment and experience, determine operational sales targets, that is, how much sales are needed month by month (or week by week) to hit the ultimate (strategic) target. Let's say we are in December. Our ultimate sales target for a certain product is $1 million for the next year. Based on judgment and experience, we determine we need sales of $100,000 in January, $125,000 in February, $140,000 in March, and so on to hit the ultimate target.

Step 2: Develop plans to hit operational sales targets of different months.

Step 3: At this point our immediate concern is of January. So, direct the plan toward the operational target of January, which is $100,000. Let us say that by the end of January we wind up with sales of $90,000, which means that we have to change the plans of future months, because what we did in January was not enough. We may have to spend more money on promotion, reduce prices further, and/or add more new products. We may not be able to change the plan for February because it takes time to implement, but for other months we can. Follow this process all the way through December.

This type of strategy will enable us not only to see how well we are progressing month by month toward our ultimate target, but also will allow us to make adjustments along the way. If we successfully hit our operational targets, chances are we would be able to hit our ultimate targets as well. For this strategy to work, strategic targets must be realistic, and not based on wishful thinking. Otherwise, it would be discouraging and demoralizing. In the end, we will fail to meet our strategic targets.

Supply and demand: Hitting just the operational demand forecast is not enough; we have to have the supply to meet the demand. Therefore, to manage demand we have to align supply with demand to maximize revenue/profit. If there is a gap, what options do we have to close it? If demand of a particular product is expected to be greater than supply, supply planners may have to add a second or third shift to expand production, or outsource it. If that does not work, demand planners may decide to reduce demand through demand shaping, that is, by cutting the promotion on a product that is short in supply and increasing promotion of substitute products. If these measures are not adequate, limited supply has to be allocated among different customers. If, on the other hand, supply is expected to be greater than demand, again demand shaping will be needed, though this time to increase demand through promotion, price management, timing of new product introductions, etc. In the worst case, it may decide to close the plant for a limited period of time, or build inventory for future use. If Dell Computer finds certain inventory is not moving, it offers a special discount on its website. Tupperware does the same. It sends an announcement by e-mail to its sales force about a special offer.

At times, it may be in our best interest to manage the demand of different customers and different products differently. At the time of allocation, when products are short in supply, it may be in our best interest to treat certain customers differently. We may decide to allocate more to large and long-term customers and less to others. When we have excess supply, we may decide to make some special deals with a few selected customers to get rid of it, and/or reduce price and increase media spending to boost its demand.

Further, if, at any given time, a customer orders certain products in a quantity that is significantly more than what was forecasted, it could be a problem. It could cause a disruption in production. But a decision has to be made whether or not to fulfill that order. For example, once a confectioner was asked to supply candy for World Youth Day in Canada. The celebration brought more than 200,000 young men and women to Canada. It won't be celebrated again for many years. One million pieces of candy was needed. The company had to decide which way to go. The upside was it would boost the sales and promote the company's name. The downside, of course, was it would disrupt production because it had to be re-planned. In any case, the sooner we decide, the more options and control we have over sales revenue, and manufacturing and transportation costs.

Product portfolio: This is another issue that has to be resolved for managing demand effectively. A garden looks beautiful as long as flowers, shrubs, and trees grow in an orderly fashion. But once you allow them to grow unplanned and unrestricted, the garden becomes a jungle. In the same vein, demand planners cannot allow products to grow in an unplanned way. So they need to prune them. There are two aspects of product portfolio management: (1) Product line management, and (2) SKU management. Certain product lines may have to be discontinued because they no longer fit in the company's strength and/or offer little or no opportunity in the future. Maybe the introduction of some new products by competitors has cannibalized their demand.

SKU reduction, often called SKU rationalization, is another part of portfolio management. More and more companies are now reducing the number of their SKUs to reduce costs and improve forecasts. The cutback in SKUs reduces costs because it reduces the cost of inventory, warehousing, and transportation. Forecasts improve as well because they will now be forecasted at a higher level of aggregation. Recently, Walmart, among other products, replaced Glad and Hefty bags with SC Johnson's Ziploc, and its own private label. According to John Fleming, Executive Vice President and Chief Merchandising Officer, Walmart in 2010 reduced SKUs by 10-15 percent. Kroger, one of the largest food stores in the United States, has already eliminated 30 percent of all SKUs in the breakfast cereal category. Recently, General Mills reduced the number of flavors of Hamburger Helper meals brand from 75 to just 30. Clorox has a cross functional SKU management process team, sponsored by the CFO, and led by the director of supply planning. This team meets every month to evaluate the performance of different SKUs to determine which ones to keep and which ones to let go.

Ultimately, profit is the main consideration in SKU rationalization. If a SKU is profitable after all the costs are factored in, it may not make sense to rationalize it. On the other hand, if a SKU does not meet the company's predetermined profitability threshold, then it becomes a candidate for rationalization. However, in some cases, a company may decide to keep a SKU even though it is not profitable because it drives the sales of complementary SKUs that are highly profitable.

Product mix: Once a company settles on a volume for the next month or next quarter, the question of product mix arises, that is, what kind of mix of different product lines is needed. This depends basically on two things: Seasonality and state of the economy. There are many products that are seasonal in nature; they are demanded more (and thus produced more) during the season and less in other times. Profit can also be the issue. The change in the mix can affect the overall profit. The state of the economy also makes a difference. During downturns there is generally less demand for premium products and more for low price alternatives. During the downturn of 2008-2009, companies like L'Oréal diverted their product mix more and more toward low-price alternatives such as hairspray, skincare, and men's care to reach a broader market.

New product introductions: For most companies new products are the engine of growth because they significantly increase both sales and profit. According to the 2009 survey of the Institute of Business Forecasting and Planning, about 18 percent of a company's sales come from new products. At the same time, risks are very high with new products, because a large percentage of them fail. Plus, they take resources away from other products. Therefore, there could be a problem if they are not properly managed.

There are two types of forecasts that are needed for a new product. One, what would be the overall sales over its life span? This is used to determine whether or not such a product should be introduced. Two, what would be the shape of its demand over time? In other words, how orders would be coming in over different phases of its life cycle. Normally, a product goes through five phases: Phase 1, introductory phase where sales increase though slightly; Phase 2, where sales increase at an increasing rate; Phase 3, where sales increase at a decreasing rate; Phase 4, where sales reach a peak and then start declining; and Phase 5, where the product becomes almost obsolete. Life spans of products are becoming shorter and shorter. Because of that, if a product is successful, we have to be sure there would be enough capacity available to meet the demand. Also, there have to be enough financial resources available to promote it further. In a recent survey by AMR (now Gartner) Research, 32 percent of the participants believe that the key reason a new product launch fails is that it reaches the market too late, followed by product price, quality, and not meeting customer needs.

To make sure that enough production capacity and financial resources are available, and that there is enough time to synchronize operational plans with the strategic ones, new products should be brought to the planning process as early as possible. P&G, for example, brings a new product to the planning process 12 to 18 months ahead of its launch.

Companies often start out a new product with a limited quantity, and then watch the market very closely, week by week and month by month. The objective here is to determine as quickly as possible whether or not the product will be successful. We cannot go on forever with wishful thinking. Based on past experience, we may be able to determine how many minimum weeks or months of sales data are needed to make that decision. Companies may use the Walmart test to determine the success of a new product, which is, if Walmart refuses to put a certain new product on its shelf, the product is less likely to succeed. This is purely because of its massive purchasing power. Recently, Clorox came out with a detergent as a new product, and Walmart refused to put it on its shelf.

The forecast of a new product is often made by using an analog, that is, by following the demand pattern of a similar product or a group of similar products introduced in the past. To manage the demand of a new product effectively after it is launched, it would be better to refit its actual demand data of certain periods with the pattern of the analog initially used, as well as with other similar products launched in the past. It is possible it may now fit better with other product(s).

If pre-orders of a new product are available, they can also be used to predict its demand. Pre-orders are the orders received before the product is launched. In the case of products such as DVDs and books, pre-orders are accepted.

Products that are difficult to forecast: There are many products that are difficult to forecast, including new products, products with intermittent demand, products with a short life cycle, products that are highly promoted, and products that are highly volatile. In the case of intermittent demand, orders come in sporadically. Orders may come in for one or two months, and then for next number of months there is no order. This is very true with products such as spare parts of a car.

Generally speaking, how well we can forecast depends on how volatile the data are. The more volatile the data, the more difficult they are to forecast. Some products are inherently volatile, and in others we create volatility through activities such as promotion and performance incentives. When a manufacturer offers a special discount to meet a quarterly or annual target, it increases the sales of that month, but, the sales of the following month will drop sharply. The minimum order policy also adds to volatility. The customer has to wait until it is ready to meet the minimum requirement. How the performance of salespeople and production people is evaluated also makes a difference. If the performance of salespeople is based on how well they meet their quotas and quotas are based on forecasts, they would create a downward bias in forecasts. Further, if in any quarter they have already met their quota, they would try to push the additional sales to the next quarter. Production people would have an upward bias if their performance is measured by customer service, and a downward bias, if measured by inventory levels. By taking corrective action we can reduce volatility, particularly that comes from our own action.

Another way to deal with products that are difficult to forecast is to plan their demand at a category/family level, without making a commitment to the product mix. Category-level information is communicated to production, but the item-level information is communicated only a few weeks before delivery.

Communication: Among all the stakeholders, communication is crucial for effective demand management. Without the input from salespeople, it would be difficult to correct the imbalance between supply and demand. At times, a salesperson may know that a large order will be coming in, though the exact date is uncertain. Demand planners need such information to factor it in their forecasts. Sometime salespeople are hesitant to communicate the bad news without realizing that giving the bad news early on is better than giving it late. If they expect a large order they should communicate it right away to demand planners along with the probability of getting it and expected date of delivery. Communication among other functions is also important. In 1998, Marketing at Volvo ran a special promotion to get rid of excess inventory of green cars, but they did not communicate this information to Production. This gave a signal to Production that green is the color of customer choice, and they increased the production of cars with that color.

Also, remember that communication is not a one-time thing; it is a continuous process. It is rare for a demand to be stable. Promotion plans may over- or under-achieve, product introductions may be postponed, competitors may change their strategy, and the economy may shift. All these will require a corrective action. Therefore, to manage demand in such an environment, good communication is essential.

Performance: To manage demand we have to monitor and manage performance. To do that, we need to establish key performance indicators (KPIs)—the ones we can quantify, measure, and monitor on a regular basis. Monitoring and managing performance should include:

1. **Reviewing forecast accuracy.** Which products are we forecasting well and which ones not? If a given product is not forecasted well, try to find out why. It may be because we used the wrong data, wrong model, and/or wrong assumptions. Or, the error resulted from the bias of one particular individual. If we know the cause, we may be able to correct it. The KPI here may be Mean Absolute Percentage Error (MAPE), Weighted Mean Absolute Percentage Error (WMAPE), and/or any other metric. (For more detail on forecasting error metrics, read Chapter 26.)

2. **Managing changes.** Before uploading forecasts for supply chain planning, review and discuss forecast changes proposed by Marketing, Sales, or by any other function. Those changes may have to be incorporated into the forecasts. While doing that, make sure all the changes and rationale behind them are documented and each change is monitored against the actual. You may find that changes made by one function tend to improve forecasts, while by another worsens them. Establish a threshold for forecast accuracy, that is, forecast

is acceptable as long as its accuracy is above 70 percent, or by any other number, which may vary from one brand to another. Flag SKUs/categories with accuracy below the threshold, investigate them, and then take the necessary action.

3. **Comparing forecasts to business plans and act.** The objective here is to see whether forecasts are consistent with our operational, strategic, and financial targets. If not, what options are available to make it happen?

4. **Reviewing customer service and inventory performance.** The objective here is to see if our customer service and inventory levels are on target. If not, identify what is causing the problem so that necessary action can be taken. The problem may very well be poor forecasts, disruptions in the supply chain, or demand is not properly managed. Whatever the reason may be, find the root cause.

5. **Tracking performance of new products.** It is important to track closely how new products are doing. Because of their shorter life span, it is important to capitalize on them if they are doing well. If not, you have to take them off the production line and get rid of their inventory.

All these reviews should be done on a monthly cycle; possibly as a part of the Sales and Operations Planning (S&OP) process, which we will discuss in Chapter 8.

BUSINESS POLICIES

To run demand planning effectively and efficiently, demand planners must have some policies (rules) in place for dealing with different issues. Otherwise, whenever an issue arises, we would wind up wasting lot of time going back and forth to have a resolution. Here are some of the policies that should be set.

Profit objectives: The business has to decide about profit objectives. Do we want to make profit on every product or maximize it in total? On new products, we may need time before they start generating profit. Some products may be complementary, which may yield profit collectively and not individually. Further, it is not unusual to have a product that is not profitable but does bring in a great deal of business from other products. Square D, a division of Schneider Electric, for example, at one time, wanted to discontinue E-Stop for diesel locomotives because of its poor performance, but decided against it because one customer that buys it also buys the breaker cells in large volume. E-stop type product was not available elsewhere. The company was afraid, without it, it would lose that customer.

Limited supply: When supply is limited, the business policy may require a longer lead time. If expediting cost is involved, it should state who gets charged and how much. You may decide not to charge customers who are more important to the company, and ship collect or don't expedite at all to others. It should also state how to handle allocation among customers when necessary. Should the limited supply be allocated evenly among all customers or more to those who are more important to the company, and less to others?

If a product is high in value and well established with a steady flow of customers, then a shortage may breed value and increase demand. A company like Decker Outdoor Corporation intentionally creates shortages for its high-end Decker boots (e.g., UGG) to increase its demand. Instead of meeting the customer demand, it allocates its supply among different customers.

Apple does the same thing. In 2010, it successfully used this strategy when it launched its iPad1 tablet computer. It restricted its supply by selling it only through selected outlets. It did the same thing when it launched iPad2 in 2011. By doing that, it created a sense of urgency and created long lines of buyers at many outlets.

Small orders: There may be need for a policy on how to handle small orders. It may require a minimum order. There may also be a need for a policy on handling less than truck load (LTL). The company may want to charge a premium on bulk goods to cover additional transportation cost.

Customer service: There also is a need for a policy for customer service, which may vary from product to product, customer to customer, and from one geographical location to another. A company may like to offer high customer service on products that are high in value as well as to top customers.

Criteria for pruning products: To maximize profit, it is important for demand planners along with other stakeholders to review regularly the product portfolio to determine which products to keep and improve, as well as which new products to introduce and when. Demand planners must have a set criterion in place when to let a product go—maybe when it starts performing below a certain level and/or when there are too many SKUs in the same category. In some cases, the company may decide to offer only on a make-to-order basis.

Cannibalization by new products: New products often cannibalize the old ones, but they have to be introduced to compete effectively in the market place. Here again some guidelines are needed. Under what circumstances a new product should be introduced to replace the old one? A company may have to replace the existing product with a new and better one; otherwise, it may lose its competitiveness.

Difficult to forecast products: A company also needs guidelines for dealing with products that are difficult to forecast. Generally, the more volatile the demand of a product, the more difficult it is to forecast. The volatility is often measured by the coefficient of variation (COV), which is equal to:

$$\text{Coefficient of Variation} = \frac{\text{Standard Deviation}}{\text{Mean}}$$

The company may decide to designate a product difficult to forecast if its coefficient of variation (COV) is greater than 0.8. There are products, however, that have a high volatility, but we know how to handle them. For example, we have models to handle volatility arising from seasonality, and thus such products should not be categorized as difficult to forecast. Here are some suggestions for dealing with difficult to forecast products:

1. As mentioned earlier, very often we create volatility ourselves through promotional activities including product loading. In the past, the cigarette manufacturers were creating volatility in the demand by loading products to meet their quarterly targets. They did this by raising prices, that is, you will pay the same prices, if you buy now. But if you buy next month or next quarter, you will have to pay higher prices. This type of strategy was aimed at hitting their quarterly targets, but added volatility to the demand. To control such volatility, we have to discontinue or reduce such activities.

2. Pay more attention to products that are high in value and difficult to forecast and less to others. Usually, a large percentage of sales come from a few products.

3. Consolidate products at fewer locations instead of keeping them stored at multiple locations. If offered in multiple packages/configurations, consolidate them into fewer packages/configurations. If, for example, a company has 10 different packages of a product with different quantities, it may decide to consolidate them into one. Forecasts generally improve when forecasted at a higher level of aggregation. With these initiatives, the quantity required for safety stock as well as risk associated with them will decrease.

4. Set a policy about the order quantity and lead time for delivery. A company may ask for a longer lead time for larger orders. Such a policy will help in handling peak demand without adding significant safety stock. Furthermore, with that policy, the customer will know how much lead time is required for delivery.

Exceptions: Exceptions are anomalies that must be identified so that corrective actions can be taken. These include having a forecast error of a product above a certain level; a product having a significant over- or under-forecast, say, three consecutive periods in a row; a product having a zero demand even though its forecast was positive; a product with an inventory level far above or below a certain threshold, and so on. So we need rules of exceptions (that is, how large a deviation has to be to qualify as an exception), a computerized system that flags them, a process that investigates them, and rules that enable us to take a corrective action. The over-forecast of a certain product might have been caused by an override of one individual. The retailer's demand for a certain product was zero because it decided to discontinue it without communicating that information to the supplier. It could be that the product had an intermittent demand, and thus its demand was zero in one or more periods. At one time, the demand for a certain product was far below the forecast because its promotion was delayed. The objective here is to ensure that process is in place to find exceptions and flag them so that corrective action can be taken before it is too late.

Natural disasters also need a policy to deal with them. Although they don't occur often, when they do, they badly disrupt the supply chain. The natural disaster in Japan in March 2011 resulting from a combination of earthquake, tsunami, and nuclear accident is a reminder of why an exception-based process is needed. The disaster not only took the lives of thousands of people but also severely wounded the industrial infrastructure, the breadbasket of Japan. Japan produces, among other things, 20 percent of the world's computer chips, 60 percent of silicon wafers, and 90 percent of BT resin for circuit boards, according to *The Wall Street Journal*. Therefore, it is important to have a policy in place to deal with exceptions swiftly and cost-effectively. There are three lessons learned from the past disasters: One, companies should diversify their portfolio of suppliers so that they can use alternate sources when disaster strikes. Two, for some key materials with very few suppliers, companies should move from "just-in-time" to "just-in-case" so that they have enough inventory on hand to cover the period of disruption. Three, there should be an agile marketing strategy that can quickly steer customers away from products that are short in supply to substitutes that are readily available.

In March 2000, the Philips facility in Albuquerque (New Mexico) went up in flames. That plant made radio frequency chips, which are the key components for mobile telephones. When this happened, Nokia quickly made design changes so that other back-up companies could manufacture them. According to Dr. Hau L. Lee, Professor of Operations, Information, and Technology at the Stanford Graduate School of Business, two suppliers, one in the United States and the other in Japan, needed only five days to fulfill the orders for those chips. Ericsson, on the other hand, had no such process in place, and was unable to find new chip suppliers. As a result, Ericsson had to cut back its production and lost some of the market to Nokia.

Another case in point is the earthquake in Taiwan in September 1999 that delayed shipments of computer components to the United States by weeks and, in some cases, by months. Unlike other PC manufacturers, Dell had a marketing policy in place to deal with it. It immediately steered customers away from the PCs that used those components by raising their prices on its website, and at the same time boosted the sales of substitutes by lowering their prices. So, the exception based-process is essential for effectively managing demand.

Price discrimination: Price discrimination is charging different prices in different markets and to different customers. It is practiced in every market and in every business to increase sales and profit. The pharmaceutical companies, for example, charge higher prices in developed countries and lower prices in developing countries. Airlines charge a lower price when reservations are made early on and a higher price when made close to the flight date. To do that, a company needs a policy that states how much to charge, when, and where.

The recent trend in price discrimination is not only related to charging different prices in different markets and to different customers but also to come up with a product with a price that consumers can afford. Gillette (a division of P&G), for example, dominates the world's razor and blade market (70 percent by the most recent estimate) but it lagged behind its rivals in India. To increase its market share in 2010, it launched a new razor, Gillette Guard, which was sold for just 34 cents (15 rupees) and the blade that went with it for just 11 cents (5 rupees).

With that, the business strategy has changed. Instead of first coming up with a product and then deciding on the price, now businesses first decide on what consumers can afford and then produce a product that fits that price.

Thus, we can see that demand planning is a must. Without that we will be giving up profit margin, shareholder value, customer service, and market position. Having demand plans for all products and services is a best practice. Otherwise, turmoil caused by one product that was poorly managed may disrupt production of others.

SUGGESTED READING

1. Birchall, Jonathan. "Wal-Mart Product Purge Sets Worrying Trend for Suppliers." ***Financial Times.*** August 10, 2009, p. 15.
2. Dowell, Andrew. "Japan: The Business Aftershocks." ***The Wall Street Journal.*** March 25, 2011, p. B1.
3. Lee, L. Hau. "The Triple-A Supply Chain." ***Harvard Business Review.*** October 2004, pp. 102-112.
4. Milliken, Alan. "Demand Planning Process Beyond Forecasting." 2009. (Slides prepared for in-house training)
5. Milliken, Alan. "Demand Planning: Managing the Unforecastables." ***Journal of Business Forecasting.*** Summer 2006, pp. 3-9.
6. Milliken, Alan. "Use of Volume-Variance Analysis to Develop Demand Planning Strategies."2009. (Slides prepared for in-house training)
7. Montgomery, David. "Flashpoints for Changing Your Forecasting Process." ***Journal of Business Forecasting.*** Winter 2006-2007, pp. 35-37.
8. Simon, Robin. "New Product Development and Forecasting Challenges." ***Journal of Business Forecasting.*** Winter 2009-2010, pp. 19-21.
9. Wiggins, Jenny. "General Mills Eyes Return to Inflation." ***Financial Times.*** October 28, 2009, p. 19.

QUESTIONS FOR REVIEW

1. What is demand planning and what purpose does it serve?
2. What is demand management, and how does it work?
3. Why do we need to establish business policies to run an effective and efficient demand planning process?
4. Why do we need a monthly demand review process, and what should be reviewed in that meeting?
5. How should we deal with products that are difficult to forecast?
6. How should we handle products that are short in supply in an effectively run demand planning process?
7. Why are highly promoted products difficult to forecast?
8. Why is it important to decide on profit objectives before starting demand planning?
9. How does the accuracy of forecasts affect customer service and inventory? Explain.

10. Explain in brief:
    a. The more volatile a product, the more difficult it is to forecast
    b. List three different product types that are difficult to forecast
    c. Product mix
    d. Price discrimination

CHAPTER 5

POINT-OF-SALE-BASED DEMAND PLANNING

The effectiveness of demand planning depends, among other things, on the data stream used in forecasting and planning. Among the three data streams—shipment, customer order (demand), and Point of Sale (POS)—POS is the best. Before we explain why, it is important to know what POS data are and how they differ from the syndicated data. The POS data are the data of sales to end-consumers—sale transactions entered at the checkout counter. When we buy a product, the person at the counter scans the product, which not only generates the bill but also records the information into the database—the product we bought, price we paid, the store we bought from, and the day we purchased it. That information is called POS data.

SYNDICATED DATA VS. POS DATA

Syndicated data are also POS data, but they are provided by a third party data vendor. They differ from the POS data in number of ways:

1. Manufacturers (suppliers) get POS data only from those customers with whom they have an information-sharing agreement. But, there are many other customers who also sell their products but their sales transaction data are not available. Syndicated data providers such as AC Nielsen and Symphony IRI Group provide such data, though at a price. The

POS data obtained from their own customers as well as from syndicated data vendors cover most but not all of the data. This is because there are customers who still use traditional methods of recording sales, and thus their data are not available. Also, there are customers who, for one reason or another, don't want to share their data with anyone including syndicated data providers. Further, POS data of military entities and international consumers are not available. Retailers that give their POS information to syndicated data vendors do not provide it free; they want to be compensated. They are either paid directly or receive some kind of market analysis in return.

2. Customers (retailers) who provide data directly to their suppliers do so only of their products, and not of competitors. Syndicated data providers provide data of their products as well as of their competitors.

3. Data received directly by suppliers from their customers are generally at a SKU level, whereas data received from syndicated data vendors are usually at a higher level of aggregation such as at a brand level.

4. POS data provided directly to suppliers by their customers often have to be cleaned, standardized, and grouped before using, whereas data provided by syndicated data vendors require minimal processing because they perform most of these processes before sending them. Daily transaction data may have to be aggregated into weekly or monthly buckets, categories, channels of distribution, and geographical markets, depending on the need. Some of the products are sold in multi-packs of two or three units, which have to be converted into the exact number of units sold. Products sold in different sizes such as 8-oz and 15-oz cans have to be equalized. Furthermore, syndicated data vendors provide user-friendly software, making it easier to access, process, and use the data, which is not the case where suppliers get directly from customers. There are, however, some customers who do some cleaning and formatting before sending the data. In some cases, they also provide the software too.

Syndicated data vendors provide much more than POS data. They also track retailers' feature ads in newspapers, as well as manufacturers' Free-Standing Inserts (FSIs), to find out who is promoting what, and their effect. They make their analysis available to their clients at a price. Feature ads include coupons and discounts. FSIs include coupons that typically come in Sunday newspapers. AC Nielsen and Symphony IRI Group subscribe to almost 300 newspapers to get that information.

Syndicated data vendors, such as AC Nielsen and Symphony IRI Group, also track the impact of in-store circular and in-store displays. Displays can be on the end-aisle, beginning of the aisle, or center of the aisle. They estimate the effect of each type on the sale. In addition to AC Nielsen and Symphony IRI Group, there are several other specialized syndicated data providers, such as SPINS that provides consumption data of natural and specialty products, and Intercontinental Marketing Services (IMS) that provides consumption of different drugs based on prescriptions issued.

POS data are important because what matters most to suppliers is not how many orders they receive from customers but how much their customers have sold to ultimate consumers. The other factors that have increased the use of this type of data are consolidation of retail stores into larger chains; availability of technology to store a large amount of data, ability to transmit data from one location to another safely and quickly, as well as ability to easily access, process, and analyze the data. The use of scanners to record sale transactions, even by small stores, has also increased their use. In recent years, there has been a massive consolidation of retail stores into larger chains, which consolidate the POS data from all of their stores in a database at regional locations or at the headquarters, making it easier to access data of thousands of stores from one or a few locations. Furthermore, data warehouses have become more sophisticated and less expensive, and data transmission engines have become powerful enough to move even terabytes of data from one location to another at the speed of light. Many of the Mom and Pop shops have also started scanning and recording their sale transactions.

DATA TRANSMISSION

POS data are transmitted in a number of ways, but the ones that are used most often are: (1) Private exchange such as Retail Link and Partners Online, (2) EDI 852 transmission, and (3) the Internet.

Private exchange: The big box retailers often use their own exchange to transmit data to their suppliers. For example, Walmart uses its Retail Link, and Target, its Partners Online. Information that is often made available includes not only daily and weekly POS transactions, but also inventory levels by SKU and location/store. Retailers typically transmit POS data weekly, though some retailers such as grocery stores do it daily. To safeguard the information, Walmart requires that its information must stay either within Retail Link or behind a vendor's own firewall, but not on a third party's server. Other companies that provide such information also have similar conditions.

EDI 852 transmission: Most small accounts and regional departmental stores chains transmit their product activity data electronically through EDI 852 (Electronic Data Interchange). However, the data are often sent in weekly or monthly buckets, aggregated at different levels including category, customer, and distribution center (DC).

Internet: Where neither private exchange is available nor is there access to EDI, the Internet is used as a last resort. Here data are provided on a spreadsheet such as Microsoft Excel. The data so provided may not be quite reliable. If a customer you are working with does not have an online portal or is not capable of sending via EDI, it may mean that POS data are not important to that customer. The chances of getting the data in a consistent and timely manner will be slim. It may require numerous phone calls and follow-ups just to receive the data, and many additional follow-ups to interpret. If you receive data that cannot be formatted even on an Excel spreadsheet or on any other spreadsheet, then you have a real problem. In that case, you have to decide whether or not it is worth the effort.

WHY POS-BASED DEMAND PLANNING?

The best driver for demand planning is not any forecast, but the POS-based forecast (forecast of sales to end-consumers). Your customers (whether distributors, wholesalers, dealers, or retailers) won't buy from you unless they can sell them to their end-consumers. Therefore, you as a supplier want to forecast not how many orders you would receive from your customers but how much end-consumers would buy from them. As such, data used for demand planning have evolved from shipment to demand (customer orders) to POS.

POS-based forecasts are more accurate than forecasts based on shipment or demand data: Both suppliers and retailers would like to forecast sales based on POS information rather than on anything else because it is a true indicator of the market, and is more stable. The more stable the data are, the more accurate the forecasts will be. Backlogs, stock-outs, machine breakages, switchovers, and stoppages—they all add volatility to the shipment data. The bullwhip effect further adds volatility when a customer (retailer, for example) places an order larger than what it actually needs. Inventory decisions of retailers also add volatility in shipments. If sales to consumers are flat and the retailer decides to reduce inventory and places no order to the supplier, then the supplier's shipment data will show a decline in sales, even though there is no change in consumer sales. This is also true with new products. Retailers initially build inventories to levels that are well above expected sales to make sure they do not run out of stock in the first week of sales. Then, if sales are not depleting the inventory fast enough, they will order less and less until inventory reaches a reasonable level.

Since there is not a one-to-one relationship between a shipment and POS, shipments by themselves cannot be regarded as an indictor of the market. Usually, there is a gap between them, because shipments occur first and then comes POS. Also, a shipment is usually greater than POS. There are, however, some businesses, such as Amazon.com, which hold very little inventory. The orders are mostly fulfilled directly by their vendors. In those cases, shipments are the same as the end-consumer demand, and are a good indicator of the market. Further, with POS forecasts, a supplier can determine whether the customer is ordering more than or less than what it actually needs.

The supplier's business policy also distorts the shipment pattern. If a supplier penalizes a customer for giving an order for less than a case, the customer will wait until it is ready to place an order for a case, thereby causing volatility in shipment. The consumer demand, on the other hand, is free of inventory decision, and thus more stable, because consumers rarely make explicit decisions to build or deplete their inventory.

There are also more variations in the customer order demand than in consumer demand. Customer order demand changes widely from one period to the next because of a change in the company's inventory policy, its perception about the market, and promotional efforts of its suppliers. To meet a quarterly or annual target, suppliers often offer special incentives to push the products to customers, thereby causing variations in customer order demand. Figure 5.1 gives the data of customer order demand and consumer demand of a Swedish grocery supplier, spanning 110 weeks. It clearly shows that fluctuations in order demand are much more than

Figure 5.1 | Consumer Demand vs. Order Demand

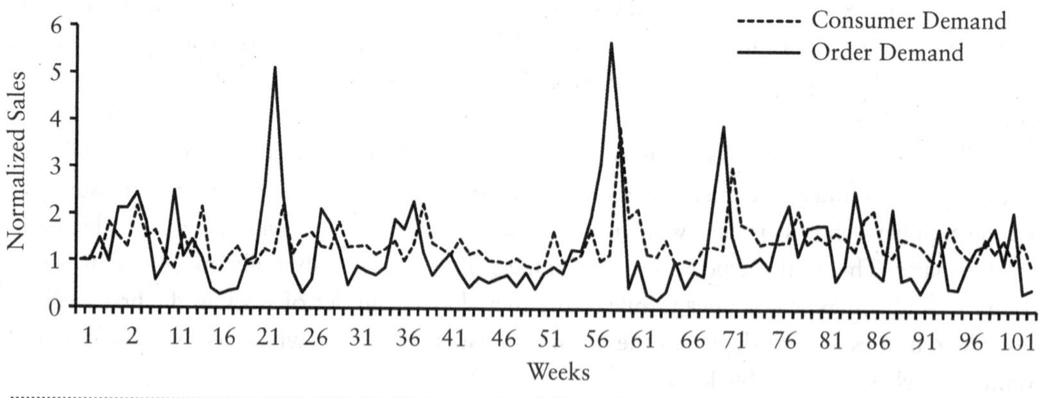

Source: Larsson, Magnus. "Forecasting Improves with Scanner Data: A Swedish Grocery Supplier's Journey." ***Journal of Business Forecasting***. Winter 2002-2003, pp. 19-21, 30.

in consumer demand.

POS data provides the best market intelligence: No data—whether of shipment or customer demand—can provide as good market intelligence as POS, and do it at the most granular level. With that you can determine seasonality of a brand by day, week, and month, as well as by location. Not only that, within a brand you can determine if certain SKUs have a different seasonal pattern from others. One manufacturer of jewelry products found from its POS data that white pierced earrings peak in June and other colors in December; they are sold more in March in the South but more in June and July in the East; and they are sold more in the third week of a month than in any other week. The reason why people buy more earrings in the third week of a month may be because payroll payments are often made twice a month, the first check might be used to pay for more necessary items (such as mortgage and car payments), and the second check for non-essential items.

Above all, POS data can be used to develop the right assortment plan, that is, which SKU to produce, by how much, and for which season. It also gives more reliable information about the effect of a promotion—which promotion works and which one does not, and in which location/store. Not only that, one can determine the impact of an in-store display—which type of display is most and least effective. This kind of information helps in increasing sales, reducing markdowns, and improving profit margin.

POS data aids in taking full advantage of the market: Brown Shoe sells close to 90 million pairs of shoes globally, owns and operates over 1,100 Famous Footwear stores, 300 specialty retail stores, and distributes footwear worldwide to more than 2,000 departments, mass merchandisers, and independent stores. Most shoes have a very short life cycle. Sandals, for example, are popular with consumers between March and August in the United States, and after that their sales drop dramatically. So, it is critical to synchronize closely their anticipated demand with supply. If a certain style or size is doing well in season, the company wants to know right away so that it can react. The same is true if a certain style or size is not doing well. POS forecasts signal the change in the market quickly and correctly, thereby enabling businesses to react. Furthermore, Brown Shoe improved its forecast accuracy of sandals by size and color, 13 weeks into the future, to 80 percent by implementing the POS-based forecasting system. Not only that, it reduced its lead time by 50 days for its core shoe items sold at Famous Footwear. The lead time went down because it started placing orders with its manufacturing plants, which were more firm, thereby enabling them to make firm commitments with their suppliers of raw material. In the past, it used to revise its orders frequently. Further, with POS-based forecasts, the company started ordering weekly instead of monthly, and giving smaller orders.

In the fashion industry, one needs weekly forecasts in order to detect changes in the consumer demand early enough to react. The same is true with new product launches. The supplier wants to know quickly whether consumers have accepted or rejected its product. POS data provide that information. Additionally, the supplier can optimize its limited production capacity by producing the right product at the right time.

Above all, with the use of POS data, the orders the supplier will receive will not be constrained by the behavior of customers, but by the behavior of consumers, the main driver. Knowing the consumer demand, demand planners both of suppliers and customers can do a better job in aligning the supply with the consumer demand. If a customer is not ordering enough, the supplier can bring it to its attention.

POS-based demand planning nurtures collaboration: It will nurture collaboration when everyone uses the same data (POS data). At Kraft Foods, for example, consumption data are the language of communication among different functions for discussing the status of its brands, categories, and competitiveness, as well as the overall U.S. market, regions, and major accounts. It also nurtures collaboration among suppliers and customers. The initiatives such as Collaborative Planning, Forecasting and Replenishment (CPFR®) and and Vendor Managed Inventory (VMI) very much revolve around POS data. Many customers encourage their suppliers to "suggest" alternative forecasts to those already in their system, thereby letting the demand planners of their suppliers to influence their demand when necessary.

POS lets you separate consumer appetite from store expansion: An increase in sales can come from an increase in consumer appetite or from opening of new stores. But from the customer's and supplier's perspectives, it makes a difference. When sales increase because of an increase in sales in practically every store of every customer, then it means that the consumer's appetite for a product has increased. In other words, the supplier can assume that the overall sales of its products are growing, which may not be the case if it resulted from the opening of new stores by one customer. In that case, it may mean that its sales only to that customer have grown. Thus, it is important to examine sales of each store, which is possible only with POS data.

CHALLENGES WITH POS DATA

Although POS data are rich in information, getting the right information and managing them in a timely manner is extremely difficult. There are many problems with the data. To begin with, there is no single standard format in which data are available. Some of the items are sold in a multi-pack of two or three units, which have to be converted into single units by using the average price. Some provide data in daily buckets, and others, in weekly or monthly buckets. Some provide POS data at a regular interval, and others, irregularly. Some provide data at a SKU level, and others, at a category level. Syndicated data vendors usually provide data at a category level. Also, their data do not include the data of major retailers (such as Walmart) nor those of global markets and military entities. Recently however, Walmart has decided to make this data available to third party vendors. There are many small or medium-size stores that either do not generate POS information or do not make their POS data available even to third party vendors. To arrive at the overall demand of a category, companies have to inflate the data to compensate for what is missing—data of customers with either no POS facilities or reluctant to share, and of international and military related customers.

Data coming from different customers are not the same either. In one case, a week may end on Saturday, and in another case, on Sunday. In one case, a year may be made up of 13 periods, 4 weeks in each period. In another case, a year may be made up of 12 periods, with each quarter of 4-4-5 weeks. In some cases, the month may end on the last day of a month, and, in another case, on the 15th of a month. Holidays also create problems. In some years, Thanksgiving, for example, falls earlier on the calendar than in other years, making it difficult to make year-to-year weekly comparisons. Therefore, for best results, it is important that the product, geography, periods, and volume measures are comparable. If you want to determine the market trend of a given SKU, make sure that the same SKUs are aggregated. If you want to get a handle on a product category, make sure right SKUs are aggregated. If the objective is to determine the demand trend by geography, region, and/or country, makes sure that SKUs of appropriate customers and stores are aggregated.

Self-scanner programs present another challenge, making it difficult for a manufacturer to determine how much sales resulted from a special promotion directed only to those who use it. For example, a local food store has a self-scanner program. With that, the consumer scans its loyalty card and uses the mobile scanner throughout the store. The consumer then scans a product as it puts it in the basket. (This way the consumer does not need to unload products at the checkout counter and then reload.) To encourage self-scanning, stores make special offers to those who use it. For example, consumer may get $1.00 off from a regular price on a box of frozen pancakes. This deal is not advertised in the store or anywhere, nor is it available to other shoppers. Since that information is not available, manufacturers find it difficult to decipher the impact of a special offer from the POS data.

The accuracy of data is another issue that has to be dealt with. However, over the past five years or so, accuracy of POS data has vastly improved as a result of technology upgrades and cashier training.

From time to time, the transmission problem occurs as a result of hardware and software problems, or for any other reason. When that happens, it has to be properly addressed. If you have a transmission problem and you did not notice it until the following week, you can simply hope that the account has retained its weekly data and can re-transmit. On the supplier's end, it is important that there is a process in place to accept the re-transmission and reload it.

KEY TAKEAWAYS

The key takeaways for using POS and syndicated data in demand planning can be summarized as follows:

1. POS forecasts are the leading indicators of market trends, which can tell ahead of time which products or categories are expected to do well or poorly, and in which market. This information can help both suppliers and retailers in identifying risks and opportunities. They also provide a better handle for determining the impact of various marketing efforts including pricing, trade spending, and advertising.

2. The experience of Brown Shoe Company is that the first two weeks of sales is not a true predictor of the success or failure of a new product. You need three to four weeks of POS data to make that determination.

3. You can determine whether or not your customer's inventory is in or out of balance. This can be accomplished by having a sales report, which shows how much weekly sales of a SKU is as a percentage of its total family and how much the inventory of that SKU is as a percentage of that family. If a given SKU accounts for 10 percent of the weekly sales of its family, whereas the on-hand inventory is 20 percent of the family, then the inventory is out of balance. To keep track of out-of-stock, you have to require the retailer to give you the sales report that shows how many SKUs it has on hand with an inventory balance of zero.

4. To use effectively the POS data, you have to automate your POS-based demand planning process. POS generates massive amount of data, which are very difficult to handle manually. You need technology to automate the data, which does exist. It is just a matter of finding which one is the best fit for you.

5. With POS analysis, suppliers can see whether variations in demand are resulting from a change in the consumer behavior or from variations in retail inventories. Wide fluctuations

in retail inventories can cause a disconnect between retail sales and replenishment orders. The variations in inventories can occur because of opening and closing of customers' distribution centers, product loading for an upcoming season or promotion, or customers' changes in their inventory target levels. The variations in inventories can also occur because the implementation of a new plan-o-gram was delayed at some or all stores; execution of certain promotions were uneven or incomplete; customers did not replenish them in an orderly fashion; and/or inventory of a customer was aligned more to its inventory policy and less to the consumer demand. (Plan-o-gram is how product is displayed and stocked on the retail floor.) Once you know the source of a problem, then you may know what to do to fix it.

6. Shipment and POS data will not be the same in any specific week, month, or quarter, but it will be close over a 12-month period. Usually, a shipment is larger than POS by anywhere from 5 percent to 10 percent. If the gap is more than that, you may need to investigate. The shipment is larger than POS because shipment occurs before POS. To determine the size of a shipment from a POS forecast, you have to use a factor, that is, what takeaway (consumer sale) is as a percentage of shipment over the last 12-month period, and use it as a guide. If the factor is .90 (90 percent), you have to divide POS forecast by .90 to determine how much shipment should be. But, if a supplier sells its product directly to end-consumers or to customers who do not hold inventory, then shipments would be the same as POS.

FUTURE OF POS DATA

Knowing how effective POS-based demand planning is, its use will grow over time. It will be used not only in sensing demand but also in shaping and re-shaping it to meet operational and strategic goals. Companies like Dell Computer and Tupperware are already using it in sensing the demand and then taking an appropriate action.

The use of POS data in demand planning will move the planning process from a monthly to a weekly cycle, thereby minimizing risks and maximizing sales. With POS data, you can make fairly reliable weekly forecasts, making it possible to adjust the replenishment activities weekly. Furthermore, we expect to see in the near future the development of standard measures with respect to products and periods, making it easier to process and analyze POS data.

There are still some channels of retail sales that do not have good POS data because the products they sell cannot be easily classified by the UPC number. (The UPC is the standardized bar code used to identify a product at the cash register.) An example of such a channel is restaurants.

Even though they sell an item with an UPC number like a bottle of beer, but when served in a glass it does not have that number printed on it. This may change in the future.

The POS data are great for knowing the current consumer demand but not future demand, says Steve Keifer, Vice President of Industry and Marketing at GXS. In this respect, online retailers have an advantage over others because they allow consumers to order before the launch date. Sites such as Amazon.com, and Barnesandnoble.com allow consumers to order before the launch date. With that, marketers can assess fairly well the future consumer demand. Many online retailers have access to pre-order data on products such as books, DVD movies, music, mobile phones, and video games, which will expand over time. Further, since a large percentage of sales of these products occur within a few weeks of the product launch; their accurate demand forecasts are critical to maximize revenue and profit.

The data of newborns and newlyweds can also help in forecasting. In the United States, it is a common practice for engaged couples and expecting parents to create an online gift registry, which contains a list of items they would like to have. Expecting parents might request baby clothes, toys, books, and food utensils. Engaged couples might request silverware, fine china, linens, and other housewares. Such registries not only tell what is going to be purchased, but also about when they would be bought. Most baby registry items are purchased shortly before or after the due date. If friends and family did not purchase those items, most likely they would be bought later on by them. Similarly, with wedding registries, most of the purchases will occur shortly before or after the nuptial date. Retail chains, which offer gift registry options, can leverage such data.

SUGGESTED READING

1. Andres, Fred. "Demand Planning and Forecasting with POS Data: A Case Study." ***Journal of Business Forecasting.*** Winter 2008-2009, pp. 29-32, 38.
2. Borgos, Mike. "More Power with Point of Sale Data." ***Journal of Business Forecasting.*** Winter 2008-2009, pp. 19-21.
3. Brown, Jeff. "Consumer Driven Forecasting to Improve Inventory Flow: Brown Shoe Company's Journey." ***Journal of Business Forecasting.*** Winter 2008-2009, pp. 24-25.
4. Bursa, Karin. "How to Effectively Manage Demand with Demand Sensing and Shaping Using Point of Sale Data." ***Journal of Business Forecasting.*** Winter 2008-2009, pp. 26-28.
5. Gallucci, John A. and Hugh J. McCarthy. "Enhancing the Demand Planning Process with POS Forecasting." ***Journal of Business Forecasting.*** Winter 2008-2009, pp. 11-14.
6. Keifer, Steve. "Beyond Point of Sale Data: Leveraging Demand Signals for Forecasting."

Journal of Business Forecasting. Summer 2010, pp. 14-22.
7. Lapide, Larry. "Use POS Information to Address What, Why, and How?" *Journal of Business Forecasting*. Winter 2008-2009, pp. 17-18.
8. Park, Sara. "How Point of Sale Data are Used in Demand Forecasting at Heinz North America." *Journal of Business Forecasting*. Winter 2008-2009, pp. 39-40.
9. Shapiro, Richard. "How to Use POS Data in Demand Planning." *Journal of Business Forecasting*. Winter 2008-2009, pp. 36-38.
10. Sichel, Bill. "Forecasting Demand with Point of Sale Data—A Case Study of Fashion Products." *Journal of Business Forecasting*. Winter 2008-2009, pp. 15-16.
11. Simon, Robin. "The ABCs of Point of Sale (POS) Data." *Journal of Business Forecasting*. Winter 2008-2009, pp. 4-10.
12. Tolbert, Fred. "Why Point of Sale Data Matters for Demand Management." *Journal of Business Forecasting*. Winter 2008-2009, pp. 33-35.

QUESTIONS FOR REVIEW

1. What are POS data? How do they differ from the syndicated data? Explain.
2. What are the benefits of using POS data in demand planning? Explain.
3. Describe in detail the problems encountered in using POS data, and how they can be overcome.
4. What are the key takeaways of using POS data in demand planning? Explain.
5. Why are POS data more stable than shipment and demand data?
6. How are shipment data related to POS data?
7. From a demand planning perspective, does it make a difference if a customer's orders increase by 20 percent because of a 20 percent increase in sales in each and every store or because of opening of new stores by that customer? Explain.
8. Describe how retailers transmit POS data to suppliers.
9. Does the use of POS data strengthen or weaken collaboration both within and outside the organization? Explain.
10. Describe in detail the market intelligence gained from the POS data.

PART II

THE FORECASTING PROCESS

INTRODUCTION

Models are important in forecasting, but process is just as important, if not more so. Process deals with issues such as what kind of information is needed to prepare forecasts; who has it; how that information would be collected and then transmitted to a forecaster; where the forecasting function would reside; which forecasting philosophy would be followed—one number or multiple numbers; which forecasting approach would be used; who would participate in the forecasting process; and, after forecasts are prepared, how their performance would be evaluated for further improvement. These are all part of the forecasting process, which has evolved over time from Silo to Consensus Forecasting to Sales & Operations Planning (S&OP) to now Collaborative Planning, Forecasting and Replenishment (CPFR®) to further improve forecasts as well as plans. No matter how good the plans are, they won't add any value unless they are implemented. A good forecasting process sees to it that they are implemented effectively, efficiently, and in a timely manner.

CHAPTER 6

THE PROCESS

The key components of a successful forecasting operation are people, process, information, and technology. Of these, the people are probably the most important, which include not only the forecaster who prepares statistical forecasts but also the others who participate in the process. They must know fairly well the products they forecast and the markets they operate in. The forecaster must have some background in statistics, enough to evaluate models. If other participants also have some knowledge about statistics, that would be a big plus. They all should understand the importance of forecasting in decision making, and work together for a common goal, which is not what is good for a specific function, but what is good for the company as a whole. Information/data are another component that we discuss in Chapters 11-13. Technology, which also plays an important part not only in generating forecasts but also in automating the process, is discussed in Chapters 29 and 30. This chapter discusses the role that process plays in forecasting.

Very often when we think of forecasting, the first thing that comes to our mind is models. Models are important, but the process is just as important, if not more so. The forecasting process includes, among other things, what information/data will be needed to prepare forecasts; who has it and how to obtain it; where to place the forecasting function; once information/data are received by the forecaster how to analyze it; which approach and model to use to prepare forecasts; which forecasting philosophy to follow—one number or multiple number forecasts; and after statistical forecasts are prepared, how judgment, if necessary, would be overlaid to arrive at the final forecasts. Judgment is used to account for elements that have a bearing on forecasts but cannot be quantified and for information that was not available at the time the forecasts were generated. The final part of the process—how forecasts will be monitored and updated—comes after the forecasts are finalized.

Process matters. Take a case in point. In the year 2000, Nike implemented the i2 Technology (now a part of JDA Software) expert system to prepare forecasts. (The expert system is the one that automatically tests different models embedded in a software package, and then prepares forecasts with the best one.) Nine months later, Nike declared that it lost $400 million because of inaccurate forecasts. It over-forecasted certain shoes and under-forecasted others. Who should be blamed — the system, the process, or both? Maybe the expert system was not up to par and gave wrong forecasts. Maybe there was no process in place to monitor forecasts. Maybe the forecasting system was used as a black box. Regardless, the problem remained undetected for nine months. If a good process had been in place, the problem would have been discovered much sooner and corrective actions could have been taken. In other words, when the error of a certain product went over the threshold two to three periods in a row, had the process been in place, the error would have been flagged. Carroll Mohan, former Manager of Analytical Methods in Corporate Market Research for Coca-Cola, says that businesses should revise their forecasts when the error far exceeds the average, occurs two times in a row in the same direction, or exceeds the adjustment capability of a company.

In recent years, market dynamics have changed dramatically, which have made the job of forecasting even more challenging. The explosion in the number of products, proliferation in the number of channels of distribution, shorter life cycles, aggressive advertising to allure customers, declining consumer loyalty, increasing economic uncertainty and globalization—all these factors have complicated the task of forecasting. To counter it, organizations are re-engineering their processes of forecasting and supply chain management to reduce costs and increase sales and profit.

Before setting up a forecasting process, various issues have to be resolved. What types of forecasts are needed (demand forecasts, shipment forecasts, financial forecasts, and/or a combination of these) and in what buckets (monthly, weekly, daily, or any other)? What levels of detail (by SKU, category, region, and channel of distribution, customer, and the like) are required? How often and how far ahead should forecasts be prepared? How should forecasts be updated and revised? What information/data are needed, from where it would come, and in what manner? Where should we place the forecasting function? Who should participate in the process? Which models and forecasting software/systems should we use? Which forecasting philosophy should we follow one-number or multiple numbers? Which forecasting approach should we use—bottom-up, top-down, or middle out? All these issues have to be resolved before implementing a process.

WHAT FORECASTS ARE REQUIRED

The types of forecasts that are needed vary from company to company and function to function. Companies may need demand forecasts, shipment forecasts, and/or financial forecasts. Companies like UPS and AAA may need, among other things, forecasts of the number of phone calls coming in every hour on the hour in order to staff the call centers appropriately. Banks with ATM facilities may like to have a forecast of, among other things, how much money would be taken out from each machine, each day. The need also varies from function to function. Some functions may need short-term forecasts, others long-term forecasts. Production people need forecasts in units, and Finance in dollars. As to the level of detail, Production needs forecasts at an item level, and Marketing at a category level. Salespeople may need forecasts by category/item, broken down by customer, trade channel, and region. Senior management may want forecasts of total revenue, profit margin, and market share.

Whether forecasts should be prepared at a category, subcategory, and/or item level depends not only on who would be using them and for what purpose, but also at what level they can be prepared most accurately. As we know, the quality of forecasts tends to deteriorate as we forecast at a more and more granular level. Forecasts are more accurate at a category level than at a subcategory level; more accurate at a subcategory level than at an item level, and so on.

FORECAST HORIZON AND FORECAST BUCKETS

How far ahead to forecast (forecast horizon) is another decision that has to be made before setting up a forecasting process. The answer depends very much on the cycle time; that is, how far ahead decisions have to be made. If the cycle time is two months, meaning it will take that much time to purchase raw material and manufacture the final product, then you will need forecasts at least two months ahead. Usually the supply chain has a frozen lead time, determined by the speed of procurement of products (whether they are produced internally or externally). The next question is in what bucket should forecasts be prepared—weekly, monthly, and/or quarterly? This depends on how replenishment is managed. If it is managed monthly (that is, you make a monthly production plan), then you will need forecasts in monthly buckets; if it is managed weekly, you will need them in weekly buckets.

No matter what your planning cycle is, it is always a good idea to prepare forecasts in monthly buckets, at the very least. If, for example, your planning cycle is two months or longer, monthly forecasts can help to detect a problem sooner so that you can fix it. Let us say your cycle time is three months. If you are in the beginning of January, you will need forecasts of April and beyond. At the beginning of February, you will need forecasts of May and beyond. If forecasts are prepared monthly, you can compare each month's forecast with the actual and, if there is any problem, you can revise them as well as the plans for upcoming months. In the above example, if you are in early February, the production plans has been locked for two months—that is, through April—but you can make a change for the month of May and beyond. In some cases, you may have a little more flexibility. In the case of one manufacturer of steel doors, which had a cycle time of two months, demand planners could not make any change in the production plan in the first month, but in the second month it could make a change up to 10 percent. After that, it could make any change. So, forecasts prepared on a monthly cycle can help to improve forecasts, as well as plans.

PLACEMENT OF THE FORECASTING FUNCTION

Because every function has a bias of its own, where to place the forecasting function is another issue that has to be resolved before setting up a forecasting process. Sales would have a downward bias if forecasts are used for setting quotas; otherwise, they would have an upward bias to make sure products are available to fulfill the orders. Marketing would have an upward bias if the advertising budget is tied to forecasts; the higher the forecast number, the larger would be the amount sanctioned for advertising. Finance is generally conservative and prefers under-forecasting, partly because it wants to keep the shareholders' confidence. Production prefers under-forecasting if it is evaluated on the basis of inventory; otherwise, it would have an upward bias to make sure orders are fulfilled on time and there is no backlog. Therefore, the best thing may be to have an independent forecasting department, which would be free from any bias. But this may be possible only within a large corporation; small or mid-size companies may not be big enough to justify one whole department for this job. There are, however, some companies that are against an Independent Forecasting Department. They believe this would mean to other departments that the Forecasting Department is not a part of their team, and thus refuse to cooperate or lend any support, which is essential in forecasting.

As it stands, the forecasting function resides all over. Some companies have it in Sales, others in Marketing, Supply Chain, or Finance. About 13 percent of the companies have an independent forecasting department, according to the 2009 survey of the Institute of Business Forecasting and Planning. (See Figure 6.1.) There are two things that are worth noting: One, Supply Chain

Figure 6.1 | Where the Forecasting Function Resides

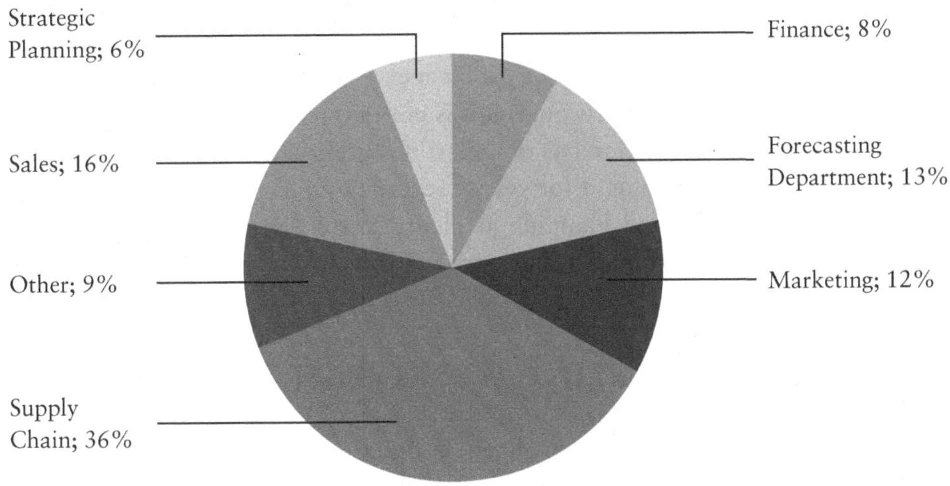

Source: Based on the 2009 IBF survey data.

dominates with respect to the placement of the forecasting function. This is probably because most of the forecasting done in business is of operational forecasts, and the largest user of such forecasts is Supply Chain. They want to keep the forecasting function close to where major operational decisions are made. Two, more and more companies have moved their forecasting function out of Finance.

Despite these biases, it may not make much difference where you place the forecasting function provided there is a good Consensus Forecasting process in place where all the functions work together to arrive at the final numbers, which we will discuss in the next chapter.

ONE NUMBER VS. MULTIPLE NUMBER FORECASTS

As we will explain in the next chapter, one rational for having a Consensus Forecasting process is to have a one number forecast to overcome problems associated with multiple number forecasts. The multiple number forecasts imply that every department within an organization creates its own forecasts for its own use. Production people prepare their own forecasts for their production plan;

Salespeople for their sales plan; Marketing people for their market plan; and so on. With a one number forecast, on the other hand, there is only one forecast that everyone uses. What we need is one forecast, and not multiple forecasts; with multiple forecasts it is very difficult to align supply with demand, which is necessary for running a lean and profitable operation. How can we align supply with demand if supply is based on one set of forecasts and demand on another? At times, it becomes a problem even for a President/CEO to decide which forecast to use when making a decision. But it is not easy to implement a one number policy, because by doing so each function has to impart its authority to forecast to someone else, which can be difficult after owning it for years. According to Sara Park, former Senior Manager of Forecasting and Demand Planning at Heinz North America, it is difficult to implement a policy of one number forecast, but once implemented, it is even more difficult to maintain it.

FORECASTING APPROACH

The forecasting approach is another issue that has to be decided. There are several approaches that are used, but a company may decide to use anyone of these or a combination of them. The approaches most often used are as follows:

1. Top-down, bottom-up, and middle-out
2. Product life cycle
3. Size of customers
4. Product classification

Top-down, bottom-up, and middle-out: In the top–down approach, we first prepare forecasts at higher levels of product, market, and period, and then disaggregate or allocate them down into categories and SKUs, customers, DCs, and weeks/days. For example, we may decide to first prepare the forecast of a company as a whole (aggregate forecast), and then break down into categories to arrive at category level forecasts, then categories into SKUs to arrive at SKU-level forecasts. One way to break down forecasts is by using their past ratios—the ratio of a category sales to the total and the ratio of a SKU sales to its category. If a category "A" is 10 percent of the total, we will apply a factor of 10 percent to the total to get its forecast. Similarly, we can breakdown each category forecast into SKUs.

In the bottom-up approach, we start from the bottom. We first prepare a forecast of each SKU, and then aggregate all the SKU forecasts of a category to arrive at its category forecast, and aggregate all the category forecasts to arrive at a company level forecast. In the middle-out approach, we start from the middle, that is to say, from a category. To get the forecast of a company as a whole, we aggregate all the category forecasts. To get forecasts of SKUs, we break down each category forecast into SKUs, again by using their past ratios. Many companies in the consumer products industry use this approach.

Each of these approaches has its pros and cons. The top-down approach is good because forecasts prepared at an aggregate level are generally more accurate than at a category and SKU level. It will work well if the aggregate demand as well as the demand of products at both a category and SKU level is fairly stable, which is often not the case. The bottom-up approach will be better if the demand pattern of different SKUs is very different.

Some companies like Ocean Spray Cranberries use a hybrid approach, which combines both bottom-up and top-down approaches. It first prepares both sets of forecasts, and then reconciles them to arrive at one set of numbers.

Product life cycle: The product life cycle approach is most appropriate where products have a distinct life cycle pattern. Here products are first categorized into different stages of development, and then forecasts are prepared by using the best model for each stage. For example, Howmedica, Division of Stryker Corporation, which is a manufacturer of orthopedic implants, uses such an approach. It categorizes products into four stages: (a) newly introduced products, (b) mature products, (c) products with a declining demand, and (d) obsolete products. It defines mature products as ones that have been in existence for two or more years. Products with declining sales are those that are still selling, but their demand is beginning to taper off. Obsolete products are those that are almost at the end of their life cycle.

Size of customers: If you have large customers, you may like to prepare their forecasts separately to make sure that they get the best customer service. Preparing forecasts by customer is called Account Based Forecasting. Companies such as Nabisco (now a part of Kraft Foods) do their forecasting by customer.

Product classification: It is not unusual for a company that has to prepare forecasts of hundreds and thousands of different products, but doesn't have enough resources to do the job. One way to get around this problem is to classify the products by the level of their importance, and pay the most attention to those that are highly important and the least attention to ones that are least important. ABC is one such approach for classification. Here products that are most important to the company are classified as "A," and the least, "C." Products that fall between the two are classified as "B." Forecasts of "C" products are often prepared by the expert system, which automatically selects the best model for each product from a series of models, and then prepares their forecasts.

Some companies like Syngenta, world leader in agribusiness, groups its products into: (1) products that are high in business importance but easy to forecast, (2) products that are high in business importance but difficult to forecast, (3) products that are low in business importance but easy to forecast, and (4) products that are low in business importance but difficult to forecast, according to Richard Herrin, formerly with Syngenta, and now Director of Supply Chain at Georgia Gulf Corporation. Syngenta found that 45 percent of its products, comprising 59 percent of total sales are easy to forecast and thus don't need much attention. Within the group of products that are difficult to forecast, 17 percent (6 percent of total sales) have low business importance and thus don't deserve much attention. What requires the most attention are products that are high in business importance but difficult to forecast, which in this case constituted 38 percent of all products, yielding 35 percent of total sales. Therefore, it is important to categorize products to determine where we should spend most of our forecasting resources.

A company may like to prepare forecasts by the channel of distribution, that is, prepare separate forecasts for drug stores, grocery stores, warehouse clubs, etc. This may be important where there is an opportunity to optimize sales/profit by promoting products differently in difference channels.

MONITORING AND REVISING FORECASTS

Monitoring and revising forecasts are also important parts of the forecasting process. If there is a problem in our forecasts, and a monitoring process is in place, we are more likely to detect the problem much sooner and be able to take the necessary action in a timely fashion. This raises the question of how often we should monitor and revise forecasts. It depends partly on the bucket in which we prepare forecasts, partly on a period that can give a fair reading about the performance, and partly on the importance of a product. Weekly forecasts are fine if we need them, but they may not provide a good handle on the forecasting performance. Sales may go down in one week, but make it up in the following week or the week after. Most of the companies (69 percent of them according to the 2009 survey of the Institute of Business Forecasting and Planning) monitor and update forecasts monthly. A period less than a month may be too short to give a good reading and longer than that may not give you enough time to react. The importance of a product also makes a difference. You may like to monitor and update forecasts of high value products more frequently than others.

These are the key decisions we have to make before designing a forecasting process. In the next three chapters we will discuss different forecasting processes that have evolved over time—what they are, and how each one improved the one before it.

SUGGESTED READING

1. Gelly, Paul. "Managing Bottom-Up and Top-Down Approaches: Ocean Spray's Experience." ***Journal of Business Forecasting***. Winter 1999, pp. 3-6.
2. Herrin, Richard. "Managing Products via Demand Variability and Business Importance." ***Journal of Business Forecasting***. Spring 2007, pp. 6-10.
3. Koster, Cynthia. "A Case Study of Two Forecasting Organizational Options." ***Journal of Business Forecasting***. Spring 2000, pp. 14-15.
4. Lapide, Larry. "A Simple View of Top-Down versus Bottom-Up Forecasting." ***Journal of Business Forecasting***. Summer 1998, pp. 28-29.
5. Milliken, Alan. "Demand Planning: Managing the Unforecastables." ***Journal of Business Forecasting***. Summer 2006, pp. 3-9.
6. Mohn, N. Carroll. "Forecast Performance of An Audit Service: Coca Cola's Experience." ***Journal of Business Forecasting***. Winter 1988, pp. 6-7.
7. Worthen, Ben. "Future Results Not Guaranteed," CIO. July 15, 2003.

QUESTIONS FOR REVIEW

1. What is the forecasting process? How does it affect the quality of forecasts?
2. What is forecast horizon? How should a company decide about it?
3. What are the benefits of having an independent forecasting department?
4. Why is it important to classify products into groups before setting up a forecasting process? Give two different ways of classifying products, and the rationale behind them.
5. How is product life cycle used as a way of classifying products for best forecasting results?
6. How often should forecasts be monitored and revised, and why?
7. In which department does a large percentage of companies have their forecasting function, and why?
8. What kind of forecasts does each one of the following functions need and why?
   a. Salespeople
   b. Finance people
   c. Production people
   d. Marketing people
9. Among four different types of products listed below, where should the forecaster spend the

most and the least time?

a. Products that are important to the company but difficult to forecast
b. Products that are important to the company but easy to forecast
c. Products that are not important to the company but easy to forecast
d. Products that are not important to the company but difficult to forecast

10. Discuss in brief the following:
    a. ABC classification
    b. Top-down vs. bottom-up approach
    c. Demand vs. shipment forecasts
    d. Middle-out approach to forecasting
    e. Account-based forecasting

CHAPTER 7

SILO TO CONSENSUS FORECASTING

Over the last three decades or so, market dynamics have changed significantly and so has the forecasting process. It has changed from Silo Forecasting (SF) to Consensus Forecasting (CF) to Sales and Operations Planning (S&OP) and now to Collaborative Planning, Forecasting and Replenishment (CPFR®). In this chapter, we will discuss the Silo Forecasting and Consensus Forecasting processes. The other two will be discussed in the following chapters.

In the Silo Forecasting process, we have multiple forecasts because each function prepares its own forecasts for its own use. Production prepares its own forecasts for its production plan, Sales for its sales plan, Marketing for its marketing plan, and Finance for its financial plan. Since no one is accountable and no one is watching the numbers, there is no incentive to improve them. This was fine when manufacturers were king. Whatever they produced, they sold. If something was left over, marketing would make it go away. Those days are gone. Consumers are now more demanding and less loyal. They have many more choices. If you cannot give them what they want, someone else will. To make sure they produce and hold in inventory what consumers want, companies have to improve their forecasts, which was not possible in the Silo structure.

Another problem that resulted from the Silo structure was difficulty in aligning supply with demand, because each one's plan was based on a different set of forecast numbers. Demand was based on one set of forecast numbers prepared by demand planners, and supply, on another, prepared by supply planners. To align supply with demand we need not only one set of forecast numbers but also forecasts that are more accurate.

The multiple forecast numbers also created a problem for people at the top. At times, the CEO didn't know which forecast to use because each function had a different number. The Consensus Forecasting process helped to overcome this problem by generating one set of forecasts.

WHY CONSENSUS FORECASTING?

The key benefits of a Consensus Forecasting process are collaboration, ability to overlay judgment over statistical forecasts, and one number forecasts. To improve forecasts we need cross-functional collaboration because no one has all the information. Salespeople are the eyes and ears of the market because they are closest to the market. They can provide visibility of their customers' demand, feedback on their promotional activities, and competitive activities. Marketing people can provide information on products they plan to introduce or abandon, territories they plan to enter or exit, and promotional plans. Finance controls the budget. Input from the Supply Chain does not add much value as far as demand forecasts go, because it deals with supply, not demand. But it can tell whether or not the expected demand will be met. At times, the presence of people from operations can also help in demand forecasting. Take the example of a steel door manufacturer whose sales rose sharply when one of the competitors went out of business. With the result, the customized doors, which were previously delivered in two weeks, were now delivered in three. After four months, when statistical forecasts were presented in a monthly consensus meeting, operations informed the committee that they had implemented a second shift. The doors that required three weeks would now again be available in two weeks. In that case, the sales guy responded that we had to raise the forecast because they were not accepting orders from customers who wanted delivery in two weeks. So, forecasts were intuitively raised, and for a good reason.

Judgmental overlay on statistical forecasts (called baseline forecasts) often improves forecasts because it accounts for elements that have a bearing on forecasts but cannot be quantified, and for information that was not available at the time they were prepared. For example, in 2007 Menu Foods, a manufacturer of dog and cat food, had to recall 60 million containers of "Cut and Gravy" food because of contamination. When the Menu Food's competitor, Evanger's Dog and Cat Food, learned about the recall, it intuitively raised its forecasts to fill the gap. It is important, however, that people responsible for adjusting forecasts have the domain knowledge about the product and the market.

One number philosophy means that every department within an organization uses the same forecasts. In the consensus meeting, one number emerges because all the departments have to agree on one number.

GETTING STARTED

Here are six steps to be followed for preparing forecasts with the Consensus Forecasting process:

Step 1: Gather the historical data of what you wish to forecast. If you wish to forecast shipments, you need shipment data. If you wish to forecast demand (orders), you will need demand data. If you wish to forecast end-consumer sales, you will need end-consumer sales data. More and more companies now have started forecasting end-consumer sales, often called Point of Sale (POS), because this is what ultimately drives the demand and shipments.

Step 2: Obtain input from all the functions including Sales, Marketing, and Finance, along with the historical sales data. Sales may provide input about the plans of their customers and competitive information. Marketing may provide information about its promotional plans, products it plans to introduce and abandon, and so on.

Step 3: As much as possible, have an agreement on the assumptions to be made, and then prepare statistical forecasts. Each forecast is based on assumptions such as what price we will charge, how much we will spend on advertisement, what kind of state of the economy we expect in the period we wish to forecast, and so on. It would be great if all the stakeholders including top management agree on assumptions.

Step 4: Manage exceptions. No matter how forecasts are prepared, when a forecaster looks at the computer printout, he or she may find certain forecasts that don't make sense; they are either too high or too low. These numbers have to be adjusted, which is called managing the exceptions. Such adjustments can be made either by the forecaster him/herself or collectively in the consensus meeting.

Step 5: Send statistical forecasts to all the stakeholders for their review. This will enable the forecaster to take care of any issue or concern they may have about the data, model, and/or assumptions before the consensus meeting, thereby preparing him or her better for the meeting.

Step 6 Present statistical forecasts at the consensus meeting, which is cross functional, and is often held once a month. (Some companies call the consensus meeting a compromise meeting, because here different functions have to compromise on one set of forecast numbers.) Here the forecaster presents not only forecasts but also the assumptions he or she made. Forecasts and assumptions are thoroughly discussed and debated. If any number needs to be adjusted, it is done collectively. Once forecasts are jointly agreed upon, every function uses the same numbers.

Forecasts so finalized are called Consensus Forecasts because they are based on consensus, but not necessarily on unanimity, because every person may not wholeheartedly agree to each and every number. When forecasts are prepared this way, their quality improves. According to the 2009 survey by the Institute of Business Forecasting and Planning, 80 percent of the companies follow this process in preparing forecasts.

INGREDIENTS OF A SUCCESSFUL CONSENSUS FORECASTING PROCESS

It is without any question that we need a Consensus Forecasting process because it improves forecasts as well as plans. Following are the key ingredients for a successful Consensus Forecasting process.

Collaboration among different functions: For this process to work, we need close collaboration from all the functions involved. To prepare them, the forecaster needs input from all the functions, which is not easy, because each function has its own agenda. Salespeople would go for under-forecasts if their quotas are based on them. Otherwise, they would prefer over-forecasts to make sure that products are available when orders come in. Marketing people will go for over-forecasts if their advertising budget is tied to them. Above all, different functions have been preparing forecasts for their own use for many years; it won't be easy for them to part with their authority.

Equal voice: Each group must have an equal voice in the consensus meeting. If one powerful group or individual dominates the meeting, it would defeat the purpose, according to John Hellriegel, Vice President of Demand Planning & Replenishment North America, The Estee Lauder Companies. Silence does not necessarily mean consent. Each group (business function) must say openly whether or not it agrees with the forecasts or wish to make some changes, and why.

Blessing from the top: The support from top management is a must because without it we cannot expect collaboration from other functions. It is not easy to move the organization from a silo structure to collaboration, where all the functions work together as a team, are sympathetic to the concerns of others, and think holistically. In fact, it requires a culture change, which is not possible without commitment from the top.

To win the support of upper management we have to educate them, which also is not easy. They have to understand how much value improved forecasts would add. Even a 1-percent improvement in forecasts can mean millions of dollars of savings in terms of lower inventory, stock-outs, shrinkage and obsolescence, increased sales, and better customer service. Winning the support of upper management requires patience, persistence, and hard work. In 1986, for example, Parke-Davis had a forecasting function in place, but nobody knew its role. Its forecasts were used in production and distribution, but they were not considered a part of the management review process. People in the forecasting function were determined to change that. To accomplish it, they first decided to improve further the quality of their own forecasts. If they had confidence in their own numbers, it would be easier to sell. Then they started comparing their own forecasts with those of management to make sure that their forecasts were more accurate. After they were satisfied with their own numbers, they started introducing them to the management. In the beginning, management showed no interest, but the forecasting people continued submitting their forecasts. They also started reporting on how their numbers compared to management forecasts. After a while, management started looking at their forecasts and began asking why their numbers were different. This was the turning point, says, Debra M. Schramm, Forecasting Manager at the time. Five years later, their forecasts became an integral part of the management review process.

Understanding the mutual benefits: To get cooperation from different functions/departments, you must be able to answer one important question, which is, "What is in it for me?" Every function wants to know this before extending its hand for cooperation. Salespeople, for example, believe that their primary function is to sell; so, forecasting is not a part of their responsibility. If they understand that getting orders is not enough unless they can be fulfilled, their attitude might change. When Sean Reese, Demand Planner at Ocean Spray Cranberries, after months of frustration with no response from Salespeople, approached their manager and explained to him how improved forecasts would help them, the information started flowing in. It will further help if the forecaster, off and on, visits salespeople face to face; attends their national or regional sales meetings; and ask them to make demand planning a part of their agenda. You can also expect more cooperation from other functions, such as Marketing and Finance, if they recognize how improvements in forecasts will help them too in their efforts.

Independent forecasting department: It will also make a difference where the forecasting function is placed, that is, who is given the responsibility for preparing statistical forecasts, because each function has a bias of its own as described earlier. The best thing, of course, is to have an independent forecasting department; it will have no ax to grind. At present, only 13 percent of the companies have an independent forecasting department, according to the 2009 survey of the Institute of Business Forecasting and Planning.

Monitoring forecasts: To improve forecasts further, we need to monitor them regularly to determine if there is any problem. The problem may be with the data, assumptions, model, or bias of a particular participant in the consensus process. There is a bias in a forecast if the error is consistently one directional (maybe two to three times in a row). In other words, the error is consistently resulting either from over-forecasting or from under-forecasting. Once you know the source, you may know how to handle it.

There are several other things that can also help to improve the Consensus Forecasts. Technology is one of them. You need cutting edge technology for retrieving, analyzing, filtering, and slicing and dicing data; preparing forecasts; and receiving feedback from stakeholders. Forecasting software rather than spreadsheet packages are needed for forecasting. It is cumbersome, if not impossible, to store and manipulate data of thousands of items on a spreadsheet. Furthermore, all the models are not available in a spreadsheet package, nor are they available in a form forecasters can easily use. Also, it is difficult to receive input and feedback from all the stakeholders without the appropriate technology in place.

SUGGESTED READING

1. Hellriegel, John. "Getting Past the Plateau Driving Performance from an Established Demand Planning Process." ***Journal of Business Forecasting.*** Spring 2009, pp. 12-16.
2. Jain, Chaman L. and Thomas P. Chen. "The Role of Judgment in Business Forecasting." ***Industrial Management.*** November/December 1992, pp. 1-3.
3. Reese, Sean. "The Human Aspects of Collaborative Forecasting" in ***Practical Guide to Business Forecasting,*** edited by Chaman L. Jain and Jack Malehorn. New York: Graceway Publishing Company, 2005, pp. 180-188.
4. Schramm, Debra M. "How to Sell Forecasts to Management" in ***Practical Guide to Business Forecasting,*** edited by Chaman L. Jain and Jack Malehorn New York: Graceway Publishing Company, 2005, pp. 460-461.
5. Simonelic, Ken. "Successfully Managing and Executing Change." ***Journal of Business Forecasting.*** Fall 2009, pp. 20-21.

QUESTIONS FOR REVIEW

1. What is Consensus Forecasting? How does it differ from Silo Forecasting?
2. What are the key ingredients of a successful Consensus Forecasting process?
3. Explain in brief the following:
   a. Under what circumstances would Production people prefer over- and under-forecasts?
   b. Under what circumstances would Marketing people prefer over-forecasts?
   c. What is the usual preference of Finance people—over- or under-forecasts, and why?
   d. Are Consensus Forecasts based on consensus or unanimity?
4. How can you win the support of Salespeople for setting up a forecasting function? Explain.
5. Why is the support of upper management necessary for a successful Consensus Forecasting process? Explain.
6. Why is monitoring of forecasts essential for improving them? Explain.
7. Why is judgmental overlay over statistical forecasts important? Explain.
8. Explain why it is important to have an independent forecasting department.
9. Explain why the collaboration of various functions is important for improving forecasts.
10. Explain how to win the support of upper management.

CHAPTER 8

THE SALES AND OPERATIONS PLANNING PROCESS

The Consensus Forecasting process is fine for improving forecasts, but it is not adequate for managing a business. Forecasts, no matter how accurate they are, won't help unless we quickly act on them. If, for example, we find that demand will be greater than supply, to capitalize on it we have to move quickly to expand our supply either by adding in a second/third shift or by outsourcing. If no participant of the consensus meeting has the power to act (which is usually the case), the consensus team members will send the proposal to a high-ranking individual (who may be the President) for action. But by the time he or she is ready to act, it may be too late. So, we had the best forecasts, but we could not take advantage of them. The S&OP process provides the mechanism not only to foresee the opportunities and problems but also enables an action quickly.

The S&OP process is not just good to have, market dynamics dictate that we need it to survive. In the last three decades or so, the number of products has exploded, the number of sales and distribution channels has proliferated, the life cycle of products has shortened, and lead-time has become much longer. Furthermore, consumers have become less loyal and more demanding. As such, the competition has become more intense. To stay competitive, there must be a process that allows us to not only foresee opportunities and risks, but also to act on them fast. The S&OP process, if properly designed and implemented, does it all.

OBJECTIVES OF AN S&OP PROCESS

Before going into how the S&OP process works, it is important to know its key objectives, which are the following:

1. Align demand with supply and budget (financial plans)
2. Integrate operational plans with strategic plans
3. Integrate product mix with total volume
4. Ability to act pro-actively

Align demand with supply and budget (financial plans): The key objective of the S&OP process is to align expected demand with expected supply and budget (financial plans) in an effort to reduce cost, increase sales, and improve profit margin. The cost goes up if demand is greater than supply because of overtime, smaller runs, switchovers, outsourcing, and expediting delivery. The cost also goes up if supply is greater than demand because of an increase in inventory, underutilized fixed assets, and excess labor. Further, if expected demand is greater than expected supply, the company will miss the opportunity if it fails to manage it. Similarly, if expected supply is greater than expected demand, the company needs to find ways to increase demand to optimize profit or, in the worst case, minimize losses. Additionally, demand and supply plans help to develop an integrated financial plan about revenue, margin, profit and loss, balance sheet, and cash flow.

If expected demand is greater than expected supply, the company needs to expand its supply; if this is not possible, it has to find other ways to manage the demand. The company may decide to dampen the demand of products that are expected to be short in supply by cutting down their promotion (a part of demand shaping). If shortages still persist, it has to decide about the allocation of available quantity to different customers. (The allocation problem also occurs at the launch of a new product because every customer wants to be the first to sell, yet it is produced in limited quantity.) If expected supply is greater than expected demand, then the company has to decide whether to increase the demand through promotion, build inventory for future use, close the plant for a few weeks, and/or find other ways to utilize the excess capacity.

The objective of S&OP is not only to align demand and supply but also have to be consistent with the budget (financial plans). The gaps between demand and supply versus budget are most often addressed in the Pre-Executive meeting and Executive meeting—generally six or nine months ahead. The alignment process may call for modifying demand and supply plans, the budget, or both. At times, a change in the budget may be needed, but the top management may not be ready for that.

Integrate operational plans with strategic plans: To meet the overall objectives, a company needs to align not only expected supply with expected demand but also to integrate its operational plans with strategic ones. Operational plans are short term, whereas strategic plans are long term. There is no set time horizon for operational and strategic plans; they vary from company to company and from industry to industry. Usually, 1 to 3 months are regarded as operational, and 3 to 18 months, strategic. Strategic goals may include meeting budget/financial plans and/or hitting a certain market share target. If operational forecasts are off and are not consistent with the strategic ones, it means that something has to be done with the operational forecasts/plans to hit the strategic targets. We may decide to promote some products more heavily, introduce a few more new products, and/or look for new markets or channels of distributions to boost the demand.

In recent years, companies have started bringing new products under the purview of the S&OP process much earlier so that operational plans could be well aligned with strategic plans. At Procter & Gamble (P&G), for example, in the past, the introductions of new products were brought to the process only 6 to 12 months before the launch date, making it difficult to align operational plans with strategic ones. Now they are brought to the S&OP process 12 to 18 months ahead of the launch date, giving enough time to make changes in operational plans to align them with strategic plans.

Align product mix with total volume: When we talk about demand and supply in the context of S&OP, we are primarily concerned with the volume and not the mix. Volume here includes the overall demand of a company as a whole, as well as the overall demand of a brand/category. Product mix, on the other hand, includes both product lines (brand/categories) and individual products. In S&OP, we deal only with product lines and not individual products. (A product line is a group of products within the product mix that are closely related. Individual products—often called SKUs—within a product line are distinguished by size, price, appearance, or by some other attribute.) Once the expected volume is identified, the next step is to decide on the product mix, because it is the volume that drives the mix. L'Oréal, for example, during the recession of 2008-2009, decided to produce product lines with low-price alternatives to meet their targets.

Ability to act pro-actively: Now it is more important than ever to be pro-active. In the today's competitive markets, if you see any opportunity, you want to be the first one to grab it. So, you need to have a process in place that allows you to see opportunities and risks ahead of time and provides a mechanism to act. The S&OP process does just that.

HOW THE S&OP PROCESS WORKS

How the S&OP process works can be explained by the following five-step approach outlined by Thomas F. Wallace, with some minor modifications (see Figure 8.1).

Step 1: Gather historical sales data, as well as input from various functions, particularly Sales and Marketing. Sales may provide information about customers' plans regarding the opening and closing of stores, promotions, consumer feedback, and so on. Marketing may provide information about its promotional plans, products it plans to introduce and discontinue, markets it plans to exit or enter, and so on. After all the information is gathered, prepare statistical forecasts. This is done by a forecaster who may reside within the Demand Planning group or outside of it.

Figure 8.1 | Sales and Operations Planning Process

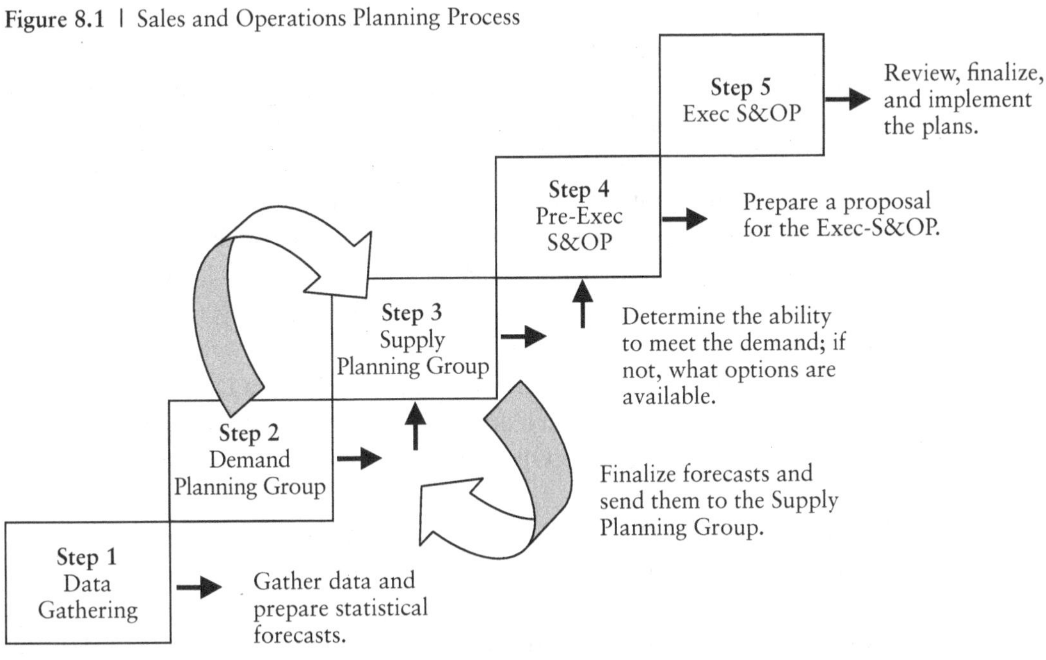

Source: Adapted from the book, Thomas F. Wallace. *Sales & Operations Planning: The How-To Handbook*. Cincinnati, Ohio: T. F. Wallace & Co., 2004, p. 59.

Step 2: Prepare Consensus Forecasts by going through the consensus process described in the previous chapter. (If you don't have a Consensus Forecasting process in place, institute one.) This is done by the Demand Planning group, which may be comprised of Sales, Marketing, Finance, etc. The Demand Planning group reviews the forecasts as well as underlying assumptions and, where necessary, collectively overlays judgment over the statistical forecasts. After forecasts are finalized, they are sent to the Supply Planning group to see if they can meet the demand. Very often a representative of the Supply Planners participates in the consensus meeting, who then conveys the concerns and issues expressed in that meeting to its own group. This type of arrangement, among other things, strengthens the relationship between Demand and Supply planners and reinforces collaboration.

Step 3: The Supply Planning group, which often includes manufacturing, purchasing, and logistics, uses demand forecasts to determine whether or not there is enough supply capability (including manufacturing capacity, inventory, and logistics capacity) to not only meet the demand but also expectations of customer service, quality, and cost objectives. If it can, the group wants to make sure that contingency plans are in place to address demand risks and opportunities identified by the Demand Planners. If demand is expected to be greater than supply, what options are available? Solutions could include putting in a second or third shift and/or outsourcing. If supply is expected to be greater than demand, options may be building inventory for future use or closing the plant for a few days/weeks. After that, the Supply Planning group sends its plan to the Demand Planning group for its review. Bear in mind, the responsibility of the Demand Planning group is not only to prepare forecasts but also to manage the demand. This helps the Demand Planning group to prepare better for the Pre-Executive meeting.

In fact, Step 2 and Step 3 are a reiterative process because both Demand and Supply planning groups need the input of each other to come up with a best plan, which they can present in the Pre-Executive S&OP meeting.

Step 4: Have a Pre-Executive S&OP meeting, which is often attended by people from the Demand Planning and the Supply Planning groups as well as from New Product Development and Finance. In this meeting, they discuss whether the overall volume of operational forecasts is consistent with strategic goals (which may be financial goals, budget, etc.); and if not, what can be done. Once they settle on that, the next step is to see whether the expected demand (forecasts) can be met. If not, what options do we have to align the demand with the supply? If, on the other hand, supply is expected to be greater than demand, what can be done to balance them? Committee members discuss and debate all these issues and then finalize their proposal. Since all the key stakeholders attend this meeting, each looks at the proposal from its own perspective. Salespeople want to be sure that there would be enough supply to meet their customers' demand. Financial people want to be sure that there would be enough revenue to meet the financial goals. For Marketing, market share may be the issue. At the end of the day, they come up with a plan, a course of action that has been jointly agreed upon, which they would present at the up-coming Executive S&OP meeting. If on any issue they could not reach agreement, it would be left to the discretion of the Executive S&OP team.

Step 5: After the Pre-Executive S&OP committee finalizes its plan, it is time for the Executive S&OP committee to meet. The meeting is attended by people from different functions. The difference between the Executive S&OP committee and the Pre-Executive S&OP committee is that members of the former are key people who are empowered to make decisions. At Pfizer, for example, even the President attends the meeting. Since the Pre-Executive S&OP committee has done all the groundwork, persons are there to respond to any question that may come up and members have the power to make a decision, whatever the decision the committee makes is implemented right away. The Executive S&OP committee goes over the recommendations of the Pre-Executive S&OP team, evaluates them against the company's strategic plans, policy and risk parameters, and then takes an appropriate action. The committee may ask questions about market share, expected revenue and profit, status of inventory and order backlogs, extent of cannibalization if a new product is to be introduced, and key performance indicators (KPI).

In some companies, particularly small ones, members of the Pre-Executive team are empowered to make most of the decisions. In that case, the Pre-Executive S&OP meeting and the Executive S&OP meeting are one and the same.

Generally, the S&OP process is on a monthly cycle, which means all these activities have to be completed within a month. After the decisions are made and implemented, and results are in, the postmortem starts. It is the way of determining what worked, what did not, and what lessons are learned to improve further the process.

With the implementation of the S&OP process, forecasts improve; inventory, shrinkage, stock-outs and obsolescence go down; customer service gets better; and sales increase. Table 8.1 shows how much these four companies—Air Products & Chemical, JohnsonDiversey, Syngenta, and On Semiconductor—benefited after they implemented the S&OP process. They improved forecast accuracy, reduced inventory, and improved customer service. According to the 2009 survey of the Institute of Business Forecasting and Planning, 73 percent of the companies have implemented this process, and the number is growing. One executive of a company remarked, "With the implementation of S&OP, strategic planning has become alive. Plus, Supply Planners have become active participants in the process."

JOHNSONDIVERSEY: A CASE STUDY

JohnsonDiversey, which sprang out of DiverseyLever and Johnson Wax Professional in 2002, recognized from the start that they had to improve customer service and reduce inventories for

Table 8.1 | Benefits Derived From the Implementation of S&OP Process

Company	Period	Improvement in Forecasts	Improvement in Inventory	Improvement in Customer Service	Source
Air Products & Chemical	2003-06	21%	20%	10%	Stephen P. Crane *Dir. of Supply Chain Performance Polymers*
JohnsonDiversey	2002-05	23%	18%	6%	Greg Reyman *Specialist in Operations Planning JohnsonDiversey*
Syngenta	2001-06	49%	5-10%	NA	Richard Herrin *formerly with Syngenta, and now Director of Supply Chain Management at Axiall Corporation*
On Semiconductor	2004-05	NA	14%	1%	Tim Williams *Demand Forecasting Mgr.*

Sources:
1. Crane, Stephen P. "How to Incorporate Market Intelligence into Statistical Forecasting," Presentation at the Demand Planning & Forecasting Best Practices Conference in Orlando, Florida, of Institute of Business Forecasting and Planning, Appeared in the Conference Manual (New York: Institute of Business Forecasting and Planning, October 2006), pp. 327-347.
2. Herrin, Richard. "Managing Products via Demand Variability and Business Importance." ***Journal of Business Forecasting.*** Spring 2007, pp. 6-10.
3. Reyman, Greg. "How JohnsonDiversey Implemented S&OP in Europe." ***Journal of Business Forecasting.*** Fall 2005, pp. 20-23, 28.
4. Williams, Tim. "Forecasting Journey at On Semiconductor." ***Journal of Business Forecasting.*** Spring 2006, pp. 29-32.

sustained growth. It was a great challenge for the company, particularly in Europe where the merging of different companies complicated the supply and distribution network. Although it had a large portfolio of products, a large portion of the revenue came only from few products. Communications among various functions were very poor. The technology that was used to support processes was outdated, and often differed from one process to another. The main interest of Sales and Marketing was in selling, not in developing a sales plan. There was little or no agreement on sales forecasts, and no accountability for customer service and inventory levels. Demand Planners did not exist at the time. A number of people were involved in the supply planning, but most of their time was spent on fulfilling orders. And so the company was not doing well. This led to the development of the S&OP process, which was implemented in two phases.

In the first phase, JohnsonDiversey focused primarily on process, people, and technology. In terms of process, the initial focus was on linking the Sales/Marketing to the Supply Chain to developing rolling mid-term demand plans. Since in Europe the sales were very much locally oriented, each country was asked to develop its local demand plans, and then send it either to its local supply units or to the European supply units. To better manage the product portfolio, the company reviewed all its items to decide which ones to keep and which ones to discontinue. To optimize its resource utilization, it introduced ABC product classification so that it could concentrate more on high-revenue generating products, and less on the others. To improve the skills of people, S&OP workshops were run with an emphasis on a country-specific demand review process. In addition, it decided to regularly review supply performance indicators such as Orders Timely in Full, Number of Days of Supply on Hand, Obsolescence Index, and Sales Forecast Error. The tool, SAP Vanilla, was rolled out in all countries as an ERP (Enterprise Resource Planning) system.

In the second phase, JohnsonDiversey took a number of new initiatives. It developed a planning review process to review all the processes across Europe, and created a program to assess the skill sets of all the Planners to determine what their strengths were and what skills they needed to develop. Wherever it found a gap, training programs run by the Planners Academy closed it. The company decided to have "One Process and One System" for its planning needs in every country. It also decided to have a strong Demand Planning and Forecasting process, which would be based on collaboration among various stakeholders including Sales, Supply Chain, Portfolio, and Finance. Since demand drives supply it decided to concentrate first on improving Demand Planning and then on Supply Planning. The Supply Planning process was based on geographical and physical characteristics (one process for bulky products with low value, and another for complex and high-value products). It further decided to use SAP technology for Forecasting and Planning, though it would first make a full use of SAP R/3, and then go to its next level version—

APO technology.

Although the company still has a long way to go, it made a significant progress in three years (2002-2005). Forecast error went down from 26 percent to 20 percent, Orders Timely in Full went up from 88 percent to 93 percent, and Number of Days of Supply on Hand went down from 67 days to 55 days. Dr. Greg Reyman, who was at the time involved with the process, offers the following advice. (1) In a multi-country organization, the S&OP process should be managed centrally. (2) Key performance indicators must be made transparent so that every country and region can see how they are doing in comparison with others. (3) The S&OP process must be aligned with the corporate strategy, which must be followed by each operating company.

INGREDIENTS OF A SUCCESSFUL S&OP PROCESS

The S&OP process works, but it can be more effective if all the ingredients are in place. In addition to what was described in the previous chapter in connection with the Consensus Forecasting process, which is a part of the S&OP process, here are the key ingredients.

Cross-functional participation: The cross-functional participation is needed at every level—in the consensus meeting, the Pre-Executive S&OP meeting, and the Executive S&OP meeting. Since no one person/function has all the information needed to make a good forecast and/or good decisions, participation by different functions ensures that all the information available or known at the time has been captured. It also serves as checks and balances. It is important to know before each meeting which process participants are uncomfortable with the current plans and/or actions so that their concerns can be addressed. It is also important that forecasts are finalized through the Consensus Forecasting process. Otherwise, some functions may distrust the numbers, and refuse to buy-in. Above all, the close cross-functional participation reduces the chances of someone later on undermining the forecasts, and consequently the process.

Involvement of key persons in the process: For an S&OP to succeed, people from top management must be actively involved with the process right from the beginning. They could be the President, Vice President of Operations or Sales, CFO, and other key persons. The more we have such people involved in the process, the better it will be. Without their involvement, the S&OP process will suffer. People may think that S&OP meetings are optional; however, it is necessary to have their full cooperation to run this process efficiently and effectively. Above all, without their active participation, resources needed to run the S&OP process may not be available.

Need for a champion: To run the process smoothly and effectively, there needs to be a champion who has the clout and power to make sure meetings are held regularly and on time. Everyone who is supposed to attend shows up, the discussion remains well within the scope of the agenda, and if and when conflict arises, it is quickly resolved. It is healthy to have a disagreement, but the champion must know how to manage it.

Strict adherence to the meetings' calendars and agendas: It is important to strictly adhere to each meeting's calendar and agenda. If at any given time one cannot attend a meeting, he or she should be available by phone or else send a personal representative. Postponing a meeting due to lack of attendance sends the wrong signal that the meeting is not important. Also, as described earlier, in the S&OP process, a number of meetings are held within a month; each meeting is linked to another. The Supply Planning group cannot do anything unless the Consensus meeting is held to arrive at demand forecasts. The Pre-Executive S&OP meeting cannot do anything unless the Supply Planning group has met and come up with its proposal based on the information provided by the Demand Planning group. Without the Pre-Executive S&OP proposal, the Executive S&OP meeting cannot act.

Concentrate on overall volume and product families/categories, not on SKUs: It would be difficult to accomplish much in a meeting if we start discussing SKUs, which may easily run into hundreds and thousands. Therefore, it is important to confine the discussion and analysis to overall volume and families/categories. If we have a good handle on product families/categories, we are likely to have a good handle on their SKUs as well, because they are part of them. However, if a given SKU(s) is a large revenue generator, it may require a special attention.

Goals and metrics must be clearly defined: Nothing will happen unless there are clearly defined goals and metrics. The goals may be of forecast accuracy that we would like to achieve, inventory-on-hand we would like to maintain, service levels we would like to provide, and a market share target we would like to hit. Goals would never be achieved unless quantifiable metrics are in place to measure and monitor them. But don't use too many metrics; just a few key ones. Whichever ones you decide to use, it is important that they are linked to the business performance—forecast accuracy, for example, is linked to inventory level, customer service, and stock-outs.

Postmortem the results: Despite all the best efforts, error occurs. Error could result from a poor forecast and/or a poor decision. So, it is important to do the postmortem after the facts are in so we can determine what went wrong and why. Once we know the cause of an error, we may find a way to correct it—at the very least, we can make sure that the same error does not occur again. In forecasting, error can result from the data we used, assumptions we made, the model we applied, and/or from the bias of a particular individual. It is equally important to learn what went well and why, because it too can help in the future.

Guidelines for resolving conflicts and courage to act on difficult issues: Conflicts among different functions are fairly common in business and are healthy. To move forward, conflicts have to be resolved and decisions have to be made. So, it is important to have some guidelines for resolving conflicts. For example, in the case of a conflict, alternative scenarios may have to be specified and their effect on the bottom line has to be assessed in terms of dollars and/or units. If that does not work, a key person from the management, maybe the CEO or President, has to step in to make the final decision.

Tom Wallace, guru of the S&OP process, strongly believes that the success of the Executive S&OP process comes not only from the use of right tools, techniques, and process but also in large part from the ability to act rather than to put off difficult decisions, which he calls "putting the moose on the table." If the team in the Executive S&OP meeting does not do that, it would be creating a negative energy, which would impede the progress.

Centralizing data and using standard global product identification: For an effective S&OP process, it is important that data are centralized in a global warehouse, and products have a standard identification possibly under the umbrella of UCCnet. (UCCnet is a global repository where enterprises register their items and share standardized supply chain information.) The process works effectively and efficiently if data are maintained in a centralized data warehouse. Collecting data from different sources makes the job of a forecaster much harder. Plus, data become more transparent if they are stored and maintained at one place. In companies where different data are maintained at different places and on different platforms, people including forecasters often don't know exactly what is available, and where.

Technology to facilitate the process: To make the most of an S&OP process , we need appropriate technology to collect, analyze, and disseminate information, as well as to prepare forecasts and develop plans. To start the process, the technology used may be as simple as Microsoft Excel and the Internet. But as the process progresses, we may need a little more advanced technology. For a process to work efficiently, many of the processes have to be automated. Technology facilitates automation. To make the process more efficient, we may need three types of tools—demand planning tools, supply planning tools, and a workbench. The demand planning tools include "Demand Collaborator," which is used to gather information from various sources such as Sales, Marketing, and Finance, and the forecasting engine to prepare forecasts. The supply planning tools include tools for planning production, inventory, procurement, and logistics. For that, we may need tools such as "Supply Collaborator," "Distribution Resource Planning" (DRP), and

"Material Requirement Planning" (MRP). The "Supply Collaborator" helps to gather information from various sources such as suppliers of raw materials and contract manufacturers. The DRP enables the setting of certain inventory control parameters (like safety stock) and calculate the time-phased inventory requirements. The MRP is a system for managing material requirements in a manufacturing process. The Advanced Planning System (APS) is a recent development that takes care of such things as production and inventory planning as well as provides, though somewhat limited, "what-if" scenario capability. The S&OP Workbench makes transparent various performance metrics of supply and demand to all the stakeholders. The Scorecards provide the historical metrics, whereas Dashboards provide the future metrics, but both are needed. The metrics may include profit margin, inventory level, customer service, and capacity utilization. The demand-related metrics are forecast errors, order back-logs, etc. The supply-related metrics are plant utilization, critical material shortages or surpluses, inventory level, customer service, etc.

Both demand and supply planning will be most effective if a plan is finalized through a "what-if" simulation rather than through a single pass-through determination. With that, both Demand and Supply Planning groups are likely to come up with the best plans. The Demand Planning group can go through a number of simulations to determine the best plan—the plan that will yield the maximum revenue/profit. It can go through simulations such as these: What would happen if the company lowers or raises the price, lowers or raises the advertising budget, introduces X or Y number of new products, enters into a new market, and/or exits from the old one? The Supply Planning group can also arrive at the best plan through simulations. If demand is expected to be greater than supply, the company might look into what would be the most efficient way to increase supply. Would it be by putting in an extra shift or by outsourcing? If supply is expected to be greater than demand, the firm might look for the best way to minimize costs; for example, it may consider closing the plant for a certain period of time or using the capacity to produce products for future use. Simulations, if done with a click of button, can be used effectively in the Pre-Executive S&OP and Executive S&OP meetings. (Such a sophisticated technology may not exist at the moment, but it is needed.)

Giving incentives and celebrating successes: Rewards help in meeting and exceeding goals, but they can be counterproductive if they are based on a specific activity. If production people are rewarded on the basis of maintaining low levels of inventory, it may hurt logistics by increasing expediting costs. Also, at times, products will be moved around from one warehouse to another for no reason other than to meet inventory targets, thereby unnecessarily increasing the company's transshipment costs. If salespeople are rewarded for meeting or exceeding their quotas, and quotas are tied to forecasts, they would bias their forecasts downward. So, for the best interest of a company, rewards should be based on overall performance such as overall profit or overall sales, and not on the performance of a specific activity. Keep in mind, our competitor is not across the hall, but outside the company. Therefore, the reward based on overall performance will not only improve overall performance but also bring harmony among different functions.

It is also important to celebrate successes because they give a sense of accomplishment and raise the morale and spirit of those involved. Furthermore, it gives an opportunity to recognize those who made it possible. Adtran, supplier of advanced transmission products, celebrates successes with lunch parties to which senior management is invited.

Aim for continuous improvement: There is no such thing as a perfect process. So, it is important to challenge assumptions, processes, technologies, and "Best-in-Class" benchmarks in an effort to make further improvements. Also, the world we live in is continually challenged by changing market dynamics, consumer behavior, and technology. To meet these challenges, we may have to change the process, too. In our continuous improvement efforts, it would also help if we regularly track all the changes when they occurred, action taken, and results achieved. Such information is vital for future improvement.

P&G has a rigorous annual audit process for assessing the performance of the Sales & Operations Planning process of every Business Unit across the globe. A Business Unit is a specific category of products like Oral Care and Skin Care. P&G has over 20 such categories that generate over a billion dollars in sales a year. The auditing process calls for the assessment and scoring of "Work Processes, Metric Tracking, and Capability." The assessment that is done every year is called Category ERP Assessment (CERPAT). The results of the assessment and action plans are shared with the GMs and other key functional leaders. Remember, S&OP is a journey and not a destination. There would always be a room for improvement.

In summary, S&OP is an alignment process that not only aligns demand and supply but also pushes all different functions of an organization in the same direction. Further, it moves the organization to a much shorter planning process—from a traditional annual planning process to a monthly planning process.

MYTHS ABOUT S&OP

As described above, S&OP is a must to run a business smoothly and efficiently. But there are some myths about it, resulting primarily from a lack of understanding. Tom Wallace from T. F. Wallace & Company, Fred Baumann from JDA Software, and Colleen Crum from Oliver Wight Americas share some of the myths they have encountered over time, which follow:

Myth No. 1: We don't need S&OP; it's a supply chain thing. This is not true. The S&OP is about managing the business. As such, it touches every function including the supply chain. We cannot have a demand plan without the help of Sales, Marketing, and Finance. We cannot come up with a supply plan without the help of the supply chain. Both the plans—demand and supply—are needed to run a business. Also, the basic premise of S&OP is cross-functional collaboration; it cannot work without the active participation of all the functions.

Myth No. 2: We don't need S&OP because we don't manufacture; everything is outsourced. This is not true either because S&OP is for every business including manufacturing, retail, and service related. In fact, it is needed where supply and demand have to be aligned for optimum results, which is the case with manufacturing companies, as well as with retail companies, banks, hotels, and others.

Myth No. 3: S&OP won't work because we have a silo structure. Accepting it means giving up on the future of organization. If we want the organization to grow, we have to break up the silos that separate one function from the other. S&OP helps to achieve that by creating a spirit of collaboration.

Myth No. 4: S&OP won't work for us because our business changes too quickly. On the contrary, S&OP is very agile. It responds to changing market dynamics promptly and efficiently. In fact, this is the main intent of this process.

Myth No. 5: S&OP is not suitable for big companies. In fact, large companies are the first ones who recognized the value of this process and implemented it. Now it is being adopted more and more by mid-size companies.

Myth No. 6: S&OP takes too long to implement. The experience of a number of experts in the area is that one can implement the basics in less than six months, and start reaping the benefits. V&M Star (producer of tubular products for oil and gas applications such as finished oil country tubular goods, line pipes, and standard pipes) did it from the beginning to the end in six months, according to Amy Mansfield, Production Planning Manager. The most difficult part in S&OP is to get buy-in from the senior management. Once we have that, every thing will go smoothly and quickly.

Myth No. 7: We have to improve our forecasts before we think about S&OP. It is true that good forecasts are the key to a successful S&OP process, but it is not a prerequisite. In fact, forecasts improve with the implementation of this process because it promotes collaboration, consensus process, and one number philosophy. Above all, it makes forecasts transparent, which further helps in improving forecasts.

Myth No. 8: We need an advanced technology to support it. It is true that the more advanced technology is used in S&OP, the better it is. But we can start with the existing technology including Microsoft Excel, Access, and the Internet. Even then we can reap some of the benefits. A number of companies have done that. We can upgrade the technology as we go along.

Myth No. 9: S&OP should be owned or sponsored either by supply planners or demand planners. This is a huge misunderstanding about S&OP. It should be owned by everyone. In fact, the first and foremost owner of this process should be the leader of the business, which may be President, General Manager, CEO, or COO. Further, if it is owned just by Demand Planners, Supply Planners won't engage seriously in the process. The same would happen if it is owned just by Supply Planners or by any other function. Therefore, for this process to work, it should be owned by everyone including the leader of the business.

Myth No. 10: S&OP is just another time-consuming meeting with little action. This would be true if it was not implemented in its true spirit, if there is no buy-in from senior management, if the trading partners either don't participate at all or participate half heartedly because they have not yet fully recognized its value, and if there is no champion to lead the process. So, if the process does not add any value, it is not the fault of S&OP, but of those who implemented it. If S&OP exists only by name, the process will still have all the attributes of a silo structure.

SUGGESTED READING

1. Baumann, Fred and Colleen Crum. "The Top 10 Myths and Realities of S&OP." White paper, JDA and Oliver Wight. 2009.
2. Bounds, Gwendolyn. "Peril and Gains of Unexpected Demand." ***The Wall Street Journal.*** April 10, 2007, p. B9.
3. Bower, Patrick. "How the S&OP Process Creates Value in the Supply Chain." ***Journal of Business Forecasting.*** Summer 2006, pp. 20-32.
4. Boyer Jr., John E. "10 Proven Steps to Successful S&OP." ***Journal of Business Forecasting.*** Spring 2009, pp. 4-10.

5. Herrin, Richard. "Managing Products via Demand Variability and Business Importance." ***Journal of Business Forecasting.*** Spring 2007, pp. 6-10.
6. Lapide, Larry. "Sales and Operations Planning: A Diagnostics Model" in ***Practical Guide to Business Forecasting,*** edited by Chaman L. Jain and Jack Malehorn. New York: Graceway Publishing Company. 2005, pp. 137-142.
7. Milliken, Alan L. "Demand Planning: Managing the Unforecastables." ***Journal of Business Forecasting.*** Summer 2006, pp. 3-9.
8. Reyman, Greg. "How JohnsonDiversey Implemented S&OP in Europe." ***Journal of Business Forecasting.*** Fall 2005, pp. 20-23, 28.
9. Wallace, Thomas F. "Eight Elementary Errors about S&OP." Newsletter of Tom Wallace. September 2009.
10. Wallace, Thomas F. ***Sales & Operations Planning: The How-To Handbook.*** Cincinnati, Ohio: T. F. Wallace & Co., 2004.
11. Wallace, Thomas F. and Robert A. Stahl. ***Sales & Operations Planning: The Executive's Guide.*** Cincinnati, Ohio: T. F. Wallace & Co., 2006.

QUESTIONS FOR REVIEW

1. What is the difference between the Consensus Forecasting process and the S&OP process? What led to the development of the S&OP process?
2. What are the key ingredients of a successful S&OP process? Explain.
3. What are the key objectives of an S&OP process? Explain.
4. What is the objective of establishing metrics and goals in the S&OP process? Explain.
5. Does volume drive product mix or product mix drive the volume in an S&OP process, and why?
6. Who should own the S&OP process, and why?
7. Why is product segmentation necessary in demand planning? Explain.
8. Which one is better—proactive or reactive demand planning, and why?
9. Describe in detail five myths about S&OP.
10. Explain in brief the following:
    a. Product mix vs. volume
    b. Operational plan vs. strategic plan
    c. Three Key Performance Indicators (KPI) of the supply chain
    d. Value added activities

CHAPTER 9

COLLABORATIVE PLANNING, FORECASTING AND REPLENISHMENT

The Collaborative Planning, Forecasting and Replenishment (CPFR®) process is an extension of S&OP. Both are based on the concept of collaboration, though the S&OP's collaboration is within the organization and the CPFR's is outside the organization. It was pioneered by Walmart and Warner-Lambert when they realized they had more to gain by working together and sharing information. The pilot program was started with Listerine, a key product of Warner-Lambert, which proved to be highly successful.

With CPFR®, the suppliers (or manufacturers) don't need to guess how many products their customers have sold to consumers, how much inventory they are holding, what their business plans are about promotion, opening and closing of stores, and holding inventory; all this information is available. Since the consumer sales data (Point of Sale or POS) are more stable than demand (customer orders placed with a supplier) and shipment data (products shipped by the supplier to a customer), forecasts based on them are more accurate. With more accurate forecasts, there would be fewer stock-outs, less inventory, and more sales. Furthermore, the quick access to POS data enables a supplier to act quickly. If a product is doing well, the company will know right away what action it has to take to increase supply. If, of course, it is not doing well, it would help to minimize the risk. The risk can be minimized by cutting down production, writing off aged inventory, and marking down prices to get rid of excess inventory. The kind of market intelligence that can be gained from the POS data can neither be gained from the demand data nor from the shipment data. In the case of stock-outs, both suppliers and retailers lose, though the former lose more than the other, because consumers, in the absence of a product, may buy a competitive product.

The collaboration between suppliers and customers did not emerge overnight; it grew gradually from Vendor Managed Inventory program (VMI, 1985) to Efficient Consumer Response (ECR, 1992) to Co-Managed Replenishment (1995) to Collaborative Planning, Forecasting and Replenishment (CPFR®, 1996). Under the VMI program, the supplier takes full responsibility for managing the inventory of a retailer. The retailer, however, sets conditions about such things as inventory level and customer service. The customer, for example, may require seven days of inventory and seven days on order. The retailer in turn regularly provides information about the sales of its products and inventory. The ECR is another collaborative initiative that integrates suppliers, retail distribution centers, and retail stores into one common system. It is also demand driven, and initiates manufacturing and shipments based on the consumer purchase activities. Electronic cash registers transmit sales and other retailer's information to the manufacturer. It was introduced in the grocery industry in 1992. But non-standardized operational practices and the rigid separation of roles of manufacturers and retailers failed to exploit the synergy that was expected from this initiative. Co-Managed Replenishment improves the process over VMI because here demand is jointly managed. Both agree on forecasts and shipment orders.

The CPFR® program is also based on collaboration with trading partners, but it is much more structured and comprehensive, and brings both parties even closer. As such, CPFR® is the most advanced form of an inventory management program where suppliers and their customers work together to replenish inventories at the customer sites. The program was initiated by the Walmart's Vice President of Supply Chain and Benchmarking Partners, a software and research firm located in Cambridge, Massachusetts. It was started out as CFAR (Collaborative Forecasting and Replenishment), but later on changed to CPFR® to emphasize the role of "planning" in the collaborative process. To get the most from CPFR®, Voluntary Interindustry Commerce Standards Association (VICS) has established guidelines for starting this process, its scope, product lines that are included, the level of sophistication required, what is expected from each other, and ways to measure success. The level of sophistication varies from company to company, depending on how much support it has from senior management, how much internal collaboration exists, and the kind of technology is available for use. (For more details, see the website of VICS.)

There is also a trend in collaboration towards Scan-Based Trading (SBT) where the supplier owns the inventory until it is scanned at the point of sale, meaning until it is sold by the customer (retailer). Although it has been there for over 20 years, but it has not been embraced as a common business practice.

BENEFITS OF CPFR®

Undoubtedly the benefits of CFPR® are significant. With it, suppliers have access not only to the consumption data but also to the customers' business plans, which further help to improve forecasts (further than S&OP) and, consequently, customer service, in-stocks, inventory, and productivity. According to VICS, companies that implemented it by linking S&OP to CPFR® have improved their in-stocks anywhere from 2 to 8 percent, and reduced their inventory anywhere from 10 to 40 percent across the supply chain.

Further, the implementation of CPFR® boosts all types of collaboration both within and outside the organization. The companies that adopted CPFR® have seen an increase in internal collaboration between sales and marketing and supply chain teams, and external collaboration not only between customers and suppliers but also between suppliers and next-tier suppliers, and suppliers and transportation carriers. Some even believe that today's increased interest in S&OP was sparked by CPFR®. When companies started their CPFR® initiatives, they first had to look internally to determine whether or not they would fulfill the commitments they would make with customers. In most cases, what they found was not that pretty. This forced them to embark on ways to correct it. In that sense, CPFR® helped to improve S&OP even further.

Over time, we have made tremendous progress in CPFR® considering where we were and where we are. Early on, when Walmart offered POS data to Procter & Gamble (P&G), it showed no interest because what mattered to P&G were orders from a customer and not sales to consumers. As such, suppliers at the time were customer centric, and not consumer centric. Today P&G very much regards its consumer sales as "first moment of truth." However, there are still several companies that don't make use of consumption data for one reason or another—the process is not in place, they don't have the tools to retrieve and process them, they don't recognize their value, and/or they don't have people with a skill to process and use them. Some manufacturers instead use customer's warehouse withdrawal data for preparing forecasts, while others use customers' forecasts. All these may be because the CPFR process is fairly new (about 10-years old), and thus has not been widely adopted. Generally, it takes about 20 to 25 years before a process is fully adopted.

HOW DOES THE CPFR® PROCESS WORK?

Although numerous companies (41 percent of them according to the 2009 survey of the Institute of Business Forecasting and Planning) have a CPFR® program in place, their form and the information they share vary from company to company, and from industry to industry. Some may share just the POS data; others, POS data and inventory information; and still others, all these plus business plans and forecasts. VICS initially developed a nine-step approach for implementing an efficient and effective CPFR® program, but later on reduced it to four to make it more flexible and easy to understand and implement. Here are the nine original steps:

Step 1: *Front-end agreements.* For any collaboration to work we must have some front-end agreements, which are essential for any program. These agreements are just commitments made by both parties to each other but have no legal binding. It is true that we cannot foresee all the problems but we know a number of them that are likely to occur. An agreement about them would make the process smoother and more effective. Here are the key issues that require a resolution:

i. *Mission statement.* The objectives of CPFR® must be stated upfront. The objective may be to reduce inventory, improve customer service, increase sales and market share, reduce cost, and/or improve profit margin. Whatever they may be, they must be quantified so that we can monitor the progress.

ii. *Information to be shared.* We need an agreement on the information to be shared. The customer may agree to share POS data, inventory situation, warehouse withdrawal, business plans, and/or forecasts. The supplier, on the other hand, may agree to share production capacity, availability of products, products to be launched and discontinued, and/or forecasts.

iii. *Roles and responsibilities.* For a smooth operation of the CPFR® program, the roles and responsibilities of each individual on both sides of the aisle must be described in detail so that everyone knows who will provide which information/data, who will receive it, and who is the contact person in case there is a problem. It will further help if the availability of each piece of information/data by hour of each day for timely delivery is documented in detail.

iv. *Metrics to be used.* What metrics will be used to measure performance is also critical. In this way each party will know exactly how they would be measured. We may decide to measure market share by category, forecast error based on POS data measured by Mean Absolute Percentage Error (MAPE), the level of inventory by Days of Inventory, customer service by percentage of orders filled in full, and so on. Furthermore, metrics agreed upon must have the same time horizon. For example, if both parties agree on MAPE, it should be based on the same time horizon. It would be difficult to determine whether time and resources committed to this process are paying off if the customer prepares weekly MAPEs and the supplier, monthly MAPEs.

v. *Technology standard and resources.* For the process to work efficiently, technology used by both trading partners must be compatible so that information/data can flow smoothly and quickly. If, for example, the customer sends the POS information via EDI (Electronic Data Interchange), the supplier must have the capability to retrieve it. For these, some commitments for resources may be needed.

vi. *Confidentiality.* Confidentiality is at the heart of collaboration; without that, it won't work. Therefore, it is important to spell out clearly what information can and cannot be disclosed.

vii. *Time fence.* Some agreements on time fence are also needed. Time fence is viewed as a long-time range, a medium-time range, and a short-time range. The agreement may be that in the long-time range, there will be no commitment. Forecasts will be only used for determining future capability. In the case of a medium-time range, there will be limited flexibility; whereas in the case of a short-time range, there will be no flexibility. If the two-month-ahead forecasts correspond to a medium-time range and one-month-ahead forecasts to a short-time range, we may agree that in the two-month-ahead forecasts/two-month-ahead demand plan a maximum of a 10-percent change can be made, whereas in the one-month-ahead forecasts/one-month-ahead demand plan no change can be made. We also need an agreement on things such as when orders will be firmed up and when the performance of CPFR® will be reviewed.

viii. *Managing supply and demand.* Perhaps the most important activity in any process including CPFR® is to manage supply and demand. The best way, of course, is to first have an agreement on a sales (demand) forecast and then on a supply plan, because it is the demand that drives the supply. The supply plan has to be consistent with capacity limitation and targets about on-time delivery and inventory level. Bear in mind that a CPFR® arrangement is based on the honor system. Neither the retailer nor the supplier is under any legal contract to act according to the mutually consented arrangement.

ix. *Forecasts.* An agreement on forecasts is also needed between the manufacturer and the customer, that is, which forecasts would be prepared (POS forecasts, demand forecasts, and/or shipment forecasts), how they would be prepared, what kind of feedback would be provided, and how consensus would be reached. Also, in preparing forecasts of promoted products, which causal drivers (price, promotion, etc.) would be used and how their impact would be factored in. After both parties prepare their forecast, there would be a joint meeting to review each other's forecasts and, if there is a gap between the two, how it would be closed. Further, how often forecasts would be prepared—weekly, monthly, or quarterly (though they are often prepared monthly)—and in what buckets.

x. *Converting forecasts into orders and shipments.* For a smooth operation, it is important to have an agreement on how these jointly agreed upon forecasts would be transitioned into firm orders, how the firm orders would be produced and shipped, and how products received would be put on the retailer's shelves, sales transactions recorded, and payments made.

xi. *Order policy.* The order policy deals with minimum order, lead-time, safety stock settings, order points, customer service level, pack size, and truck loading. An agreement on each of them will also help. But, whatever you decide to agree on make sure that they are consistent with the optimization goals such as reducing the cost of manufacturing and optimizing transportation.

xii. *Monitoring performance.* To determine whether or not we are making progress, we have to regularly monitor the Key Performance Indicators (KPI). For these we need an agreement on which KPIs we would be monitoring.

xiii. *Sharing savings.* Although it is neither a part of VICS' recommendations nor is it practiced here, sharing savings resulting from collaborative efforts between two parties can further strengthen this program. ARASCO, a company based in Saudi Arabia with a core business of animal feeds, wanted to use "push strategy" in collaboration with its distributors to improve its supply chain. As soon as products come off the production line, ARASCO wanted to ship them to distributors in accordance with the jointly agreed upon forecasts. This would significantly cut down its cost of warehousing. As a result, its cost of handling products from the production line to a warehouse including palletizing would drop. At the same time, it would provide space for storing raw materials (90 percent of the raw materials come from abroad, which have to be stored). At times the company had to rent space at the port because the space at the manufacturing plant was limited. Plus, the company would benefit by stabilizing production and logistics. ARASCO started this program with selected distributors in 2006, promising to share with them the savings by offering a discount on sales price anywhere from 2 to 4 percent. The program was so successful that in 2007 it expanded the program to other distributors, as well as to their customers of raw material. Collaboration works only if we genuinely look after not only our own interests, but also the interests of our trading partners.

Step 2: *Joint business plans.* The next step is to develop both tactical and strategic joint business plans to achieve jointly agreed upon targets such as targets for individual categories, service level, and sales revenue. The tactical plans may include promotional and special event plans. The strategic plans, on the other hand, may include plans for new product launches, opening and closing of stores, entering new markets and channels of distribution, SKU reduction, and capacity planning. With CPFR®, the manufacturer does not need to guess about the customer plans, they are available. Since most of these plans have a bearing on forecasts, the quality of forecasts improves, making it easier to align supply with the demand.

Step 3: *Create forecasts.* Once all the information is available, then ideally the next step for each partner is to prepare its own forecasts. The customer prepares its forecasts and sends them to its supplier along with assumptions for a review. The supplier does the same—prepares its own forecasts based on the information it has, and then sends them to the customer. Then, they meet together to reconcile forecasts to arrive at one set of forecasts. In practice, says Louis C. Winsman, Whirlpool's Senior Manager of Lowe's Trade Partner Collaboration, whenever there is a CPFR® arrangement, often both parties prepare some kind of baseline numbers. There are cases, however, where just one party—the customer or supplier—prepares forecasts and then sends them to another party for a review. Bear in mind, no one is perfect. The objective here is to leverage as much as we can: the insight, knowledge, and experience of each other. Nikhil Sagar, Vice President of Inventory Management at OfficeMax, believes that manufacturers can make a better product category forecast than customers, because they have the industry insight across all the retail outlets. Although they don't share explicitly the marketing plans of others, whatever they know is embedded in their forecasts.

Step 4: *Identify exceptions in forecasts.* Until recently collaborative efforts were mostly limited to VMI and ECR, which were primarily data driven and exceptions were not a part of the process. Forecasts were not collaboratively reviewed. They were prepared mostly by using the historical data and the ERP (Enterprise Resource Planning system). If there were any outliers, missing values, and/or structural changes in the data, the system was expected to take care of them. As such, issues about the data or forecasting methodology never surfaced. Nor were forecasts enriched by the insight/knowledge of in-house sales and marketing teams or of the trading partner. Now, very often both parties independently prepare some kind of a forecast, and then compare them. If there is a gap above an allowed tolerance limit, they try to find out why. Maybe what insight/knowledge one partner had, the other partner did not. Maybe one partner knew zero sales in a number of periods were not because of lack of demand but because of stock-outs. Maybe the customer at the time prepared a forecast of a certain product did not know that the manufacturer has discontinued it. Further, if one partner uses the lift of a promotion in its forecast above a certain percentage, it has to explain why. So, the whole objective here is to find out why.

As a precaution, in the joint review of forecasts, make sure that each party knows exactly what is being compared. If we compare the CPFR® demand plan of sell-through (sale to consumers) with sell-in (orders placed with a manufacturer), then the missing element may be inventory, which can explain the gap. Let's say that the forecast for sell-through was 40,000 units versus sell-in of 25,000 units. In that case, it would be a great mistake on the part of a manufacturer to assume that the retailer would order the same as the amount it would sell. The retailer may order just 25,000 units because it intends to bring down the inventory or has a huge amount of on-order that has not landed in the inventory yet.

Step 5: *Resolve exceptions.* Once we know the problem and what is causing it, it is easier to resolve it. In the pilot program of Walmart with Warner-Lambert, Warner-Lambert recognized that Walmart forecasts did not account for seasonality and planned promotion. Nor did it synchronize its distribution centers' forecasts with the store-level forecasts. Walmart immediately recognized the problem and corrected it.

Step 6: *Create order forecasts.* Once forecasts are jointly agreed upon, the next step is to generate order forecasts that are consistent with inventory and order policies, as well as with joint business plans. The volume of orders is time phased that reflects the inventory objectives by product and receiving location. The short-term portions of order forecasts are used for generating orders, and the long-term portion for future planning.

Step 7: *Identify exceptions for order forecasts.* The objective here is to identify those order forecasts that fall outside the constraints jointly established by the customer and the supplier. For example, orders generated for certain products are significantly less than the forecasts, or above the level that cannot be fulfilled. There are cases, however, where only one party prepares forecasts, which then become the basis for order forecasts. West Marine, for example, does this, and its suppliers are responsible for meeting the demand created by its forecasts. If there is any exception, that is, if one or more suppliers cannot fulfill for one reason or another, they report to West Marine for resolution.

Step 8: *Resolve/collaborate on exception items.* This step requires investigating the order forecast exceptions by querying the shared data as well as talking to people involved on the other end of the business, and then arriving at a joint solution. This may require some negotiations between the two parties. Further, if production is expected to be insufficient to meet the customer's forecasted demand, the supplier is expected to issue an alert early on so that the customer can take action to control the damage.

Step 9: *Generate orders.* This last step calls for converting the order forecasts into committed orders. Based on that, suppliers develop shipment schedules, and then ship them to customers.

Although the underlying philosophy of CPFR® was sound, its implementation structure was perceived to be very rigid. Many companies believed that if they did not implement all the nine steps and in the sequence VICS has described, they would not be "CPFR® compliant," and thus wouldn't get all the benefits. Since the needs of different companies and industries vary, they did not feel it necessary to follow all the steps. For example, Steps 3, 4, and 5 focus on sharing and resolving conflicts about sales forecasts, and Steps 6, 7, and 8 focus on order forecasts. Some companies felt that they only wanted to share their order forecasts, and thus there was no need to follow other steps. Others wanted only the customer's forecasts (as in the case of Arrow Electronics described in the case study later on in this chapter) to use as an input to their own forecasts. One size does not fit all. So, they needed some flexibility, which VICS gave them by consolidating broadly the nine steps into four.

1. ***Strategy and Planning:*** This calls for establishing ground rules for the collaborative relationship, and developing joint business plans.

2. *Demand and Supply Management:* This calls for creating sales forecasts, identifying exceptions, and resolving them with an ultimate goal of balancing the demand with supply for an optimum profit.

3. *Execution*: This calls for placing orders, delivering shipments, receiving and stocking products on retail shelves, recording sales transactions, and making payments.

4. *Analysis:* This calls for monitoring plans and the execution of activities for exception conditions caused by unforeseen environmental or competitive activities, supply chain disruptions, as well as looking for new opportunities. This also calls for maintaining a score card of key metrics, and sharing them with trading partners. Insight gained from these may require adjusting current plans and/or help in improving the future ones.

INGREDIENTS OF A SUCCESSFUL CPFR® PROCESS

It is without any question that the process works. However, to maximize the benefits, in addition to the top executive sponsorship, the following things are needed.

Choosing the right partner: In selecting a trading partner, answer these three very important questions:

1. Does your trading partner has some collaborative experience within the organization and/or with another organization? The collaborative experience may be that the trading partner already has a CF (Consensus Forecasting) process and/or S&OP process in place. It may have a VMI and/or CPFR® arrangement with other organizations. In that case, your partner has some idea of what would it take to succeed.

2. Is your partner willing to commit time and resources? Without that, this type of relationship won't work.

3. Do you have a significant amount of your business with that partner? Otherwise, it may not be worth the effort.

Trust and transparency between trading partners: Trust and transparency are the basis of a successful collaborative process. Many of the organizations have shied away from it simply because they are afraid information they provide to suppliers may leak out to their competitors. So, they hold back much of the information. But without trust, this process won't work. Therefore, the best way is to start out with trust until it is violated. Benefits that result from it far exceed the risk for not doing it. The golden rule of Bill Fields, former President of Walmart, is "Trust, but verify," meaning start out with trust, and then see whether or not it is maintained.

Crawl, walk, and run: The best way to start this program is to start it with a pilot program using one or two products/categories. If that works, then rollout to other products/categories. Maybe we want to start out with just sales forecasting collaboration and then move on to order forecasting collaboration. In the process, we may find that our trading partner does not have the culture that values cooperation and communication among departments as well as with a trading partner. We may realize that our trading partner is neither fully committed nor trustworthy. If this is the case, then no matter what we do, it won't work. For a pilot program, we must have a cutoff, that is, a time when it will end. The duration of the program must be long enough to assess it adequately. In the case of a seasonal product, it should go through the whole season. In the case of a promoted product, time allowed should be enough to cover its full effect. Further, we can start a pilot program with minimum technology, which can be upgraded later on. To run this program, the greatest emphasis should be placed on people—their roles and responsibility, accountability, and trust—followed by process and technology.

Linking CPFR® with S&OP: The objectives of both S&OP and CPFR® are the same, that is, to reduce costs and increase sales and profit, though the former works by having collaboration with trading partners within an organization, while the latter with another organization. The best results can only be achieved if both these processes are integrated, because the success of one depends on the other. Once the CPFR® process is completed with respect to sales and order forecasts, the information about them has to be communicated to respected S&OP teams for review and action. The S&OP team will be able to work much more effectively if they know before taking any action about sales and order forecasts agreed upon by the CPFR® team. This will happen only if the calendar of both CPFR® and S&OP are aligned. If, for example, CPFR® is completed in the second week of a month, then the internal S&OP calendar may require demand plans to be completed for review in the third week of a month.

Further, to ensure alignment of CPFR® and S&OP, we need one individual (say, a champion) from each trading partner (one from the manufacturer and one from the retailer) who holds the organization accountable for hitting deadlines and meeting the stated objectives. The champions will ensure not only that the CPFR® process is aligned with their internal S&OP but also take the responsibility for reviewing the outcomes of CPFR®.

When S&OP and CPFR® are combined, VICS calls it Integrated Business Planning (IBP).

However, Oliver Wight defines IBP as the planning process that includes demand review, supply review, product management review, management business review, financial reconciliation, and business strategy.

Minimum expectations: The best way to proceed with CPFR® is to start with minimum expectations, which can be easily met. Success builds on success. Otherwise, we may be disappointed. As mentioned earlier, we should not start it in a big way; maybe with one or two products or categories only. Also, we don't need to invest heavily in technology to start this process. Many companies have leveraged their existing technology in the early stages of its implementation, and upgraded it as they progressed.

Constantly looking for new ways to grow: The opportunities that come with collaboration are endless. To make the most of a CPFR® program, always be on the lookout. Suppliers like P&G are constantly looking for opportunities for Joint Value Creation (value created jointly by the supplier and the customer) to drive savings into the supply chain as well as to increase business. To grow business, supply chain people are currently working along three lines: One, to reduce shrinkage at the retailer's stores; two, provide products that are shelf ready; and three, cut down the cost of warehousing and speed up delivery. If the supply chain can identify ways to minimize shrinkage and keep high value products like Mach3 Turbo Power Razors and Blades on the retail shelf and not locked behind a glass counter, the impulse sales will increase. The burden of reducing or eliminating shrinkage falls somewhat on the suppliers. Retailers like Walmart require suppliers to put a special anti-theft tags on high value products.

Suppliers are also coming up with products and packages that are shelf ready—easy to put on shelves and packed in cases that are just right for the customer's shelf-holding capacity. If a customer opens a case, and the shelf space is not large enough to hold all the items, the remaining ones in the open case will be stored away in the back room. Items in an open case are more likely to be a target for theft and/or become a part of misplaced inventory. Recently, some suppliers such as Kraft Foods in Western Pennsylvania have reduced their customers' cost of warehousing and speeded up their delivery by loading products into a truck, arranged by the customer's stores. The truck takes the products to a customer's distributor centers, where they are loaded onto a customer's truck, which delivers to its stores. With that, products don't touch the customer's warehouse, and are shipped right away to stores where they are needed.

Recently, companies that do outsourcing have reduced their shipping costs and speeded up their delivery time by consolidating merchandise at the point of origin by the shipper, and then sending it directly to the final destination—stores in the United States. Windbrella, a U.S. umbrella company that imports umbrellas from Guangdong, China, previously required its manufacturers to ship umbrellas to its distribution center in Boynton, Florida, where they were repacked and relabeled, and then shipped to stores. Now packaging and labeling for stores is done in China. The manufacturers ship their umbrellas to the UPS facility in Guangdong, China. The UPS, on the behalf of its customer, consolidates and ships them to the final destination in the United States. By doing this, the company reduced its delivery time anywhere from 15 to 30 days, and cut down its operating cost anywhere from 5 to 10 percent. The Chinese manufacturers of another company, Red Wing, a U.S. shoe company, now requires its suppliers to ship shoes to the UPS facility in Yantian, southern China, which consolidates them on the behalf of its customer and then ships directly to its stores in the United States. This way the company reduced its shipping cost by not having a separate container for each manufacturer as well as lead time by bypassing the distribution center in Salt Lake City.

Above all, companies should keep a score card of what went well and what did not, and when and why, so that they can figure out what they have to do in the future to make their process more robust. Openness among trading partners is the key to success. Did the supplier maintain the agreed upon days of supply with the retailer/distributor? Did the retailer/distributor give the supplier insight into their promotional plans in a timely manner? Lack of linked information technology is the most cited problem in the success of CPFR®. We are likely to experience physical and cultural problems in our efforts to balance supply with demand. They can be removed only if a person with authority steps in and takes the necessary action. Further, a periodic review is needed to identify and evaluate problems.

ARROW ELECTRONICS—A CASE STUDY

Arrow Electronics, one of the world's largest distributor of electronic and computer products, with $10 billion annual sales, and 12,000 employees worldwide, uses collaboration mostly to minimize risk and maximize profit. Its supply chain is fairly complex with 600 suppliers, and lead time varies anywhere from 1 to 43 weeks. That is not all. Every month it adds over 13,000 new part numbers. New products come to the market with very short notice, which cannibalizes the sales of other products. In this type of environment, the stakes are high. So, it is very important to minimize the risk.

Arrow Electronics has two sets of forecasts—Corporate Forecasts, developed internally, and Customer Forecasts, developed by customers. It is good to have forecasts of your customers, says Charles Bonomo, former Vice President of Strategic Programs at Arrow Electronics, even though they are not quite accurate. Arrow uses Customer Forecasts as just another input to its forecasting process. It manages its inventories with its own forecasts, i.e., Corporate Forecasts. However, it has made the supply chain transparent to its customers so that they know at any given time where they stand. The Supply Demand Imbalance screen, within the Collaborator tool, which Arrow has implemented, enables customers to see shortages and excesses in inventories, specifically what has been reserved for them over the next four weeks. Here a green up-arrow implies that it will meet its customer's forecasted demand, and a red arrow indicates a potential shortage. If there is a shortage, customers can check into the system about the publicly available inventory to see if its demand can be met from that source. If the shortage still exists, the system displays the date when the potential shortage will occur. Also, the Part Status Page of the Collaborator tool sends a notification when a customer's forecasted part changes from an active life cycle status to a liability status. This simply means that Arrow is not comfortable with a particular customer's forecast, and wants to hold inventory against the customer's forecast only if it is willing to sign on a dotted line, that is, it will pay for the unused quantities. The Forecast Response page within the Collaborator tool shows graphically Arrow's current ability to cover a customer's forecasted requirements, month by month, over the next six months. With this approach, both Arrow and customers have become proactive. Customers know ahead of time where they stand and what they have to do to meet their needs. Arrow makes the best decision about such things as pricing and safety stock. When Arrow sees an increase in planned orders and customer forecasts, it means that its supply would start tightening. To optimize its position, it starts firming up its prices, and adjusting safety stocks and Corporate Forecasts.

THE FUTURE OF CPFR®

What does the future hold for CPFR®? We envision many developments in the area. We expect CPFR® to become more strategic, and with more emphasis on "P" (Planning). Originally, as we know, it started out with CFAR (Collaborative Forecasting and Replenishment) without "P," as was the case with the pilot program of Warner-Lambert's Listerine. Collaboration meant only improving forecasts and consequently replenishment. Today, although we call this program CPFR®, the role of "P" is still limited and confined mostly to short-term planning, particularly promotional planning. This will eventually change.

Because CPFR® links the S&OP of both customers and suppliers, and executives are involved in the S&OP process, there is going to be more and more focus on strategic planning, according to Ronald Ireland, a Managing Principal with Oliver Wight Americas, Inc. The role of CPFR® will change from a traditional planning horizon of 1 to 13 weeks at a SKU planning level to a 1 to 24 month at an aggregate planning level. The issues about strategic planning may include new product design, store format changes, warehouse expansions, global initiatives, and other commercial opportunities. Further CPFR® and S&OP processes will become more and more integrated because their success depends on it.

The CPFR® also will expand outside traditional big-box retailers, to industries such as high-tech, telecommunications, as well as retailers and suppliers in the apparel industry. In fact, it was the apparel industry, according to Ronald Ireland, that was among the early adopters of Co-Managed and CPFR®, and companies that adopted it were Fruit of the Loom, Sara Lee, and Levi Strauss. But this industry drifted away from CPFR® commitments because their lead time was longer than many other consumer products. But now they are showing a renewed interest because of the renewed focus on strategic collaboration that allows an industry with a longer lead time to collaborate beyond 12 to 24 months, which is often the case with apparel and fashion products.

As such, we expect this process to be widely adopted in the future. Not only will more and more companies start using it because of enormous benefits that come with it, its use will expand to other products, regions, and countries. Also, this process will become more structured and technology used more advanced.

We expect to see more collaboration not only among different functions within an organization and between customers and suppliers but also between suppliers and sub-tier suppliers. Further, many companies currently use warehouse withdrawals instead of Point-of-Sale (POS) data. This may be due to incompatibility of technology among suppliers and customers, and/or customers are reluctant to share information, fearing it may fall in wrong hands, especially competitors. Forecasts based on POS data provide better forecasts because they are more stable than the customers' warehouse withdrawals. Also, we see the emergence of more advanced "what-if" simulation software, which will not only speed up the decisions but also improve them as well. With that, they can easily determine the best course of action if demand is greater than supply, supply is greater than demand, or for any other similar issue.

More and more companies with an international presence will globalize their collaborative processes, though not without challenges. Dealing with different cultures presents its own problems. Further, the name of the game in forecasting is visibility of products—how much is sitting in the customers' and distributors' warehouses, and how much has been sold to ultimate consumers. The difference in culture and marketing practices in emerging markets has made this visibility very murky. In China, for example, a large percentage of consumer goods are sold to distributors who further sell to sub-distributors and sub-sub-distributors, making it difficult to determine how much inventory each one is holding. However, with time, more and more big-box retailers like Walmart will enter the market, making it easier for suppliers to access the information they need.

We will also see collaboration among suppliers in the area of logistics. In recent years, in an effort to bring down the cost of working capital and minimize risk, customers are cutting back on the size of orders, but are giving them more frequently. This has somewhat increased the shipping costs because, at times, trucks have to go less than full. To counter it, suppliers may work together. The unused space in one truck may be used by another supplier provided their products are going to the same customer and are complementary. An example of this could be shipping together Clorox Bleach of The Clorox Company and Tide Laundry Detergent of P&G to the same customer, say, Walmart.

SUGGESTED READING

1. Bonomo, Charles. "Forecasting from the Center of the Supply Chain" in ***Practical Guide to Business Forecasting,*** edited by Chaman L. Jain and Jack Malehorn. New York: Graceway Publishing Company, 2005, pp. 154-161.
2. Khadar, S. A. "VMI Program Improves Forecasting and Supply Chain: ARASCO's Experience." ***Journal of Business Forecasting.*** Fall 2007, pp. 29-32.
3. Ireland, Ronald K. "ABC of Collaborative Planning, Forecasting and Replenishment." ***Journal of Business Forecasting.*** Summer 2005, pp. 3-4, 10.
4. Ireland, Ronald K. and Colleen Crum. ***Supply Chain Collaboration: How to Implement CPFR® and Other Best Collaborative Practices.*** Boca Raton, Florida.: J. Ross Publishing & APICS. 2005.
5. Lapide, Larry. "How About Collaborative Forecasting." ***Journal of Business Forecasting.*** Fall 2008, p. 5.
6. Lapide, Larry. "Use VMI to Improve Forecasting." ***Journal of Business Forecasting.*** Fall 1998, p. 28-30.
7. Voluntary Interindustry Commerce Standards Association. ***Roadmap to CPFR®.*** Voluntary Interindustry Commerce Standards Association: Website.
8. Ward, Andrew. "New Logic to Shipping Merchandise." ***Financial Times.*** November 7, 2005.

QUESTIONS FOR REVIEW

1. Explain how CPFR® differs from S&OP and CF.
2. Explain how CPFR® adds value to the business.
3. What are the ingredients of a successful CPFR® program? Explain.
4. What does the future hold for collaboration between customers and suppliers? Explain.
5. Explain how CPFR® tends to reduce inventory and decrease stock-outs.

6. Describe why the approach of "Crawl, Walk, and Run" is important to start a CPFR® program.
7. Describe how P&G is working on "Joint Value Creation" to improve its supply chain.
8. Describe why trust is important in the success of a CPFR® program.
9. Would you start a CPFR® program with a company that has no collaborative experience? Why or why not?
10. Explain in brief the following:
    a. Front-end-agreement as used in CPFR®
    b. Demand, shipment, and POS data
    c. "What-if" simulations
    d. Consumer centric demand vs. customer centric demand

CHAPTER 10

BUILDING COLLABORATION

As explained in the previous chapters, for a forecasting function to succeed, it needs collaboration from both within and outside the organization. But the question remains: How? For years, different departments within an organization have been working independently, preparing their own forecasts for their own use, without being monitored. If forecasts were wrong, so what? No one other than their own department would know it. As such, there was no motivation to improve them. Working together, on the other hand, means parting with their independence and authority, but it would improve forecasts. Forecasts would become transparent. There would be one set of numbers, in contrast to multiple sets of numbers. If anyone biased forecasts, everyone would know it. But to convert the silo structure into a collaborative one is not easy. There are, however, some steps we can take to facilitate the process and increase the probability of success.

SUPPORT FROM THE TOP

The first and foremost step to bring a change is to get the support from the top, without that nothing will happen. When seeking top management support, it is important to quantify the benefits of forecast improvements in dollars and cents. How much are we paying every year for holding unnecessary inventory? How much are we spending every year on expediting products because they were not in stock when orders came in? How much are switchovers in production costing us because of shortages? How much sales are we losing because of stock-outs? If we have lost one or more customers because of poor customer service, bring this to their attention.

A recent study of 15 companies (ranging in sales from $52 million to $3 billion) by the authors shows that a company can save on average as much as $2.37 million per year by reducing just one percentage point error of under-forecasting, and $1.3 million by reducing one percentage point error of over-forecasting. (Losses that were accounted for in under-forecasting were lost sales because of stock-outs and increases in expediting and production costs; whereas in over-forecasting, losses resulting from markdowns, holding extra inventory, obsolescence, transshipments, and warehousing.)

Top management wants to learn, but it does not want to be taught. Some efforts have to be made so that it recognizes that forecasts are not prepared in isolation; to prepare them, the forecaster needs input from various functions, which won't be forthcoming without top-management's blessing. The management also has to understand that it is difficult to align supply with demand with multiple forecasts, because with that supply will be based on one set of forecasts, and demand on another. Not only that, with multiple forecasts, it would be difficult to decide—even for the management—which numbers to use for making their decisions.

Before approaching top management for a change, it is important to understand the chain of command. The best way to start, says John Gallucci, Senior Director of Product Planning for the Birds Eye Division of Pinnacle Foods Group, is to schedule an hour-long meeting with a VP of Supply Chain, VP of Sales, and/or any other key person, and go over with them why collaboration is needed. Listen carefully to what their thoughts are. Provide documentation of how it would work, and what impact it would have on the bottom line. Give some recent examples of how much profit we missed because of excess inventory or lost because of lack of it. Those misses would have been avoided if all the functions worked together in preparing forecasts, and followed the one number forecast philosophy. Once functional leaders are convinced, they will drive the message to the President or to the Board. Gaining acceptance might take months or even years, but be persistent. Once the top management accepts it, the rest of the road would be easier to navigate.

DEVELOP DOWNSTREAM SUPPORT

The mandate from the top will help to get downstream support (support from Sales, Marketing, Finance, and Production) but not enough to get them emotionally involved in the collaborative forecasting process. We need them to collaborate not just because they have a mandate from the top but also because they truly believe in it. To create that spirit we need to educate them. In the beginning, we will experience some resistance. We are likely to hear, "What is in it for me?" Salespeople might say that their function is to sell, not to forecast. Production people might say that they are evaluated on the basis of production cost, customer service, or inventory levels, not on forecasting. So, we have to educate them. Salespeople have to understand what would happen if they bring in an order but is lost because we could not fulfill it. Production people have to understand that good forecasts will help to reduce their production cost, improve customer service, and lower inventory. Once they recognize the value of forecasts, they will give all the support the process needs. Further, they will be even more supportive if they get forecasts in the format they need and when they need.

CLEARLY DEFINED ROLES

Collaboration works when the roles of each individual, department, and party along with metrics to evaluate their performance are clearly defined and understood. Sales may be asked to provide market intelligence; Marketing, information on market trends, new launches, promotional plans, and so on; Finance, profit and revenue statements along with funds available for promotion; and Production, inventory, backlog, customer service, and production capacity. Specifying roles won't help unless there are metrics in place to evaluate their performance. If, for example, Marketing is given the responsibility to prepare forecasts, some metrics of forecast accuracy have to be specified which would be used to evaluate its performance. Further, it has to be clearly specified what is expected from each one when they come to a Consensus meeting, and Pre-executive and Executive S&OP meetings. For a CPFR® program, the role of each party has to be specified, that is, who would be responsible for what. Otherwise, we would end up wasting time and energy on negotiating their roles and protecting their turf rather than focusing on the task on hand.

CONFLICT MANAGEMENT PROCESS IN PLACE

No matter what we do, at times, conflicts among different teams members will arise, which have to be resolved. Otherwise, they will cause confrontation and arguments on who is right or wrong, as well as create ill-will among team members. To avoid this, we need a conflict management process, which determines possible conflicts that could arise, and their best solutions. In the Consensus meeting, for example, there may be a conflict between Sales and Production. Sales may say that the forecast of a certain SKU or category is too low and it should be raised. Production, on the other hand, may be strongly against that because it believes it would unnecessarily increase inventory. Sales may have a very compelling reason why sales of that SKU or category should be raised. If the argument is strong and convincing, adjust the forecast. If not, ask the forecaster to revisit the forecast in light of input provided at the meeting; whatever the number he or she comes up with will be final. So, it is important to set clearly rules for resolving different conflicts, and make them transparent so that everyone knows what they are. This process will not root out conflicts, but will certainly make it easier to handle them.

Very often conflicts pertaining to demand plans are resolved or minimized if they are validated through a cross-functional process using consensus decision-making techniques. Exceptions to past demand patterns are reviewed and discussed openly.

CREATE A SENSE OF URGENCY

Create a sense of urgency. People respond quickly and with less resistance if there is a sense of urgency, because it makes a compelling case for action. If we have instances where the company was adversely impacted or where impact would be felt in the future, bring them to their attention. Maybe we recently lost a significant amount of sales because of stock-outs. Along with it, expediting and production costs shot up. Maybe because of over-stock, we lost a large sum of money in markdowns, obsolescence, and shrinkage, as well as in warehousing. Maybe we lost one large customer or one is threatening to leave because of our poor customer service. Whatever the case may be, dollarize its impact because this is what people understand better. Show them that poor forecasts are the root cause of these problems. Forecasts will improve if everyone works together.

STAY FOCUSED

Rome was not built in one day. To bring about change, especially of changing a culture, takes time. So, be patient and persistent. We will encounter numerous obstacles along the way—political, technical, and people and process related. Deal with them as quickly as possible. This will encourage and empower those who are committed to the change. If obstacles are not dealt with right away, you will lose the momentum, people will become cynics, and eventually change efforts will collapse. Further, people want to see evidence of success to ensure that they made the right decision. So, monitor and publicize successes; where possible celebrate them, no matter how small they may be. They will add credibility and increase further support. If a mistake is made along the way, confess it and move forward. Remember, the path to better forecasting is a "journey" not a "destination." Continuous review and improvements are required to maintain an efficient and effective forecasting process.

A CASE STUDY

A multinational instruments company wanted to improve its logistics and procurement capability for its $400 million North American sales and service operation. It faced many challenges, but one that prohibited from doing was a lack of collaboratively built and widely accepted forecasts. The SKU level demand history and expected future sales were owned and managed by a warehouse planning manager, different from the department that manages products.

Marketing leaders, product managers, and logistics leaders had no input whatsoever into demand planning, which drove procurement, shipping, and warehouse storage of expensive instruments and accompanying spare parts. Also, the warehouse planner had a different set of incentives than Marketing—its main goal was to keep inventory down. As such, there were frequent complaints from Marketing / Sales:

> ***"We don't have enough stock to satisfy our customers!"***
> ***"Our customers have to wait too long!"***
> ***"We don't have input into the expected demand!"***
> ***"We can't incorporate market data into the forecast!"***
> ***"The warehouse has no incentive to meet customer demand!"***

Further, Marketing questioned the way the warehouse manager calculated future demand. He simply pulled the historical demand data from the ERP system, plugged them into a homemade Access database, estimated future demand using extrapolation techniques such as moving averages, and then made intuitive adjustments where necessary, as well for the known manufacturing capacity. There existed neither better tools nor a collaborative process for adding market data into the forecasts. Further, the warehouse manager wasn't apprised of such things as sales, discounts, large upcoming customer contracts, and the like. The company faced many other forecasting challenges: No concentration of efforts on "A" items, no collaboration, and no metrics for performance review to drive improvement.

Due to budget constraints and lack of top management buy-in to invest in forecasting, the logistics leader for the Marketing team (which was Lad A. Dilgard, now an independent consultant) built a minimal, short-term solution. The objective was, at the very least, to have a vehicle for integrating marketing input into the forecast. He built an Excel-based tool with a minimal statistical capability (moving averages, seasonal adjustment calculations, etc.), and devoted efforts to items that mattered the most—the ones that represented the top 80 percent of total sales.

Every month, the system sent a rough forecast (through the end of year plus one year) to product managers and asked them to make adjustments based on their market information. They also were asked to document market information for future reference, and start tracking forecast errors. The forecasts were then pushed to factories in China. With this, not only did manufacturing planning greatly improve, but also the problem associated with a lack of forecast collaboration diminished.

Interestingly, once product managers got involved in the process, the team prodded them to provide their input. They were concerned that their input would be used to alter their warehouse buying plan or the plant production plan. Even after proving to them the benefit of their input, obtaining product managers' input was still somewhat difficult because providing that information was not part of their job description or incentive plan. They also did not understand how better forecasts could translate into more and correct inventory for their customers. These were the huge obstacles to forecast improvement, which are witnessed as well by many other organizations.

SUGGESTED READING

1. Charan, Ram. "Home Depot's Blueprint for Culture Change." ***Harvard Business Review.*** April 2006, pp. 61-70.
2. Dilgard, Lad A. "Worst Forecasting Practices in Corporate America and Their Solutions—Case Study." ***Journal of Business Forecasting.*** Summer 2009, pp. 4-13.
3. Gratton, Lynda and Tamara J. Erickson. "Ways to Build Collaborative Teams." ***Harvard Business Review.*** November 2007, pp. 101-109.
4. Weiss, Jeff and Jonathan Hughes. "Want Collaboration: Accept and Actively Manage Conflict." ***Harvard Business Review.*** March 2005, pp. 93-101.

QUESTIONS FOR REVIEW

1. Why are collaborative efforts necessary for building an effective and efficient forecasting process? Explain.
2. Why is top management sponsorship essential in building a collaborative forecasting process? Explain.
3. Describe the key steps required for bringing a change in a corporation.
4. Explain why do we need collaboration both within and outside the organization to improve forecasts.
5. Why do we need to create a sense of urgency to have collaboration from functional leaders, and how can it be created? Explain.
6. Describe why it is important to deal with obstacles right away in a collaborative forecasting process. What would happen if no serious efforts are made to deal with them?
7. What do we mean by downstream support? What are the best ways to get it? Explain.
8. Explain what kinds of complaints can we expect from Marketing and Sales if the forecasting function is controlled and managed by a warehouse manager.
9. Explain why warehouse managers are reluctant to provide input to forecasting.
10. In what form would Production, Sales, and Finance like to have forecasts, and why? Explain.

PART III

DATA

INTRODUCTION

Forecasts are as good as the data/information used in preparing them. With the advancement of technology, combined with the willingness of trading partners within and outside the organization to share information, forecasters now have access to more data/information than ever before—POS, warehouse withdrawals, demand, customer forecast, shipment, etc. But mere availability of data is not enough. One has to know the data before using them; one has to know which data to use and how much; and which model is appropriate? Also, see if there is any problem in the data that has to be taken care of before applying a model. This part describes not only what kinds of data are available—internally and externally—but also what to look for in the data, and, if there is a problem, how to handle it.

CHAPTER 11

WHAT YOU NEED TO KNOW ABOUT DATA

Before applying data to a model it is important to know what kinds of data are available, which data are needed to prepare a forecast, and what their characteristics are. We also need to know if there is any problem in the data; if yes, how to handle it. Knowing all this will help not only in preparing and improving forecasts but also in understanding the output. In this chapter we will discuss some of the basics of data.

DATA STREAMS

In business, data of four different streams are used in forecasting and planning, which are:

1. Shipment data
2. Demand data
3. Warehouse withdrawals
4. Point-of-Sale data

Shipment data: Shipment data include shipments made by a manufacturer (supplier/vendor) to a customer (retailer, wholesaler, or distributor). Shipment data can be used not only for forecasting shipments but also for forecasting cash flow, because shipment information can be easily converted into cash flow. Shipment data are often obtained from financial transactions recorded in the invoicing system. But what matters most to a manufacturer is not how much it shipped to a customer or how many orders were received from it, but how much the customer has sold its products to end-consumers. Shipment data do not give that information. Furthermore, in forecasting, the more volatile the data, the more difficult it is to forecast. Backlogs, stock-outs, machine breakages, switchovers, and stoppages—they all add volatility in the shipment data. The volatility is further exacerbated by the promotional plans of a manufacturer and the bullwhip effect. Furthermore, because of the lag between when a shipment is made to a store and when POS occurs, it is difficult for a supplier to determine consumption demand from the shipment data.

Demand data: Demand data represent orders received by the manufacturer from a customer. Demand can be constrained and unconstrained. Unconstrained demand is the number of orders received irrespective of whether or not they would be fulfilled. If an order was not accepted because it could not be fulfilled or was canceled for one reason or another, it would still be a part of the unconstrained demand, but not of constrained demand. Further, an order is entered when it is received and not when it is delivered. If, for example, an order of 1,000 units is received in June but shipped in September, it would be entered into the demand data of June when the order was received, and not into the month of September when it was fulfilled. In other words, demand represents the data of orders received, irrespective of whether or not they were accepted, and/or when delivery was made or requested.

Although demand data are better than shipment data in predicting consumer demand, they are not a true substitute for POS because they don't represent consumer takeaways. Consumer demand changes gradually, whereas customer demand changes widely from one period to the next because of a change in inventory levels, replenishment policies, buyer's perception about the market, and promotional plans of suppliers. Further, if forecasts are based on POS, the customer demand will be more stable.

Point-of-Sale data: POS data are the data of sales to ultimate consumers, which are captured when a salesperson at the sales counter scans a product. It is the best data for forecasting consumer demand because they truly represent the demand of end-consumers. They are more stable than demand and shipment data, and thus forecasts based on them are more accurate. There is one problem, however. They are still a proxy (though a good one) of total sales to ultimate consumers, because there are outlets that don't have the scanning facility, and also ones that don't make their data available for one reason or another. Their sales data are not reflected in the POS data, which the company purchases from AC Nielsen or Symphony IRI Group. Further, POS of military entities and of sales abroad are not available. (For more detail on POS data, read Chapter 5)

WAREHOUSE WITHDRAWAL DATA

Where POS data are not available, customer warehouse withdrawals (WW) are the next best alternative for forecasting consumption. The warehouse withdrawals represent the products pulled out of the warehouse racks. One problem though is that they are often provided in higher units of measure (cases or pallets), which have to be broken down into smaller units such as SKUs for forecasting purposes.

THINGS YOU SHOULD KNOW ABOUT DATA

There are a number of things you should know about data, the most important among them are:

1. More data (observations) are not necessarily better because consumption patterns change over time; with the result, the data that were relevant before, may no longer be relevant. Consumption patterns change because of changing market dynamics resulting from a proliferation of new products, intense competition, development of new markets and channels of distributions, and changing economic conditions. So, it is not necessary to go back too far in preparing forecasts. Chapter 13 explains in detail how to decide how far back to go.

2. There are more variations (noise) in the data at a granular level than at an aggregate level, but variations diminish when aggregated at a higher and higher level—for example, from a SKU to a category to a company level. When we aggregate data of two or more series, declining values in some series are offset somewhat by increasing values in others. Table 11.1 gives sales data of four different SKUs of toothpaste as well as their sum total, which is category. Here it can be seen that there are more variations at a SKU level than at a category level. In other words, when data of SKUs are aggregated, the series becomes more stable.

3. Trend becomes more visible when granular data are aggregated; again for the same reason described above. The rise in values in some granular level series is somewhat negated by a decline in the values in others; with the result, a clearer trend emerges.

4. Everyday low price makes the sales data more stable, whereas promotions and other sales incentives make them unstable. This is because sales increase during the periods of promotion and drop afterward. With everyday low price, the sales do not change significantly from one period to the next, other than because of seasonality.

Table 11.1 | Sales Data of Four Different SKUS of Tooth Paste

Period	Strawberry Flavor (Mil. of Units)	Orange Flavor (Mil. of Units)	Mango Flavor (Mil. of Units)	Grape Flavor (Mil. of Units)	Category (Sum Total) (Mil. of Units)
1	4	7	8	9	28
2	5	5	7	13	30
3	6	7	6	16	35
4	8	6	7	17	38
5	7	5	11	16	39
6	4	9	10	18	41

5. AC Nielsen and Symphony IRI Group (third party syndicated data vendors) provide POS data of our products as well as those of competitors, but the data that we get directly from our customers, with whom we have a data sharing arrangement, are only of our own products.

6. Relational databases are the ones that link disparate data tables through common references such as product codes, customer name, UPC (Unique Product Code) numbers, and geographical location. They make it easier to pull the sales information by any selection criteria.

7. Intermittent products (products with a sporadic or lumpy demand) do not form a normal distribution. Their sales occur irregularly. The manufacturer may get one order, say in January, and next one maybe in August or September. The extreme irregularity in the data makes it difficult to forecast with any reasonable amount of accuracy. Products such as spare car parts form such a pattern.

8. Bullwhip effect corrupts the data pattern. It occurs when a small change in the downstream demand near the end consumers causes a significant change in the upstream demand closer to the manufacturer. In other words, a small change in consumer demand causes a much greater change in the inventory of each participant in the supply chain, and the change becomes bigger and bigger as we move upstream, say, from inventory of finished goods to inventory of raw material. It is the result of lack of visibility in consumer demand, unusual changes in consumers' buying patterns, and poor forecasts. Increased collaboration and visibility across the chain are used to mitigate the bullwhip effect.

SUGGESTED READING

1. Kiely, Daniel A. "Synchronizing Supply Chain Operations with Consumer Demand Using Customer Data" in ***Practical Guide to Business Forecasting,*** edited by Chaman L. Jain and Jack Malehorn. New York: Graceway Publishing Company, 2005, pp. 307-312.

QUESTIONS FOR REVIEW

1. Does an "Everyday Low Price" policy make the consumption data more or less stable, and why? Explain.
2. Does the aggregation of granular level data make the data trend more or less visible, and why? Explain.
3. What is intermittent demand? Does this make it more difficult or easier to forecast the demand of such a product? Explain.
4. Between demand and POS data, which one is likely to give a relatively more accurate forecast and why? Explain.
5. Describe whether or not we can determine the market share of our product just from the POS data received directly from our customers.
6. Between SKU and category, which one generally has more noise in the data, and why? Explain.
7. What purpose does the relational database serve? Explain.
8. If we receive an order in February for a delivery in April, in which month—February or April—should we enter the order in the unconstrained demand data?
9. "The more data we have, the better it is for forecasting." Why or why not?
10. Explain in brief the following:
    a. Demand data
    b. Shipment data
    c. POS data
    d. Warehouse withdrawal data
    e. Constrained vs. unconstrained demand

CHAPTER 12

DATA ANALYSIS AND TREATMENT

Before we start modeling, it is important to study the data. Each dataset has its own problems, which have to be taken care of before preparing forecasts. The more we understand the data, the better it is. Data may have large variations because of seasonality, promotional activities, opening and closing of stores, and intermittent demand. Once we know the problems, we may know what to do about them. Preparing forecasts without examining the data is like enlisting a person in the Army without a physical checkup. The best way to start is to plot the data. It will show anomalies and missing data if there are any. It will also give us an indication if there is a trend in the data and/or seasonal factors are at work.

WHAT TO LOOK FOR IN THE DATA

Here is what we should look for in the data:

How much data do we have? The selection of a model depends, among other things, on the size of data (number of observations). Many models have a data requirement; some require more than the others. Box Jenkins, for example, requires a minimum of 36 observations, according to some authorities, to prepare a forecast. At the same time, having more data is not necessarily better. There are a certain number of observations for every product that can give the best forecast. How to arrive at that number is discussed in the next chapter.

How reliable are the data? Reliability of a forecast depends, among other things, upon the reliability of data. If the data are not reliable, so would be the forecast. To determine the reliability of data, check the source of the data. Also, check the basis on which the data were gathered, that is, whether data were based on actual enumeration of the universe or on a sample test. Data based on actual enumeration of the universe are generally more reliable than a sample test. But, often, we work with sample data.

Are the data consistent? It is important that all the data are consistent. If we are preparing a shipment forecast, make sure that all the values are of shipment. If you making a demand forecast, make sure that all the values are of demand. (You will be surprised how often companies make this mistake.) Otherwise, we will be mixing apples and peaches, and forecasts would be far from being accurate.

Which data are more appropriate—aggregated or disaggregated? Sales data of a company as a whole are aggregated; but when broken down by division, distribution center, territory, customers, category, or SKU, they become disaggregated. Generally, the more aggregated the data, the more accurate would be the forecasts. Therefore, it is better to first prepare forecasts at a category level, and then break them down into SKUs using one method or another. Usually, SKUs within a category follow the same pattern. In some cases, however, this may not be true where one SKU tends to cannibalize the other, for example, regular cake vs. sugar free cake. In that case, it would be better to prepare their forecasts separately.

Is there a missing data value? It is important to know whether any data value is missing in a dataset. Missing data may distort the true pattern. Let's say sales of four periods are as follows: Period 1, $10 million; period 2, $15 million; period 3, $20 million; and period 4, $25 million. If sales of period 3 are missing, then the computer will read that the sales increased from $15 million (in period 2) to $25 million (in period 4) over just one period, but in actual reality it happened over two periods. If we plug in zero for period 3, we will be distorting the pattern. It will show that the sales went down from $15 million in period 2 to zero in period 3 and then jumped back to $25 million in period 4. So, we need to interpolate the value for the missing period, particularly in time series modeling. The section on "Data Treatment" shows how it can be done.

Are there outliers in the data? An outlier is an unusual (abnormal) value, the value that deviates significantly from the norm. The value may be extremely low or extremely high. In one period, sales went down sharply because of riots in major cities or because of stock-outs; and in another period, sales went up sharply because of one big order from abroad, or from a special event that was not expected to occur. The values of both these periods are unusual. They are unusual because

Table 12.1 | Sales Data: Examples of Outliers

Period	Zurich Trading Co. (Mil. of $)	Bombay Trading Co. (Mil. of $)
1	80	230
2	86	238
3	95	245
4	103	550
5	54	260
6	114	275
7	125	289

they are far from the norm. In another example, in August 2009, the auto sales surged to their highest monthly total in more than a year because of the "Cash for Clunkers" program where the U.S. Government offered as much as $4,500 to a customer who traded in its old vehicle for a new one. This was a one-time thing. When the government terminated this program, sales dropped. In Table 12.1, the outlier is in period 5 in the case of Zurich Trading Company, and in period 4, in the case of Bombay Trading Company. The outlier is regarded as a temporary change in the data pattern. It happened in one particular period, but may not happen again.

Is there a structural change in the data? The structural change (shift) is an abrupt change in the data pattern and/or data relationships. The change is permanent. The structural change can occur, for example, because of a merger or acquisition, change in the line of merchandise, introduction of new products or abandonment of old ones, exit or entry of a major competitor, regulatory changes, and loss or gain of one or more large customers. The sales data pattern of the oral contraceptive, Ortho, for example, changed in 1975 because of the FDA concern about the reduced levels of estrogen. The structural change tells us that the data prior to the change is not comparable to the ones that follow. In Table 12.2, the structural change occurred in the sales data of Lucy Department Stores in periods 6 and 9. In both cases, it occurred because of acquisition of another company. In contrast to an outlier, the structural change represents a permanent change.

Is there seasonality in the data? Seasonal variations are those that occur regularly and periodically. The length of a seasonal cycle is always one year or less. For example, sales

Table 12.2 | Lucy Department Stores: An Example of Structural Change

Period	Sales (Mil. of $)
1	307.5
2	352.7
3	401.7
4	617.3
5	783.4
6	**1,449.0**
7	1,809.9
8	2,027.2
9	**3,271.1**
10	3,384.2
11	3,594.2
12	3,624.5

of department stores reach their peak in the months of November and December because of Christmas. This happens regularly (every year) and periodically (occurs every year at the same time). In other words, if we are preparing annual forecasts, we should not be concerned about seasonal variations because annualized data do not have seasonality. But, if we are preparing forecasts for a period of less than one year, say, for a month or a quarter and there is seasonality in the data, the model used must account for it. Seasonality varies from region to region, from category to category, and, in some cases, even from one SKU to another.

Is there any change in the number of trading days? The number of business days may differ from one week to another, one month to another, and one year to another, any of which can make a difference in some businesses. For them, some adjustments in the data or forecast may be needed.

When do different holidays/events fall? There are some businesses that are holiday driven; any change in them makes a difference. A number of holidays don't fall on a fixed calendar date. In one year Easter may come one week earlier, and in another year, a week later. Some categories are holiday specific, for example, candy for Halloween. Some categories are event specific, for example, beer and salty snacks for Super Bowl. For these, some adjustments in the data or forecast will be needed.

Which phase of the life cycle is the product in? The forecaster needs to know before preparing a forecast whether a product is in the introductory, mature, declining demand, or obsolescent phase. The product in each phase of a life cycle may require a different model for forecasting.

Is there abnormal distribution in the data? It is often assumed that the data are normally distributed, that is, the data form a bell-shaped distribution (normal curve). If not, one has to look for a model that does not make this assumption. Products with an intermittent (sporadic or lumpy) demand do not have a normal distribution.

Is there a cause-and-effect relationship? If there is a cause-and-effect relationship in the data, then Cause-and-Effect models such as regression have to be used. In other words, if sales are affected by the price we charge, the amount of money we spend on promotion, and the state of the economy, then data require a Cause-and-Effect model for forecasting. Here sales are the effect, and the price and the amount spent on advertisements, and the state of the economy are the causes. Further, if we find from the data that certain past events skewed the historical demand (upward or downward) and are likely to occur again, then we want to make sure that the model we select makes adjustments for those events.

HOW TO TREAT DATA

We have described above some of the problems in the data. Here we will explain how to handle them.

Missing value: If a value is missing, you have to interpolate it, that is, you have to plug in the estimated value for that period, particularly in Time Series modeling. There are a number of ways of doing it. Here are steps for the simplest one:

Step 1: Compute the change in sales from one period to another. For example, the sales in Period 2 increased from Period 1 by 6 (86-80). Do the same for other periods, which are given in column 3 of Table 12.3.

Step 2: Calculate the percentage change in sales from one period to the next. For example, the sales in Period 2 increased by 7.5% ($\frac{6}{80} \times 100$) from the previous period. The same way calculate the percentages of all other periods prior to the missing period, which are given in column 4 of Table 12.3.

Step 3: Compute the average percentage increase, which comes to 8.8% ($\frac{26.4}{3}$).

Table 12.3 | Interpolating Data for a Missing Value

Period (1)	Sales (Mil. of $) (2)	Change from One Period to the Next (3)	% Change (4)	Interpolated Value (Mil. of $) (5)
1	80	—	—	
2	86	6	7.5	
3	95	9	10.5	
4	103	8	8.4	
5	NA	—	—	112
6	121	—	—	
7	125	4	—	
Total			**26.4**	

Average % Change $= \frac{26.4}{3}$ 8.8% | Estimated Value of Period 5 = 103 × 1.088 = 112

Step 4: Estimate the value for Period 5. Here we assume if the sales continue to rise by 8.8%, what would be the value of that period. This comes to 112 (103 × 1.088), which is to be plugged in for Period 5.

Outlier: If we find an outlier in the data, the first thing to do is to account for why it happened. If we know what contributed to it, we may know whether that element is likely to recur, particularly, during the period we want to forecast. In that case, we should make a forecast by replacing the outlier with an estimated value, which can be computed the same way as shown for the missing value. But, if that particular element is likely to occur again in that period, then we have to adjust the forecast for that. For example, that element increases the sales by 10% based on past experience. Then use that factor to arrive at the final forecast. If that element is not likely to recur, then the forecast arrived earlier will be the final forecast. (Note this approach holds only for Time Series modeling. In regression, there is another way for handling an outlier, which we will discuss in Chapter 23.)

Structural change: In the case of structural change, we don't use the data prior to the change, because the pattern that existed before has changed. In Table 12.2, if we want to make a forecast of Period 13, we will use the data starting with Period 9—this is when the second acquisition took place.

QUESTIONS FOR REVIEW

1. Describe what we should look for in the data before preparing forecasts.
2. What is the best way to handle a structural change in the data for forecasting?
3. For annual forecasts, should we be concerned about seasonal variations? Why? Explain.
4. Why is it important to plug in an estimated value for the period in which the actual value is missing, particularly, in Time Series modeling? Explain.
5. Explain in detail how to handle an outlier in preparing forecasts.
6. Explain which models are appropriate where data have cause-and-effect relationships.
7. Does the product with an intermittent demand have a normal distribution? Explain.
8. Can we use the same model for different phases of a product life cycle? Why or why not?
9. What do we mean by seasonal variations? Explain.
10. Explain in brief the following:
    a. Outlier
    b. Structural change
    c. The "Cash for Clunkers" program, under which the U.S. Government gave as much as $4,500 for an old vehicle, sharply increased the sales of auto in August 2009. Does it represent an outlier or structural change?
    d. Intermittent demand

CHAPTER 13

HOW MUCH DATA TO USE IN FORECASTING

To prepare a forecast we have to decide how much data to use. The saying "the more data, the better" is a myth. Because of the changing market dynamics, we cannot go too far back to prepare a forecast. But how far back should we go? This depends on the phase of life cycle the product is in, model we plan to use, forecast horizon (how far ahead we plan to forecast), the ups and downs in the economy, and ex post forecasts.

PRODUCT LIFE CYCLE

Each product goes through the following five phases of life cycle:

Phase 1: When the product is introduced (introductory phase).
Phase 2: When the demand for a product is increasing at an increasing rate.
Phase 3: When the demand for a product is increasing at a decreasing rate.
Phase 4: When the demand for a product matures.
Phase 5: When the demand for a product starts declining.

Among all the phases, a product in the introductory phase is the most difficult to forecast, and a product in the mature phase is the easiest. Every product goes through these phases, though the life span varies. High-tech and fashion products generally have a very short life span.

How much data to use depends on the phase of cycle the product is in? If a product is in the introductory phase, we will use data only of that phase. If it is in Phase 2 (when demand is increasing at an increasing rate) and we expect it to remain in that phase during the forecast period, we will use only the data of that period, and so on. It is assumed here that a sufficient number of observations in that phase are available. There will be a problem, however, if a product shifts from one phase to the next during the forecast period. There are models like analog and diffusion that take care of this problem.

MODEL REQUIREMENT

Each model has its own data requirement. For example, the single moving average percentage change model requires less data than the double moving average percentage change model. With a three-period moving average percentage change model, we need at least four periods of data to generate a forecast, whereas with a three-period double moving average percentage change model, we need at least six periods of data. For a Box Jenkins model, a minimum of 36 data points are required according to some authorities. The requirement goes up to 72 months if the data have a monthly seasonality. The regression model has its own data requirement. It is suggested that we should have at least five observations for each independent variable.

FORECAST HORIZON

How far ahead we want to forecast (short term or long term) also makes a difference. Less data are needed for short-term forecasts. This is because what happened in the most recent past would be a good indicator of what would happen in the near future. However, for long-term forecasting, we have to use much more data. Here the forecaster is more concerned about the long-term trend than short-term ups and down in the data.

UPS AND DOWNS IN THE ECONOMY

Every economy experiences ups and downs, called business cycles, which affect businesses. Sales go up during prosperity and go down during a recession. How much they impact the business depends on how severe they are. In fact, small changes in the economy may not have a significant effect on sales, but when those changes are drastic, their effect can be significant. For example, the recession that started in 2008 in the United States was fairly severe and affected many businesses badly. In that case, we have to use the data starting with recession, because the data prior to it are not applicable to the current trend. The problem, however, will arise when we hit a turning point. At that point, we may have to make a judgment call. A turning point is a point when the economy shifts from one phase of the business cycle to another; for example, from trough to revival. Turning points are the most difficult to forecast.

EX POST FORECASTS

The best way to determine how much data to use, prepare ex post forecasts with different periods of data (i.e., one year of data, two years of data, and three years of data), and then determine which one on average gives the least amount of error. (Ex post forecasts are forecasts of those periods for which actuals are known.) Let's say we want to know how well we will forecast if we use one year (12 months) of data. Let's assume further that we have 60 months of data. In that case, we will first prepare a forecast of month 13 using first 12 months of data, and then compare it with the actual to determine the forecast error. Then, drop one month from the top and add one month from the bottom (still keeping 12 months of data) to prepare the next month forecast, which in this case would be month 14. This way prepare as many forecasts as the data allow. (The model used here should be the same as the one we normally use, and use it for preparing all other ex post forecasts.) Then, the same way, prepare ex post forecasts, using 24 months and 36 months of data at a time. Again, prepare as many forecasts as we can with the data on hand. After that, compute mean absolute percentage error (called MAPE) of all the forecasts prepared with 12 months, 24 months, and 36 months of data, and then compare their average percentage error. If ex post forecasts prepared with 12 months of data give the least amount of error, use 12 months of data; if 24 months of data give the least amount of error, use 24 months of data; and so on. In so doing, don't depend on just one or two ex post forecast errors. Prepare as many different ex post forecast errors as the data permit. This approach will give us a better handle on deciding how much data to use.

How much data are appropriate may vary from one industry to another and one company to another. In the consumer products industry, generally three years of data are used. The best way, of course, is to determine by using our own data.

A CASE STUDY

In one consumer products company the forecaster always prepared forecasts using three years of data. Maybe he was doing it because of industry practices or he felt comfortable preparing them with that amount of data. One day, the Vice President of Marketing asked him to explain why he was using three years of data. He could not give any satisfactory answer. The VP felt, since the market dynamics are changing so rapidly, it would be better to prepare forecasts with one or two years of data. So, he asked the forecaster to prepare forecasts with one and two years of data. To the surprise of every one, forecasts prepared with one year of data gave the largest number, and with three years of data, the lowest. Since upper management always looks for high numbers, the VP insisted that we should use forecasts based on one year of data. But the forecaster was uncomfortable doing that.

To have a satisfactory closure, he approached me for an answer. I didn't have the answer either. But I knew how to get it. I suggested that we should develop ex post forecast errors as explained above, and then let the numbers speak for themselves. In this case, the forecast horizon was six months, meaning they were preparing six-months-ahead forecasts. The results showed that the mean absolute percentage error (MAPE) of ex post forecast errors was the lowest when three years of data were used and the highest when one year of data was used. In fact, the mean absolute percentage error based on three years of data was less than half of what was of one year of data.

QUESTIONS FOR REVIEW

1. Explain how much data to use for forecasting when a product is in Phase 2 of its life cycle where sales are increasing at an increasing rate. It is assumed that the product will remain in that phase during the forecast period.
2. Explain how much data to use for forecasting when the economy is in a severe recession. It is assumed that the recession will continue even during the forecast period.
3. Explain in detail how we can use ex post errors to determine how many data points we should use in preparing a forecast.
4. Explain why a model we select makes a difference about the number of observations to be used for preparing a forecast.
5. Is it easier or more difficult to forecast when a product is in the Introductory Phase or in the Mature Phase of its life cycle? Explain.
6. How many years of data are normally used in the consumer products industry?
7. How many different phases does a normal product have in its life cycle? Explain.
8. Explain why it is important to decide on the number of observations to be used to prepare a forecast.
9. Do small changes in the economy make a difference in operational forecasts? Explain.
10. Explain in brief the following:
    a. Turning point
    b. Ex post error
    c. Forecast horizon
    d. Business cycle

PART IV

MODELS AND MODELING

INTRODUCTION

Before we start modeling, it is important to know what kinds of models are available as well as their key features. It is equally important to know the fundamentals of modeling. A forecaster must understand why it is not necessary for a highly sophisticated model to improve forecasts; why there is no magic model that can work with every dataset; why it is not essential for a forecast to improve when two or more models are combined; why models age with time; and why it is important that a selected model should be sound both theoretically and statistically. Understanding the key features of different models and the basics of modeling can help not only in selecting the right model but also in using it in a most effective manner. For benchmarking, companies may like to know which models are used most in business, and why.

CHAPTER 14

FUNDAMENTALS OF MODELS AND MODELING

For effective forecasting, it is important to know not only the different models and their key features but also the fundamentals of modeling, which is the subject of this chapter. A good understanding of the fundamentals will help you not only in selecting an appropriate model but also in using it effectively and efficiently.

TYPES OF MODELS

Before we start modeling, we need to know what kinds of models are available and their key features. Basically, there are three types of models:

1. Time Series
2. Cause and Effect
3. Judgmental

Time Series models: In Time Series models, we simply extrapolate the past data by using one technique or the other to arrive at a forecast. It is assumed here that the past trend/pattern will continue into the future. In Part V ("Time Series Models"), we discuss various techniques available for extrapolating the data. Time Series models are also called Univariate models because they need only the data of a series we wish to forecast. They are often used for short-term forecasting, because during that period, the data pattern/trend is less likely to change; if it changes, it is less likely to change in a significant way.

Cause-and-Effect models: Cause-and-Effect models are used where the data have a cause-and-effect relationship. If the sales of a company are affected by the price it charges and the amount of money it spends on promotion, then the sales are the effect, and the price and amount spent on promotion are the causes. Here we statistically compute the average relationships between price and sales and between the amounts spent on promotion and sales by using the historical data, and then use those relationships to prepare a forecast. In these models, we need not only the data of a variable to be forecasted, which are sales data in this case, but also of the price and the amount spent on promotion. Since in such models, data of more than one variable are needed, they are also called Multivariate models. Cause-and-Effect models provide more insight into the data than Time Series models because they give the information about the relationships that exist among the cause-and-effect variables. There are a number of models that fall in this category, but the one that is used most is regression.

Judgmental models: In judgmental models, judgment is predominant. These models are used when we don't have the historical data, such as is the case with new products; when data exist but are not applicable as in the case of fashion products where each product has its own data pattern; when we have to prepare a forecast for a period far into the future; when a large percentage of sales comes from a few customers; and/or when a forecast is needed in a hurry. Although forecasts prepared with such models are very much intuitively driven, they are by no means seat-of-the-pant forecasts. There are set procedures to be followed to prepare a forecast.

Models are also categorized as (1) Quantitative and (2) Qualitative. Quantitative models are those where a forecast is prepared using the hard data, as in the case of Time Series and Cause-and-Effect models. Qualitative models, on the other hand, are those where a forecast is prepared with little or no hard data. Judgmental models fall in this category.

MODELS USED IN BUSINESS

Among the three types of models (Time Series, Cause-and-Effect, and Judgmental), Time Series models are by and large the simplest and easiest to use. In fact, they are the ones that are used most

Figure 14.1 | Models Used in Business (All Industries Combined)

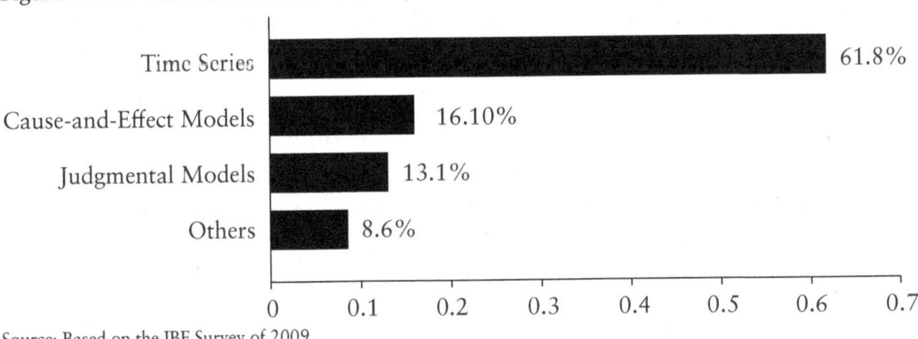

Source: Based on the IBF Survey of 2009.

Figure 14.2 | Time Series Models Used (All Industries Combined)

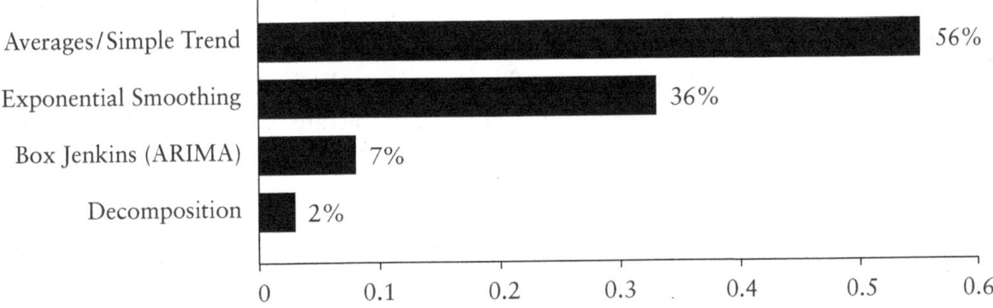

Source: Based on the IBF Survey of 2009.

in business. Figure 14.1 shows the uses of models in business based on the 2009 survey conducted by the Institute of Business Forecasting and Planning. It shows that 62% of the companies use Time Series models; 16%, Cause-and-Effect models; 13%, Judgmental models; and the remaining 9%, homegrown models.

Within Time Series, the simplest models are averages and simple trend; they are the ones that are used most (56%). (See Figure 14.2)

FUNDAMENTALS OF MODELING

To use models effectively and efficiently, it is important to know their fundamentals, which are the following:

Actual = Pattern + Error. Every dataset has its own pattern, and every model captures a specific pattern. The more a model captures the pattern, most likely, the smaller would be the error.

Therefore, the model that captures most of the pattern is the best model for forecasting. However, if we are at a turning point of the phase of a product life cycle, or the economy shifts from one phase of business cycle to the next, for example, from a recession to revival, the past pattern won't help.

The more random variations there are in the data, the more difficult it is to forecast. In an effort to find the right model, we first determine what kind of pattern exists in the data so that we can match the right model with the pattern. If data numbers are random, then there is no pattern in the data. Without a pattern, we cannot forecast because there is no model that captures randomness in the data.

Sophisticated models are not necessarily better than simple ones. It is a misnomer (or a worst practice) that the more sophisticated the model, the better it is. Just like we cannot really judge the quality of a product by its price tag, we cannot judge the capability of a model to forecast by its "level of sophistication." In the end, what matters is how well a model forecasts, not how simple or complex it is. So, the best strategy is to start with a simple model, and then move on to a more complex one until your error requirement is met. If you can tolerate the 4% error that a simple model gives, then it is not necessary to go for a complex one. The idea is if a simple aspirin can cure your headache, then why to go for a high power painkiller.

There is no such thing as magic model. There is no magic model that works with every dataset. Every dataset has a specific pattern and every model captures a specific pattern. The best thing, therefore, is to find a model that captures most of the pattern in your dataset. The more it captures, the more likely it would give good forecasts. Remember, there is no silver bullet.

No two models give the same forecast. If we apply two different models to our data, no matter which type we use, we will have two different forecasts. It would be a coincidence if we get the same result. As mentioned earlier, there are three different types of models (Time Series, Cause and Effect, and Judgmental). It won't make any difference either if we use two different models of the same type, or two different models of different types, the forecast of each would be somewhat different.

Models age with time. No matter how good a model is, it ages with time. The model that worked well in the past may not work now because of a change in the data pattern resulting from a change in the market dynamics. Maybe the market has become more competitive, the life cycle of a product has shortened, consumer behavior has changed, and/or a number of new products have emerged in the market.

A model can be improved further but at a cost. We can further improve a model and, consequently, forecasts, but there is a cost of doing it. Therefore, to make the most of our limited forecasting resources, we have to watch closely the incremental cost of improving a model, and the benefit resulting from it. Generally speaking, in the beginning, it is easier to improve a model and the forecasts. But as we continue our journey toward improvement, it will become harder and more costly.

Combining two or more different models do not necessarily improve forecasts. There is no guarantee that we can improve forecasts by combining forecasts of two or more different models, but it is worth testing. Here we prepare a forecast by each model and then get the final forecast by having a simple or weighted average of both. Whether or not it is worth it can be determined by preparing ex post forecasts. However, by using two or more models we may get different perspectives. For example, if we use two models, one Time Series and the other Cause and Effect, we may find that one model has a tendency to over-forecast and the other to under-forecast. If this is the case, they can help us in determining risks and opportunities. One model can give us the worst-case scenario, and the other can give us the best case we can hope for. The Cause-and-Effect model can also give us insight into the market, that is, how much lift in sales the promotion provides, how sensitive the sales are with respect to price, and so on.

A selected model should be sound statistically as well as theoretically. The selected model should not only be statistically sound, but also it should make sense. For example, we may find that there is a strong statistical relationship between the divorce rate in the United Kingdom and the import of potatoes. This does not mean that we can forecast the divorce rate from the import of potatoes because one has nothing to do with the other. Therefore, the model selected should be statistically valid as well as make sense.

Revise forecasts at a set interval or when there is a significant change in the market dynamics or business plans. There is a cost of revising forecasts. So, the best thing is to revise forecasts at a set interval, which may be monthly or quarterly, unless there is a significant change in the market dynamics and/or in business plans. Maybe a new competitor has entered the market, or our key customer has decided to hold back its plan for opening new stores. Maybe the company decided to cut down its promotional budget. All these will require revising the forecasts. According to the 2009 survey of the Institute of Business Forecasting and Planning, 69% of the companies revise their forecasts monthly.

Forecasts can change the plan. As described in one of the earlier chapters, each forecast is based on a plan—the price we intend to charge, the amount we plan to spend on promotion, and the state of the economy. If our plan changes, so would the forecast. If we don't like the forecast number, we may decide to change the plan to hit the target. For instance, let us say that our forecast tells us that our sales of next quarter will be $500 million, but our target is $525 million. We may decide to change our plan, perhaps by increasing the spending on promotion, lowering the price, and/or introducing more new products, to hit the target.

Managing the exceptions improves forecasts. It is not unusual for a forecaster to find from a forecast report spit out by the computer that certain forecasts don't make sense. They are either too high or too low. To take care of this problem, the forecaster intuitively adjusts those numbers, which is called managing the exceptions. This can occur either because the models selected for them were not right; there were problems with the data; or for any other reason. In those cases, the forecaster adjusts their numbers by using his or her best judgment. At the top of it, another adjustment might be made for the same and/or other forecasts in the consensus meeting described in Chapter 7 on Consensus Forecasting Process. Adjustments made by the forecaster as well as in the consensus meeting, by and large, improve forecasts.

A statistical forecast is an average forecast. Statistical forecasts are basically average forecasts because they are based on some kind of average, no matter which model we use—Time Series models, Cause-and-Effect models, or any other model. In Time Series, for example, we may use an average of changes in sales of the last three periods or the last ten periods to make a forecast of the next period. In Cause-and-Effect, the forecast is based on the average relationships with the variable we wish to forecast and the variables that affect it. Therefore, no matter which model we use, the next period forecast may not exactly be the same as actual.

The best model is not necessarily the one that yields the best result in one particular period. On the contrary, the best model is the one that yields on average the best results over a number of periods. A model may give the best forecast in one particular period, which may be just a coincidence.

Target setting is not modeling. It is not unusual to have a target that comes in the form of a directive from senior management. This is not modeling; it is merely a target setting. It is wrong to use a target or budget as a forecast. They are not the same.

QUESTIONS FOR REVIEW

1. What are the different types of models? How do they differ from each other?
2. Which models are used most in business, and why?
3. Which models are likely to give better forecasts—ones that are simple and easy to use or ones that are difficult and complex? Explain.
4. Is a forecast based on a plan or is a plan based on a forecast, or both? Explain in detail.
5. Can we improve a forecast by combining forecasts of two or more different models? Explain.
6. Do models age with time, or would a model that worked well in the past continue working in the future? Explain.
7. What do we mean when we say a model selected should be sound both statistically and theoretically? Explain.
8. Is there any model that will work well with every set of data? Why or why not?
9. Would two different models applied to the same dataset give exactly the same forecast? Explain.
10. Explain in brief the following:
    a. Statistical forecast is an average forecast
    b. Managing exceptions in forecasting
    c. Qualitative vs. Quantitative models
    d. Sophisticated models are not necessarily the best

PART V

TIME SERIES MODELS

INTRODUCTION

Time Series models are one of the three types of models that are used in business forecasting. The other two types are Cause-and-Effect and Judgmental. Here forecasts are prepared by rolling forward the numbers by using one method or the other. The assumption made here is that the past data pattern will continue into the future. Although there are a number of Time Series models, we will discuss only the ones that are most frequently used in business. A recent survey of practicing forecasters conducted by IBF (Institute of Business Forecasting and Planning) shows that about 62% of them use Time Series models. Among Time Series models, ones that are most often used are averages, exponential smoothing, and simple trend. The reasons for using Times Series models are threefold. One, they are easy to understand and use. Two, most of the forecasting done in business is short term and Times Series models are quite suitable for that. Three, forecasting in business became popular only in last 20 years or so. As such, most of the forecasters are fairly newcomers in the field. The best way to start learning forecasting is with Time Series models, which are easy to understand and use.

CHAPTER 15

AVERAGES

Time Series models are univariate models. They require only the data of a series to be forecasted. If you wish to forecast sales, you need only the data of sales. If you wish to forecast cash flow, you need only the data of cash flow. Here forecasts are prepared by extrapolating the data using one technique or the other. In so doing, the assumption is made that the past data pattern will continue into the future. These models are, by and large, easy to understand and use. Their simplicity, however, should not be construed as less effective. In many situations, they work fairly well.

Time Series models are generally good for forecasting sales of a company as a whole, forecasting the sales of mature products, and for short-term forecasting. They work well for short-term forecasting because during that period the data pattern either does not change at all or changes mildly. In other words, they are appropriate where the past trend is expected to continue into the future. However, some people view forecasting with Time Series models like driving a car with the windshield glass completely blocked, and the driver drives by looking at the rearview mirror. This is fine if you are driving in the Mojave Desert, where it does not matter which direction you go. But if you are driving on a curvy road, this will certainly be a prescription for disaster.

There is a long list of Time Series models, but the ones that are often used in business are the following.

1. Naïve
2. Average Level Change

3. Average Percentage Change
4. Weighted Average Percentage Change
5. Moving Average Level Change
6. Single Moving Average Percentage Change
7. Double Moving Average Level Change
8. Double Moving Average Percentage Change
9. Single Exponential Smoothing
10. Double Exponential Smoothing
11. Trend Line
12. Classical Decomposition
13. Sales Ratios
14. Family Member Forecasting

The first four models on the list are discussed in this chapter; models 5 through 8 are discussed in Chapter 16; models 9 and 10 are covered in Chapter 17; model 11 (Trend Line) is discussed in Chapter 18; Classical Decomposition model is the topic of Chapter 19; Sales ratio models are covered in Chapter 20; and Family Member Forecasting is discussed in Chapter 21.

Naïve: In this model the sales of the last period are assumed to be the forecast of the next period. If the sales of period 10 are $100 million, then the forecast of period 11 is $100 million. This model exists only in theory and is rarely used. The naïve model is often used as a benchmark to determine the efficiency of other models. In other words, the model you use must perform at least better than a naïve model.

Average Level Change: Each model is based on certain assumptions. The average level change model assumes that sales change from one period to the next by the average of past changes. Here is the step-by-step procedure for computing forecasts with this model, using the sales data of City Stores given in Table 15.1.

Step 1: Compute the level change in sales from one period to the next. Level changes are given in Column 3. The level change in period 2 from period 1 is $15.60 million ($371.60 – $356.00); in period 3 from period 2, $2.10 million ($373.70 – $371.60); and so on.

Step 2: Compute the average of level changes. This is the sum of all level changes divided by number of changes, which comes to $2.68 million ($24.10 ÷ 9). This implies that the sales, on average, increase from one period to the next by $2.68 million.

Table 15.1 | Average Level Change

Period (1)	Sales of City Stores (Mil. of \$) (2)	Level Change (Mil. of \$) (3)
1	356.00	—
2	371.60	15.60
3	373.70	2.10
4	380.40	6.70
5	364.80	–15.60
6	373.10	8.30
7	367.40	–5.70
8	373.40	6.00
9	374.10	0.70
10	380.10	6.00
Sum		**24.10**

$$\text{Average Change} = \frac{\$24.10}{9} = \$2.68 \text{ mil.}$$

$$\hat{Y}_{11} = \$380.10 + \$2.68 = \$382.78 \text{ mil.}$$

Step 3: Prepare the forecast. The forecast of period 11 will be the current value of period 10 plus the average level change, which comes to \$382.78 million (\$380.10 million + \$2.68 million). Incidentally, the total of the actual sales was \$393.50 million. This means that the forecast error for this period was \$10.72 million (\$393.50 million – \$382.78 million), or 2.72% [(\$10.72 million ÷ \$393.50 million) × (100)]. The forecast value in forecasting is often identified by Y hat ($\hat{Y}$).

Average Percentage Change: The average percent change model works the same way as the average level change model, except it assumes that the next period sales will increase (decrease) by the average of percentage changes. Here again, we use the data of City Stores to demonstrate the procedure. (See Table 15.2)

Here, the forecast is prepared as follows:

Step 1: Compute the level change in sales from one period to the next, the same way as before. The level changes are given in Column 3 of Table 15.2.

Step 2: Convert the level change, given in Column 3, into a percentage. The percentage change in sales in period 2 over period 1 is 4.38% [(\$15.60 million ÷ \$356.00 million) × (100)]; in period 3 over period 2, 0.57% [(\$2.10 million ÷ \$371.60 million) × (100)]; and so on. These values are given in Table 15.2, Column 4.

Step 3: Compute the average percentage change. This is calculated by dividing the sum of all percentage changes by the number of changes, which comes to 0.76% (6.81 ÷ 9). This means that sales, on average, are increasing at the rate of 0.76% from one period to the next.

Step 4: Forecast the sales of period 11. This will be the actual of period 10 plus 0.76% of it, which comes to \$382.98 million [(\$380.10 million) + (\$380.10 million × .0076)]. As mentioned earlier, the actual sales for this period were \$393.50 million. This means that the forecast error of this period is \$10.52 million (\$393.50 million – \$382.98 million) or 2.67% [(\$10.52 million ÷ \$393.50 million) × (100)].

Weighted Average Percentage Change: The two models discussed above assume that all the

Table 15.2 | Average Percentage Change

Period (1)	Sales of City Stores (Mil. of \$) (2)	Level Change (Mil. of \$) (3)	Percentage Change (4)
1	356.00	—	—
2	371.60	15.60	4.38
3	373.70	2.10	0.57
4	380.40	6.70	1.79
5	364.80	–15.60	–4.10
6	373.10	8.30	2.28
7	367.40	–5.70	–1.53
8	373.40	6.00	1.63
9	374.10	0.70	0.19
10	380.10	6.00	1.60
Sum			**6.81**

$$\text{Average \% Change} = \frac{6.81}{9}$$

$$= 0.76\%$$

$$\hat{Y}_{11} = (\$380.10) + (\$380.10 \times .0076)$$

$$= \$382.98 \text{ million}$$

periods are equally important, and thus give an equal amount of weight to each change, which is one. However, in some situations, the forecaster may feel that the most recent periods are more representative of what will happen tomorrow than the older ones, and thus may like to give more weight to the most recent periods and less to others. There is no hard and fast rule for assigning weights. It all depends upon which weighting scheme works the best. In one situation, the weighting scheme of 1, 2, 3, 4, etc., might be appropriate where the weight increases by an increment of one; while in other, of 2, 2, 3, 3, etc., The weighting scheme of 1, 2, 3, 4, etc., implies to give a weight of 1 to the first change, 2 to the second change, 3 to the third change, and so on. The weighting scheme of 2, 2, 3, 3, etc., implies give a weight of 2 to first two changes, and 3 to the next two changes, and so on. As such, the weight increases as we move toward more and more recent periods. Here is the step-by-step procedure to prepare a forecast using the weighted average percentage change model, weighting scheme of 1, 2, 3, etc., and the sales data of K-Music Stores (Table 15.3).

Step 1: Calculate the level change in sales from one period to the next, the same way we did in the case of level change model. The level changes are given in Table 15.3, Column 3.

Step 2: Convert the level change into a percentage, the same way we did in the case of average percentage change model. The percentage changes are given in Table 15.3, Column 4.

Step 3: Column 5 in Table 15.3 gives weights to be assigned to each percentage change. We have assigned a weight of 1 to the first percentage change, 2 to the second percentage change, and so on. Multiply the percentage change (C) by its weight (W), that is, Column 4 × Column 5. Their products are given in Column 6.

Step 4: Calculate the weighted average percentage change. Using the formula given below, the weighted average percentage change comes to:

$$\text{Wtd. Avg. \% Change} = \frac{\Sigma CW}{\Sigma W} = \frac{741.49}{45} = 16.48\%$$

This means that the sales on average increase at the rate of 16.48% from one period to the next.

Step 5: Prepare the forecast for period 11. This will be equal to the actual of the current

Table 15.3 | Weighted Average Percentage Change

Period (1)	Sales of K Music Stores (Mil. of $) (2)	Level Change (Mil. of $) (3)	% Change (C) (4)	Weight (W) (5)	Col. 4 × Col. 5 (CW) (6)
1	3,101.00	—	—	—	—
2	3,837.00	736.00	23.73	1	23.73
3	4,633.00	796.00	20.75	2	41.49
4	5,536.00	903.00	19.49	3	58.47
5	6,798.00	1262.00	22.80	4	91.18
6	8,382.00	1584.00	23.30	5	116.50
7	9,941.00	1559.00	18.60	6	111.60
8	11,696.00	1755.00	17.65	7	123.58
9	12,731.00	1035.00	8.85	8	70.79
10	14,204.00	1473.00	11.57	9	104.13
Sum				45 ΣW	741.49 ΣCW

Weighted Average % Change = (741.49) ÷ (45) = 16.48%

$\hat{Y}_{11}$ = (14,204.00) + (14,204.00) × (.1648) = $16,544.46 million

period plus 16.48% of it. This comes to $16,544.46 million [($14,204.00 million) + ($14,204.00 million) × (.1648)]. This compares with the actual value of $16,527.00, an error of –$17.46 million ($16,527.00 million – $16,544.46 million) or –0.11% [($17.46 million) ÷ ($16,527 million) × (100)]. The minus sign of forecast error implies that the error resulted from over-forecasting.

QUESTIONS FOR REVIEW

1. Explain the key assumption on which Time Series models are built.
2. Explain where Time Series models are most appropriate for forecasting.
3. Describe why Time Series models are viewed as looking backward rather than looking forward.
4. Explain how the average level change model differs from the average percentage change model.
5. In average level change and average percentage change models how much weight do we assign to each change? Explain.
6. What is the rational for assigning weights in the weighted average percentage change model? Explain.

GAP Stores	
Period	Sales (Mil. of $)
1	445
2	481
3	534
4	647
5	848
6	1,062
7	1,252
8	1,587
9	1,934
10	2,519

7. The table above gives the sales of GAP stores. Using the average level change model, forecast the sales of period 11.
   Answer: $2,749.44 million.

8. Using the data given in Question 7 and the average percentage change model, forecast the sales of period 11.
   Answer: $3,060.12 million.
9. Using the data given in Question 7 and the weighted average percentage change model, forecast the sales of period 11. Here it is assumed that the most recent value should get more weight than the others. As such, weights are assigned as follows: One to the first change, two to the second change, and so on. In each case, the weight increases by an increment of one.
   Answer: $3,126.84 million.
10. Again using the data given in Question 7 and the weighted average percentage change model, forecast the sales of period 11. Here weights should be assigned as follows: 1, 1, 2, 2, 3, 3, 4, 4, and 5.
    Answer: $3,122.22 million.

CHAPTER 16

MOVING AVERAGES

Moving average is another Time Series model. Unlike average level change, average percentage change, and weighted average percent change models, a moving average model assumes that the data of most recent periods, not all of the periods, are appropriate for the next period forecast. When we use three-period-moving-average change, we assume that the average of the last three-period changes is appropriate for the next period forecast. When we use a four-period moving average, we assume that the average of the last four-period changes is appropriate for the next period forecast. The data of the most recent periods are more appropriate because data patterns do change over time. What will happen in the next period depends probably more on the pattern of the most recent periods than of all the periods.

Moving average models come in all shapes and sizes. It can be a moving average of levels (moving average level model); moving average of level changes (moving average level change model); and moving average of percentage changes (moving average percentage change model). Moving average can be single and double. In a single moving average, the moving average is computed once, whereas in double moving average, it is computed twice.

SINGLE MOVING AVERAGES

In single moving averages, we will discuss two models: (1) Moving average level change and (2) moving average percentage change.

Single Moving Average Level Change: In a single moving average level change model, we use an average of a certain number of changes for making a forecast for the next period. To illustrate this, we will use the sales data of Jewel Company, given in Table 16.1. Here is the step-by-step procedure:

Step 1: Decide on the period of moving average. That is, decide on how many periods of moving average (two, three, or any other number) we wish to use. This depends on how quickly the pattern changes. If the data pattern seems to change significantly after two periods, we will use two-period moving average; if it changes after three periods, we will use three-period moving average. In the case of Jewel Company, we used a three-period moving average.

Step 2: Compute the change in sales from one period to the next. The change can be negative or positive. The change in sales in period 2 from period 1 is $210.30 million ($2,219.60 million – $2,009.30 million); and in period 3 from period 2 is $379.30 million ($2,598.90 million – $2,219.60 million). Similarly, we can compute other level changes, which are given in Column 3.

Table 16.1 | Single Moving Average Level Change

Period (1)	Sales of Jewel Company (Mil. of $) (2)	Level Change (Mil. of $) (3)	3-Period Moving Total of Changes (4)	3-Period Moving Avg. of Changes (5)
1	2,009.30	—	—	—
2	2,219.60	210.30	—	—
3	2,598.90	379.30	—	—
4	2,817.80	218.90	808.50	269.50
5	2,981.40	163.60	761.80	253.93
6	3,277.70	296.30	678.80	226.27
7	3,516.40	238.70	698.60	232.87
8	3,764.30	247.90	782.90	260.97
9	4,267.90	503.60	990.20	330.07
10	5,107.60	839.70	1591.20	530.40

$\hat{Y}_{11}$ = $5,107.60 million + $530.40 million

= $5,638.00 million

Step 3: Compute the three-period moving total of changes given in Column 3. The moving total is computed by adding the first three changes (i.e., of periods 2, 3, and 4), which comes to $808.50 million ($210.30 million + $379.30 million + $218.90 million). The value is entered next to the period 4 in Column 4. Then drop one change from the top (i.e., of period 2) and add one change from the bottom (i.e., of period 5). The moving total of period 5 comes to $761.80 million ($379.30 million + $218.90 million + $163.60 million), which is entered next to period 5 in Column 4. Similarly, compute moving total of changes of other periods.

Step 4: Compute the moving average level change. Since each moving total is a sum total of three changes, moving average will be the total divided by three. The moving average of period 4 is $269.50 million ($808.50 million ÷ 3); the moving average of period 5, $253.93 million ($761.80 million ÷ 3); and so on. All the moving averages are given in Column 5. (Note that here the moving average value is not entered the way it is done in statistics. Technically, the first moving average, $269.50, in the table should be entered next to period 3, not 4, midway between periods 2 and 4. If we do it that way, we cannot prepare a forecast of the next period, which is, period 5. For that we need the moving average of period 4, and not of period 3. Also, keep in mind that in statistics, a moving average is used to smooth the data, not for preparing a forecast. To prepare a forecast, we modify the moving average so that it can be used.)

Step 5: Prepare a forecast. In the above example, we want to prepare a forecast of period 11. This means that we are in period 10, making a forecast of period 11. The forecast of this period will be the actual sales of period 10 plus the moving average level change of the same period. This comes to $5,638.00 million ($5,107.60 million + $530.40 million). (Keep in mind we used the last moving average level change to prepare the forecast of next period.)

How accurate is this forecast? This can be determined by comparing the forecast value with the actual. The actual sale of this period is $5,650.00 million. This means that the forecast error is $12.00 million ($5,650.00 million – $5,638.00 million), or 0.21%.

Single Moving Average Percentage Change: The single moving average percentage change model works the same way as the single moving average level change model except it assumes that the next period value will increase (decrease) by the moving average percentage change instead of by the moving average level change. Here again, we use the sales data of Jewel Company to illustrate the procedure. (See Table 16.2) Steps to be followed are:

Step 1: Compute the level change from one period to the next, the same way we did in the case of single moving average level change. Level changes here are given in Column 3.

Step 2: Compute percentage change from one period to the next. The percentage change of period 2 is 10.47% [($210.30 million ÷ 2,009.30 million) × (100)]; the percentage change of period 3 is 17.09% [($379.30 million ÷ $2,219.60 million) × (100)]; and so on. All the percentage changes are given in Column 4.

Step 3: Decide on the period of moving average to be used. Here again, we decided to use a three-period moving average.

Step 4: Compute the three-period moving total of percentage changes. Do this by adding the first three changes (i.e., of period 2, 3, and 4), and entering the total next to period 4 in Column 5. The first moving total of percentage changes comes to 35.98% (10.47% + 17.09% + 8.42%). Then drop one change from the top (i.e., of period 2) and add one change from the bottom (i.e., of period 5). This moving total of percentage changes comes to 31.32% (17.09% + 8.42% + 5.81%), which is entered next to period 5. Similarly, compute moving total of percentage changes of all other periods.

Table 16.2 | Single Moving Average Percentage Change

Period (1)	Sales of Jewel Company (Mil. of $) (2)	Level Change (Mil. of $) (3)	% Change (4)	3-Period Moving Total of % Changes (5)	3-Period Moving Avg. of % Changes (6)
1	2,009.30	—	—	—	—
2	2,219.60	210.30	10.47	—	—
3	2,598.90	379.30	17.09	—	—
4	2,817.80	218.90	8.42	35.98	11.99
5	2,981.40	163.60	5.81	31.32	10.44
6	3,277.70	296.30	9.94	24.17	8.06
7	3,516.40	238.70	7.28	23.03	7.68
8	3,764.30	247.90	7.05	24.27	8.09
9	4,267.90	503.60	13.38	27.71	9.24
10	5,107.60	839.70	19.67	40.10	13.37

$\hat{Y}_{11}$ = $5,107.6 million + ($5,107.6 million × 0.1337)

= $5,790.37 million

Step 5: Compute the moving average percentage change. Since each moving total of percentage changes is a total of three changes, the average will be the total divided by three. The moving average percentage change of period 4 is 11.99% (35.98 ÷ 3), moving average percentage change of period 5 is 10.44% (31.32 ÷ 3), and so on. All the moving average percentage changes are given in Column 6.

Step 6: Prepare a forecast. Forecast of period 11 will be the actual of period 10 plus 13.37% of it. The forecast of that period comes to $5,790.37 million [($5,107.60 million) + ($5,107.60 million × 0.1337)]. (Keep in mind that we used the last moving average percentage change to prepare a forecast of the next period.)

Since the actual value of this period is $5,650.00 million, the forecast error comes to -$140.37 million ($5,650.00 million – $5,790.37 million), or –2.48%.

DOUBLE MOVING AVERAGES

As described earlier, in a double moving average model, the moving average is computed twice. Here again we will explain double moving average level change and double moving percentage change models.

Double Moving Average Level Change: Here again we will demonstrate this model by the sales data of Jewel Company. The step-by-step procedure for preparing a forecast with this model is as follows:

Steps 1-4: The first four steps are the same as in single moving average level change model. Thus, Columns 1-5 in Table 16.3 are the same as in Table 16.1. Here again, we use the moving average of three periods.

Step 5: Compute three-period double moving total of level changes given in Column 5. This is done by adding the first three single moving average level changes given in Column 5 (i.e., of periods 4, 5, and 6). Their total comes to $749.70 million ($269.50 million + $253.93 million + $226.27 million). Enter the total next to the period 6 in Column 6. Then, drop one change from the top (i.e., of period 4) and add one change from the bottom (i.e., of period 7). This total comes to $713.07 million ($253.93 million + $226.27 million + $232.87 million). Enter this total next to period 7. Similarly, compute the double moving total of level changes of other periods.

Step 6: Compute the three-period double moving average of level changes. Since each number in Column 6 is a total of three changes, the average will be the total divided by three. The double moving average level change of period 6 is $249.90 million ($749.70 million ÷ 3); the double moving average level change of period 7 is $237.69 million ($713.07 million ÷ 3); and so on. All the double moving average level changes are given in Column 7 of Table 16.3.

Step 7: Prepare a forecast, which in this case is of period 11. This will be the total of the actual sales of period 10, plus the double moving average level change of the same period. This comes to $5481.41 million ($5,107.60 million + $373.81 million).

How does this model perform? Since the actual of this period is $5,650.0 million, the error comes to $168.59 million ($5,650.00 million – $5481.41 million), or 2.98%.

Double Moving Average Percentage Change: The double moving average percentage change model works the same way as the double moving average level change model. The only difference is that this model assumes that the next period value will increase or decrease by the double

Table 16.3 | Double Moving Average Level Change

Period (1)	Sales of Jewel Company (Mil. of $) (2)	Level Change (Mil. of $) (3)	3-Period Mov. Total of Level Changes (Mil. of $) (4)	3-Period Mov. Avg. of Level Changes (Mil. of $) (5)	3-Period Double Mov. Total of Level Changes (Mil. of $) (6)	3-Period Double Mov. Avg. of Level Changes (Mil. of $) (7)
1	2,009.30	—	—	—	—	—
2	2,219.60	210.30	—	—	—	—
3	2,598.90	379.30	—	—	—	—
4	2,817.80	218.90	808.5	269.50	—	—
5	2,981.40	163.60	761.8	253.93	—	—
6	3,277.70	296.30	678.8	226.27	749.70	249.90
7	3,516.40	238.70	698.6	232.87	713.07	237.69
8	3,764.30	247.90	782.9	260.97	720.10	240.03
9	4,267.90	503.60	990.2	330.07	823.90	274.63
10	5,107.60	839.70	1591.2	530.40	1121.43	373.81

$\hat{Y}_{11}$ = $5,107.6 million + $373.8 million

= $5,481.41 million

moving average percentage change instead of by the double moving average level change. The computations are shown in Table 16.4. Steps used for preparing a forecast with this model are as follows:

Steps 1-5: The first five steps are the same as followed in the single moving average percentage change model. Therefore, Columns 1-6 in Table 16.4 are the same as in Table 16.2.

Step 6: Compute the three-period double moving total of percentage changes. Do this by adding the first three single moving average percentage changes given in Column 6 (i.e., of periods 4, 5, and 6). Their total comes to 30.49% (11.99% + 10.44% + 8.06%). Enter the total next to period 6 in Column 7. Then, drop one change from the top (i.e., of period 4) and add one change from the bottom (i.e., of period 7). Their total comes to 26.18% (10.44% + 8.06% + 7.68%). Enter that total next to period 7 in Column 7. Similarly, compute the three-period double moving percentage change total of other periods.

Table 16.4 | Double Moving Average Percentage Change

Period (1)	Sales of Jewel Company (Mil. of $) (2)	Level Change (Mil. of $) (3)	% Change (Mil. of $) (4)	3-Period Mov. Total of % Changes (Mil. of $) (5)	3-Period Mov. Avg. of % Changes (Mil. of $) (6)	3-Period Double Mov. Total of % Changes (Mil. of $) (7)	3-Period Double Mov. Avg. of % Changes (Mil. of $) (8)
1	2,009.30	—	—	—	—	—	—
2	2,219.60	210.30	10.47	—	—	—	—
3	2,598.90	379.30	17.09	—	—	—	—
4	2,817.80	218.90	8.42	35.98	11.99	—	—
5	2,981.40	163.60	5.81	31.32	10.44	—	—
6	3,277.70	296.30	9.94	24.17	8.06	30.49	10.16
7	3,516.40	238.70	7.28	23.03	7.68	26.18	8.72
8	3,764.30	247.90	7.05	24.27	8.09	23.82	7.94
9	4,267.90	503.60	13.38	27.71	9.24	25.00	8.33
10	5,107.60	839.70	19.67	40.10	13.37	30.69	10.23

$\hat{Y}_{11}$ = \$5,107.60 million + (\$5,107.60 million × 0.1023)

= \$5,630.19 million

Step 7: Compute the three-period double moving average percentage change. Do this by dividing the moving total given in Column 7 by three. Since each total in this column is a sum total of three changes, the average will be computed by dividing each by three. The double moving average percentage change of period 6 is 10.16% (30.49% ÷ 3). The value is entered next to the period 6 in Column 8. The double moving percentage change of period 7 is 8.72% (26.18% ÷ 3). This way we can compute double moving average percentage change of other periods.

Step 8: Prepare a forecast. The forecast of period 11 will be the actual of period 10, plus 10.23% of it. The forecast comes to $5,630.19 million [($5,107.60 million) + ($5,107.60 million × 0.1023)].

How did this model perform? This can be determined by comparing the forecast with the actual of this period. The error comes to $19.81 million ($5,650.00 million – $5630.19 million), or 0.35%.

DATA REQUIREMENTS

The data requirements of moving average models depend on the: (1) Periods of moving average, and (2) type of moving average—single or double. The larger the periods of moving average, the greater will be the data requirement. In a single moving average level change model, for two-period moving average, at least three periods of data will be needed to prepare a forecast; and for a three-period moving average, at least four periods of data will be needed. The use of single or double moving average also makes a difference. The double moving average needs more data than the single moving average. In the single moving average level change model, for a three-period moving average, at least four periods of data will be needed to prepare a forecast, whereas, for the double moving average level change model, for the same moving average, at least six periods of data will be needed.

QUESTIONS FOR REVIEW

1. Describe in what way the moving average level change model differs from the average level change model.
2. Explain how much weight is given to each change both in the average level change model and the moving average percentage change model.
3. Describe how the single moving average change model differs from the double moving average change model.

4. What is the difference between the single moving average level change model and single moving average percentage change model? Explain.
5. Are moving averages used in forecasting the same way as they are used in statistics? Explain.
6. What determines the number of periods to be used for moving average in moving average change models? Explain.

Sales Data of Tim John Shoe Company

Period	Sales (Mil. of $)
1	3,501
2	3,594
3	4,701
4	4,205
5	4,001
6	4,481
7	5,422
8	5,272
9	5,515
10	6,474

7. The table above gives the sales data of Tim John Shoe Company. Using two-period single moving average level change model, compute the forecast of period 11.
Answer: $7,075.00 million.

8. Using the sales data of the Tim John Shoe Company given in Question 7 and a two-period single moving average percentage change model, compute the forecast of period 11.
Answer: $7,186.08 million.
9. Using the sales data of the Tim John Shoe Company given in Question 7 and a two-period double moving average level change model, compute the forecast of period 11.
Answer: $6,797.75 million.
10. Using the sales data of the Tim John Shoe Company given in Question 7 and a two-period double moving average percentage change model, compute the forecast of period 11.
Answer: $6,859.87 million.

CHAPTER 17

EXPONENTIAL SMOOTHING

Exponential smoothing models are also members of the Time Series family. They differ from average change and moving average change models in one important way. In the average change and moving average change models, each observation gets the same weight, which is one. But in exponential smoothing, more weight is given to the most recent observations and less to others, and the weight exponentially decreases as we go back in time. Further, the exponential smoothing technique did not originate as a forecasting model; rather, it was for smoothing out the data. It was converted into a forecasting model.

There are different types of exponential smoothing models: Single, double, and triple. Within single exponential smoothing, we have a standard single exponential smoothing model and single exponential smoothing model with an adapted approach. In the latter model, the alpha (α) value (smoothing constant) changes with a change in the pattern of data. Double exponential smoothing model (Holt's exponential smoothing and Brown's exponential smoothing with one parameter) is the extension of the single exponential smoothing model that accounts for trend in the data. Triple exponential smoothing model (Holt-Winters' exponential smoothing) further expands on smoothing models by accounting for both trend and seasonality in the data. Because of the complexity in their computation, we will describe only two models: (1) Single exponential smoothing and (2) double exponential smoothing. However, forecasting packages available in the market (for instance those of SAS, John Galt Solutions, and Smart Software) cover all these models.

Single Exponential Smoothing: There are two basic properties of the single exponential smoothing model. One, it gives more weight to the most recent data and less to others. In fact, this is true with all exponential smoothing models. Two, it automatically adjusts for the error experienced in the current period. We can demonstrate both these properties with the help of a formula of single exponential smoothing, which is:

$$F_{t+1} = \alpha X_t + (1-\alpha) F_t \qquad \text{...(17.1)}$$

where

F_{t+1} = Forecast of the next period

α = Smoothing constant

X_t = Actual value of the current period

F_t = Forecast (smoothed) value of the current period

Property 1: It gives more weight to the most recent value and less to others. The amount of weight decreases exponentially as we go back. How much weight is given to each value depends on the size of the α value used in the formula, which varies between 0 and 1. The larger the α value, the greater will be the weight. The sum total of all the weights is approximately one.

Let us say that there are four observations. If $\alpha = .2$, then the weights assigned to past observations will be as follows:

$$X_t = .2 = (.2)(1-.2)^0$$
$$X_{t-1} = .16 = (.2)(1-.2)^1$$
$$X_{t-2} = .128 = (.2)(1-.2)^2$$
$$X_{t-3} = .1024 = (.2)(1-.2)^3$$

Property 2: It automatically adjusts for the error experienced in the current period. The size of adjustment depends on the size of the α value. The larger the α value, the greater will be the adjustment for the error. As mentioned earlier, the α value varies between 0 and 1. There will be no adjustment for the error if $\alpha = 0$, and maximum adjustment, if $\alpha = 1$. We can demonstrate this with the help of the formula of a single exponential smoothing model, which is:

$$F_{t+1} = \alpha X_t + (1-\alpha) F_t \qquad \text{...(17.2)}$$

This can be re-written as:

$$= \alpha X_t + F_t - \alpha F_t$$

or

$$= F_t + \alpha X_t - \alpha F_t$$

or

$$= F_t + \alpha(X_t - F_t) \qquad ...(17.3)$$

The difference between $X_t - F_t$ (actual – forecast) is the error. If we label $X_t - F_t$ as e_t (forecast error of the current period), then it becomes:

$$X_t - F_t = e_t \qquad ...(17.4)$$

Substituting Equation 17.4 into Equation 17.3, we get:

$$F_{t+1} = F_t + \alpha(e_t) \qquad ...(17.5)$$

This equation states that the forecast of the next period (F_{t+1}) is equal to the forecast of the current period (F_t) plus alpha (α) times forecast error (e_t) experienced in the current period. In other words, the forecast of the next period is equal to the forecast of the current period plus the adjustment factor for the error experienced in the current period. The adjustment factor for the error depends on the size of the α value. The larger the α value, the greater will be the adjustment for the error. Also, the adjustment is made opposite to the direction of the error made in the current period. In other words, if we over-forecasted in the current period, it will dampen somewhat the forecast of the next period. If, on the other hand, we under-forecasted in the current period, it will inflate somewhat the forecast of the next period.

Here is the step-by-step procedure for preparing a forecast with the single exponential smoothing model, using sales data of Jewel Company (See Table 17.1):

Step 1: Determine the optimal α value. As mentioned earlier, the α value varies between 0 and 1. To arrive at the optimal value, one has to prepare forecasts by using all the values between 0 and 1, i.e., .1, .2, .3, and so on to find out which value, on average, gives the least amount of error. The value that gives the lowest error is the optimal value. It is difficult to go through this procedure manually. But every software package of single exponential smoothing goes through this iteration to arrive at this value. In the case of

Jewel Company, let us say the optimal value comes to .99.

Step 2: Initialize the forecast. As can be seen from the formula given in Equation 17.1, if one wishes to make a forecast of period 1, one needs a forecast of the previous period, which we don't have. Also, to make a forecast of period 11, which is the objective of this demonstration, we have to make forecasts of all the periods starting with period 1. So, we initialize the forecast by assuming that the forecast of period 1 is the same as the actual, which is $2,009.30. (See Table 17.1, Column 3)

Step 3: Prepare forecasts. First, we have to prepare a forecast of period 2. (This is the first period for which forecast can be prepared.) Keep in mind we are in period 1 and making a forecast of period 2. This can be done by plugging the values in Equation 17.1. Here:

$$\alpha = .99$$
$$X_t = 2{,}009.30$$
$$F_t = 2{,}009.30$$

The forecast of period 2 will be:

$$F_2 = (.99)\,(2{,}009.30) + (1 - .99)\,(2{,}009.30)$$
$$= 2{,}009.30$$

If we are in period 2 and wish to make a forecast of period 3, then:

$$X_t = 2{,}219.60$$
$$F_t = 2{,}009.30$$

The forecast of period 3 will be:

$$F_3 = (.99)\,(2{,}219.60) + (1 - .99)\,(2{,}009.30)$$
$$= 2{,}217.49$$

Similarly, if we are in period 10 and wish to make a forecast of period 11, then:

$$X_t = 5{,}107.60$$
$$F_t = 4{,}262.84$$

The forecast of period 11 will be:

$$F_{11} - [(.99)(5{,}107.60)] + [(1 - .99)(4{,}262.84)]$$
$$= \$5{,}099.15 \text{ million}$$

Since the actual of period 11 was $5,650.00 million, the error came to $550.85 million, or 9.75%. This does not seem to be the right model. This may be because the data have a trend, which is not captured by this model.

Table 17.1 | Single Exponential Smoothing

Period (1)	Sales of Jewel Co. (Mil. of $) (X) (2)	Forecast (Mil. of $) (F) (3)
1	2,009.30	2,009.30
2	2,219.60	2,009.30
3	2,598.90	2,217.49
4	2,817.80	2,595.09
5	2,981.40	2,815.57
6	3,277.70	2,979.74
7	3,516.40	3,274.72
8	3,764.30	3,513.98
9	4,267.90	3,761.80
10	5,107.60	4,262.84
11		**5,099.15**

Double Exponential Smoothing with Brown's One Parameter: The single exponential smoothing model does not account for trend in the data. If there is trend in the data, the forecasted value computed by this model will lag behind the Time Series changes. It will under-estimate the positive trend and over-estimate the negative trend. The double exponential smoothing overcomes this problem by adjusting the value for trend.

Here is the step-by-step procedure for preparing a forecast with double exponential smoothing. Again, we will use the sales data of Jewel Company. (See Table 17.2)

Step 1: Determine the optimal α value. Here again one has to prepare forecasts of all the periods using all α values between 0 and 1, and then determine which one, on average, yields the lowest error. Let us say the optimal α value came to .70.

Step 2: The formula for computing forecast with double exponential smoothing is:

$$Y_{t+p} = a_t + b_t\,(P) \qquad \text{...(17.6)}$$

where

Y_{t+p} = Forecast value of the "P" period

a_t = "a" value of the current period

b_t = "b" value of the current period

P = Number of periods ahead to be forecasted. (If you wish to forecast one period ahead, then P = 1, if you wish to forecast two periods ahead, P = 2, and so on.)

To compute the value of "a" and "b," we need to compute single smoothed value (S) and double smoothed value (D). Therefore, the next step is to compute S value for each period, the formula which is:

$$S_t = \alpha X_t + (1 - \alpha)\, S_{t-1} \qquad \text{...(17.7)}$$

Table 17.2 | Double Exponential Smoothing with Brown's One Parameter

Period (1)	Sales of Jewel Company (Mil. of $) (2)	S (3)	D (4)	a (5)	b (6)	Forecasts (Mil. of $) (7)
1	2,009.30	2,009.30	2,009.30	2,009.30	000.00	—
2	2,219.60	2,156.51	2,112.35	2,200.67	103.05	2,009.30
3	2,598.90	2,466.18	2,360.03	2,572.33	247.69	2,303.72
4	2,817.80	2,712.31	2,606.63	2,818.00	246.60	2,820.02
5	2,981.40	2,900.67	2,812.46	2,988.89	205.83	3,064.60
6	3,277.70	3,164.59	3,058.95	3,270.23	246.49	3,194.72
7	3,516.40	3,410.86	3,305.29	3,516.43	246.33	3,516.72
8	3,764.30	3,658.27	3,552.37	3,764.16	247.09	3,762.76
9	4,267.90	4,085.01	3,925.22	4,244.80	372.85	4,011.25
10	5,107.60	4,800.82	4,538.14	5,063.50	612.92	4,617.65
11						**5,676.43**

Notes: S = Single exponential smoothing
D = Double exponential smoothing

where

S_t = Single smoothed value of the current period
α = Smoothing constant
X_t = Actual value of the current period
S_{t-1} = Single smoothed value of one period before the current period

As can be seen from the above formula, to compute S value of period 1, we need S value of one period before (S_{t-1}), which we don't have. So, to initialize it, we assume S value of period 1 is the same as the actual ($2,009.30 million). The other S values we can compute by plugging the appropriate values in Equation 17.7. The S value of period 2, for example, comes to:

$$S_2 = (.70)(2{,}219.60) + (1 - .70)(2{,}009.30)$$
$$= 2{,}156.51$$

The S value of period 3 comes to:

$$S_3 = (.70)(2{,}598.90) + (1 - .70)(2{,}156.51)$$
$$= 2{,}466.18$$

Similarly, we can compute other S values which are given in Column 3 of Table 17.2.

Step 3: Compute the double smoothed value (D) of each period. The formula for computing D is:

$$D_t = \alpha S_t + (1 - \alpha) D_{t-1} \qquad \text{...(17.8)}$$

where

D_t = Double smoothed value of the current period
α = Smoothing constant
D_{t-1} = Double smoothed value of one period before the current period

Here again, to compute the D value, we need the D value of the previous period, which we don't have. Therefore, to initialize it, we assume that the D value (double smoothed value) of the first period is the same as the S value of that period (which is $2,009.30 million). Thereafter, we compute their values by plugging appropriate values in Equation 17.8. The D value of period 2 comes to:

$$D_2 = (.70)(2{,}156.51) + (1 - .70)(2{,}009.30)$$
$$= 2{,}112.35$$

The D value of period of 3 comes to:

$$D_3 = (.70)(2{,}466.18) + (1 - .70)(2{,}112.35)$$
$$= 2{,}360.03$$

Similarly, we can compute D values of other periods, which are given in Table 17.2, Column 4.

Step 4: Compute "a" value for all the periods. The formula for computing "a" value is:

$$a_t = 2(S_t) - (D_t) \qquad \text{...(17.9)}$$

We can compute "a" values of all the periods by plugging appropriate values in Equation 17.9. The "a" value of period 1 comes to:

$$a_1 = 2(2{,}009.30) - (2{,}009.30)$$
$$= 2{,}009.30$$

The "a" value of period 2 comes to:

$$a_2 = 2(2{,}156.51) - (2{,}112.35)$$
$$= 2{,}200.67$$

Similarly, we can compute other "a" values, which are given in Column 5 of Table 17.2.

Step 5: Compute "b" value of all the periods. Its formula is:

$$b_t = \frac{\alpha}{1-\alpha} \times (S_t - D_t) \qquad \text{...(17.10)}$$

Here again, we can compute "b" values of all the periods by plugging the appropriate values in Equation 17.10. The "b" value of period 1 comes to:

$$b_1 = \frac{.70}{1 - .70} \times (2{,}009.30 - 2{,}009.30)$$

$$= 0$$

The "b" value of period 2 comes to:

$$b_2 = \frac{.70}{1 - .70} \times (2{,}156.51 - 2{,}112.35)$$

$$= 103.05$$

Similarly, we can compute "b" values of other periods, which are given in Table 17.2, Column 6.

Step 6: Prepare forecasts. Forecasts can be prepared by plugging the "a" and "b" values in Equation 17.6. Let us say we are in period 1 and wish to make a forecast of period 2. Here P will be 1 because we are making one period ahead forecast. The forecast will come to:

$$F_2 = (2{,}009.30) + (0.00)\,(1)$$
$$= \$2{,}009.30$$

If we are in period 2 and wish to make a forecast of period 3, then:

$$F_3 = (2{,}200.67) + (103.05)\,(1)$$
$$= \$2{,}303.72$$

Similarly, if we are in period 10 and wish to make a forecast of period 11, it will be:

$$F_{11} = (5{,}063.50) + (612.92)\,(1)$$
$$= \$5{,}676.43$$

Since the actual of period 11 was $5,650.00 million, the error comes to –$26.43 million ($5,650 million – $5676.43 million), or –.47%.

OTHER EXPONENTIAL SMOOTHING MODELS

The two models discussed above are not the be all and end all of exponential smoothing models. There are many other variations in exponential smoothing, though the ones discussed above are most often mentioned in the forecasting literature. Others include single exponential smoothing with an adaptive approach, Holt's double exponential smoothing with two parameters, and Holt-Winters' triple exponential smoothing with three-parameters. The single exponential smoothing model with an adaptive approach allows the α value to change in a controlled manner to capture a change in the data pattern. Though both double exponential smoothing models, one of Brown with one parameter and the other of Holt with two parameters, adjust the forecast value for level and trend, the former uses the same smoothing weight for both and the latter uses one for level and another for trend. The triple exponential smooth model (Holt-Winters), unlike double exponential smoothing models, captures not only trend but also seasonality in the data.

STERLING IRON WORKS—A CASE STUDY

As mentioned earlier, a single exponential smoothing model is used where there is no trend and seasonality in the data; double exponential smoothing model is used where there is a trend but no seasonality; and triple exponential smoothing model is used where there is trend and seasonality. To demonstrate this, we use the data of Sterling Iron Works, which have both trend and seasonality. Figure 17.1 gives a plot of its net sales running from Q1, 2007 to Q4, 2010. It shows that although sales have ups and downs, on the whole, the trend is upward. Also, the data have seasonality; sales tend to rise in Q1. For that type of data, the triple exponential smoothing model would be most appropriate for forecasting.

To test it, we keep the last four quarters (Q1, 2010 – Q4, 2010) as holdout periods and prepare their ex post forecasts with all the three models—single, double, and triple exponential smoothing. We use Brown's linear trend model for double exponential smoothing and the Holt-Winters' multiplicative model for triple exponential smoothing. We prepare ex post forecasts for holdout periods using as much data as are available at the time. In other words, we first prepare

Figure 17.1 | Sterling Iron Works

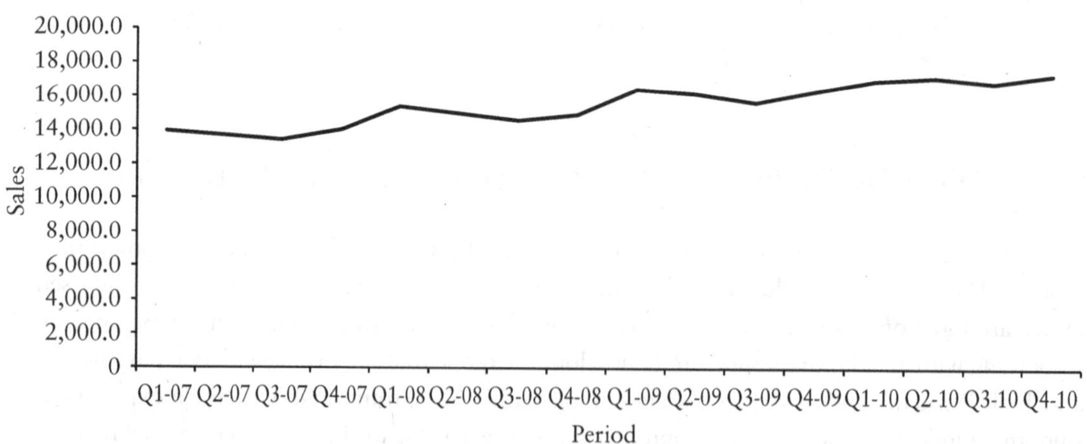

Table 17.3 | Sterling Iron Works

Model	Actual Sales (Mil. of $)	Forecast (Mil. of $)	% Error
Single Exponential Smoothing			
Q1, 2010	16,987.0	16,364.9	3.66
Q2, 2010	17,199.0	16,986.9	1.23
Q3, 2010	16,870.0	17,199.0	1.95
Q4, 2010	17,344.0	16,870.0	2.73
MAPE			**2.39**
Double Exponential Smoothing			
Q1, 2010	16,987.0	16,536.8	2.65
Q2, 2010	17,199.0	17,087.9	0.65
Q3, 2010	16,870.0	17,452.3	3.45
Q4, 2010	17,344.0	17,324.2	0.11
MAPE			**1.72**
Triple Exponential Smoothing			
Q1, 2010	16,987.0	17,792.5	4.74
Q2, 2010	17,199.0	17,152.8	0.27
Q3, 2010	16,870.0	16,700.6	1.00
Q4, 2010	17,344.0	17,262.0	0.47
MAPE			**1.62**

the forecast of Q1, 2010 using the data of Q1, 2007 – Q4, 2009, with all these three models. Then we prepare a forecast of Q2, 2010 using the data of Q1, 2007 – Q1, 2010, again with all the three models. Similarly, we prepare forecasts of Q3 and Q4 of 2010. The results are given in Table 17.3. It shows that the average forecast error (Mean Absolute Percentage Error—MAPE) of all the four quarters of 2010 is highest with the single exponential smoothing model and lowest with the triple exponential smoothing model.

SUGGESTED READING

1. Chase Jr., Charles W. ***Demand-Driven Forecasting: A Structured Approach to Forecasting.*** Hoboken, New Jersey: John Wiley and Sons. 2009.
2. Kress, George J. and John Snyder. ***Forecasting Market Analysis Techniques: A Practical Approach.*** Westport, Connecticut: Quorum Books. 1994.

3. Makridakis, Spyros, Steven C. Wheelwright, and Rob J. Hyndman. ***Forecasting: Methods and Applications.*** New York: John Wiley and Sons. 1998.
4. Wilson, J. Holton, Barry Keating, and John Galt Solutions, Inc. ***Business Forecasting.*** New York: McGraw Hill. 2007.

QUESTIONS FOR REVIEW

1. Explain in what way moving average models differ from exponential smoothing models.
2. What are the main characteristics of single exponential smoothing models? Explain.
3. What role does the alpha (α) value play in a single exponential smoothing model? Explain.
4. Describe the ways the single exponential smoothing model differs from the double exponential smoothing model.
5. Describe in what way triple exponential smoothing model differs from single and double exponential smoothing models.
6. Describe which model will be most appropriate among three exponential smoothing models—single, double, and triple—where:
   a. Data has neither trend nor seasonality.
   b. Data has trend but no seasonality.
   c. Data has trend and seasonality.
7. What do we mean by optimum alpha value, and how it is derived?
8. What values of alpha can take in exponential smoothing?

Earnings Per Share of Surrey Plastic Company			
Period	**Earnings Per Share (Mil. of \$)**	**Period**	**Earnings Per Share (Mil. of \$)**
1	1.59	6	3.53
2	1.86	7	4.10
3	2.19	8	4.39
4	2.40	9	3.02
5	2.71	10	2.60

9. The table above gives 10 periods of earnings per share (EPS) data of Surrey Plastic Company. Using the single exponential smoothing model, forecast the EPS of period 11. Here alpha value is assumed to be 0.9.
   Answer: \$2.66.

10. Using the data of earnings per share of Surrey Plastic Company, as given in question 9, forecast the earnings per share of period 11 using the Brown's double exponential smoothing model with one parameter. Alpha value is here assumed to be 0.74. **Answer:** \$2.04.

CHAPTER 18

TREND LINE

The trend line forecasting model is used either directly as a tool to prepare a forecast or as a part of another model. When used directly it is often used for long-term forecasting. Sales may fluctuate from one period to the next but overall it may form a trend going either upward or downward. The objective here is to fit a best line to the data, called trend line or fitted line, as shown in Figure 18.1. The best-fitted line is the one that yields the least sum total of squared deviations from the line. The points on the

Figure 18.1 | Actual vs. Trend Line/Fitted Line

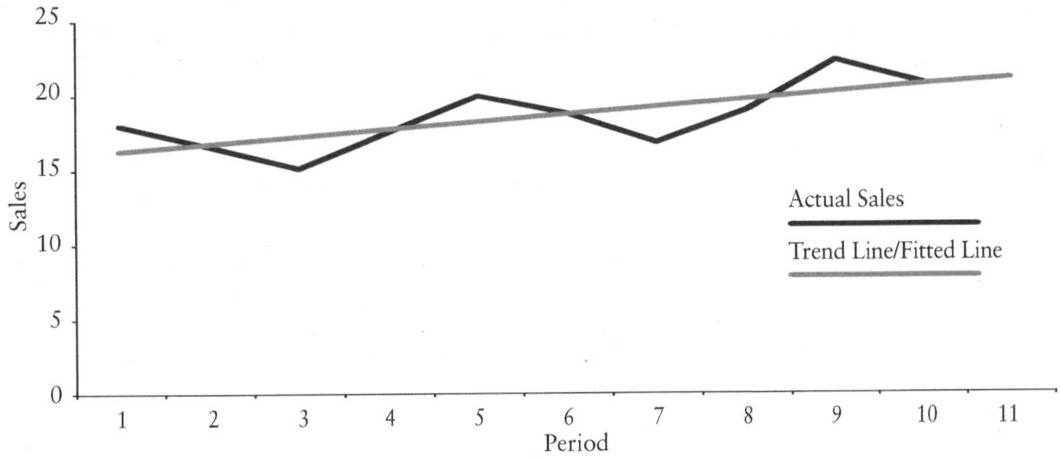

fitted line are called fitted values or forecasts. The model that is often used is the least squares. How to manually prepare a forecast with the least squares trend line model depends on whether there is an odd or even number of observations. We will show how to prepare a forecast with both.

PREPARING A FORECAST WHERE THE NUMBER OF OBSERVATIONS IS ODD

Here is the step-by-step procedure for preparing a forecast with a trend line model where the number of observations is odd. We will use the data of Home Furniture, Inc., given in Table 18.1. We have sales data of nine periods, and will make a forecast of the tenth period. The trend line equation is written as follows:

$$T = a + bX \qquad \dots(18.1)$$

where

T = Trend value (forecast)
a = Intercept
b = Slope of the line
X = Coded value which we assign

If we know the values of a, b, and X, we can get the trend value, which in this case would be the forecast. The steps are as follows:

Step 1: Assign code values, which are X values (See Table 18.1, Column 3). The assignment of code values depends on whether the number of observations is odd or even. In this example, the number of observations is nine, which is odd. In that case, take the mid period, which is period 5, and assign it the value of zero. Then decrement by one going backward and increment by one going forward. In other words, the code value of period 4 will be –1, of period 3, –2, and so on. Similarly, code value of period 6 will be +1, of period 7, +2, and so on (See Table 18.1, Column 3). There are a number of ways of assigning code values, but this is the one most often used.

Step 2: Compute "a" and "b" by plugging the values in their respective formulas:

$$a = \frac{\Sigma Y}{N} = \frac{164.09}{9} = 18.23$$

$$b = \frac{\Sigma XY}{\Sigma X^2} = \frac{28.97}{60} = 0.48$$

here

Y = Sales
N = Number of observations
Σ = Symbol of "sum of"

Step 3: Forecast the value of period 10. Once values of "a" and "b" are computed, the trend line equation, as shown in Equation 18.1, becomes:

$$T = 18.23 + 0.48X$$

The "X" value of period 10 will be 5, as it increases from one period to the next by one. By plugging its value in the above equation, we get the forecast value of period 10, which comes to:

$$T_{10} = 18.23 + (0.48)(5) = \$20.65 \text{ million}$$

Table 18.1 | Computation of Trend-Based Forecast (where the number of observations is odd) Home Furniture, Inc.

Period (1)	Sales (Mil. of $) Y (2)	X (3)	XY (4)	X^2 (5)
1	17.99	–4	–71.96	16
2	16.60	–3	–49.80	9
3	15.13	–2	–30.26	4
4	17.55	–1	–17.55	1
5	19.96	0	0	0
6	18.77	+1	18.77	1
7	16.81	+2	33.62	4
8	18.97	+3	56.91	9
9	22.31	+4	89.24	16
Total	**164.09 ΣY**		28.97 ΣXY	60 ΣX^2

$$a = \frac{\Sigma Y}{N} = \frac{164.09}{9} = 18.23$$

$$b = \frac{\Sigma XY}{\Sigma X^2} = \frac{28.97}{60} = 0.48$$

$$T = 18.23 + 0.48X$$

$$T_{10} = 18.23 + 0.48 \times 5 = \$20.65 \text{ million}$$

The actual of period 10 was \$20.77 million. Thus the error comes to \$0.12 million (\$20.77 million – \$20.65 million) or 0.60%. (Note that the data used here is real, but to hide the identity, the name of the company was changed.)

PREPARING A FORECAST WHERE THE NUMBER OF OBSERVATIONS IS EVEN

The procedure of forecasting where the number of observations is even is the same as described for when the number of observations is odd except the way coded values (X) are assigned. Here is the step-by-step procedure:

Step 1: Assign code values, which are X values (Table 18.2, Column 3). Here we have an even number of observations—10 in total. Take two central periods, which in this case are periods 5 and 6. Assign a value of –1 to period 5 and +1 to period 6. Then decrement by two going backward, that is, assign a value of –3 to period 4, –5 to period 3, and so on. Also, increment by two going forward, that is, assign a value of +3 to period 7, +5 to period 8, and so on.

Table 18.2 | Computation of Trend-Based Forecast (where the number of observations is even) Home Furniture, Inc.

Period (1)	Sales (Mil. of \$) Y (2)	X (3)	XY (4)	X^2 (5)
1	17.99	–9	–161.91	81
2	16.60	–7	–116.20	49
3	15.13	–5	–75.65	25
4	17.55	–3	–52.65	9
5	19.96	–1	–19.96	1
6	18.77	+1	18.77	1
7	16.81	+3	50.43	9
8	18.97	+5	94.85	25
9	22.31	+7	156.17	49
10	20.77	+9	186.93	81
Total	184.86 ΣY		80.78 ΣXY	330 ΣX^2

$$a = \frac{\Sigma Y}{N} = \frac{184.86}{10} = 18.49$$

$$b = \frac{\Sigma XY}{\Sigma X^2} = \frac{80.78}{330} = 0.24$$

$$T_{11} = 18.49 + (0.24) \times (11) = \$21.18 \text{ million}$$

Step 2: Compute "a" and "b" by plugging values into their respective formulas:

$$a = \frac{\Sigma Y}{N} = \frac{184.86}{10} = 18.49$$

$$b = \frac{\Sigma XY}{\Sigma X^2} = \frac{80.78}{330} = 0.24$$

Step 3: Forecast the value of period 11 by plugging the values of "a," "b," and "X" in Equation 18.1. The X value of period 11 will be 11 because it is an increment of 2. The forecast comes to:

$$T_{11} = 18.49 + (0.24) \times (11) = \$21.18 \text{ million}$$

Since the actual of period 11 is \$19.49 million, the error comes to –\$1.69 million (\$19.49 million – 21.18 million), or –8.66%.

QUESTIONS FOR REVIEW

1. What do we mean by fitted values? Explain.
2. Which method is normally used to fit a line to a dataset so that the sum total of squared deviations from the fitted line is the least?
3. What do "a" and "b" values represent in a trend line equation? Explain.

Sales Data of Simpson Brewing Company

Period	Earnings (Mil. of \$)
1	9.24
2	11.51
3	11.04
4	11.27
5	10.64
6	16.11
7	15.97
8	15.01
9	17.80
10	13.85

4. The table above gives the sales of Simpson Brewing Company. Using the trend line forecasting model, forecast the sales of period 11.

   Answer: \$17.41 million

Sales Data of Woodruff Stores	
Period	Sales (Mil. of $)
1	3,929
2	4,887
3	3,668
4	3,721
5	3,980
6	4,898
7	3,626
8	3,716
9	3,860

5. The table above gives the sales of Woodruff Stores. Using the trend line forecasting model, forecast the sales of period 10.
   Answer: $3,807.00 million

CHAPTER 19

CLASSICAL DECOMPOSITION

Classical decomposition is another model of Times Series. It assumes that each value has four components: (1) Seasonal, (2) trend, (3) cyclical, and (4) random/irregular. To make a forecast for the next period, one has to first estimate the values of these components. The decomposition model can be additive or multiplicative. In additive, we add these components to get a forecasted value, whereas in multiplicative, we multiply them. The approach that is most often used is multiplicative, the one we will discuss in this chapter. This model is often called classical decomposition model.

Before proceeding further, one has to understand what these components are and what they imply. The seasonal component measures seasonal variations, which occur regularly and periodically, and the length of a cycle is always less than one year. The sales of a department store reach their peak in the month of December because of Christmas. This occurs regularly (because it happens every year) and periodically (because it happens at the same time).

The seasonal variations are caused by customs and traditions (as in the case of Christmas), as well as by weather. The sales of certain sporting goods such as tennis rackets go up during summer and go down during winter. This happens regularly and periodically.

The trend component refers to a long-term trend in the data, the same as we discussed in the previous chapter. The sales move up and down from one period to the next but the overall linear (long-term) trend will mostly likely be either upward or downward.

The cyclical component (often called business cycle) also represents variations in the sales data but over a longer period of time—more than one year. The length of a cycle can be measured either from trough to trough or from peak to peak; that is, how much time it takes for sales to go from one trough to the next, or from one peak to the next. In the case of a seasonal cycle, the cycle is completed within a year. For a department store, sales reach their peak in the month of December. Its seasonal cycle is completed within a year; that is, from December of one year to November of the next year. This means if we are preparing forecasts for a period of less than one year, say, for weeks, months, and quarters, we have to be concerned about seasonality.

The cyclical variations occur regularly but not periodically. The length of a cycle is always more than one year. The sales, for example, go up for a certain period of time, hit the peak, and then start falling. The cyclical variations do not occur periodically because it is not certain how much time it will take for sales to go from a trough to a peak, and then from a peak to a trough. One time sales may take three years to complete the cycle, and in another time, five years. As such, the length of a cyclical cycle varies from one cycle to the next.

The random/irregular component measures variations that occur randomly/irregularly. The sales of a company in one period may go down because of a labor strike, riot, snowstorm, or hurricane. In another period, sales may go up because of a visit by the Pope, Olympic games, or World's Fairs. Such events have a strong impact on certain businesses. For example, between 1:00 and 1:15 P.M. on October 3, 1995, the TV ratings of all the major channels shot up because that was the time of the announcement of the verdict of a nationally publicized case, People vs. O.J. Simpson. At that time 49.4% of the nation's 95.9 million households tuned in to their TV set. This compares with the 30% normal viewing at that time of a day. Since such events occur randomly/irregularly, they are by definition unpredictable. We make adjustments in the historical data for such variations but we do not include them in the computation of forecasts. In other words, forecasts are prepared with an assumption that normal conditions will prevail, that is, no random event will occur during the forecast period. Next, we will show how to compute each of these components.

SEASONAL

The seasonal component refers to a seasonal index. The seasonal indices are based on the average of 100. If the seasonal index of January is 120, it means that January performs 20% better than the average of 12 months. If it is 85, it means it performs 15% poorer than the average. The average, which is 100, is the average of all the indices of 12 months. Any month having an index of more than 100 implies that it performs better than the average. Any month having an index of less than 100 implies that it performs poorer than the average.

Since there are 12 months in a year and the average of their indices is 100, the sum total of all the indices has to be 1,200. Similarly, the sum total of quarterly indices has to be 400, because there are four quarters in a year.

There are two types of seasonal indices—specific and typical. The specific seasonal index is based on the data of just one year, whereas the typical seasonal index is based on the data of two or more years. The typical seasonal index is an average of specific seasonal indices.

Specific Seasonal Index: We will demonstrate the computation of the specific seasonal index using the sales data of a specific year of Fantastic Rubber Company as given in Table 19.1. There are several ways of doing it. The one we will show is the simplest one. Let us start with Year 1. Here is the step-by-step procedure:

Step 1: Add up the sales of all the months, which comes to 196 (see Table 19.1, Column 2).

Step 2: Determine the factor for the year 1, which is computed as follows:

$$\text{Factor} = \frac{1{,}200}{\text{Total Sales}}$$

or

$$= \frac{1{,}200}{196} = 6.1224$$

Since we are computing monthly seasonal indices, the numerator will be 1,200 (100 × 12). This is because there are 12 months in a year, and the average value of a seasonal index is 100. Similarly, if we wish to compute quarterly seasonal indices, the numerator will be 400 (100 × 4).

Step 3: Multiply the sales of each month by the factor, which is 6.1224. This will give us the seasonal index of each month. The sales index of January comes to 110.2 (18 × 6.1124), the sales index of February comes to 98.0 (16 × 6.1224), and so on. This way we can compute all the specific seasonal indices of this and other years, which are given in Table 19.1.

Table 19.1 | Sales Data of Fantastic Rubber Company

Mos	Year 1						Year 2						
(1)	Sales (Mil. of $) (2)		Seasonal Factor (3)		Specific Seasonal Index (4)	Sales (Mil. of $) (5)		Seasonal Factor (6)		Specific Seasonal Index (7)	Sales (Mil. of $) (8)
Jan	18	×	6.1224	=	110.2	25	×	4.4776	=	111.9	32
Feb	16	×	6.1224	=	98.0	23	×	4.4776	=	103.0	29
Mar	15	×	6.1224	=	91.8	22	×	4.4776	=	98.5	27
Apr	15	×	6.1224	=	91.8	23	×	4.4776	=	103.0	27
May	16	×	6.1224	=	98.0	18	×	4.4776	=	80.6	23
Jun	13	×	6.1224	=	79.6	16	×	4.4776	=	71.6	20
Jul	12	×	6.1224	=	73.5	15	×	4.4776	=	67.2	20
Aug	15	×	6.1224	=	91.8	21	×	4.4776	=	94.0	23
Sept	17	×	6.1224	=	104.1	23	×	4.4776	=	103.0	25
Oct	19	×	6.1224	=	116.3	26	×	4.4776	=	116.4	26
Nov	22	×	6.1224	=	134.7	30	×	4.4776	=	134.3	35
Dec	18	×	6.1224	=	110.2	26	×	4.4776	=	116.4	31
SUM	196				1200.0	268				1200.0	318
			Factor = 1,200 ÷ 196 = 6.1224					Factor = 1,200 ÷ 268 = 4.4776			Fa

Table 19.2 | Typical Seasonal Indices

(1)	Line (2)	Rank (3)	Jan (4)	Feb (5)	Mar (6)	Apr (7)	May (8)
Lowest	1	1	110.2	97.0	90.9	91.8	80.6
	2	2	111.4	98.0	91.8	93.9	84.9
	3	3	111.9	103.0	95.2	95.2	86.8
	4	4	115.2	104.4	98.5	101.9	90.5
Highest	5	5	120.8	109.4	101.9	103.0	98.0
Total of 3 Central Value	6		338.5	305.4	285.5	291.0	262.2
Modified Average	7		112.8	101.8	95.2	97.0	87.4
Typical Seasonal Index	8		112.5	101.5	94.8	96.7	87.1

Factor $= \dfrac{1,200}{1,204} = 0.9967$

ar 3			Year 4					Year 5				
asonal 'actor (9)		Specific Seasonal Index (10)	Sales (Mil. of $) (11)		Seasonal Factor (12)		Specific Seasonal Index (13)	Sales (Mil. of $) (14)		Seasonal Factor (15)		Specific Seasonal Index (16)
.7736	=	120.8	38	×	3.0303	=	115.2	48	×	2.3211	=	111.4
7736	=	109.4	32	×	3.0303	=	97.0	45	×	2.3211	=	104.4
.7736	=	101.9	30	×	3.0303	=	90.9	41	×	2.3211	=	95.2
7736	=	101.9	31	×	3.0303	=	93.9	41	×	2.3211	=	95.2
.7736	=	86.8	28	×	3.0303	=	84.9	39	×	2.3211	=	90.5
.7736	=	75.5	27	×	3.0303	=	81.8	35	×	2.3211	=	81.2
.7736	=	75.5	28	×	3.0303	=	84.8	38	×	2.3211	=	88.2
.7736	=	86.8	31	×	3.0303	=	93.9	41	×	2.3211	=	95.2
7736	=	94.3	33	×	3.0303	=	100.0	43	×	2.3211	=	99.8
.7736	=	98.1	37	×	3.0303	=	112.1	48	×	2.3211	=	111.4
7736	=	132.1	42	×	3.0303	=	127.3	52	×	2.3211	=	120.7
7736	=	117.0	39	×	3.0303	=	118.2	46	×	2.3211	=	106.8
		1,200.0	396				1,200.0	517				1,200.0
1,200 ÷ 318					Factor = 1,200 ÷ 396					Factor = 1,200 ÷ 517		
3.7736					= 3.0303					= 2.3211		

Jun (9)	Jul (10)	Aug (11)	Sept (12)	Oct (13)	Nov (14)	Dec (15)	Sum (16)
71.7	67.2	86.8	94.3	98.1	120.7	106.8	
75.5	73.5	91.8	99.8	111.4	127.3	110.2	
79.6	75.5	93.9	100.0	112.1	132.0	116.4	
81.2	84.8	94.0	103.0	116.3	134.3	117.0	
81.8	88.2	95.2	104.1	116.4	134.7	118.2	
236.3	233.8	279.7	302.8	339.8	393.6	343.6	
78.8	77.9	93.2	100.9	113.3	131.2	114.5	= 1,204
78.5	77.7	92.9	100.6	112.9	130.8	114.1	= 1,200

Typical Seasonal Index: The typical seasonal index is the average of specific seasonal indices. There are several ways of computing it. Here is the simplest way:

Step 1: Compute specific seasonal indices of sales of all the five years, the same way as described above. The specific seasonal indices are given in Columns 4, 7, 10, 13, and 16 of Table 19.1.

Step 2: Rank the index values of each month given in Columns 4, 7, 10, 13, and 16 of Table 19.1, from the lowest to the highest so that there are five values appearing under each month. The ranked index values are given in Table 19.2, Columns 4–15.

Step 3: Sum up the three central values of each month. In other words, eliminate one value from the top and one value from the bottom. The sum of three central values of January is 338.5; of February, 305.4; and so on. (See Table 19.2, Line 6) The objective of this step is to remove extreme values (the lowest and the highest) that may represent periods of abnormal sales—periods of extremely high or low sales. The three central values are most likely the representative of the "norm."

Note: There is no hard and fast rule about eliminating the highest and lowest values. It would not have been necessary to eliminate any value if the year-to-year variations in each month were very small. Since we had just five values of each month, we could not afford to eliminate more than one value from the top and one value from the bottom. If we had just three values, we could not afford to eliminate even a single value. On the other hand, if we had more values, say, seven or more, we could afford to eliminate more than one value from the top and the bottom.

Step 4: Compute the modified average of the three central values by dividing their sum by the number of central values, which in this case is three. The modified average of January comes to 112.8 (338.5 ÷ 3); of February, 101.8 (305.4 ÷ 3); and so on. (See Table 19.2, Line 7)

Step 5: Sum up the modified averages of all the months. This comes to 1,204. (See Table 19.2, Column 16, Line 7) But this total should be 1,200. To bring the total to 1,200, we will re-compute seasonal indices the same way as we did before.

Step 6: Compute the factor. This is done dividing 1,200 by the sum total, 1,204. This comes to:

$$\text{Factor} = \frac{1{,}200}{1{,}204} = 0.99667$$

Step 7: Find the typical seasonal index for each month by multiplying the modified average of each month with the factor (.99667) computed above. The typical seasonal index of each month is given in Table 19.2, Line 8. (The sum of this line now comes to 1,200.)

TREND

The next step is to compute trend values, that is, T. To do this, we have to deseasonalize the sales data. We will compute trend values from the deseasonalized sales data. Since we are using the multiplicative decomposition model, sales (Y) = T × S × C × R, or TSCR. If we divide the actual sales (Y) by S (seasonal index), it will leave with us TCR (TSCR ÷ S)—deseasonalized sales or sales without a seasonal component. Column 4 of Table 19.3 gives typical seasonal indices of all the months, which we computed earlier—Line 8, Table 19.2. The only thing we did here is that we divided each index by 100. In other words, we listed the seasonal index of January as 1.124 (112.4 ÷ 100); of February, 1.015 (101.5 ÷ 100); and so on. Also, note that we have listed the same seasonal index for each month of each year. In other words, the index of January Year 1 is the same as of January Year 2, January Year 3, January Year 4, and January Year 5. The 112.4 index of January means that, on average, January performs 12.4% better than the average. This is true with January of Year 1, January of Year 2, as well as of any other year. This will remain so until we re-compute the index. For this reason, we list the same index of each month for each year of all five years. We deseasonalize the sales data dividing the sales of each month by its seasonal index. For example, the value of the deasonalized sales of January Year 1 is 16.01 (18 ÷ 1.124); of February Year 1, 15.76 (16 ÷ 1.015); and so on. The deseasonalized sales data of all the months of all the five years are given in Column 5. The next step is to compute the trend value (T) from the deseasonalized data. The equation of trend line is:

$$T = a + bX$$

where

T = Trend
a = Constant
b = Slope of the line
X = Coded value that we assign

X (coded) values were assigned the same way as we described in Chapter 18. Here are the steps for computing the trend values:

Step 1: Determine whether there is an odd or even number of observations. In our example, the number of observations is 60, which is even. In that case, we find two central periods in the series, which are months 30 and 31. (See Table 19.3)

Step 2: Assign a negative 1 (–1) to the first central period (month 30 in this case) and positive 1 (+1) to the second central period (month 31).

Step 3: Going backward, decrement by two, and going forward, increment by two. In other words, period 29 will get a value of –3; period 28, a value of –5; period 27, a value of –7; and so on. Similarly, period 32 will get a value of +3; period 33, a value of +5; period 34, a value of +7; and so on.

All the X values (coded values) are given in Column 6 of Table 19.3. The next step is to find the values of "a" and "b" in the trend line equation. Their formulas are:

$$a = \frac{\Sigma Y}{N} \qquad \ldots(19.1)$$

$$b = \frac{\Sigma XY}{\Sigma X^2} \qquad \ldots(19.2)$$

where

Y = Deseasonalized sales (Column 5, Table 19.3)
N = Number of periods
X = Coded values of periods (Column 6, Table 19.3)
Σ = Symbol for "sum of"

By plugging values in Equations 19.1 and 19.2, we get:

$$a = \frac{1{,}697.36}{60} = 28.29$$

$$b = \frac{18{,}595.07}{71{,}980} = 0.26$$

The trend line equation then becomes:

$$Y = 28.29 + 0.26X \qquad \ldots(19.3)$$

By using Equation 19.3, we can compute the trend value of each month of each year.

The only thing we have to do is to plug in the value of X. For example, the X value of January Year 1 is –59 (See Column 6), its trend value comes to 13.05 (28.29 + 0.26 × –59). The X value of February Year 1 is –57, its trend value comes to 13.56 (28.29 + 0.26 × –57). This way we can compute the trend values of all other months. All the trend values are given in Column 9.

Since we have trend values now, we can determine the combined values of cycle and random factors (CR) of each month. Recall that TCR represents deseasonalized sales. Thus, dividing deseasonalized sales in Column 5 by the trend values in Column 9, we will arrive at the combined values of cycle and random components (CR), which appear in Column 10 (TCR ÷ T = CR). For example, the CR value of January Year 1 comes to: 1.23 = 16.01 (Period 1, Column 5) ÷ 13.05 (Period 1, Column 9); and of February Year 1, 1.16 = 15.76 (Period 2, Column 5) ÷ 13.56 (Period 2, Column 9). Next step is to eliminate irregular (random) variations in the data to arrive at "C" values, which we show in the next section. The random variations can be caused by events such as a fire in the warehouse and/or a strike at the plant.

CYCLICAL

The cyclical component (C) is computed by applying the moving average to CR values. In statistics, moving average is used to smooth the data, but here it is used to eliminate irregular variations (R) from the CR. In this example, we use three-period moving average to smooth the data. The process works as follows:

Step 1: Compute the moving total by summing the first three data points of a series for which moving average is required. In this case, we want moving averages of CR given in Column 10, Table 19.3. The sum of the first three values of CR in this example comes to 3.51 (1.23 + 1.16 + 1.12).

Step 2: Enter the first moving total in the column adjacent to the CR value (Column 11 in Table 19.3) but in the period immediately following the last data point included in the sum (which is Period 4). Then compute the second moving total by dropping one value from the top and adding one value from the bottom. This comes to 3.35 (1.16 + 1.12 + 1.06). All the moving totals are given in Column 11.

Step 3: Compute moving averages dividing each moving total by the number of data points included in the moving total, which is 3. The first moving average comes to 1.17 (3.51 ÷ 3). The second moving average comes to 1.12 (3.35 ÷ 3). This way we can compute

Table 19.3 | Computation of Trend and Cyclical Values

Period (1)	Year & Month (2)		Sales (Mil.of $) (3)	Seasonal Values Based on 5yr Avg. (4)	TCR (Col. 3 ÷ Col. 4) (Y) (5)	Code (X) (6)
1	Year 1	Jan	18	1.124	16.01	−59
2		Feb	16	1.015	15.76	−57
3		Mar	15	0.949	15.81	−55
4		Apr	15	0.967	15.51	−53
5		May	16	0.871	18.37	−51
6		June	13	0.785	16.56	−49
7		July	12	0.776	15.46	−47
8		Aug	15	0.929	16.15	−45
9		Sept	17	1.006	16.90	−43
10		Oct	19	1.129	16.83	−41
11		Nov	22	1.308	16.82	−39
12		Dec	18	1.141	15.78	−37
13	Year 2	Jan	25	1.124	22.24	−35
14		Feb	23	1.015	22.66	−33
15		Mar	22	0.949	23.18	−31
16		Apr	23	0.967	23.78	−29
17		May	18	0.871	20.67	−27
18		June	16	0.785	20.38	−25
19		July	15	0.776	19.33	−23
20		Aug	21	0.929	22.60	−21
21		Sept	23	1.006	22.86	−19
22		Oct	26	1.129	23.03	−17
23		Nov	30	1.308	22.94	−15
24		Dec	26	1.141	22.79	−13
25	Year 3	Jan	32	1.124	28.47	−11
26		Feb	29	1.015	28.57	−9
27		Mar	27	0.949	28.45	−7
28		Apr	27	0.967	27.92	−5
29		May	23	0.871	26.41	−3
30		June	20	0.785	25.48	−1
31		July	20	0.776	25.77	1
32		Aug	23	0.929	24.76	3
33		Sept	25	1.006	24.85	5
34		Oct	26	1.129	23.03	7
35		Nov	35	1.308	26.76	9
36		Dec	31	1.141	27.17	11
37	Year 4	Jan	38	1.124	33.81	13
38		Feb	32	1.015	31.53	15
39		Mar	30	0.949	31.61	17
40		Apr	31	0.967	32.06	19
41		May	28	0.871	32.15	21
42		June	27	0.785	34.39	23
43		July	28	0.776	36.08	25
44		Aug	31	0.929	33.37	27
45		Sept	33	1.006	32.80	29
46		Oct	37	1.129	32.77	31
47		Nov	42	1.308	32.11	33
48		Dec	39	1.141	34.18	35
49	Year 5	Jan	48	1.124	42.70	37
50		Feb	45	1.015	44.33	39
51		Mar	41	0.949	43.20	41
52		Apr	41	0.967	42.40	43
53		May	39	0.871	44.78	45
54		June	35	0.785	44.59	47
55		July	38	0.776	48.97	49
56		Aug	41	0.929	44.13	51
57		Sept	43	1.006	42.74	53
58		Oct	48	1.129	42.52	55
59		Nov	52	1.308	39.76	57
60		Dec	46	1.141	40.32	59
					ΣY=1697.36	

XY (7)	X^2 (8)	Trend Value (T) (9)	(CR)(Col. 5 ÷ Col. 9) (10)	3-Month Moving Total (11)	3-Month Moving Average (12)
-944.84	3,481	13.05	1.23	—	—
-898.52	3,249	13.56	1.16	—	—
-869.34	3,025	14.08	1.12	—	—
-822.13	2,809	14.60	1.06	3.51	1.17
-936.85	2,601	15.11	1.22	3.35	1.12
-811.46	2,401	15.63	1.06	3.40	1.13
-726.80	2,209	16.15	0.96	3.34	1.11
-726.59	2,025	16.66	0.97	3.23	1.08
-726.64	1,849	17.18	0.98	2.99	1.00
-689.99	1,681	17.70	0.95	2.91	0.97
-655.96	1,521	18.21	0.92	2.90	0.97
-583.70	1,369	18.73	0.84	2.86	0.95
-778.47	1,225	19.25	1.16	2.72	0.91
-747.78	1,089	19.76	1.15	2.92	0.97
-718.65	961	20.28	1.14	3.14	1.05
-689.76	841	20.80	1.14	3.45	1.15
-557.98	729	21.31	0.97	3.43	1.14
-509.55	625	21.83	0.93	3.26	1.09
-444.59	529	22.35	0.86	3.05	1.02
-474.70	441	22.86	0.99	2.77	0.92
-434.39	361	23.38	0.98	2.79	0.93
-391.50	289	23.90	0.96	2.83	0.94
-344.04	225	24.41	0.94	2.93	0.98
-296.23	169	24.93	0.91	2.88	0.96
-313.17	121	25.45	1.12	2.82	0.94
-257.14	81	25.96	1.10	2.97	0.99
-199.16	49	26.48	1.07	3.13	1.04
-139.61	25	27.00	1.03	3.29	1.10
-79.22	9	27.51	0.96	3.21	1.07
-25.48	1	28.03	0.91	3.07	1.02
25.77	1	28.55	0.90	2.90	0.97
74.27	9	29.06	0.85	2.77	0.92
124.25	25	29.58	0.84	2.66	0.89
161.20	49	30.10	0.77	2.59	0.86
240.83	81	30.61	0.87	2.46	0.82
298.86	121	31.13	0.87	2.48	0.83
439.50	169	31.65	1.07	2.51	0.84
472.91	225	32.16	0.98	2.82	0.94
537.41	289	32.68	0.97	2.92	0.97
609.10	361	33.20	0.97	3.02	1.01
675.09	441	33.71	0.95	2.91	0.97
791.08	529	34.23	1.00	2.89	0.96
902.06	625	34.75	1.04	2.92	0.97
900.97	729	35.26	0.95	3.00	1.00
951.29	841	35.78	0.92	2.99	1.00
1,015.94	961	36.30	0.90	2.90	0.97
1,059.63	1,089	36.81	0.87	2.77	0.92
1,196.32	1,225	37.33	0.92	2.69	0.90
1,580.07	1,369	37.85	1.13	2.69	0.90
1,729.06	1,521	38.36	1.16	2.92	0.97
1,771.34	1,681	38.88	1.11	3.20	1.07
1,823.16	1,849	39.40	1.08	3.40	1.13
2,014.93	2,025	39.91	1.12	3.34	1.11
2,095.54	2,209	40.43	1.10	3.31	1.10
2,399.48	2,401	40.95	1.20	3.30	1.10
2,250.81	2,601	41.46	1.06	3.42	1.14
2,265.41	2,809	41.98	1.02	3.36	1.12
2,338.35	3,025	42.50	1.00	3.28	1.09
2,266.06	3,249	43.01	0.92	3.08	1.03
2,378.62	3,481	43.53	0.93	2.94	0.98
ΣXY = 18,595.07	X^2=71,980			2.85	

moving averages of other months, which are given in Column 12.

Here, one has to decide how many periods one has to use in computing moving averages. In theory, one has to do trial and error to arrive at the optimum number. The best way is to prepare ex post forecasts with different numbers of moving periods, and use the one which on average gives the best forecasts. As mentioned earlier, the moving average smoothes the data. When data are smoothed, it means that irregular (random) variations are removed.

PREPARING A FORECAST

The next step is to prepare a forecast of the next period, which in this case is period 61 or January Year 6. As described before, in the decomposition model:

$$\text{Forecast} = T \times S \times C$$

In the above equation, R is missing. As described earlier, R (irregular or random component) by definition is unpredictable. We prepare a forecast with the assumption that there would be a normal condition. Therefore, we remove irregular variations in the data, but we don't put them back when we prepare a forecast. As such, we need only the values of T, S, and C for the period for which we wish to prepare a forecast. Since we are making a forecast of January Year 6, we need these values for that period. First we compute the T value of January Year 6 by using the Equation 19.3, which is:

$$Y = 28.29 + 0.26\,X$$

For this, we need the value of X for January Year 6 (period 61), which comes to 61 (59 + 2), where 59 is the X value of December Year 5. The trend value then becomes:

$$Y_{\text{Jan Year 6}} = 28.29 + 0.26 \times 61 = 44.05$$

We already know the S value, which is 1.124. C value for that period can be derived by computing the three-month moving average of the last three months (October, November, and December of Year 5), which is computed as follows:

$$C_{\text{Jan Year 6}} = \frac{1.00 + 0.92 + 0.93}{3}$$

$$= 0.95$$

Now we have all the values we need to prepare a forecast. The forecast of January Year 6 will be:

$$\text{Forecast}_{\text{Jan Year 6}} = 44.05 \times 1.124 \times 0.95$$
$$= \$47.05 \text{ million}$$

Bear in mind that with this model one can make a forecast of only one period ahead. We can compute T and S values for any period in the future, but not the C value. A forecasting software that prepares forecasts beyond one period assumes that the C value will continue to be same in the future. In the above example, we cannot make a forecast beyond January Year 6. Also, seasonal variations exist only in the data of less than one year, that is, in the quarterly, monthly, weekly, or daily data. Where seasonal variations exist, we have to include S in the computation of a forecast. However, if we are making an annual forecast, we don't need S. In that case, the decomposition model will look like this:

$$\text{Forecast} = T \times C \times R$$

SUGGESTED READING

1. Makridakis, Spyros, Steven C. Wheelwright, and Rob J. Hyndman. ***Forecasting: Methods and Applications.*** New York: John Wiley and Sons. 1998.
2. Wilson, J. Holton, Barry Keating, and John Galt Solutions, Inc. ***Business Forecasting.*** New York: McGraw Hill. 2007.

QUESTIONS FOR REVIEW

1. What is the main philosophy behind the classical decomposition model? In what ways does it differ from moving average and exponential smoothing models?
2. What do we mean by seasonal variations? What kind of information do we get from seasonal indices?
3. How do seasonal cycles differ from cyclical cycles? Explain.
4. What are the sums of seasonal indices of quarterly and monthly data?
5. What does the index of 110 for January imply, and what does the index of 75 for March imply?
6. Do cyclical fluctuations occur regularly and periodically?
7. Which component in the decomposition model accounts for the impact of rare events?

Sales Data of Johnson Sugar Manufacturing Company (Mil. of $)				
Month	Year 1	Year 2	Year 3	Year 4
January	10	20	30	35
February	8	23	25	32
March	11	22	28	30
April	12	25	30	30
May	14	26	31	28
June	13	28	30	27
July	12	25	33	28
August	14	22	34	31
September	16	23	35	33
October	17	26	36	37
November	20	29	34	40
December	18	26	31	38

8. The table above gives the sales data of Johnson Sugar Manufacturing Company. Using the classical decomposition model forecast the sales of January Year 5. In computing typical seasonal indices, don't eliminate any value. Also, use three-period moving average to eliminate irregular variations in the data.
   Answer: $30.04 million.
9. GE forecasted the sales of November 2011, which came to $420 million. In making this forecast, the model did not account for seasonality. What would be the seasonally adjusted forecast for November 2011, if the seasonal index for that month is 125?
   Answer: $525 million.
10. The forecaster of Novak Enterprise forecasted the sales of August and September 2011, which came to $30 million for each month. The model used in preparing this forecast did not account for seasonality. If the seasonal indices for August and September are 90 and 120 respectively, would the sales for the month of September be smaller or larger than $30 million?
    Answer: Larger than $30 million.

CHAPTER 20

SALES RATIOS

The sales ratio is another Time Series model of forecasting. It assumes that each month or quarter contributes a certain percentage to the total sales of a year, and that percentage remains fairly stable over time. If we know the sales of one month or one quarter, we can predict the sales of the whole year. This is a quick and easy way to determine how sales are coming along and/or to verify the accuracy of a forecast prepared by another model.

AVERAGE SALES RATIO

Here is the step-by-step procedure for preparing a forecast with the average sales ratio. The sales data of Delphi Enterprise are used to illustrate the procedure. (The data are real, but because of confidentiality, the name of the company was changed.)

Step 1: Table 20.1 gives two years of monthly sales data (Year 1 and Year 2). First step is to compute the sales ratio of each month to the total of that year. For example, the sales ratio of January Year 1 is 0.074 [(194,529 ÷ 2,637,598)] and sales ratio of February Year 1 is 0.068 (180,053 ÷ 2,637,598). This way we can compute sales ratios of all the months for both years, that is, of Year 1 and Year 2. They are given in Columns 3 and 5 in Table 20.1.

Step 2: Compute average sales ratio of each month of both years. The average sales ratio of January is 0.075 [(0.074 + 0.077) ÷ (2)]; of February, 0.071 [(0.068 + 0.074) ÷ (2)];

Table 20.1 | Average Sales Ratios | Delphi Enterprise

Month (1)	Year 1 Sales (Mil. of $) (2)	Sales Ratios (3)	Year 2 Sales (Mil. of $) (4)	Sales Ratios (5)	Average Sales Ratios (6)
January	194,529	0.074	204,011	0.077	0.075
February	180,053	0.068	197,708	0.074	0.071
March	193,489	0.073	186,805	0.070	0.072
April	178,690	0.068	173,225	0.065	0.0.66
May	175,083	0.066	183,138	0.069	0.068
June	245,968	0.093	273,495	0.103	0.098
July	203,194	0.077	186,384	0.070	0.074
August	233,556	0.089	225,785	0.085	0.087
September	252,654	0.096	259,797	0.098	0.097
October	243,747	0.092	259,425	0.098	0.095
November	295,889	0.112	265,051	0.100	0.106
December	240,746	0.091	244,524	0.092	0.092
Total	**2,637,598**	**1.000**	**2,659,348**	**1.000**	**1.000**

Note: All the calculations were made with the Microsoft Excel, and the numbers were rounded.

and so on. All the average sales ratios are given in Column 6, Table 20.1. What do these ratios tell us? The average sales ratio of 0.075 of January implies that, on average, 7.5% of the annual sales comes from the month of January; the average sales ratio of 0.071 of February implies that, on average, 7.1% of the annual sales comes from the month of February; and so on. We compute the average because monthly ratios change somewhat from one year to the next. The average tends to give us a better idea as to what percentage each month contributes to the total of a year. At times, it may be advisable to eliminate a certain month(s) of a year from the average if, for one reason or the other, that month had an unusual contribution (positive or negative) to the total. In that month, sales might have gone up sharply because the company received one large order from Saudi Arabia, the Olympic games were in the town, and/or one of the competitor's plants caught fire; or, the sales might have gone down sharply because of a snowstorm, a strike at the factory, or for any other reason. Such occurrences distort the normal pattern. Therefore, when you notice such values, the best thing to do is to eliminate those months from the average.

Note that here we use the average of two sales ratios, the model is called average sales ratio. If we use a ratio based on just one year (this is, what is available at the time) to make a forecast, it will be called sales ratio model.

Step 3: Prepare forecasts. Let's say that we just finished January of Year 3, and we want to forecast the sale of the whole year on that basis. We can do it by dividing the sale of January by the average ratio of that month. The total of the actual sales in January of Year 3 is $198,947 million, and the average sale ratio of that month is 0.075. Then the forecast for Year 3 will be $2,644,394 million ($198,947 million ÷ 0.075). (See Table 20.2) This compares with the actual sale of $2,564,944 million (an error of –3.10%). When the sales of February of Year 3 are in, we can once again make a forecast for the year to see if the number is similar to what we projected earlier. The average sales ratio of February is 0.071. Then the forecast of the year will be $2,602,327 million ($185,557 million ÷ 0.071). This gives an error of –1.46%. We can do the same when the sales for the month of March are in. Table 20.2 gives annual forecasts of Year 3 based on the sale data of all the months and their average percentage errors. As we can see from the table, error ranged anywhere from 1.20% to –22.86%. (See Column 5 of Table 20.2) The error went up in the months when the sales ratio was not quite stable. In other words, the annual forecast only of those months would be reliable, which have a fairly stable ratio. (A minus error refers to the error resulting from an over-forecast, and a positive error, from an under-forecast.)

Table 20.2 | Forecasts of Year 3 Based on The Average Sales Ratio | Delphi Enterprise

Month (1)	Year 3 Sales (Mil. of $) (2)	Avg. Sales Ratios Based on the Data of Year 1 & Year 2 (3)	Projected Sales of Year 3 (4)	% Error (5)
January	198,947	0.075	2,644,394	–3.10
February	185,557	0.071	2,602,327	–1.46
March	177,166	0.072	2,467,447	3.80
April	179,221	0.066	2,697,377	–5.16
May	168,905	0.068	2,497,755	2.62
June	226,617	0.098	2,311,270	9.89
July	231,820	0.074	3,151,358	–22.86
August	241,445	0.087	2,784,012	–8.54
September	214,259	0.097	2,214,776	13.65
October	240,701	0.095	2,534,167	1.20
November	256,150	0.106	2,418,233	5.72
December	244,156	0.092	2,665,116	–3.91
Total	**2,564,944**	**1.000**		

Note: All the calculations were made with the Microsoft Excel, and the numbers were rounded.

CUMULATIVE AVERAGE SALES RATIO

Among other things, sales in any given month are affected by the promotional calendar because many companies turn on and off their promotions in certain months of a year. If the promotional calendar were to change, so would the sales ratios. In any one year, a company may decide to change the promotional calendar. It used to do promotions in January, but last year it decided to do them in February. With the result, the sales ratio of January went down and of February went up. The annual forecasts based on them became less accurate. This problem can be overcome somewhat by using cumulative sales ratios. Here is the step-by-step procedure for forecasting annual sales with cumulative sales ratios:

Step 1: Column 2 of Table 20.3 gives sale ratios of Year 1, copied from Column 3 of Table 20.1. Cumulate the monthly sales ratios of each year. The cumulative sales ratio of January of Year 1 will be the same as the sales ratio, which is 0.074. The cumulative ratio of February will be 0.142 (0.074 + 0.068); of March 0.216 (0.142 + 0.073), and so on. This way we can compute the cumulative sales ratios of all the months of both

Table 20.3 | Cumulative Average Sales Ratios | Delphi Enterprise, Inc.

	Year 1		Year 2		
Month (1)	Year 1 Sales (Mil. of $) (2)	Cumulative Sales Ratios (3)	Year 2 Sales (Mil. of $) (4)	Cumulative Sales Ratios (5)	Average Cumulative Sales Ratios (6)
January	0.074	0.074	0.077	0.077	0.076
February	0.068	0.142	0.074	0.151	0.147
March	0.073	0.216	0.070	0.222	0.219
April	0.068	0.283	0.065	0.287	0.285
May	0.066	0.350	0.069	0.356	0.353
June	0.093	0.443	0.103	0.458	0.451
July	0.077	0.520	0.070	0.529	0.524
August	0.089	0.609	0.085	0.613	0.611
September	0.096	0.704	0.098	0.711	0.708
October	0.092	0.797	0.098	0.809	0.803
November	0.112	0.909	0.100	0.908	0.909
December	0.091	1.000	0.092	1.000	1.000
Sum	**1.000**		**1.000**		**1.000**

Note: All the calculations were made with the Microsoft Excel, and the numbers were rounded.

years. They are given in Columns 3 and 5 of Table 20.3.

Step 2: Compute the average cumulative sales ratios. The average cumulative sales ratio of January is 0.076 [(0.074 + 0.077) ÷ (2)], of February, 0.147 [(0.142 + 0.151) ÷ (2)], and so on. Average cumulative sales ratios of all the months are given in Table 20.3, Column 6.

Step 3: Prepare forecasts. To do that, we need to cumulate the monthly sales of Year 3, which are given in Column 3 of Table 20.4, because the sales ratios we are going to use will be cumulative. When the sales of January are in, we can forecast the total sales of Year 3, which will be the same as computed on the basis of its monthly sales ratio. The actual sales of January, Year 3, are $198,947. The projected sales for the year will come to $2,635,060 ($198,947 ÷ 0.076). When the sales of February come in, we cumulate the sales of January and February because our average cumulative sales ratio is based on both these months. The cumulative ratio of January and February is 0.147, meaning that, on average, the sales of January and February represent 14.7% of the annual sales. Then the projected sales of the year will be $2,619,161 ($384,504 ÷ 0.147). Since the total of the

Table 20.4 | Forecasts of Year 3 Based on Cumulative Average Sales Ratios | Delphi Enterprise, Inc.

Month (1)	Year 3 Sales (Mil. of $) (2)	Year 3 Cumulative Monthly Sale (3)	Cumulative Sales Ratio (4)	Projected Sales of Year 3 (5)	% Error (6)
January	198,947	198,947	0.076	2,635,060	–2.73
February	185,557	384,504	0.147	2,619,161	–2.11
March	177,166	561,670	0.219	2,569,330	–0.17
April	179,221	740,891	0.285	2,599,177	–1.33
May	168,905	909,796	0.353	2,579,730	–0.58
June	226,617	1,136,413	0.451	2,521,329	1.70
July	231,820	1,368,233	0.524	2,609,729	–1.75
August	241,445	1,609,678	0.611	2,634,466	–2.71
September	214,259	1,823,937	0.708	2,577,100	–0.47
October	240,701	2,064,638	0.803	2,572,020	–0.28
November	256,150	2,320,788	0.909	2,554,092	0.42
December	244,156	2,564,944	1.000	2,564,261	0.03
Total	**2,564,944**				

Note: All the calculations were made with the Microsoft Excel, and the numbers were rounded.

actual sales of Year 3 is $2,564,944, the percentage error comes to –2.11%. Similarly, we can prepare forecasts of Year 3 based on the cumulative sales ratios of other months. Columns 5 and 6 of Table 20.4 give forecasts of Year 3 based on different months of cumulative sales ratios and their percentage errors respectively. The percentage error here ranges between 0.03% and –2.73%, much lower than what we experienced when we used average sales ratio. Also, the mean absolute percentage error (MAPE) of the cumulative sales ratio was much lower than the mean absolute percentage error (MAPE) of the average sales ratios (1.19% against 6.83%).

QUESTIONS FOR REVIEW

1. What are the principles on which models of average sales ratio and cumulative average sales ratio are based? Explain.
2. How can we decide which month's average sales ratio is likely to give a better annual forecast than others?
3. How do we decide which month's cumulative average sales ratio is likely to give a better annual forecast than others?

Demand of Electricity | Albany Electric Company (Bil. of kWh)				
Quarter	Demand (Year 1)	Demand (Year 2)	Demand (Year 3)	Demand (Year 4)
Q1	26.21	25.76	25.91	27.08
Q2	23.45	22.88	24.07	24.99
Q3	31.85	34.02	36.60	41.29
Q4	25.28	25.80	26.43	26.69
SUM	**106.79**	**108.46**	**113.01**	**120.05**

Note: Data given above are real, but because of confidentiality, the name of the company was changed.

4. Explain why the cumulative average sales ratio model tends to give lower forecast errors than the average sales ratio model.
5. The table above gives the demand of electricity by quarter over four years (Years 1–4) of Albany Electric Company. Using the demand of the first three years and average sales ratio model, forecast the annual sales of Year 4 on the basis of: An actual demand of the first quarter of Year 4; actual demand of the second quarter of Year 4; and actual demand of the third quarter of Year 4. The actual annual demand of Year 4 is given at the bottom of the column

Quarter	Forecast (Bil. of kWh)	% Error
1	114.05	4.99
2	116.50	2.96
3	132.37	-10.27

of that year. Also, compute the percentage forecast error for each projected annual demand.

Answer: Annual forecasts of Year 4 and their forecast errors are:

6. Using the first three years of data given in Question 5 and average cumulative sales ratio model, forecast the annual sales of Year 4 on the basis of: Actual demand of first quarter of Year 4; actual demand of first and second quarters of Year 4; and actual demand of first, second, and third quarters of Year 4. The actual annual demand of Year 4 is given at the bottom in the column of that year. Compute also the percentage forecast error for each projected annual

Cumulative Quarters	Forecast (Bil. of kWh)	% Error
1	114.05	4.98
1 & 2	115.21	4.02
1, 2 &3	122.22	–1.81

demand.

Answer: Annual forecasts of Year 4 and their forecast errors are:

7. In computing average sales ratio or average cumulative sales ratio, which ratio should be eliminated from the average, and why?

CHAPTER 21

FAMILY MEMBER FORECASTING

For production planning and scheduling purposes, forecasts have to be broken down to the most granular level, that is, by SKU (stock keeping units, item) level. Generally, forecasts are categorized into three: (1) Aggregate, (2) category/brand, and (3) SKU. The aggregate-level forecast is the forecast of the company as a whole. The category/brand-level forecast is a forecast of all the SKUs combined within a category/brand. The SKU-level forecast is a forecast by SKU (item). For example, a clothing manufacturer manufactures gent's suits as well as lady's suits. Both are quite different from each other. So, we have two categories, one for gent's suits and the other for lady's suits. Each category may have a number of SKUs within it. Gent's suits, for example, come in different designs, colors, and sizes. A suit with stripes, a blue color, and size 38 regular is one SKU, and a suit with stripes, a blue color, and size 40 regular is another SKU. So, there can be hundreds of SKUs within a category. For production planning, we need a forecast for each and every SKU.

As mentioned in Chapter 6, forecasts can be initiated from the top (top-down approach), the bottom (bottom-up approach), or somewhere in the middle (category/brand—middle-out approach). If a forecast is initiated from the top, then the forecast has to be broken down into categories/brands, and then each category/brand into SKUs. Very often in business, forecasts are initially prepared at a mid-level, that is, at a category/brand level, and then broken down into SKUs. Of course, if forecasts are initiated from the bottom (bottom-up), then we have the SKU level forecasts right from the beginning. The family member forecasting is a way of breaking down the aggregate level forecast into category/brand level forecasts, and category/brand level forecasts into SKU level forecasts.

METHODOLOGY

There are several ways of disaggregating an aggregate or category/brand-level forecast. The method we explain here is the one that is commonly used and is easy to work with. Let us say that we have prepared a forecast at a category/brand level. The category/brand is also called family, because a number of SKUs fall within it. Let us say that we have prepared a forecast of a category/brand/family of shirts for the month of March 2012, using one model or the other. The forecast came to 25 million units. The family of shirts is keyed as 5200. (See Table 21.1) There are five SKUs within that family, which are 5200-1 (size 14), 5200-2 (size 15), 5200-3 (size 16), 5200-4 (size 17), and 5200-5 (size 18). We want to break up the family (category/brand) level forecast into five SKUs. Here is the step-by-step procedure:

Step 1: Column 3 of Table 21.1 gives the actual monthly sales of the most recent 12 months of all the five SKUs, along with their family total. The first step is to compute the ratio of each SKU to the total sales of that family (category/brand). For example, the ratio of SKU 5200-1 comes to 0.252 (35 ÷ 139); of SKU 5200-2, 0.072 (10 ÷ 139); and so on. All these ratios are given in Column 4. The ratio 0.252 of 5200-1 means that during last 12 months 25.2% of the total sales of that family (category/brand) came from that SKU.

Step 2: Let us say that the projected sales of the whole family of March 2012 came to 25 million units, which were derived using one model or the other. The next step will be to breakdown the 25 million units into five SKUs using their ratios. The forecast

Table 21.1 | Family Member Forecasting

Product Code (1)	Description (2)	Rolling 12 Month Total of Actual Sales (Mil. of Units) (3)	Ratio of a Member to the Family (4)	March 2012 (Mil. of Units) (5)
5200-1	SKU	35	.252	6.3
5200-2	SKU	10	.072	1.8
5200-3	SKU	9	.065	1.6
5200-4	SKU	64	.460	11.5
5200-5	SKU	21	.151	3.8
5200	**Family**	**139**		**25.0**

of SKU 5200-1 comes to 6.3 million units (25 × 0.252), the forecast of SKU 5200-2 comes to 1.8 million units (25 × 0.072), and so on. The forecasts of all the SKUs are given in Column 5. Here we assume that the ratios of the last 12 months will hold in the future. There is no hard and fast rule as to how many months should be used to develop these ratios. If the market dynamic of a product changes very rapidly, you may like to use fewer months, say, nine months or six months, in creating these ratios.

It is important that we use the rolling total of a certain number of months, which is 12 months in our example, and update it when the data of the next month become available. Let us say at present we are in January and our rolling total includes the data of last 12 months, say, from January to December of last year. When the data of January of this year become available, our rolling total will have the data from February to December of last year and January of the current year. In other words, in our rolling total we drop one month from the top and add one month from the bottom, still maintaining a total of 12 months for developing ratios.

QUESTIONS FOR REVIEW

1. Explain why it is important to disaggregate the category/brand level forecast into SKUs.
2. What is the rational behind using ratios for disaggregating a category/brand forecast into SKUs? Explain.
3. Which function needs forecasts at a highly granular (SKU) level, and why?

King Kong Manufacturing Company | Sales of Detergent | Year: 2011 (Mil. of Units)			
Month	**SKU-1**	**SKU-2**	**SKU-3**
January	5	10	25
February	7	10	34
March	9	13	23
April	11	14	22
May	4	18	41
June	5	22	38
July	8	27	9
August	9	29	45
September	11	30	67
October	21	8	80
November	10	9	55
December	11	10	34

4. The table above gives 12 months of sales data of a detergent made by King Kong Manufacturing Company, year 2011, which comes in three sizes SKU-1, SKU-2, and SKU-3. Using the family

member forecasting method and 12-month ratios, forecast the sales of each of the three SKUs for the month of January 2012. The forecasted sales of the detergent category for the month of January 2012 is 985 million units, which the forecaster derived by using the regression model.

Answer: SKU-1: 139.5 million units.
SKU-2: 251.3 million units.
SKU-3: 594.3 million units.

PART VI

CAUSE-AND-EFFECT MODELS

INTRODUCTION

With the increasing recognition of the importance of forecasts in decision-making and the rising level of sophistication of business forecasters, more and more forecasters are now using Cause-and-Effect models. The advancement in computer technology and the development of various forecasting software in the area have further increased their use. At present, even the spreadsheet packages such as Microsoft Excel and Lotus have a regression model embedded in them, the model most used within the family of Cause and Effect. Further, where there is a causal relationship, Cause-and-Effect models are a must. Above all, no model provides as much insight into the interrelationships between the drivers and the business as Cause-and-Effect models, thereby helping managers to make better decisions.

CHAPTER 22

SIMPLE REGRESSION MODELS

The Cause-and-Effect models are one of the three types of forecasting models. The other two are Time Series and Judgmental models. Within Cause-and-Effect models, regression, econometric and artificial neural network models are often used in business. Within these three, the one that is most used is regression. (See Figure 22.1) In all of these models, we identify the variable to be forecasted (called the dependent variable), and variables that affect it (called the independent variables), develop relationships among them by using the past data, and then use the relationships to prepare a forecast. (In this book, we will cover only regression and artificial neural network models—regression in this and the next chapter, and artificial neural network model in Chapter 25.) Econometric models are primarily used for macro forecasting. Based on our conversation with many forecasters, companies that claim they use econometric models are in fact using regression, and nothing more.

WHERE CAUSE-AND-EFFECT MODELS ARE USED

Cause-and-Effect models are most appropriate:

1. Where strong causal relationships exist, and relationships are fairly stable. If sales are a function of advertisement and their relationship is fairly strong and stable, then

Figure 22.1 | Cause-and-Effect Models Used in Business (All Industries Combined)

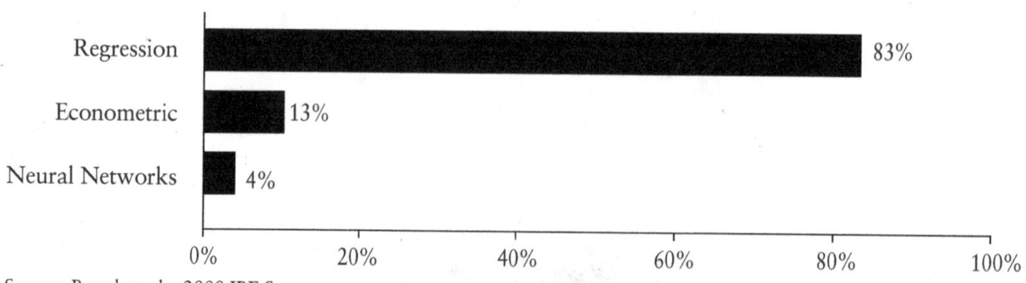

Source: Based on the 2009 IBF Survey.

every time we increase the amount spent on advertisements, the sales will increase, and vice versa. If, however, the relationship between them changes significantly, then forecasts developed by using the historical data won't provide accurate forecasts.

2. Where independent variables are either known or highly predictable. Independent variables are the causal factors (explanatory variables/drivers). If the sales depend on advertisements and GDP to predict sales of the next period, we will need to know not only how much money would be spent on advertisements, but also what would be the GDP in that period. We may know the amount to be spent on advertising, but for GDP we have to forecast. Therefore, how accurate our sales forecast would be depends, among other things, on how accurate the GDP forecast is.

3. Where "what-if" scenarios are needed for optimization. That is, what would happen if we raise the media spending by 5%, and/or reduce the price by 2 cents? The Cause-and-Effect models provide such insights, thereby helping managers in their efforts to hit the operational and strategic targets.

4. Where sensitivity analysis is needed, that is, how sensitive the dependent variable is to an independent variable. If, for example, demand is highly price sensitive (elastic), a small change in price will cause a large change in demand, there the company has to think twice before raising the price. The Cause-and-Effect models provide such information.

REGRESSION MODELS

To understand regression models it is important to understand the variables, which are: (1) dependent and (2) independent. The dependent variable is the one that we want to forecast, and

Table 22.1 | Independent Variables

Internal/Endogenous	External/Exogenous
Price of a product	Competitive price
Media spending	New competitive product to be launched
Number of new products to be introduced	Gross Domestic Product
Number of products to be discontinued	Consumer price index
Number of stores	Unemployment
FSI (Free Standing Insert) coupons distributed	Auto sales
Etc.	Etc.

independent variables (also called explanatory variables/drivers) are those that influence the dependent variable. The independent variables can be one or more. If, for example, we believe that the sale of a product is a function of price and GDP, then we have two independent variables —price and GDP. The dependent variable is always one, which is sales in this case. There are two categories of independent variables: Internal (endogenous) and external (exogenous). The internal variables are those over which we have control, that is, we can change them if needed. In the above example, price is an internal variable. We can change it if necessary. But the other independent variable, GDP, is not within our control. We cannot change it. We have to accept it as it is. Table 22.1 gives a list of various internal and external independent variables.

TYPES OF REGRESSION MODELS

The regression models come in all shapes and colors. The ones that are often discussed in the literature are:

1. Simple and multiple regression models
2. Linear and curvilinear regression models
3. Time Series and cross-sectional regression models
4. Dynamic regression model
5. Logit and probit regression models

Simple and Multiple Regression Models: A simple regression model is used where there is only one independent variable. If there is more than one independent variable, it is called a multiple regression model. In other words, if the model assumes that sales are a function of price only, then it is a candidate for simple regression model, because there is only one independent variable. If sales are a function of price and GDP, then we have two independent variables, and the model will be a multiple regression model.

Linear and Curvilinear Regression Models: Linear regression models assume that the relationship between the independent and dependent variables is linear. If a regression model shows that there exists a relationship of 1:2 between price (in cents) and sales (millions of $), and is negative; then, other things remaining constant, if the price goes down by one cent, sales will go up by $2 million; if it goes down by 2 cents, sales will go up by $4 million; and so on. This is a case of linear regression model. If, on the other hand, the relationship between them is non-linear, then it is a case of curvilinear regression. Here the relationship between them will vary; with a one cent decrease in price, sales may increase by $2 million dollars; with a 2 cents decrease in price, sales may increase by $1.5 million; and so on.

Time Series and Cross-Section Regression Model: The Time Series regression model is based on consecutive time periods. For example, a sales model of Eastman Kodak Company is based on its sales data of last 36 months. The cross-section regression model, on the other hand, is based only on one time period. For example, if we want to predict the height of a son based on the height of a father, we will need the data of height of fathers and sons over one time period, say, of 2011.

Dynamic Regression Model: The dynamic regression is a model that includes lagged values of independent variables, dependent variable, or both. For example, certain promotional activities affect sales only after one or two months. In that case, the model will become more efficient if the promotional spending is lagged.

Logit and Probit Regression Models: These types of models are used where the objective is to estimate the probability of the occurrence of an event (dependent variable), which takes the value of 1 and 0 —1 for "Yes" and 0 for "No." These are used for developing models for such things as bankruptcy to determine the probability of a company going bankrupt, and payment-default to predict the probability of a person defaulting on credit card payment.

FOUR STEPS TO BUILD A MODEL

There are four steps to build a regression model, which are:

1. Specification
2. Estimation
3. Validation
4. Forecast

Before starting the specification process, it is important to study the data to see if there are any

Figure 22.2 | Lovely Pharmacy Stores

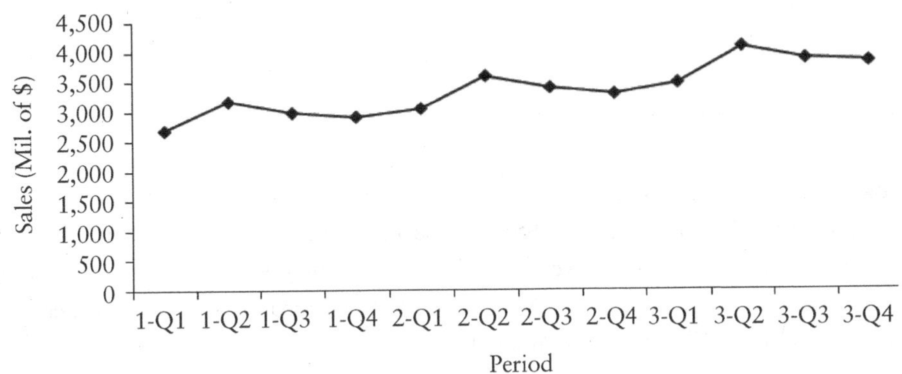

problems. For that, the best way is to plot the historical data of a dependent variable over time. It may tell us whether the data contain outliers (unusual values), seasonality, and/or structural change. If we know what kinds of problems the data have, we may know how to deal with them. For a structural change (permanent change in the data pattern because of merger/acquisition, introduction of a revolutionary new products, etc.), for example, we may have to eliminate the data prior to the change. Figure 22.2 gives a plot of sales data of Lovely Pharmacy Stores. It shows that the data do not seem to have either an outlier or a structural change. However, they do have seasonality. Every year, for one reason or the other, sales are the highest in the second quarter. Since the seasonality can be handled only in a multiple regression environment, we will discuss it in the next chapter.

Specification: Let us first specify the linear population regression model with one independent variable (case of simple regression), which is expressed as:

$$Y = \alpha + \beta X + u \qquad \ldots(22.1)$$

Here Y is the dependent variable (what we want to forecast), α is the intercept (constant) of the regression equation, X is the independent variable (that drives Y), β is the slope of the regression line (often called regression coefficient), and u is the error term. Here α represents the value of Y when $X = 0$, and β shows how much Y changes with one unit of change in X. No matter what we do, there would be some error, which is represented by u. The other way of saying it is that $\alpha + \beta X$ represents the forecast, and u represents the error in the forecast.

Here α and β represent population parameters. But, when we forecast we would be using sample data. Since the error is realized only after the actual is materialized, the simple regression model for a sample data becomes:

$$Y = a + bX \quad \ldots(22.2)$$

Here Y is a dependent variable.

After the data are studied and treated, the specification process starts. Let us say we want to build a sales model for Lovely Pharmacy Stores. The first thing is to think about all of the possible factors that, in our judgment, drive the sales of this company. Let us say we come up with four factors: Price (P), media spending (M), Gross Domestic Product (GDP), and Personal Consumption Expenditures (PCE). Then the model becomes:

$$\text{Sales} = f(\text{P, M, GDP, PCE}) \quad \ldots(22.3)$$

Here f stands for function, that is, sales are a function of P (Price), M (Media Spending), GDP (Gross Domestic Product), and PCE (Personal Consumption Expenditures). One way to determine which variable(s) to use in a model is to calculate coefficients of correlation. In our example it would be between sales and price, sales and media spending, sales and GDP, and sales and PCE. The coefficient of correlation gives the degree of association between variables, that is, how sales are associated with price, media spending, GDP, and PCE. The higher the association, the better it is. The absolute value of the coefficient of correlation runs between zero and one. Zero means that there is no association whatsoever. One means that there is perfect association.

The coefficient of correlation can be negative or positive, which describes the direction of correlation. Price usually has a negative coefficient of correlation, meaning when price increases, sales drop, and vice versa. The sign of a coefficient is important in regression-based modeling. If a coefficient's sign is contrary to the common belief, then one should check very closely the validity of the model.

The coefficient of correlation can be computed with Microsoft Excel; the instructions for doing so are given in Appendix A. Table 22.2 gives quarterly sales data of first three years plus Quarter 1 of Year 4. The coefficients of correlation of independent variables with sales of Year 1-Q1 through Year 3-Q4, are given in Table 22.3. It shows that although price has a negative correlation, its coefficient is very poor, which is -0.56. GDP has the highest coefficient of correlation with sales (0.89), followed by PCE (0.88). Let us say we decide to use GDP as a driver for sales. Then the model becomes:

Table 22.2 | Lovely Pharmacy Stores | Sales, Average Price, Media Spending, GDP, and PCE

Period	Sales (Mil. of $)	Average Price Per Unit	Media Spending (Mil. of $)	GDP (Bil. of $)	PCE (Bil. of $)
Year 1-Q1	2,693	15	49	7,630	5,131
Year 1-Q2	3,179	14	48	7,783	5,218
Year 1-Q3	2,989	15	50	7,859	5,264
Year 1-Q4	2,917	15	51	7,981	5,338
Year 2-Q1	3,054	14	54	8,124	5,430
Year 2-Q2	3,603	13	54	8,280	5,471
Year 2-Q3	3,403	14	53	8,391	5,576
Year 2-Q4	3,303	14	56	8,479	5,641
Year 3-Q1	3,485	15	55	8,635	5,713
Year 3-Q2	4,093	14	56	8,722	5,811
Year 3-Q3	3,887	14	58	8,829	5,893
Year 3-Q4	3,840	14	57	8,972	5,986
Year 4-Q1	4,016			9,104	6,095

Notes: 1. GDP stands for Gross Domestic Product.
2. PCE stands for Personal Consumption Expenditures.

$$\text{Sales} = f(\text{GDP}) \qquad \ldots(22.4)$$

Now the model has been specified, that is, sales are a function of GDP. The next step is to estimate the model, that is, to calculate the values of a and b.

Estimation: The regression model can be easily computed with Microsoft Excel. The step-by-step instructions for doing it are given in Appendix B. The Excel-based regression output, using the same data, (i.e., from Year 1-Q1 through Year 3-Q4) of Lovely Pharmacy Stores, is given in Table 22.4. It gives, among other things, values of a and b. The estimated model becomes:

$$\hat{Y} = -3{,}888.922 \text{ (intercept)} + 0.8739 \text{ (coefficient of X variable 1) } X \qquad \ldots(22.5)$$

Now the model has been estimated. Before we use it for making a forecast, we want to know

Table 22.3 | Coefficients of Correlation

Between Variables	Coefficient of Correlation
Sales and Price	-0.56
Sales and Media Spending	0.80
Sales and GDP	0.89
Sales and PCE	0.88

how good the model is. In other words, we want to know whether or not the model is valid, which is the subject of the next section.

Validation: The next step is to validate a model, that is, determine how good it is. We can evaluate it by using the following diagnostics, which are:

1. R^2
2. t test
3. F test
4. Durbin-Watson (DW) test
5. Standard error of regression
6. Ex post forecasts
7. Diagnostic beyond statistics

Since it is very time consuming to compute these statistics manually, we will use the Microsoft Excel-based output, as given in Table 22.4.

R^2: R^2 (also called coefficient of determination) shows what percentage of the variations in the dependent variable (sales in our example) can be explained by the model. The more it explains the variations in the dependent variable, the better it is. Table 22.4 shows that here R^2 is 0.79. It means

Table 22.4 | Lovely Pharmacy Stores | Sales Model Summary Output (Year 1-Q1 – Year 3-Q4)

Regression Statistics						
Multiple R				0.8901		
R Square				0.7924		
Adjusted R Square				0.7716		
Standard Error				205.2593		
Observations				12		
ANOVA						
	Df	**SS**		**MS**	**F**	**Significance F**
Regression	1	1,607,729.1		1,607,729	38.159889	0.0001045
Residual	10	421,313.89		4,2131		
Total	11	2,029,043.0				
	Coefficient	**Stand. Err**	**t Stat**	***p*-Value**	**Lower 95%**	**Upper 95%**
Intercept	-3,888.922	1,176.6569	3.3051	0.0079	6,510.6774	1,267.167
X Variable 1	0.8739	0.1415	6.1774	0.0001	0.5587	1.1891

Notes: 1. GDP stands for Gross Domestic Product.
2. PCE stands for Personal Consumption Expenditures.

that 79% of the variations in the sales of Lovely Pharmacy Stores can be explained by the model, and the other 21% are due to other factors (variables) not included in the model. The closer the R^2 comes to one, the better it is.

For model evaluation, we should always use adjusted R^2 instead of R^2, because the former adjusts for the degrees of freedom. The degrees of freedom show the data points that are available to provide useful information—the more the better. The formula for computing degrees of freedom is n-k, where n is the number of observations, and k is the number of independent variables, which is one in the case of simple regression. With every additional independent variable, the degree of freedom decreases by one, meaning the number of data points that contribute useful information to the model are reduced by one. So, the increase in R^2 resulting from more variables does not necessarily mean that the model has improved. The best thing, therefore, is to use adjusted R^2, even in the case of simple regression. The interpretation, of course, is the same. The closer the adjusted R^2 is to one, the better it is. In our example, the adjusted R^2 is 0.77.

t test: The t test is used to determine whether a regression coefficient (b) is significantly different from zero. If not, it means that there is little or no slope, and thus X has no impact on Y. We keep only that variable whose b value is significantly different from zero. Otherwise, we eliminate it from the model. In our example, the t value of GDP (X) is 6.1774. (See Table 22.4) To determine whether its value is significantly different from zero, statisticians start with a null hypothesis, that is, β value is not significantly different from zero, and then using the t distribution table and a critical value (level of confidence) to make that determination. The null hypothesis takes this form:

Null hypothesis $H_0: \beta = 0$
Alternative Hypothesis $H_a: \beta \neq 0$

Here H_0 stands for null hypothesis, and β for the regression coefficient of the population. The null hypothesis states that its value is zero, implying it is not significantly different from zero. The other is the alternative hypothesis, which states that it is significantly different from zero. To determine that we look at the table of t distribution at a critical value, say, 5% (implying chances of wrong is 5%, or 95% level of confidence) at a given degrees of freedom. Also, the critical value of 5% means alpha =.05. The degrees of freedom simply imply the number of data points that are available for producing useful information. The formula for determining degrees of freedom is df = n – k – 1. Here df stands for the degree of freedom; n, the number of observations; and k, the number of independent variables. In our example, df = (12 - 1 -1) = 10. Then we look at the table value of t distribution at 10 degrees of freedom and critical value of 5%, which is 1.81. (See

Appendix C) Since the calculated value of t, which is 6.18, is greater than the table value, we reject the null hypothesis, implying β is significantly different from zero. In other words, X (GDP) has a significant effect on Y (sales). So, we decide to keep that variable in the model. Usually, the constant term is not the focus of hypothesis testing.

Rule of thumb: If the calculated t value of the coefficient of a variable is equal to or greater than 2 (positive or negative) for 20 or more observations, the coefficient is significantly different from zero. We should keep that variable in the equation. The higher the t value, the better it is.

Since p value is the cumulative probability for getting a t value equal to or greater than the calculated t value in absolute terms, we can also determine whether or not a variable is significant by inspecting the value of p. As a rule of thumb, a variable is statistically significant if its p value is equal to or less than 0.05. In our example, p value is equal to 0.0001, which is much lower than 0.05. So, the model with a GDP variable is good. The output of Microsoft Excel gives p values.

F test: The F test measures the overall significance of a model. It is useful only in testing multiple regression models because in a simple regression the relationship between F and t is fixed, which is, $F = t^2$. Therefore, we will discuss it in the next chapter.

Durbin-Watson statistic (DW) test: The Durbin-Watson statistic (DW) measures the presence of autocorrelation in the residuals. The residual (error term) is the difference between the actual and the fitted (predictive) values of a dependent variable. The fitted values are the values computed by the regression model. (The autocorrelation measures how well successive residuals are related.) To meet the criteria of a robust regression model, residuals have to be random, that is, they don't form any pattern. If there is autocorrelation, it means that independent variable(s) does not fully explain the variations in the dependent variable. Excel output does not give a DW value but it does give residuals, which can be used to calculate DW as shown in Table 22.5. In our case, DW comes to 2.17. The value of DW varies between 0 and 4, and 2 is the best. Further, if DW is less than 2 (or approaches zero), then residuals are positively related. If it is greater than 2 or approaches 4, then they are negatively related. The issue of autocorrelation is often treated with the Cochran-Orcutt iterative procedure.

Rule of thumb: If DW is between 1.75 and 2.25, it is safe to say that there is not much autocorrelation among residuals. With 2.17 value of DW for the model we computed, we can say even though the value is on the borderline, it is acceptable.

Table 22.5 | Computation of Durbin Watson (DW) Statistic | Lovely Pharmacy Stores | Model: Y = f (GDP)

Period	Residuals (e_t) (Mil. of $)	$(e_t)^2$ Per Unit	$(e_t - e_{t-1})$ (Mil. of $)	$(e_t - e_{t-1})^2$ (Bil. of $)
Year 1-Q1	-85.81	7,363.04	—	—
Year 1-Q2	266.49	71,015.70	352.30	124,112.36
Year 1-Q3	10.07	101.46	-256.42	65,748.72
Year 1-Q4	-168.54	28,406.14	-178.61	31,902.88
Year 2-Q1	-156.51	24,494.29	12.03	144.83
Year 2-Q2	256.17	65,621.88	412.67	170,299.99
Year 2-Q3	-40.83	1,667.36	-297.00	88,209.63
Year 2-Q4	-217.74	47,408.58	-176.90	31,294.22
Year 3-Q1	-172.06	29,604.96	45.67	2,086.13
Year 3-Q2	359.91	129,536.09	531.97	282,994.37
Year 3-Q3	60.41	36,48.85	-299.51	89,703.56
Year 3-Q4	-111.56	12,445.55	-171.97	29,572.07
Sum		**421,313.89**		**916,068.76**

$$DW = \frac{\sum_{t=2}^{n}(e_t - e_{t-1})^2}{\sum_{t=1}^{n} e_t^2}$$

$$DW = \frac{916{,}068.76}{421{,}313.89} = 2.17$$

Standard error of regression: The standard error of regression measures deviations around the regression line. In other words, it describes the degree of closeness between the actual and fitted values estimated by the regression equation. The smaller the standard error of regression, the better the model is. It can also be used to prepare range forecasts (low and high forecasts) at different levels of confidence. The lower the standard of error of regression, the smaller will be the gap between the low and high forecasts, suggesting a high degree of confidence in the estimated model. How to compute the range forecast, we will show after we prepare a forecast.

Ex post forecasts: This is another diagnostic tool, probably the most important one, which tells us how well the model forecasts the holdout periods. This tells not only how well it forecasts but also what kind of error we can expect. But selecting holdout periods is more art than science. The ConAgra Foods typically uses 13 weeks of holdout periods particularly where 2 years of weekly

POS history for a regression-based modeling is used, according to Richard Gordon, Director of Analytics at Symphony IRI Group. If a product is highly seasonal, it makes sure that holdout periods include a sufficient number of seasonal observations. He further adds that such a test is essential because it helps in getting users' buy-in.

Diagnostic beyond statistics: Statistical diagnostics are fine. Some consumer product companies go one step further and evaluate a statistical model with the results of market research of a consumer product/category. Some analytic vendors such as Symphony IRI Group and AC Nielsen do detailed price and promotion analyses of certain brands based on the consumption data of certain stores, which they provide to their customers for a fee. They can give a range of elasticity of price and promotion of a brand based on their market research. Let us say their research shows that price elasticity of Brand A ranges between -0.5 and -0.9. The -0.5 elasticity means if price decreases by 1%, sales will increase by 0.5%. The model will be validated if its statistical elasticity falls within that range. We will show in the next chapter how to calculate statistical elasticity.

Preparing a Forecast: After going over all the diagnostic tests, we have to decide whether or not the model we have developed is satisfactory. If a model is validated; we can go ahead and make a forecast for the next period or any other period. Otherwise, we have to go back and re-specify the model, meaning test other independent variables, and then follow all the steps again. Let's assume that we are satisfied with the model we have built, and want to make a forecast of the next period, Year 4-Q 1. The forecast can be prepared by plugging the value of GDP of that period ($9,104 billion, given in Table 22.2) in the Equation 22.5, which we estimated. The forecast comes to:

$$\begin{aligned}\hat{Y}_{04\text{-}Q1} &= -3{,}888.922 + 0.8739\ (9{,}104) \qquad \ldots(22.6)\\ &= \$4{,}066.91 \text{ million}\end{aligned}$$

Incidentally, since the actual value for that period was $4,016 million, the error came to -1.3%.

If we wish to have a range forecast for Year 4-Q1, we can do so by applying the standard error of regression (which is $205.26, given in Table 22.4) to the forecast. Assuming Y values are normally distributed around the mean, at a 68% level of confidence (meaning we want to be right 68 times out of 100), the range forecast will be: $4,066.91 ± (1) (205.26), that is, as low as $3,861.65 million and as high as $4,272.17 million. At a 95% level of confidence (we want to be right 95 times out of 100), the forecast range will be: $4,066.91 ± (2) (205.26), that is, as low as

\$3,656.39 million and as high as \$4,477.43 million. Again, at a 99% level of confidence (we want to be right 99 times out of 100), the forecast range will be \$4,066.91 ± (3) (205.26), that is, as low as \$3,451.13 million and as high as \$4,682.69 million. The range is based on the characteristics of a normal distribution, that is, at a 68% level of confidence, it would be within ± 1 standard error of regression; at a 95% level of confidence, within ± 2 standard errors of regression; and at a 99% level of confidence, within ± 3 standard errors of regression.

ASSUMPTIONS OF AN ORDINARY LEAST SQUARES MODEL

The efficiency of a model depends on how well the assumptions of the Ordinary Least Squares (OLS) model are satisfied. All the model statistics, described above, such as adjusted R^2, t value, and DW are merely symptoms of the assumptions. The more a model satisfies the assumptions, the better would be the model statistics. The OLS model is based on five assumptions, which are:

1. There is a cause-and-effect relationship between Y and X(s).
2. The residuals are normally distributed with a zero mean.
3. The successive residuals are not correlated, that is, there is no autocorrelation (serial correlation).
4. The residuals have a constant variance, that is, there is no heteroscedasticity.
5. The X values are fixed (given).

The first assumption states that there is a cause-and-effect relationship between Y and X(s), and the relationship is linear. If there is no cause-and-effect relationship, then the independent variable(s) cannot explain anything about the dependent variable. A model, even if well fitted to the data and with excellent R^2, t, F, and DW values, won't give the best results unless the variables used truly describe the relationship. The divorce rate in England may be highly statistically related to the import of potatoes, but we cannot predict the divorce rate from the import of potatoes because one has nothing to do with the other. Therefore, a model should not only be statistically valid but also be theoretically sound.

The second assumption of a zero mean of residuals is always fulfilled because of the least squares estimation. Residuals have to be normally distributed, and thus do not pose a problem because the Gauss-Markov theorem, the basis of the least squares method, does not require residuals to be normally distributed. However, for hypothesis testing, using the t distribution, this assumption is necessary.

The third assumption requires that there is no autocorrelation (also called serial correlation); that is, the successive residuals are not correlated. In a Time Series regression model, the consecutive residuals are often correlated. (If the sales of a current month are affected by the sales of the previous month, it would show up in the residuals.) Its presence increases the variance in the residuals as well as in the estimated coefficients, thereby reducing the efficiency of a model to forecast. One way to detect autocorrelation is to plot the residuals. If they form some kind of pattern, then there is autocorrelation. The Durbin-Watson test (described earlier) is used to test the presence of first order of autocorrelation. The elimination of autocorrelation can improve the forecasts. Generalized Least Squares procedures, including Cochran-Orcutt, Hildreth-Lu, and Maximum Likelihood, can be used to deal with this problem. Most of the software packages available in the market have one or more of these procedures.

The fourth assumption is that residuals have a constant variance, that is, there is no heteroscedasticity. In statistical terminology, the constant variance property is called homoscedasticity (i.e., no heteroscedasticity). The constant variance means if residuals are divided into different time periods, the variance calculated from each period of residuals has a similar value. Lack of that means that data have a heteroscedasticity. The heteroscedasticity results when data values have a large range between the smallest and the largest value; when the growth rate between the dependent and independent variables varies significantly during the modeling period; and when the data are highly heterogeneous. Its presence increases the variances in the OLS estimates. In repeated samples (when data are updated for forecasts), the estimated coefficients will fluctuate widely, thereby making the forecasts less reliable. It is often found more in the cross sectional data than in time series data. The problem of heteroscedasticity is often taken care of by some kind of transformation such as inverse and logarithmic. We will discuss some of the transformations in the next chapter. However, if we compute the residual as a percentage of the actual dependent variable and with that their pattern becomes random, then the solution is a logarithmic transformation of all values. If all that fails, re-specify the model.

The fifth assumption is that Xs are fixed, meaning their values don't change. But in the real world, it does not always happen that way. Variables that are within our control also change. We assumed that we would spend $10 million on advertising, but we spent only $9 million. We assumed that we would not raise the price, but we did. Often, we also have variables in a model that are not within our control. For example, we expected that the economy would grow by 3%, but it grew only by 2%. So, the best thing is to firm up the values at least of those variables that are within our control. Where we have no control, we should use them only if they are very vital to the model.

The OLS model will be the Best Linear Unbiased Estimator (BLUE) if all the above mentioned five assumptions are satisfied in the case of a simple regression model, and plus one more assumption, which is, X variables are not linearly correlated (i.e., there is no multicollinearity/collinearity), in the case of a multiple regression model.

SUGGESTED READING

1. Makridakis, Spyros, Steven C. Wheelwright, and Rob J. Hyndman. ***Forecasting: Methods and Applications.*** New York: John Wiley and Sons. 1998.
2. Wang, George C. S. and Chaman L. Jain. ***Regression Analysis: Modeling & Forecasting.*** New York: Graceway Publishing Company. 2003.
3. Wang, George C. S. "What You Should Know about Regression Based Forecasting." ***Journal of Business Forecasting.*** Winter 1993-'94, pp. 15-21.
4. Wang, George C. S. and Charles K. Akaby. "Heteroscedasticity: How to Handle in Regression Modeling." ***Journal of Business Forecasting.*** Summer 1994, pp. 11-17.
5. Wang, George C. S. "How to Handle Multicollinearity in Regression Modeling." ***Journal of Business Forecasting.*** Spring 1996. pp. 23-27.
6. Wang, George C. S. "Autocorrelation: Problems and Solutions in Regression Modeling." ***Journal of Business Forecasting.*** Winter 1994-'95, pp. 18-25.
7. Wilson, J. Holton, Barry Keating and John Galt Solutions, Inc. ***Business Forecasting.*** New York: McGraw Hill. 2007.

QUESTIONS FOR REVIEW

1. Explain where Cause-and-Effect models are most appropriate for forecasting.
2. What are the different models that fall in the category of Cause and Effect? Within that category of models, which one is used most in business, and why?
3. What steps are usually followed to develop a regression model?
4. What are the different diagnostic tests used in regression to validate a model? Explain three of the key diagnostic tests.
5. What are the key assumptions made in building an OLS regression model? Explain in detail four of them.
6. In what situations, are logit and probit models used? Explain.
7. Explain the assumption made in the OLS modeling that Xs are fixed.
8. Explain in brief the following:

a. Autocorrelation
b. Regression coefficient
c. Heteroscedasticity
d. Coefficient of determination

Simon Retail Store		
Period	Sales (Mil. of $)	Amount Spent on Advertisements (Mil. of $)
1	50	2
2	60	2
3	65	3
4	72	4
5	80	6
6	82	6
7	89	6
8	96	7
9	110	10
10	112	11

9. Simon Retail Store believes that its sales very much depend on the amount of money spent on advertisement. The table above gives the sales data and amount spent on advertising over the last 10 periods. Using the regression model, make a forecast of period 11, assuming that the amount spent on advertisements during that period would be $12 million. Answer: $122.71 million.

10. Explain in brief the following:
   a. Simple vs. multiple regression model
   b. Linear vs. curvilinear model
   c. Cross-sectional regression model
   d. Significance of F value in regression modeling

CHAPTER 23

MULTIPLE REGRESSION MODELS

In the previous chapter, we described simple regression models. In this chapter, we will discuss multiple regression models, where two or more independent variables are involved. In today's environment, business is affected not only by one single factor but also by multiple factors. The sales of a company may be driven by various internal factors such as advertising, price, and the number of new product launches, as well as by external factors such as GDP, interest rates, and competitive prices. The multiple regression models enable us to prepare forecasts where multiple factors are involved. There are different ways to build a multiple regression model; the one that is used most is the Ordinary Least Squares (OLS). This is the one we used in the previous chapter and this is the one we will describe here. The steps to build a model are the same as described in the previous chapter, which are: specification, estimation, validation and forecast.

Like simple regression, an OLS-based multiple regression model also makes the same five assumptions, plus one more. The sixth assumption is that X variables are not linearly correlated (i.e., no multicollinearity/collinearity). Multicollinearity makes the regression coefficients less stable, but it does not affect the ability of a model to forecast. However, it is difficult to isolate the contribution of X to Y. There are ways to handle this problem. Multicollinearity is a problem of multiple regression, not of simple regression because in that there is only one X.

BUILDING A MULTIPLE REGRESSION MODEL

Let us build a multiple regression model for Lovely Pharmacy Stores. The first step, like simple regression, is to plot the data of the dependent variable over time to see if the data have an outlier, seasonality, structural change, etc. To account for seasonality and outliers, the forecaster can use dummy variables, which we will describe later on. For a structural change, the forecaster may have to ignore the data prior to the change. To determine which independent variables to use, the forecaster, like simple regression, may like to first intuitively select all the variables that in his or her best judgment have a bearing on Y, and then verify them by correlating each with Y. Eliminate those variables that have a poor correlation.

Stepwise regression is another procedure for selecting variables that fit well. There are two approaches to stepwise regression: (1) Forward selection and (2) backward elimination. In the forward approach, we test variables one by one and include those in the model that are statistically significant. In the backward elimination, we start out with all the variables, and then weed out one at a time, keeping those that are statistically significant. This approach is particularly used where a large number of variables are involved.

Let us go back to the same example of Lovely Pharmacy Stores, used in the previous chapter, and make a forecast of Year 4-Q1, using multiple regression. As shown in Table 22.3 in the previous chapter, we intuitively selected four independent variables, which are average price per unit (P), media spending (M), gross domestic product (GDP), and personal consumption expenditure (PCE). From these, we selected two with the highest coefficient of correlation, GDP ($R = 0.89$) and PCE ($R = 0.88$). Quarterly data of sales, GDP and PCE are given in Table 23.1.

With two independent variables, the model becomes:

$$\text{Sales} = f(\text{GDP, PCE}) \qquad \ldots(23.1)$$

or

$$Y = a + b_1X_1 + b_2X_2 \qquad \ldots(23.2)$$

Here X_1 stands for GDP and X_2 for PCE. The next step is to estimate the model using the data of Year 1-Q1 through Year 3-Q4. We will use Microsoft Excel to perform the calculations. Table 23.2 gives output of the regression model, computed by Microsoft Excel. The estimated model becomes:

$$\hat{Y} = -3{,}708.4867 + 1.2559\, X_1 - 0.6054\, X_2 \qquad \ldots(23.3)$$

Table 23.1 | Lovely Pharmacy Stores | Sales, GDP, and PCE

Period	Sales (Mil. of $)	GDP (Bil. of $)	PCE (Bil. of $)
Year 1-Q1	2,693	7,630	5,131
Year 1-Q2	3,179	7,783	5,218
Year 1-Q3	2,989	7,859	5,264
Year 1-Q4	2,917	7,981	5,338
Year 2-Q1	3,054	8,124	5,430
Year 2-Q2	3,603	8,280	5,471
Year 2-Q3	3,403	8,391	5,576
Year 2-Q4	3,303	8,479	5,641
Year 3-Q1	3,485	8,635	5,713
Year 3-Q2	4,093	8,722	5,811
Year 3-Q3	3,887	8,829	5,893
Year 3-Q4	3,840	8,972	5,986
Year 4-Q1	4,016	9,104	6,095

Notes: 1. GDP stands for Gross Domestic Product.
2. PCE stands for Personal Consumption Expenditures.

Here Y hat ($\hat{Y}$) stands for a predictive value. The next step is validation to see how good the model is. Let us first look at the adjusted R^2, which is 0.75. It shows that the model explains only 75% of the variations in Y, and the rest are due to something else. The t values of both X_1 (0.7169) and X_2 (-0.2188) are far below the threshold of 2, and thus don't have a significant effect on Y. There *p* values also support the same conclusion. In each case, the value is above 0.5. (See Table 23.2) The insignificant t values of both X_1 and X_2 are the result of multicollinearity. Both GDP and PCE are highly correlated. Further, the negative regression coefficient of X_2 does not make any sense either. It is hard to imagine that sales are negatively related to PCE. This again is a result of multicollinearity.

***F Test*:** The F test measures the overall significance of a model. In other words, it measures the goodness of fit. Generally speaking, the larger the F value, the better it is. To conduct this test, we need two different degrees of freedoms, one associated with the numerator of F statistic (NDF), and the other associated with the denominator of F statistic (DDF), where:

$$NDF = k$$
$$DDF = n - k - 1$$

Again, n is the number of observations (which is 12, from Year 1-Q1 to Year 3-Q4), and k is the number of independent variables (which is 2). We also have to decide about the critical value. In our example, NDF is 2; DDF is equal to 9 = (12 - 2 - 1); and the critical value is 0.05 (95% level of confidence). With these, the F table gives a value of 4.26. (See Appendix D) But the calculated value of F is 17.29 (see Table 23.2). Since the calculated value is significantly greater than the table value, it means that we have a good regression model.

The DW statistic, which measures the autocorrelation, is 2.13. The model is valid if it falls between 1.75 and 2.25. It is within that limit. (Microsoft Excel does not give DW statistic. We manually computed it the same way as described in Table 22.5 in the previous chapter). Further, it states that PCE is inversely related to sales, which is contrary to the common belief.

Plus, in our model, there is an issue of multicollinearity because the coefficient of correlation between GDP and PCE is close to one. The standard error of this model is 215.79. When we compare these statistics with the model developed in the previous chapter with one independent variable, the model did not do well.

Forecast: In the real world, it is rare for a model to satisfy all the diagnostic tests. Despite some of the weaknesses, it is likely that the model may still yield a forecast, which is acceptable. Therefore, let us prepare the forecast of Year 4-Q1 with this model. To do that, we need GDP and PCE numbers of that period, which are given, and are $9,104 billion and $6,095 billion,

Table 23.2 | Lovely Pharmacy Stores | Sales Model Summary Output (Year 1-Q1 – Year 3-Q4)

Regression Statistics						
Multiple R				0.8908		
R Square				0.7935		
Adjusted R Square				0.7476		
Standard Error				215.7890		
Observations				12		
			ANOVA			
	Df		**SS**	**MS**	**F**	**Significance F**
Regression	2		1,609,958.826	804,979.4	17.28725	0.00082707
Residual	9		419,084.174	46,564.91		
Total	11		2,029,043.000			
	Coefficient	**Stand. Err**	**t Stat**	**p-Value**	**Lower 95%**	**Upper 95%**
Intercept	-3,708.4867	1,486.6496	-2.4945	0.0342	-7,071.5242	-345.452
X Variable 1	1.2559	1.7519	0.7169	0.4916	-2.7072	5.2189
X Variable 2	-0.6054	2.7666	-0.2188	0.8317	-6.8640	5.6531

Notes: 1. GDP stands for Gross Domestic Product.
2. PCE stands for Personal Consumption Expenditures.

respectively (see Table 23.1). The forecast comes to:

$$\hat{Y}_{04\text{-}Q1} = -3{,}708.4867 + (1.2559 \times 9{,}104) - (0.6054 \times 6{,}095) \quad \ldots(23.4)$$
$$= \$4{,}034.66 \text{ million}$$

Since the actual of this period is $4,016 million, the error comes to -0.46%, which is lower than what we experienced with the simple regression model developed in the previous chapter. From that we can conclude that diagnostic tests should be used as a guide, not as a bible. What matters in the end is how well a model forecasts. Also, whether or not a model is good should not be concluded just on the basis of one ex post forecast, but from a number of them—maybe from three or four ex post forecasts. Further, the regression models are based on average relationships. So, a good forecast in one period does not necessarily mean it is a good model. It may be just a coincidence. We will discuss this issue in more detail in the latter part of this chapter.

DUMMY VARIABLES

In regression modeling, seasonality and outliers are often handled with dummy variables. So it is important to know what they are and how they are used. The data of Lovely Pharmacy Stores, as mentioned before, has seasonality (see Figure 22.2 in the previous chapter), which has to be accounted for. Every year sales are the highest in the second quarter. We will demonstrate how to use dummy variables to account for seasonality by using the sales data of Lovely Pharmacy Stores.

Seasonality: Dummy variables assume the value of "zero" and "one." In the case of quarterly data, we add three independent variables, one less than the total number of quarters in a year. In the case of monthly data, we add 11, again, one less than the total number of months in a year. Table 23.3 shows how dummy variables were assigned in the model of Lovely Pharmacy Stores. It has now a total of five independent variables (X_1 through X_5): X_1 for GDP; X_2 for PCE; X_3 for Q1; X_4 for Q2; and X_5 for Q3. For the sales of Year 1-Q1, we put "one" under Q1 (X_3) and "zero" under all others, that is, for Q2 (X_4) and Q3 (X_5). For the sales of Year 1-Q2, we put "zero" under Q1 (X_3), "one" under Q2 (X_4) and "zero" under Q3 (X_5). Similarly, for the sales of Year 1-Q3, we put "zero" under Q1 (X_3) and Q2 (X_4), and "one" under Q3 (X_5). For the Year 1-Q4, we put "zero" under each, that is, for Q1 (X_3), Q2 (X_4), and Q3 (X_5). We do the same for all other periods. (See Table 23.3) Let us now build a model using five independent variables (X_1 through X_5) and the sales data from Year 1-Q1 through Year 3-Q4, as shown in the table. The output of this regression model is given in Table 23.4.

Table 23.3 | Lovely Pharmacy Stores | Using Dummy Variables to Capture Seasonality

Period	Sales (Mil. of $) Y	GDP (Bil. of $) X_1	PCE (Bil. of $) X_2	Q1 X_3	Q2 X_4	Q3 X_5
Year 1-Q1	2,693	7,630	5,131	1	0	0
Year 1-Q2	3,179	7,783	5,218	0	1	0
Year 1-Q3	2,989	7,859	5,264	0	0	1
Year 1-Q4	2,917	7,981	5,338	0	0	0
Year 2-Q1	3,054	8,124	5,430	1	0	0
Year 2-Q2	3,603	8,280	5,471	0	1	0
Year 2-Q3	3,403	8,391	5,576	0	0	1
Year 2-Q4	3,303	8,479	5,641	0	0	0
Year 3-Q1	3,485	8,635	5,713	1	0	0
Year 3-Q2	4,093	8,722	5,811	0	1	0
Year 3-Q3	3,887	8,829	5,893	0	0	1
Year 3-Q4	3,840	8,972	5,986	0	0	0
Year 4-Q1	4,016	9,104	6,095	1	0	0
Year 4-Q2	4,691	9,191	6,213	0	1	0
Year 4-Q3	4,571	9,341	6,320	0	0	1
Year 4-Q4	4,560	9,560	6,446	0	0	0

Table 23.4 | Lovely Pharmacy Stores | Sales Model Summary Output (Year 1-Q1 – Year 3-Q4)

Regression Statistics	
Multiple R	.9983
R Square	0.9966
Adjusted R Square	0.9937
Standard Error	33.89
Observations	12

ANOVA

	Df	SS	MS	F	Significance F
Regression	5	2,022,151	404,430.3	352.1047	2.56155E-07
Residual	6	6,891.648	1,148.608		
Total	11	2,029,043			

	Coefficient	Stand. Err	t Stat	*p*-Value	Lower 95%	Upper 95%
Intercept	-4,812.712	261.5929	-18.3977	1.66E-06	-5452.8074	-4172.617
X Variable 1	-0.0844	0.2899	-0.29128	.7806	-0.7937	0.6249
X Variable 2	1.5707	0.4608	3.4082	0.0144	0.44300	2.6983
X Variable 3	56.6822	29.5331	1.9193	0.1034	-15.5827	128.9472
X Variable 4	496.5429	29.5859	16.7831	2.86E-06	424.1488	568.9369
X Variable 5	184.2675	27.8667	6.6125	0.0006	116.0801	252.4550

Let us see how this model output (given in Table 23.4) compares with the output of the previous one, given in Table 23.2. It shows that the model has improved significantly over the previous one. The adjusted R^2 is now 0.99 (against 0.75); F value, 352.10 (against 17.29); t values are above 2 with the exceptions of X_1 and X_3; and standard error, 33.89 (against 215.79). The improvement resulted primarily from the inclusion of seasonality in the model. However, there is one problem. The regression coefficient of GDP (X_1) is negative, which is contrary to the common belief.

The revised model that accounts for seasonality comes to:

$$\hat{Y} = -4{,}812.712 - 0.0844\, X_1 + 1.5707\, X_2 + 56.6822\, X_3 + 496.5429\, X_4 + 184.2675\, X_5 \qquad \text{...(23.5)}$$

Let us now forecast the sales of Year 4-Q1 with this model. GDP and PCE of this period are \$9,104 billion and \$6,095 billion, respectively. For X_3, we plug in "one," because this is the forecast of Q1 period, and for all others, "zero." The revised forecast comes to:

$$\begin{aligned}\hat{Y}_{04\text{-}Q1} &= -4{,}812.712 + (-0.0844 \times 9{,}104) + (1.5707 \times 6{,}095) + \\ &\quad (56.6822 \times 1) + (496.5429 \times 0) + (184.2675 \times 0) \qquad \text{...(23.6)} \\ &= \$4{,}048.93 \text{ million}\end{aligned}$$

The forecast of \$4,048 million against the actual of \$4,016 million gives us an error of -0.82%. Since the error is fairly low, it raises a question: Which model should we use and why? We will discuss this later in the section, "Improving A Regression Model."

Outlier: If there is an outlier (unusual value) in the data, it has to be taken care of. Otherwise, it would weaken the efficiency of a model. In the previous section, we showed how to use dummy variables for capturing seasonality in the data. In this section, we will show how to handle an outlier(s), again with dummy variables. Since the data of Lovely Pharmacy Stores don't have any outlier, we will use the data of Goodwill Jewelry Company to demonstrate it. Table 23.5 gives 10-year data of sales and media spending for the company. The company had a strike in years 5 and 8. As such, sales in these two years dropped sharply. Therefore, they are not normal periods; they are outliers. To account for outliers, we add another independent variable, X_2. In the X_2 column, we assign a dummy variable of "zero" for periods with no strike, and "one" for those that had a strike. In other words, periods 5 and 8 get "one," and all other periods, "zero." Then the model becomes:

$$Y = a + b_1X_1 + b_2X_2 \qquad \text{...(23.7)}$$

Here Y stands for sales, X_1 for media spending, and X_2 for strike. The model when estimated, using the data given in Table 23.5, comes to:

$$\hat{Y} = 3.1289 + 4.4308X_1 - 18.1442X_2 \qquad \ldots(23.8)$$

To prepare a forecast of Year 11, we need to know how much would be spent on the media in that year, which is \$20 thousand (i.e., $X_1 = 20$). We are not expecting a strike in that year. In that case, X_2 will be "zero." With that, forecast of Year 11 will be:

$$\begin{aligned}\hat{Y}_{11} &= 3.1289 + 4.4308 \times 20 - 18.1442 \times 0 \qquad \ldots(23.9)\\ &= \$91.74 \text{ million}\end{aligned}$$

If the company had outliers resulting from a strike as well as from a fire at the plant, then we would have added two additional independent variables, one for strike and another for fire. A fire at the plant would also have created an outlier because with that sales would have dropped sharply. Dummy variables for a fire will be assigned the same way as for a strike, that is, "one" for the year in which there was a fire, and "zero" for others.

IMPROVING A REGRESSION MODEL

Although there is quite a science behind regression modeling, and modelers have developed ways to overcome problems including of autocorrelation, heteroscedasticity, and multicollinearity, they still have to make a judgment call at one point or the other because there is no such thing as

Table 23.5 | Goodwill Jewelry Company | Using Dummy Variables for Strike

Year (1)	Sales (Mil. of \$) Y (2)	Media Spending (Thou. of \$) X_1 (3)	Dummy Variables X_2 (4)
1	10	2	0
2	15	2	0
3	14	2	0
4	12	3	0
5	7	4	1
6	30	7	0
7	40	8	0
8	25	10	1
9	60	12	0
10	70	15	0
Average	**28.3**	**6.5**	

a perfect model, the model that satisfies all the OLS assumptions. It is not unusual for forecasters to go through numerous trials and errors to come up with the right model, a model they can live with. There are, however, simple ways that can help to improve a regression model beyond taking care of data-related problems such as of seasonality, outlier, and structural change. The ultimate objective is to satisfy the OLS assumptions; the more we do, the better would be the model statistics and, consequently, the forecasts. The model statistics are merely the symptoms of how well assumptions are satisfied. In our efforts to improve a model, we will concentrate on model statistics and forecasts.

Before attempting to improve a model, it is important to establish an error we can live with. With more and more efforts, we are likely to improve our model further, and, consequently, the forecasts. However, in the beginning, it would be easier to improve the forecast, but later on it would become more and more difficult and costly. Therefore, the objective should not only be to improve a forecast, but also at what cost. It won't pay if the incremental cost far exceeds the benefit. Here are three simple things we can do to improve a model:

1. Add or delete variables
2. Transform data
3. Try different regression models

Add or Delete Variables: As described earlier, we can determine which variable to use by calculating the coefficient of correlation between X and Y, but at times this may not be adequate. There are situations where a given variable alone may not work, but when combined with another it works. This may require some trials and errors. To alleviate somewhat the problem of multicollinearity, we can compute correlation coefficients of different independent variables, and then eliminate one of those that exhibits a strong relationship. Stepwise regression can also help in screening variables.

Data Transformation: Some of the model statistics (adjusted R^2, F value, t values, DW, etc.) may improve and, consequently, the forecasts, when data of one or more variables are transformed. In simple terms, the objective is to transform the data in such a way so that it becomes more and more associated with the dependent variable. Here are some of the transformations that can be used:

1. *Breaking down or aggregating some of the independent variables.* For example, total media spending can be broken down into direct mail, space, TV and radio, and then use each one as a separate independent variable. In other cases, we may do just the opposite, aggregate them.

2. *Converting current dollars into constant dollars, or the other way around.* For example, using GDP in current dollars instead of constant dollars, or the other way around.

3. *Using an interaction variable.* The interaction variable is the product of two variables. In Table 23.6, the product of GDP and PCE is used as one variable. In this case, we will have four independent variables, the interaction variable plus three dummy variables for seasonality.

4. *Using inverse transformation.* This is one divided by an independent variable (1/X). (See Table 23.7) It shows the inverse transformation of GDP and PCE. Here we have five independent variables in total. We can also divide one independent variable by another, which gives us another type of transformation.

5. *Using the second order polynomial.* Here we square each value of an independent variable. (See Table 23.8, where we square each value of GDP and PCE.). Here again we have a total of five independent variables.

6. *Using two different transformations.* We can also use two different transformations such as GDP/PCE as one transformation and GDP × PCE (interaction) another, as shown in Table 23.9.

Table 23.6 | Lovely Pharmacy Stores | An Example of Interaction Transformation

Period	Sales (Mil. of $) Y	GDP × PCE X_1	Q1 X_2	Q2 X_3	Q3 X_4
Year 1-Q1	2,693	39,145,715.0	1	0	0
Year 1-Q2	3,179	40,611,694.0	0	1	0
Year 1-Q3	2,989	41,367,418.3	0	0	1
Year 1-Q4	2,917	42,601,779.9	0	0	0
Year 2-Q1	3,054	44,112,507.6	1	0	0
Year 2-Q2	3,603	45,298,224.0	0	1	0
Year 2-Q3	3,403	46,787,376.0	0	0	1
Year 2-Q4	3,303	47,826,647.4	0	0	0
Year 3-Q1	3,485	49,328,301.0	1	0	0
Year 3-Q2	4,093	50,687,030.8	0	1	0
Year 3-Q3	3,887	52,032,828.6	0	0	1
Year 3-Q4	3,840	53,706,392.0	0	0	0
Year 4-Q1	4,016	55,491,611.2	1	0	0
Year 4-Q2	4,691	57,105,521.2	0	1	0
Year 4-Q3	4,571	59,034,185.9	0	0	1
Year 4-Q4	4,560	61,625,672.0	0	0	0

Table 23.7 | Lovely Pharmacy Stores | An Example of Inverse Transformation

Period	Sales (Mil. of $) Y	1/GDP X_1	1/PCE X_2	Q1 X_3	Q2 X_4	Q3 X_5
Year 1-Q1	2,693	0.00013106	0.00019491	1	0	0
Year 1-Q2	3,179	0.00012849	0.00019164	0	1	0
Year 1-Q3	2,989	0.00012724	0.00018998	0	0	1
Year 1-Q4	2,917	0.00012530	0.00018734	0	0	0
Year 2-Q1	3,054	0.00012309	0.00018417	1	0	0
Year 2-Q2	3,603	0.00012077	0.00018279	0	1	0
Year 2-Q3	3,403	0.00011918	0.00017934	0	0	1
Year 2-Q4	3,303	0.00011794	0.00017729	0	0	0
Year 3-Q1	3,485	0.00011581	0.00017505	1	0	0
Year 3-Q2	4,093	0.00011465	0.00017208	0	1	0
Year 3-Q3	3,887	0.00011326	0.00016968	0	0	1
Year 3-Q4	3,840	0.00011146	0.00016706	0	0	0
Year 4-Q1	4,016	0.00010984	0.00016406	1	0	0
Year 4-Q2	4,691	0.00010880	0.00016095	0	1	0
Year 4-Q3	4,571	0.00010705	0.00015823	0	0	1
Year 4-Q4	4,560	0.00010460	0.00015513	0	0	0

Table 23.8 | Lovely Pharmacy Stores | An Example of Second Order Polynomial Transformation

Period	Sales (Mil. of $) Y	$(GDP)^2$ X_1	$(PCE)^2$ X_2	Q1 X_3	Q2 X_4	Q3 X_5
Year 1-Q1	2,693	58,216,900	26,322,030.3	1	0	0
Year 1-Q2	3,179	60,575,089	27,227,524.0	0	1	0
Year 1-Q3	2,989	61,763,881	27,706,537.7	0	0	1
Year 1-Q4	2,917	63,696,361	28,493,176.4	0	0	0
Year 2-Q1	3,054	65,999,376	29,483,814.0	1	0	0
Year 2-Q2	3,603	68,558,400	29,929,652.6	0	1	0
Year 2-Q3	3,403	70,408,881	31,090,660.8	0	0	1
Year 2-Q4	3,303	71,893,441	31,816,368.4	0	0	0
Year 3-Q1	3,485	74,563,225	32,633,798.8	1	0	0
Year 3-Q2	4,093	76,073,284	33,772,370.0	0	1	0
Year 3-Q3	3,887	77,951,241	34,732,163.0	0	0	1
Year 3-Q4	3,840	80,496,784	35,832,196.0	0	0	0
Year 4-Q1	4,016	82,882,816	37,152,682.1	1	0	0
Year 4-Q2	4,691	84,474,481	38,603,854.2	0	1	0
Year 4-Q3	4,571	87,254,281	39,941,136.0	0	0	1
Year 4-Q4	4,560	91,393,600	41,553,494.4	0	0	0

7. *Converting a variable into a natural log.* We don't have to convert all the variables. We can convert one or more variables depending on what works.

8. *Lagging the data.* Independent variables can be lagged by one or more periods. If it is lagged by one period, then we can say that sales of current period are a function of, say, the GDP of the previous period. In other words, the sales of Year 1-Q2 are affected by the GDP of Year 1-Q1, sales of Year 1-Q3 are affected by the GDP of Year 1-Q2, and so on. (See Table 23.10)

This is by no means a complete list of ways the data can be transformed. In fact, every time we modify the data one way or the other, we land on a different transformation. We can try different transformations to see which one works, and which one does not.

Try Different Regression Models: The best way to arrive at the best model is not to test one model at a time but a number of them. With the technology we have, we can easily do it. Compare their model statistics as well as their ex post forecasts, and then choose the one that appears to be the best. (Ex post forecasts are forecasts of those periods for which actuals are known.) The best model should perform well not in just one period, but in a number of periods. Let us test nine

Table 23.9 | Lovely Pharmacy Stores | An Example of Two Transformations

Period	Sales (Mil. of $) Y	GDP/PCE X_1	GDP × PCE X_2	Q1 X_3	Q2 X_4	Q3 X_5
Year 1-Q1	2,693	1.4872	39,145,715.0	1	0	0
Year 1-Q2	3,179	1.4916	40,611,694.0	0	1	0
Year 1-Q3	2,989	1.4931	41,367,418.3	0	0	1
Year 1-Q4	2,917	1.4952	42,601,779.9	0	0	0
Year 2-Q1	3,054	1.4962	44,112,507.6	1	0	0
Year 2-Q2	3,603	1.5135	45,298,224.0	0	1	0
Year 2-Q3	3,403	1.5049	46,787,376.9	0	0	1
Year 2-Q4	3,303	1.5032	47,826,647.4	0	0	0
Year 3-Q1	3,485	1.5116	49,328,301.0	1	0	0
Year 3-Q2	4,093	1.5008	50,687,030.8	0	1	0
Year 3-Q3	3,887	1.4981	52,032,828.6	0	0	1
Year 3-Q4	3,840	1.4988	53,706,392.0	0	0	0
Year 4-Q1	4,016	1.4936	55,491,611.2	1	0	0
Year 4-Q2	4,691	1.4793	57,105,521.2	0	1	0
Year 4-Q3	4,571	1.4780	59,034,185.9	0	0	1
Year 4-Q4	4,560	1.4830	61,625,672.0	0	0	0

different models, given below, using the data of Lovely Pharmacy Stores, and test each one with four holdout periods:

1. $Y = f(X_1, X_2)$
2. $Y = f(X_1, X_2, DV)$
3. $Y = f(X_1, DV)$
4. $Y = f(X_2, DV)$
5. $Y = f(X_1 \times X_2, DV)$
6. $Y = f(1/X_1, 1/X_2, DV)$
7. $Y = f\{(X_1)^2, (X_2)^2, DV\}$
8. $Y = f(X_{1(t-1)}, X_{2\,(t-1)}, DV)$
9. $Y = f\{(X_1/X_2), (X_1 \times X_2), DV\}$

Here Y stands for sales, X_1 for GDP, X_2 for PCE, and DV for three dummy variables to capture seasonality. The objective here is to determine, among these nine models, which one is the best on the basis of model statistics as well as on their ex post forecasts. Since we don't want to depend on one set of observations, we create four different sub-models from each using four different time periods. In each case, we do not use the data of the period for which we want to forecast.

Table 23.10 | Lovely Pharmacy Stores | An Example of One Period Lag Transformation

Period	Sales (Mil. of $) Y	GDP Lagged by One Period X_1	PCE Lagged by One Period X_2	Q1 X_3	Q2 X_4	Q3 X_5
Year 1-Q1	2,693	—	—	1	0	0
Year 1-Q2	3,179	7,630	5,130.5	0	1	0
Year 1-Q3	2,989	7,783	5,218.0	0	0	1
Year 1-Q4	2,917	7,859	5,263.7	0	0	0
Year 2-Q1	3,054	7,981	5,337.9	1	0	0
Year 2-Q2	3,603	8,124	5,429.9	0	1	0
Year 2-Q3	3,403	8,280	5,470.8	0	0	1
Year 2-Q4	3,303	8,391	5,575.9	0	0	0
Year 3-Q1	3,485	8,479	5,640.6	1	0	0
Year 3-Q2	4,093	8,635	5,712.6	0	1	0
Year 3-Q3	3,887	8,722	5,811.4	0	0	1
Year 3-Q4	3,840	8,829	5,893.4	0	0	0
Year 4-Q1	4,016	8,972	5,986.0	1	0	0
Year 4-Q2	4,691	9,104	6,095.3	0	1	0
Year 4-Q3	4,571	9,191	6,213.2	0	0	1
Year 4-Q4	4,560	9,341	6,319.9	0	0	0

Therefore, with each model, we first create a sub-model using the data of Year 1-Q1 through Year 3-Q4, and prepare the forecast of the next quarter, which is, Year 4-Q1. Then, we add one more quarter, that is, we generate another sub-model using now the data of Year 1-Q1 through Year 4-Q1, and prepare the forecast of Year 4-Q2. Now we add one more quarter, and generate another sub-model by using the data of Year 1-Q1 through Year 4-Q2, and prepare the forecast of Year 4-Q3. Again, we generate another model using now the data of Year 1-Q1 through Year 4-Q3 to prepare the forecast of Year 4-Q4. The output of each model of each period is given in Table 23.11.

Table 23.11 | Lovely Pharmacy Stores | Results of Nine Different Models

Yr–04	X_1,X_2 1	X_1,X_2, DV 2	X_1,DV 3	X_2,DV 4	$X_1 \times X_2$, DV 5	$1/X_1$, $1/X_2$, DV 6	$(X_1)^2$, $(X_2)^2$, DV 7	$X_{1(t-1)}$, $X_{2(t-1)}$, DV 8	(X_1/X_2), $(X_1 \times X_2)$, DV 9
					Adjusted R^2				
Q1	0.748	0.994	0.984	0.995	0.994	0.990	0.995	0.992	0.995
Q2	0.792	0.995	0.986	0.995	0.995	0.992	0.995	0.994	0.996
Q3	0.826	0.997	0.981	0.997	0.995	0.995	0.997	0.995	0.997
Q4	0.864	0.997	0.979	0.997	0.995	0.995	0.998	0.996	0.997
Avg.	**0.808**	**0.996**	**0.983**	**0.996**	**0.995**	**0.993**	**0.996**	**0.994**	**0.996**
					F Statistic				
Q1	17.29	352.10	173.74	506.30	472.66	214.14	429.42	235.23	431.28
Q2	23.78	459.93	214.27	657.04	638.91	296.87	524.20	338.68	532.61
Q3	31.89	776.92	174.67	1010.36	677.81	505.29	875.29	530.15	859.25
Q4	45.66	930.11	164.42	1043.65	697.49	510.04	1149.30	726.36	1088.94
Avg.	**29.65**	**629.76**	**181.77**	**804.34**	**621.72**	**381.59**	**744.55**	**457.60**	**728.02**
					t Value				
Q1	X_1 = .7 X_2 = -.2	X_1 =-0.1 X_2 = 1.6	X_1=23.1	X_1=39.5	X_1=38.2	X_1 = 1.2 X_2 = 3.6	X_1 = 0.4 X_2= -3.1	X_1 = 0.5 X_2 = 2.3	X_1 = -1.4 X_2 = 34.5
Q2	X_1 = .9 X_2 = -.3	X_1 = 00 X_2 = 3.8	X_1=28.1	X_1=49.2	X_1=48.6	X_1 = 1.4 X_2 = -4.5	X_1 = 1.0 X_2= -3.1	X_1 = 0.5 X_2 = 2.9	X_1 = -1.2 X_2 = 46.3
Q3	X_1 = -.5 X_2 = 1.3	X_1 = 0.2 X_2 = 0.3	X_1=23.4	X_1=56.4	X_1=46.2	X_1 = 2.7 X_2 = -7.1	X_1 = 0.5 X_2 = 5.6	X_1 =-0.1 X_2 = 3.9	X_1 = -2.5 X_2 = 58.0
Q4	X_1 = -.5 X_2 = 1.5	X_1 =-1.5 X_2 = 7.8	X_1=23.2	X_1=58.4	X_1=47.8	X_1 =-3.4 X_2 = -7.9	X_1 = 0.1 X_2 = 7.0	X_1 = -.9 X_2 = 6.6	X_1 = -3.2 X_2 = 63.7
					Absolute % Error				
Q1	0.48	0.82	1.54	0.63	0.24	0.18	1.12	0.20	1.03
Q2	13.49	1.06	4.55	1.06	2.08	1.20	1.09	1.47	1.18
Q3	0.80	1.25	4.37	1.61	1.97	2.21	0.80	1.03	0.95
Q4	4.44	0.72	2.73	1.04	0.47	2.57	0.25	0.80	0.16
Avg.	**4.80**	**0.96**	**3.30**	**1.09**	**1.19**	**1.54**	**0.82**	**0.88**	**0.83**

Note: DV= Dummy variables

To select the best one from these nine models is not that straight forward. As we will see, there will be some judgment involved. To evaluate each model, we will look at their adjusted R^2, F value, and t values, along with their ex posts. Since we have four outputs of each model, we will concentrate on the averages of four (with the exception of t values) rather than on their individual values.

Adjusted R^2: The average highest adjusted R^2 is .996, which is fairly good. The model explains 99.6% of the variations in the dependent variable, which is great. The models that have this value are model no. 2, 4, 7, and 9.

F value: The F value, as mentioned before, measures the overall significance of a model; the higher the value, the better it is. Model no. 4 has the highest value, which is 804.34.

t values: The t values measure the significance of a variable; the higher the value, the better it is. Normally, the variable with a t value of two or more is considered significant. In the table, we have t values only of X_1 and X_2 variables, and not of dummy variables. In terms of t values, it appears that the best model is no. 4.

Ex post forecasts: Among all the nine models, the model with the lowest Mean Absolute Percentage Error (MAPE) is model no. 7 (.82%).

So, we can see that the selection is not that straight forward. On the basis of MAPE, the winner is model no. 7. But if we evaluate on the basis of adjusted R^2, and F and t values, model no. 4 appears to be the best, even though its MAPE is not the lowest.

"WHAT-IF" SCENARIOS

The regression model is used not only to prepare a forecast but also to provide answers to "what-if" scenarios to determine the best course of action to achieve a given objective. If, for example, the forecast is not meeting the sales objective of management, it can help to determine the course of action needed to hit it. In other words, how much should the price be lowered, how much should the media spending be increased, and/or how much any other variable over which the company has control should be changed to accomplish the objective. Suppose the sales of a company depend on the price it charges and the amount it spends on different media. Hypothetically, the model developed from the historical data comes to:

$$\hat{Y} \quad = \quad 120 - .4\, X_1 + 5\, X_2 \qquad \ldots(23.10)$$

where

$$\hat{Y} = \text{Predicted sales (millions of dollars)}$$
$$X_1 = \text{Average price}$$
$$X_2 = \text{Media spending (millions of dollars)}$$

If

$$X_1 = \$10 \text{ per unit}$$
$$X_2 = \$\ 2 \text{ million}$$

then

$$\hat{Y}_{t+1} = 120 - (.4)(10) + (5)(2) \quad \ldots(23.11)$$
$$= 120 - 4 + 10$$
$$= \$126 \text{ million}$$

This means that if the company sticks with its current plan, total sales of the next period are expected to be $126 million. But management wants to hit the sales target of $130 million. The sales forecast won't change itself. We have to do something about it. Let us say we can change media spending. Then the question is how much must be spent on the media to hit the target? We can determine this by solving the equation 23.10 for X_2, where $\hat{Y}$= $130 million and price =$10 per unit:

$$130 = 120 - (.4)(10) + (5)(X_2) \quad \ldots(23.12)$$
$$X_2 = \$2.8 \text{ million}$$

This implies that if we raise the media spending to $2.8 million, everything else remaining constant, we will be able to hit the sales target of $130 million.

ESTIMATING THE ELASTICITY

Elasticity measures the sensitivity of a dependent variable to different independent variables. In other words, how demand is sensitive to price, media spending, or any other driver. Demand is highly sensitive (elastic) if a small change in price causes a great change in demand. If this is the case, the demand planners can significantly increase their demand by slightly lowering the price, and vice versa. If, on the other hand, demand planners find that their demand is insensitive (inelastic) to media spending, they can reduce media spending without losing much demand. Therefore, for best planning, demand planners need not only forecasts but also the elasticities of different business drivers, which the regression can provide. The formula for measuring elasticity is:

$$\text{Elasticity} = \frac{\Delta Y/\bar{Y}}{\Delta X/\bar{X}} \text{ or } b\frac{\bar{X}}{\bar{Y}} \quad \ldots(23.13)$$

where

$\bar{X}$ = Mean of X (media spending)

$\bar{Y}$ = Mean of Y (sales)

b = Regression coefficient

Let us calculate the elasticity of media spending with respect to sales based on the data given in Table 23.5 and Equation 23.8 ($\hat{Y} = 3.1289 + 4.4308\ X_1 - 18.1442\ X_2$). As shown in the table, $\bar{X} = 6.5$ and $\bar{Y} = 28.3$. Then the elasticity of advertisement comes to:

$$E(\text{Adv.Exp.}) = b\frac{\bar{X}}{\bar{Y}} = 4.4308\ \frac{6.5}{28.3} = 1.02 \qquad ...(23.14)$$

This means if we increase the media spending expenditure by 1%, the demand will increase by 1.02%. As a rule, when elasticity is more than one, it is considered elastic, and when less than one, inelastic.

THINGS TO KEEP IN MIND

In preparing a regression model, keep in mind the following:

1. The independent variables we use should not only be statistically valid but also theoretically sound. In other words, each independent variable should have a logical relationship with the dependent variable.

2. Each independent variable should have the correct sign. For example, the relationship between price and unit sales should be negative. If we come up with a positive sign, make sure we can ewplain why. Maybe a higher price gives the perception of better quality; as such, sales go up with an increase in price. In the beer industry, there are many beer packages that are rarely promoted. However, price is generally increased once or twice a year to keep up with inflation. So, if sales are growing, the coefficient on price will be positive, which may imply that the model has been miss-specified. In this case, it may be better to use price in constant dollars (deflated by CPI) rather than the current (actual) price.

3. Because of the changing market dynamics it is not unusual to find a model that worked well in the past but is not working now. So it is important to monitor regularly the performance of a model. It may be the time to re-specify it.

4. Statistics such as adjusted R_2, F, DW, and t should be used as a guide and not as a bible to arrive at an optimum model. At times, you may find that even a model with one or two

unsatisfactory statistics gives forecasts that are acceptable. In other words, don't invalidate a model just because one or two statistics are not up to par.

5. The ultimate goal of a forecaster is to come up with a model that gives forecasts we can live with. Therefore, in the model validation process, we should also look at, among other things, ex post forecasts.

6. Because of interaction among different variables, a certain independent variable may work well in conjunction with other variables, and not when used alone.

7. A good forecasting model does not have to have all the relevant variables. All it needs is a few important variables. If two models yield more or less the same result, the one with fewer variables should be preferred over the other (Principle of Parsimony). Also, keep in mind that degrees of freedom decrease as we add more variables. Other things remaining constant, the larger the degree of freedom, the better the model is.

8. How much data we need for regression modeling depends on, among other things, the number of observations. The rule of thumb is to have at least five observations for each independent variable.

9. Make sure the model we use remains stable. A model is stable if its estimated coefficients do not fluctuate widely and/or their signs do not change—from a positive to negative or from a negative to positive—when updated. Otherwise, the model structure no longer represents the true relationship. Some of the independent variables might have become less important. An unstable model often signals the presence of multicollinearity in the data.

10. To keep a model robust, it should be updated regularly. As a rule of thumb, the monthly model should be updated quarterly, and the quarterly model, twice a year. Updating includes not only updating data points but also the model structure.

11. In some cases, the independent variable has to be forecasted. If that variable is not quite forecastable, find a close substitute or lag it. If nothing works, re-specify the model.

SUGGESTED READING

1. Makridakis, Spyros, Steven C. Wheelwright, and Rob J. Hyndman. ***Forecasting: Methods and Applications.*** New York: John Wiley and Sons. 1998.
2. Ovedovitz, Albert C. ***Business Statistics in Brief.*** Cincinnati, Ohio: South-Western College Publishing. 2001.
3. Wang, George C. S. "What You Should Know about Regression Based Forecasting." ***Journal of Business Forecasting.*** Winter 1993-'94, pp. 15-21.
4. Wang, George C. S. "How to Handle Multicollinearity in Regression Modeling." ***Journal of Business Forecasting.*** Spring 1996, pp. 23-27.
5. Wang, George C. S. "Autocorrelation: Problems and Solutions in Regression Modeling." ***Journal of Business Forecasting.*** Winter 1994-'95, pp. 18-25.
6. Wang, George C. S. and Chaman L. Jain. ***Regression Analysis: Modeling & Forecasting.*** New York: Graceway Publishing Company. 2003.
7. Wang, George C. S. and Charles K. Akaby. "Heteroscedasticity: How to Handle in Regression Modeling." ***Journal of Business Forecasting.*** Summer 1994, pp. 11-17.
8. Wilson, J. Holton, Barry Keating, and John Galt Solutions, Inc. ***Business Forecasting.*** New York: McGraw Hill. 2007.

QUESTIONS FOR REVIEW

1. How do we account for seasonality in a regression model? Explain.
2. How do we account for an outlier in a regression model? Explain.
3. Describe four things a forecaster should keep in mind while building a regression model.
4. Explain what role "what-if" scenarios play in the planning process, and how does a regression model help?
5. What do we mean by data transformation? What is the purpose of doing it in regression modeling?
6. Explain in brief the following:
   a. Simple vs. multiple regression
   b. Multicollinearity
   c. Step-wise regression
   d. F test
   e. Principle of parsimony

BLAIR HOUSE ENTERPRISE			
Period	Net Sales (Mil. of $)	Advertising Exp. (Mil. of $)	R& D (Mil. of $)
1	7,014	4.24	70.30
2	6,935	4.05	77.90
3	7,224	4.52	71.80
4	8,843	5.49	85.20
5	6,773	4.16	77.40
6	7,019	4.03	114.40
7	6,874	4.10	85.50
8	8,789	4.94	98.70
9	6,625	3.94	85.50
10	6,640	4.09	94.50
11	6,939	4.41	88.00
12	9,063	5.69	105.30
13	7,396	4.66	91.90
14	8,059	5.17	97.10
15	8,403	5.57	88.50
16	10,333	6.81	105.00

7. The table above gives the sales data, as well as its advertising and R&D expenses of last 16 periods of Blair House Enterprise. The forecaster has found that the sales of its company depend very much on the amount spent on advertisement as well as on R&D.
   a. Using the data of periods 1 through 15, forecast the sales of period 16. The amounts to be spent on advertisement and R&D in that period are also given in the table.
   b. Compute the percentage error of the forecast of period 16. The actual of that period is given in the table.

   Answers: a. $10,484.01 million
   b. -1.46%

8. In the example given in question 7, the sales forecast of period 16 comes to $10,484.01 million. If the management wants to hit the target of $11,250 million, what does it have to do to achieve it? The management is willing to increase the amount spent on R&D. Answer: $194.36 million
9. What is elasticity? What role does it play in demand planning?

SLOAN TOOL COMPANY						
Period	Sales (Mil. of $) Y	Media Spending (Mil. of $) X_1	Unemployment Rate X_2	Q1 X_3	Q2 X_4	Q3 X_5
Year 1 Q1	312.80	10.13	6.4			
Year 1 Q2	329.20	10.21	6.0			
Year 1 Q3	419.30	10.40	6.0			
Year 1 Q4	534.50	10.47	5.5			
Year 2 Q1	346.70	10.57	6.1			
Year 2 Q2	355.70	10.67	5.5			
Year 2 Q3	445.00	10.75	5.4			
Year 2 Q4	560.40	10.82	5.1			
Year 3 Q1	411.90	10.91	5.6			
Year 3 Q2	401.40	11.00	5.0			
Year 3 Q3	520.70	11.12	5.0			
Year 3 Q4	687.20	11.16	4.7			
Year 4 Q1	546.80	11.32	5.0			
Year 4 Q2	571.60	11.39	4.6			
Year 4 Q3	704.90	11.43	4.7			
Year 4 Q4	961.40	11.53	4.1			

10. In the sales data of Sloan Tool Company, given above, there appears to be seasonality in the data. Indicate how in a regression based modeling dummy variables should be assigned to capture seasonality.

CHAPTER 24

BOX-JENKINS

The Box-Jenkins models, named after their authors, George Box and Gwilym Jenkins, are essentially Time Series models that are based on a single time series. Since they work very much like regression and the knowledge of regression is needed to understand them, we decided to discuss them after the chapters on regression. These models are also called ARIMA (Autoregressive-Integrated-Moving Average) models. The difference between regression models and ARIMA models is that in regression modeling we regress the dependent variable on the independent variables, whereas in ARIMA modeling, we regress the value of the current period on the past values. In other words, these models assume that the sales of a company depend on the sales of one period before (lag of one period), two periods before (lag of two periods), and so on.

The ARIMA models, like other Time Series models, are most suitable for short-term forecasting (daily, weekly, or monthly). Their models are based primarily on two assumptions: One, the data series is either stationary or can be converted into one. The data are considered stationary if there is no significant growth or decline in the data. In other words, their mean value does not change over time (meaning, the data fluctuate around a constant mean), and variance remains essentially constant over time. The reason why we need a stationary series is because with that we can develop a model with fixed coefficients estimated from the historical observations as we do in regression. Two, the behavior pattern of underlying explanatory variables that are not included in the models do not change drastically from the past. Whether or not a series is stationary usually can be determined by plotting the data. In the real world, however, we rarely come across a stationary series, which is fine as long as we can convert it into one.

OVERVIEW OF ARIMA MODELS

Before learning how to prepare a forecast with ARIMA models, it is important to know what kinds of models are available in this category, how they differ from each other, and where each one is used. Basically, there are three types of ARIMA models: (1) AR (Autoregressive), (2) MA (Moving Average), and (3) ARMA (combination of AR and MA). The letter 'I' in ARIMA implies differencing, which is used, if necessary, to make the data stationary.

AR Models: The AR models are autoregressive because here the dependent variable is regressed on a variable(s) within the series. For example, the sales of the current period are regressed on the sales of one period before, two periods before, and so on. The AR models take this form:

$$Y_t = C + B_1 Y_{t-1} + B_2 Y_{t-2} + \dots + B_p Y_{t-p} + e_t \qquad \dots(24.1)$$

where

Y_t = Dependent variable

C = Constant

$Y_{t-1}, Y_{t-2}, \dots Y_{t-p}$ = Independent variables (lagged values of the dependent variable)

$B_1, B_2, \dots B_p$ = Regression coefficients

e_t = Error term (white noise) representing the effect of random events on the dependent variable, not explained by the model

These models can have different numbers of autoregressive terms. If an AR model has only one autoregressive term, it is called an AR (1) model, meaning it is based on one independent variable, Y_{t-1}. If it has two autoregressive terms, it is called an AR (2), meaning the model is based on two independent variables, Y_{t-1} and Y_{t-2}, and so on. We will discuss later how to decide on the number of terms.

MA Models: The MA models assume that Y_t (dependent variable) depends on the past errors (residuals). They are called moving average because they use a weighted moving average of a fixed number of forecast errors produced in the past. But unlike the traditional moving average, weights assigned in the MA models do not add up to 1. In these models, the weight for each term is statistically determined by the pattern of data, and thus their weights don't add up to 1. However, in computing the weighted average the most recent value usually gets a larger weight than the more distant ones. Their models take this form:

$$Y_t = C + W_1e_{t-1} + W_2e_{t-2} - \ldots + W_qe_{t-q} + e_t \qquad \ldots(24.2)$$

where

Y_t = Dependent variable
C = Constant
W_1 = Weight assigned
e_t = Error (residual) of time period t
$e_{t-1}, e_{t-2}, \ldots e_{t-q}$ = Error value of period t_{-1}, t_{-2}, and so on
q = Number of terms

Since we use past errors as explanatory variables in MA models, we regress the dependent variable on the past errors (residuals).

ARMA Models: In these models, we combine both AR and MA models, and the model takes the form of:

$$Y_t = C + B_1Y_{t-1} + B_2Y_{t-2} + \ldots + B_pY_{t-p} + e_t + W_1e_{t-1} + W_2e_{t-2} + \ldots + W_qe_{t-q} \qquad \ldots(24.3)$$

ARIMA Models: They are another category of ARIMA models. If the data are not stationary, we convert them by differencing. With that, the model becomes ARIMA, which is often expressed as ARIMA (p, d, q), where:

p (AR) = Number of autoregressive terms
d (I) = Number of differencing
q(MA) = Number of moving average terms

Here the model is a combination of three components—p (number of autoregressive terms—AR), d (number of differences—I), and q (number of moving average terms—MA). Again, differencing is done to convert the non-stationary series into a stationary one. Table 24.1 shows how data are differenced. Column 3 gives data with first degree of differencing where data are differenced once, and Column 4, second degree of differencing where data are differenced twice. We continue differencing until the data become stationary. Normally, it is not necessary to go beyond second degree of differencing.

So far we have explained the structure of a non-seasonal ARIMA model. When we add seasonality into a model it becomes:

ARIMA $(p, d, q)(P, D, Q)^s$

Table 24.1 | Amazing Shoe Store | Differenced Sales Data

Month (1)	Sales (Mil. of $) Y (2)	Y' First Degree of Differencing $(Y_t - Y_{t-1})$ (3)	Y" Second Degree of Differencing $(Y'_t - Y'_{t-1})$ (4)
1	20	–	–
2	24	(24-20) = 4	–
3	29	(29-24) = 5	(5-4) = 1
4	31	(31-29) = 2	(2-5) = -3
5	38	(38-31) = 7	(7-2) = 5
6	39	(39-38) = 1	(1-7) = -6
7	40	(40-39) = 1	(1-1) = 0
8	43	(43-40) = 3	(3-1) = 2
9	45	(45-43) = 2	(2-3) = -1
10	49	(49-45) = 4	(4-2) = 2

Here "s" is the number of periods per season, for example, 4 for quarterly data, and 12 for monthly data. The lower case p, d, q represent the non-seasonal component of the model, that is, non-seasonal AR, I and MA. The upper case P, D, Q, on the other hand, represent seasonal AR, I, and MA. How their values are determined will be discussed in the next section.

MODELING APPROACH

There are four steps to forecasting with ARIMA models:

1. Model identification
2. Model estimation
3. Model checking
4. Forecasting

***Model Identification*:** Among these four steps, the identification of a model is the most difficult because it requires not only the knowledge of ARIMA theory but also experience in the area, because a number of trials and errors are needed to arrive at an appropriate model.

The first step in model identification is to determine whether or not the data series is stationary. The series is stationary if the data points are scattered horizontally around a constant mean, and its mean value does not change over time. If the series is not stationary, it can be converted into a stationary series by the method of differencing. If there is a trend in the data, but no seasonality, the simple differencing will do. The simple differencing could be of first order, second order or more; but often first order is enough. The moment we determine the kind of differencing needed, the value of *I* for the non-seasonal component of the model is specified. If we do first order of simple differencing, then *I* will be one for the non-seasonal component of the model, if we do second order of simple differencing, *I* will be two, and so on. If there is seasonality in the data, the seasonal differencing will be needed. For a monthly seasonality, data have to be differenced by the lag of 12 for monthly data, and for quarterly seasonality, by the lag of 4. If we do the first order seasonal differencing, irrespective of whether for monthly or quarterly data, *I* will be equal to one for the seasonal component of the model. The plot of data often gives an indication whether the data have trend, seasonality, or both. If, for example, we do first degree (order) of simple differencing as well as seasonal differencing and use the quarterly data, then the model will be expressed as:

$$\text{ARIMA}\ (p, 1, q)\ (P, 1, Q)^4$$

↙ ↘

(Non-Seasonal Component) (Seasonal Component)

Here the first component of the model is non-seasonal and the second one is seasonal. Once the value of *I* is specified, the next step is to specify the value (term) of the autoregressive and moving average, that is, the value of p (AR) and q (MA). To determine the value of p and q, we follow the theoretical distributions of autocorrelation coefficients (ACF) and partial autocorrelation coefficients (PACF). (The plot of autocorrelation and partial autocorrelation coefficients is called a correlogram.) The ACF describes the correlation between values of the same time series at different time lags, whereas, the PACF describes the correlation between current values of a variable and earlier values of the same variable when the effects of all the intervening time lags are held constant. In other words, if we calculate the partial autocorrelation between Y_t and Y_{t-2}, we keep the effect of the intervening value Y_{t-1} constant. The value of both the autocorrelation coefficient and partial autocorrelation coefficient varies between 0 and 1, which may be positive or negative. To determine the value of p and q, we have to match the distribution of coefficients of ACF and PACF of a sample series with the theoretical ones, given in Figures 24.1 through 24.3. It is difficult, however, to match 100% the distribution of coefficients of a sample series with the theoretical ones. So, we try to match as closely as we can to determine their values. Here are some rules that are used to identify the values of p and q on the basis of ACF and PACF after data have been made stationary with a simple or seasonal differencing or both. If the data are stationary to begin with, then no differencing will be needed.

AR models: Here are the rules for identifying an AR model as well as its term.

1. If the autocorrelation coefficients decrease exponentially to zero, and the accompanying partial autocorrelation coefficients have only one spike (negative or positive) significantly different from zero, then the value of *p* will be 1 (AR=1). The model will be written as (1, 0, 0), assuming the data were not differenced. The value of a coefficient is usually considered significantly different from zero if the spike is located outside the control limits of 95% confidence interval. (Most software programs that generate a correlogram also give the confidence interval). Figures 24.1A and 24.1B show such a distribution of coefficients where AR=1.

2. If the autocorrelation coefficients decrease exponentially to zero with alternating positive and negative values, and partial autocorrelation coefficients have one spike (negative or positive) significantly different from zero, then the value of *p* will be 1 (AR=1). The model will be expressed as: (1, 0, 0). Again, it is assumed here that the data were not differenced. (See Figures 24.1C and 24.1 D)

3. If the autocorrelation coefficients decrease exponentially to zero, and the accompanying partial autocorrelation coefficients have two spikes (both positive) significantly different from zero, then the value of p will be 2 (AR=2). The model will be expressed as: (2, 0, 0). Again, it is assumed here that the data were not differenced. (See Figures 24.1E and 24.1F)

4. If the autocorrelation coefficients decrease exponentially to zero with alternating positive and negative values and the partial autocorrelation coefficients have two spikes (one negative and one positive) significantly different from zero, then the value of *p* will still be 2 (AR=2). The model will be expressed as: (2, 0, 0). It is assumed here again that the data were not differenced. (See Figures 24.1G and 24.1H)

MA models: Here are the rules for identifying a MA model and determining its term.

1. If the autocorrelation coefficients have one spike (negative or positive) significantly different from zero, and the accompanying partial autocorrelation coefficients decrease exponentially to zero, then the value of q will be 1 (MA=1). The model will be expressed as: (0, 0, 1). Again, it is assumed here that the data were not differenced. (See Figures 24.2A and 24.2B)

Figure 24.1 | Theoretical Profile of AR Models | AR (1) Models

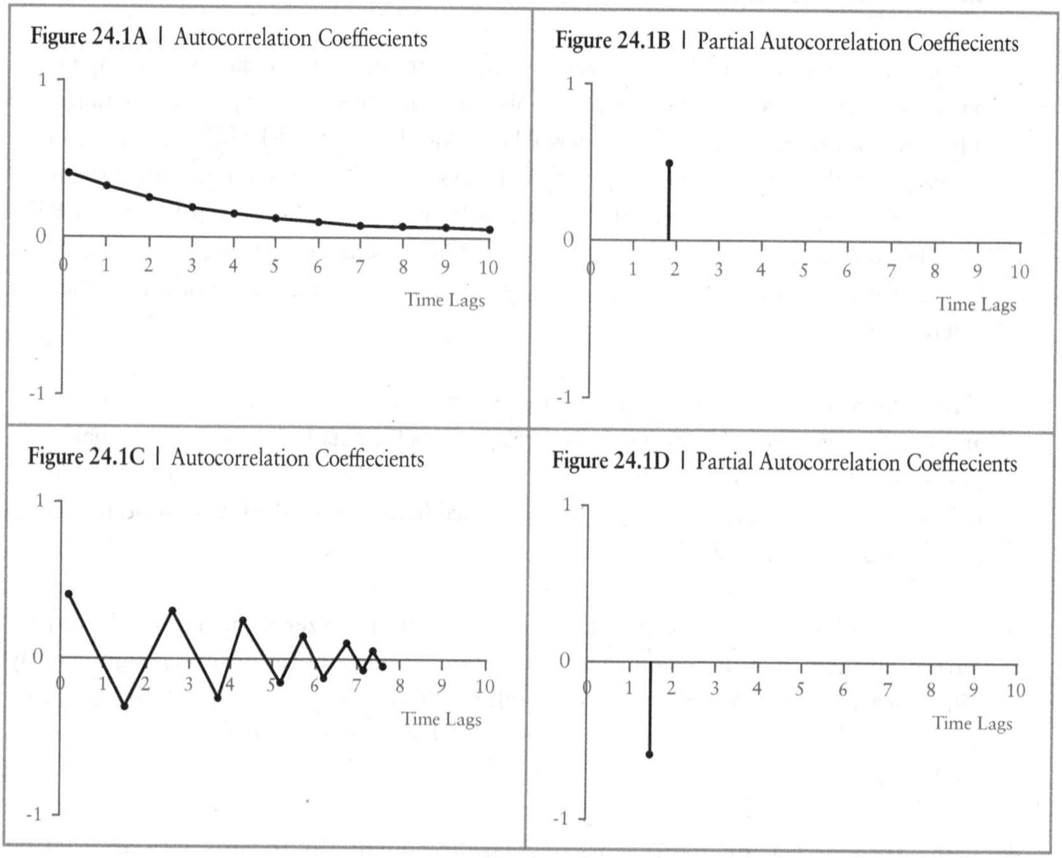

Figure 24.1A | Autocorrelation Coeffiecients

1
0
-1
0 1 2 3 4 5 6 7 8 9 10
Time Lags

Figure 24.1B | Partial Autocorrelation Coeffiecients

1
0
-1
0 1 2 3 4 5 6 7 8 9 10
Time Lags

Figure 24.1C | Autocorrelation Coeffiecients

1
0
-1
0 1 2 3 4 5 6 7 8 9 10
Time Lags

Figure 24.1D | Partial Autocorrelation Coeffiecients

1
0
-1
0 1 2 3 4 5 6 7 8 9 10
Time Lags

Figure 24.1 | Theoretical Profile of AR Models | AR (2) Models

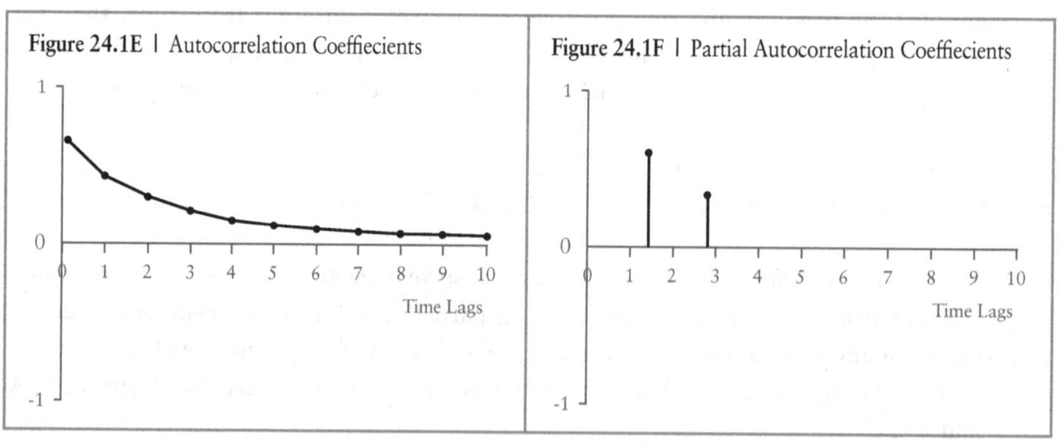

Figure 24.1 | Theoretical Profile of AR Models | AR (2) Models

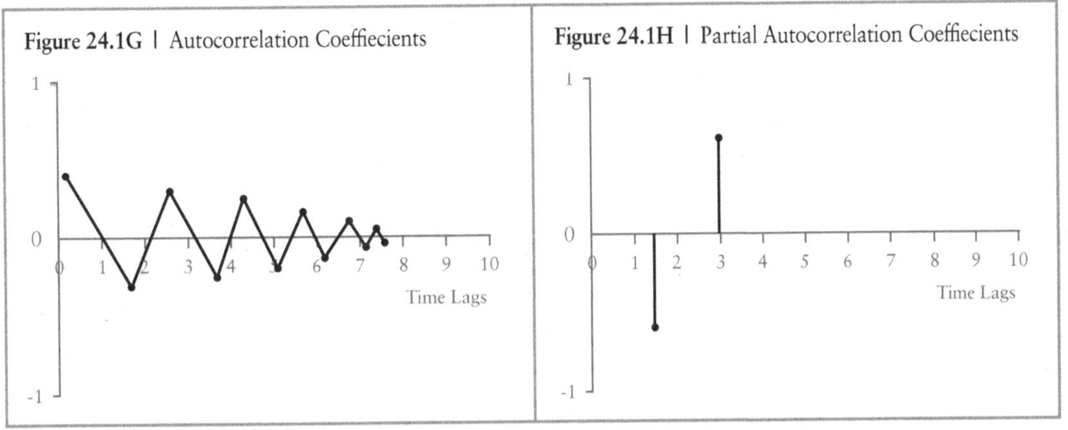

Figure 24.2 | Theoretical Profile of MA Models | MA (1) Models

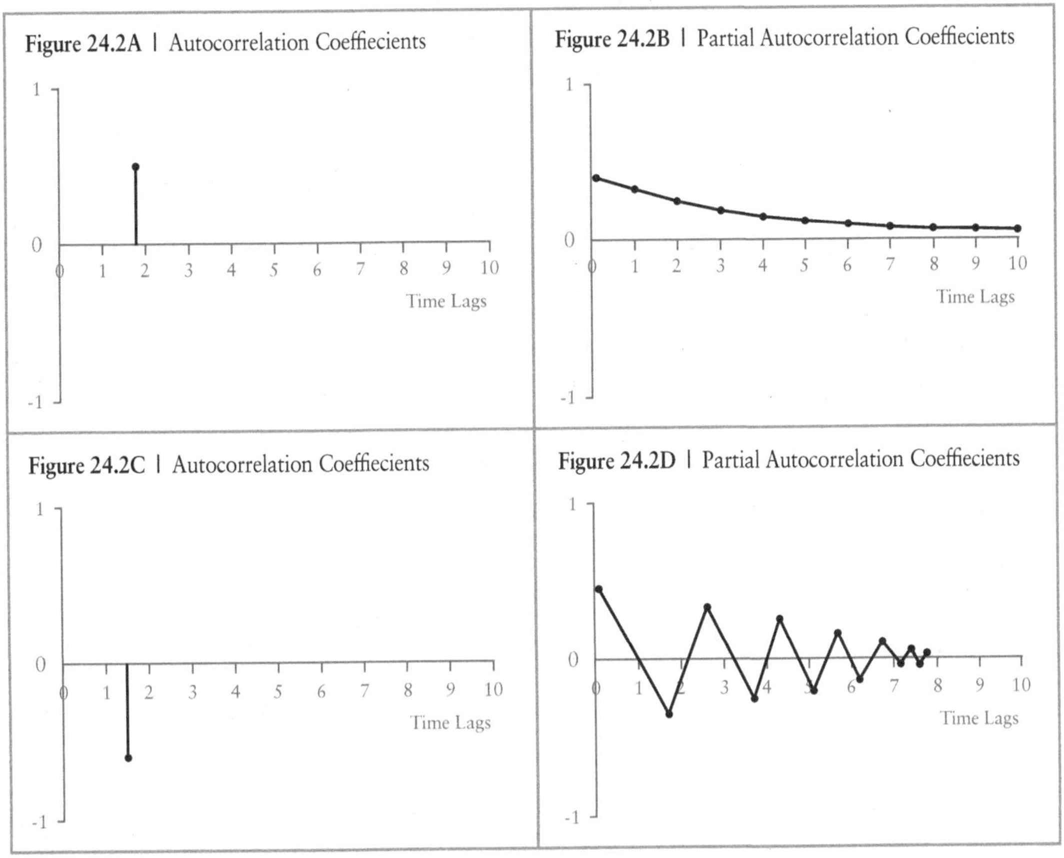

Figure 24.2A | Autocorrelation Coeffiecients

Figure 24.2B | Partial Autocorrelation Coeffiecients

Figure 24.2C | Autocorrelation Coeffiecients

Figure 24.2D | Partial Autocorrelation Coeffiecients

Figure 24.2 | Theoretical Profile of MA Models | MA (2) Models

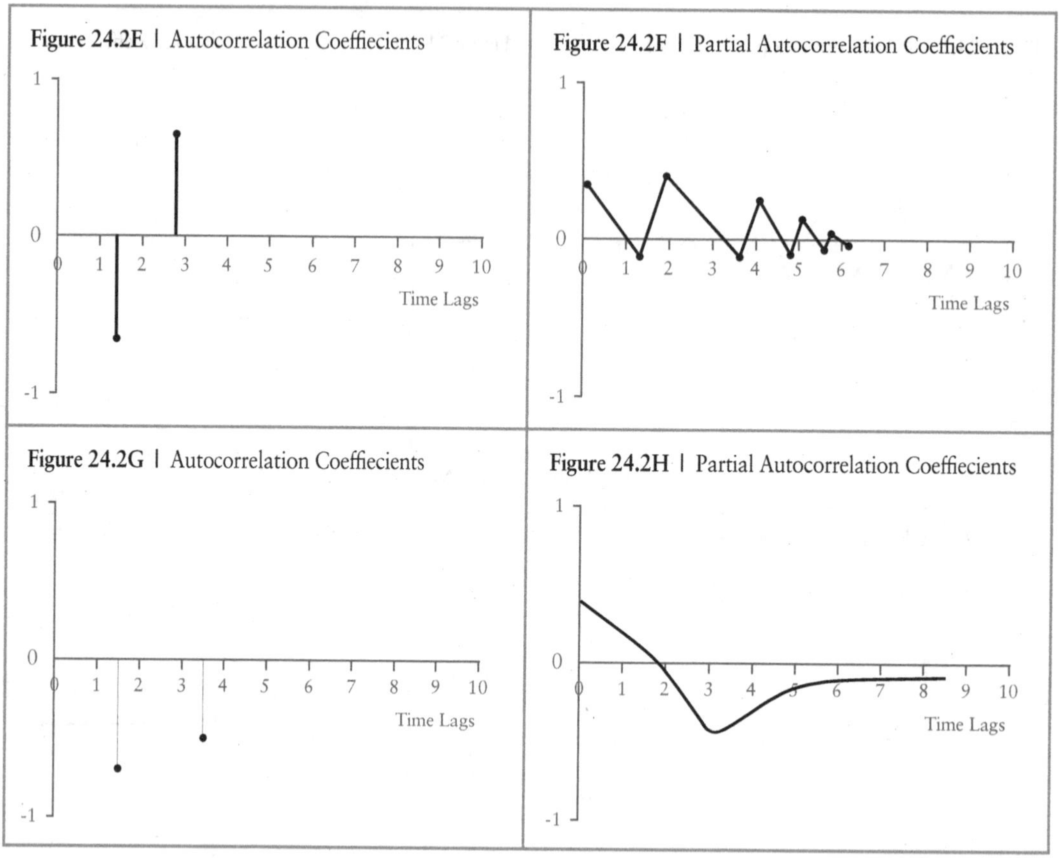

Figure 24.2E | Autocorrelation Coeffiecients

Figure 24.2F | Partial Autocorrelation Coeffiecients

Figure 24.2G | Autocorrelation Coeffiecients

Figure 24.2H | Partial Autocorrelation Coeffiecients

Figure 24.3 | Theoretical Profile of ARMA Models | ARMA (1,1)

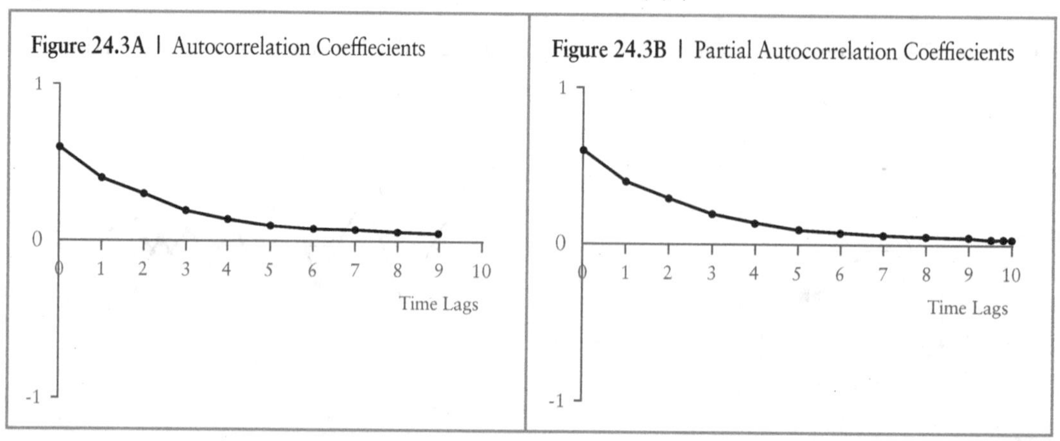

Figure 24.3A | Autocorrelation Coeffiecients

Figure 24.3B | Partial Autocorrelation Coeffiecients

Figure 24.3 | Theoretical Profile of ARMA Models | ARMA (2,2)

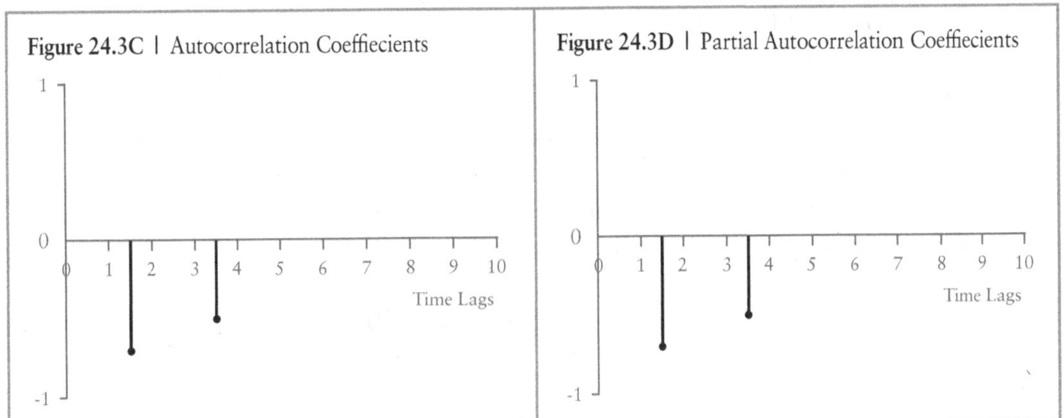

2. If the autocorrelation coefficients have one spike (negative or positive—negative as in the case of Figure 24.2C) significantly different from zero, and the accompanying partial autocorrelation coefficients decrease exponentially to zero with alternating positive and negative values, then the value of q will be 1 (MA=1). The model will be expressed as: (0, 0, 1). Again, it is assumed here that the data were not differenced. (See Figures 24.2C and 24.2D)

3. If the autocorrelation coefficients have two spikes (one negative and one positive) significantly different from zero, and the accompanying partial autocorrelation coefficients decrease exponentially to zero with alternating positive and negative values, then the value of *q* will be 2 (MA=2). The model will be expressed as: (0, 0, 2). Again, it is assumed here that the data were not differenced. (See Figures 24.2E and 24.2F)

4. If the autocorrelation coefficients have two spikes (both negative or positive, negative in the case of Figure 24.2G) significantly different from zero and the partial autocorrelation coefficients decrease exponentially to zero with positive and negative values, the value of *q* will be 2 (MA=2). The model will again be expressed as: (0, 0, 2). Again, it is assumed here that the data were not differenced. (See Figures 24.2G and 24.2H)

ARMA model: The guidelines for identifying an ARMA model and determining the terms of AR and MA are:

1. If both autocorrelation and partial autocorrelation coefficients drop exponentially to zero, but each one has one spike significantly different from zero, then it is an ARMA model with

p=1 and q=1 (AR=1 and MA=1). The model will be expressed as: (1, 0, 1). Here again, it is assumed that the data were not differenced. (See Figures 24.3A and 24.3B)

2. If both autocorrelation and partial autocorrelation coefficients drop exponentially to zero but each one has two spikes (both negative or positive, both negative in the case of Figures 24.3C and 24.3D) significantly different from zero, then it will be an ARMA model with p=2 and q=2 (AR=2 and MA=2), and the model will be expressed as: (2, 0, 2). Again, it is assumed here that the data were not differenced.

ARIMA model: As mentioned before, in ARIMA models, *I* stands for differencing (d). If we do one degree of differencing to make the data stationary, then d=1, if we do two degrees of differencing, then d=2, and so on.

ARIMA model with seasonality: If a plot of the data shows seasonality, then the model will be expressed as: ARIMA (p, I, q) (P, I, Q)^s. Here the lower case p and q represent AR and MA terms for the non-seasonal component of the model, whereas, the uppercase P and Q represent AR and MA terms for the seasonal component. The letter *I* represents differencing both in the non-seasonal and seasonal components of the model. The letter s represents the number of periods per season, 4 in the case of quarterly seasonality and 12 in the case of monthly seasonality.

The terms of AR and MA for the seasonal component of the model are determined the same way as described earlier. They are determined from the ACF and PACF, but after the data are differenced by simple differencing (if needed) as well as for seasonality. For the seasonal terms of AR and MA, we look at the spikes that are significantly different from zero at seasonal lags, for example, at the lag of 4, 8, etc., for the quarterly data; and for non-seasonal terms, we look at the spikes significantly different from zero at lags other than the seasonal ones. It should be emphasized that theoretical profiles of an ARMA model described earlier do not cover all the possibilities, but enough to guide one to determine an appropriate model. Plus, the real world situations do not behave exactly the same way as the theoretical distributions. Therefore, in selecting AR and MA terms, we should select a theoretical profile of coefficient distribution that is close enough, though not necessarily a perfect match. To select an appropriate model, we may have to go through a number of trials and errors to arrive at an appropriate model; for that experience in the area will be helpful.

PROCTER AND GAMBLE: AN EXAMPLE

Let us now use the sales data of Procter & Gamble (P&G) to demonstrate the identification process. The data run from Q1-2001 to Q1- 2010, and are given in Table 24.2.

The first step is to plot the data, which is shown in Figure 24.4, to see whether or not the data are stationary. The figure shows that data are not stationary. The data have both trend and seasonality. Despite the ups and downs, the data, on average, are trending upward. The data do have seasonality because in most of the years the sales are the lowest in Q1 and the highest in Q4. (See Table 24.2 and Figure 24.4)

The next step is to make the series stationary, which we did with the first order of differencing to get rid of trend, and seasonal differencing with a lag of 4 to get rid of seasonality (see Table 24.2). With these, the data become pretty much stationary, which can be seen in Figure 24.5.

After the data become stationary, the next step then is to specify the model, that is, determine the values of (p, I, q) $(P, I, Q)^s$. We now know the value of I of both seasonal and non-seasonal components of the model. The value of I of the non-seasonal component is one (I = 1) because of the first degree of differencing that was done to get rid of trend. The same is true with I of the seasonal component (I=1) because of the seasonal differencing. To determine the values of AR and MA for both non-seasonal and seasonal components of the model, we have to compute ACF and PACF from the differenced data (differenced for the first order and seasonality), which are plotted in Figures 24.6 and 24.7.

The patterns of ACF and PACF reveal that both have two spikes that are significantly different from zero; in each case they occur at a seasonal lag, that is, at the lag of 4 and 12 (see Figures 24. 6 and 24.7). Since there is no significant spike other than at seasonal lags, the value of AR and MA for the non-seasonal component will be zero, that is, p=0 and q=0. Further, since spikes are at a seasonal lag in both ACF and PACF, the value of both AR and MA of the seasonal component

Figure 24.4 | Procter & Gamble | Net Sales (Mil. of $)

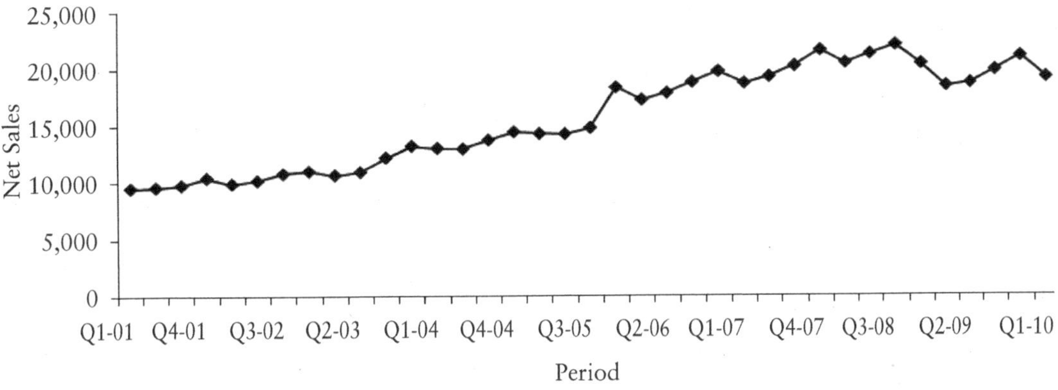

Table 24.2 | Procter & Gamble

Month (1)	Sales (Mil. of $) Y (2)	Y' First Degree Differencing $(Y_t - Y_{t-1})$ (3)	Seasonal Differencing with a Lag of 4 $(Y_t - Y_{t-1})$ (4)
Q 1-2001	9,511	—	—
Q 2-2001	9,582	71	—
Q 3-2001	9,766	184	—
Q 4-2001	10,403	637	—
Q 1-2002	9,900	-503	—
Q 2-2002	10,169	269	198
Q 3-2002	10,791	622	438
Q 4-2002	11,005	214	-423
Q 1-2003	10,656	-349	154
Q 2-2003	10,920	264	-5
Q 3-2003	12,195	1275	653
Q 4-2003	13,221	1026	812
Q 1-2004	13,029	-192	157
Q 2-2004	12,962	-67	-331
Q 3-2004	13,744	782	-493
Q 4-2004	14,452	708	-318
Q 1-2005	14,287	-165	27
Q 2-2005	14,258	-29	38
Q 3-2005	14,793	535	-247
Q 4-2005	18,337	3544	2836
Q 1-2006	17,250	-1087	-922
Q 2-2006	17,842	592	621
Q 3-2006	18,785	943	408
Q 4-2006	19,725	940	-2604
Q 1-2007	18,694	-1031	56
Q 2-2007	19,272	578	-14
Q 3-2007	20,199	927	-16
Q 4-2007	21,575	1376	436
Q 1-2008	20,463	-1112	-81
Q 2-2008	21,266	803	225
Q 3-2008	22,026	760	-167
Q 4-2008	20,368	-1658	-3034
Q 1-2009	18,417	-1951	-839
Q 2-2009	18,662	245	-558
Q 3-2009	19,807	1145	385
Q 4-2009	21,027	1220	2878
Q 1-2010	19,178	-1849	102

will be 2, that is, P=2 and Q=2. (The presence of seasonal lags validates that there is seasonality in the data.) The patterns of ACF and PACF are similar to Figures 24.3C and 24.3D. Here s is four because of the quarterly seasonality. Thus, the model becomes:

$$\text{ARIMA } (0, 1, 0)\ (2, 1, 2)^4$$

↙ ↘

(Non-Seasonal Component) (Seasonal Component)

***Model Estimation*:** Now we have specified the model, the next step is to estimate it. Most of the ARIMA models are nonlinear in nature and thus require a nonlinear solution with an iterative search for best coefficients. There are two estimation procedures that are often used: Nonlinear Least Squares that minimizes the sum of the squared errors and Maximum Likelihood that maximizes the probability so that the estimated model best represents the population. The procedure we use here is Nonlinear Least Squares. Also, in estimating the parameters of an ARIMA model with a software package we use the original data, because the model specifications take care of every thing including differencing. We use a software package because it is very difficult to manually estimate the parameters of such models. There are many such packages on the market; the one we have used is the SPSS statistics package. The parameter estimates of our P&G model are given in Table 24.3.

Figure 24.5 | Procter & Gamble | Net Sales after First Order Simple and Seasonal Differencing (Mil. of $)

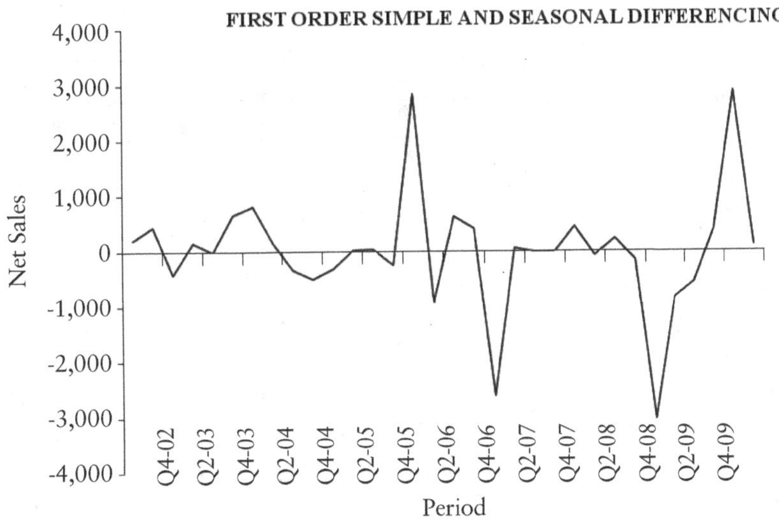

Figure 24.6 | Procter & Gamble | Autocorrelations After First Order and Seasonal Differencing of Sales Data (Q1-2001– Q1-2010)

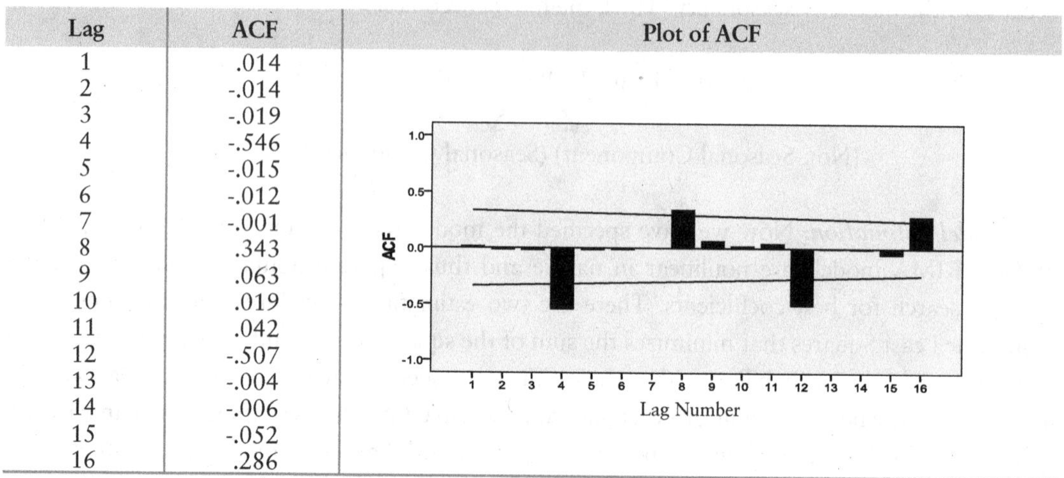

Lag	ACF
1	.014
2	-.014
3	-.019
4	-.546
5	-.015
6	-.012
7	-.001
8	.343
9	.063
10	.019
11	.042
12	-.507
13	-.004
14	-.006
15	-.052
16	.286

Figure 24.7 | Procter & Gamble | Partial Autocorrelations after First Order and Seasonal Differencing of Sales Data (Q1-2001– Q1-2010)

Lag	ACF	Plot of PACF
1	.014	
2	-.014	
3	-.019	
4	-.546	
5	-.009	
6	-.045	
7	-.027	
8	.061	
9	.071	
10	.008	
11	.060	
12	-.426	
13	.114	
14	-.034	
15	-.010	
16	-.251	

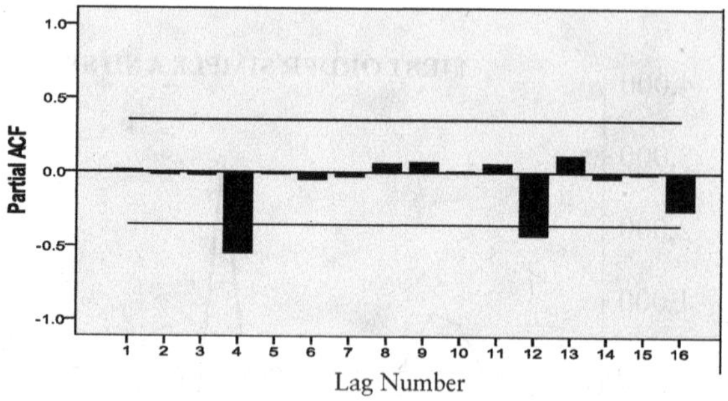

Model Checking: No matter how a model is estimated, many of the criteria for testing are the same. Here too we use R^2 to measure the degree of correlation between the dependent and independent variables and t-statistics to test the significance of coefficients. However, here we use two types of R^2: One regular and one stationary. The regular R^2 is computed before the data

Table 24.3 | Procter & Gamble | ARIMA Model Parameters

		Estimate	t
Constant		-17.337	-.208
Difference		1	
AR, Seasonal	Lag 1	-.281	-.267
	Lag 2	.626	.840
Seasonal Difference		1	
MA, Seasonal	Lag 1	.337	.049
	Lag 2	.638	.159

are differenced, and the stationary R^2 is computed after the data are differenced. We also use autocorrelations and partial autocorrelations of residuals to determine whether residuals are left with only white noise; Mean Absolute Percent Error (MAPE) to determine whether the average percent error computed from the past data is acceptable; and ex post forecasts to determine the error we are likely to experience if the same model is used in the future. If these tests fail, we have to go back and re-specify the model.

The model fit statistics of the P&G model are given in Table 24.4. It shows that the regular R^2 is .960 and the stationary R^2 is 0.520; both are extremely good. Bear in mind since that the stationary R^2 is computed from the differenced data, it has to be low. Usually, it is within 0.5. The MAPE, 3.141%, is equally good, considering the error the consumer products companies normally experience. (The 2009 survey of Institute of Business Forecasting and Planning shows that the average error at an aggregate (company) level, one-quarter ahead, experienced in the consumer products industry is 23% (see Chapter 26, Figure 26.9). However, t statistics, given in Table 24.3, are not good. In each case, it is less than two. Usually, a variable is considered significant if its value is two or above.

A model is well fitted if we are left with residuals that are nothing but white noises. To determine that, we computed ACF and PACF of residuals, which are given in Figure 24.8. The figure shows that all the residuals, both of ACF and PACF, are well within limits, and thus they are all white noise.

Table 24.4 | Procter & Gamble | Model Fit Statistics

Regular R-Squared	Stationary R-Squared	MAPE
.960	.520	3.141

Figure 24.8 | Procter & Gamble | ACF and PACF of Residuals of the Model (0,1,0) (2,1,2)

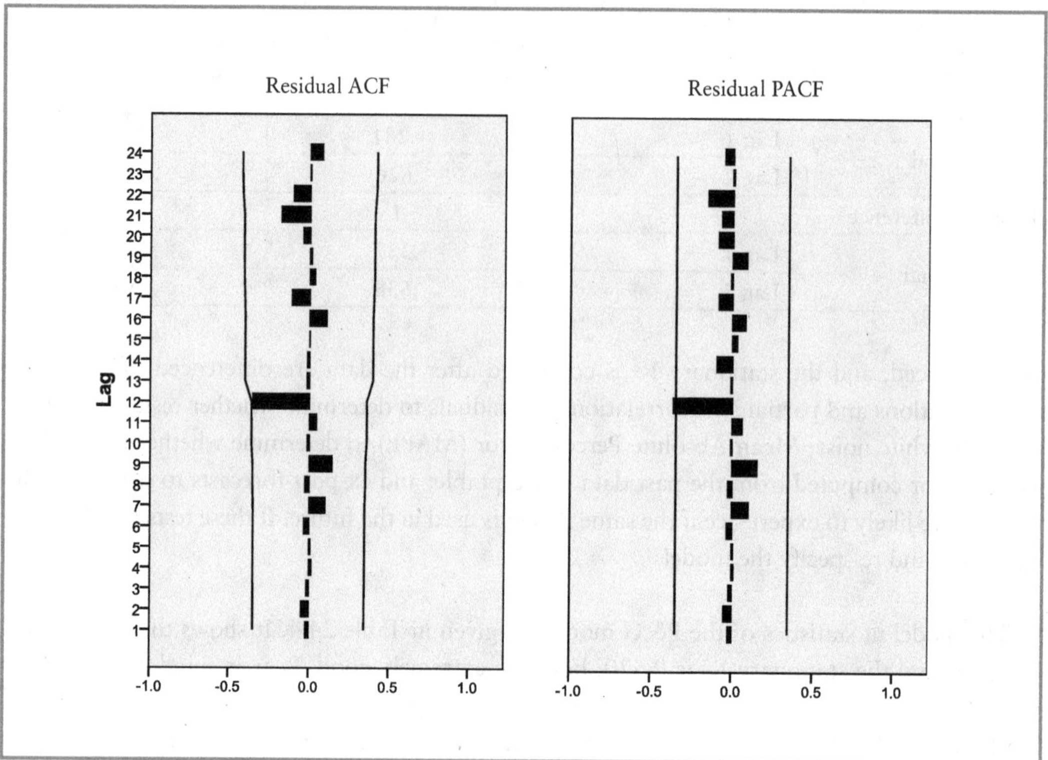

To determine how well this model forecasted, we forecasted the sales of Q2-2010, which was kept as a holdout period. The forecasted sales of this period came to $19,595 million. Since the actual of this period was $18,926 million, the error came to -3.5%, which is fairly good. From these tests, it appears that this is a fairly good model. (Caution: Here we have an ex post forecast of just one holdout period, which may be just a coincidence that we got a good forecast. To be more certain, we should, if possible, test a model with three or four holdout periods.)

There are, however, a number of other tests such as Durbin-Watson (DW) to determine if residuals are randomly distributed, that is, there is no autocorrelation, and Ljung-Box statistics (Q) to determine whether the residual autocorrelations as a set is significantly different from zero. In practice, however, tests described above are sufficient for selecting a model.

Forecasting: Once the model is validated, we are ready for forecasting. In this case, we only prepared the forecast of Q2-2010, described earlier. Since the forecasts with such models are usually prepared with software, we did not show how parameters given in Table 24.3 were used to arrive at the forecast.

WALMART: ANOTHER EXAMPLE

Let us now develop an ARIMA model for Walmart. The net sales data from Q1-2001 to Q1-2010 are given in Table 24.5. We will develop an ex post forecast of the period, Q2-2010 with the model we develop.

The first step, as before, is to determine whether the series is stationary. To make that determination, we plotted the sales data as shown in Figure 24.9. It shows that the data have both trend and seasonality. Despite the ups and downs in the data, the overall trend is upward. It has seasonality because each year the sales are the lowest in Q1 and the highest in Q4. Therefore, to make the data stationary, we did first order simple and seasonal differencing. With these, the data became quite stationary. (See Figure 24.10)

After the data are made stationary, the next step is to specify the model, that is, determine values of p and q for the non-seasonal component of the model, and P and Q for the seasonal component. To do that, we have to compute ACF and PACF of the differenced data (differenced for the first degree simple and seasonality) and then plot them, which are given in Figures 24.11 and 24.12. The plots of ACF and PACF show that each one has one spike significantly different from zero, and that spike occurs only at the lag of 4. This means that the value of both AR and MA of the

Figure 24.9 | Walmart Net Sales (Mil. of $)

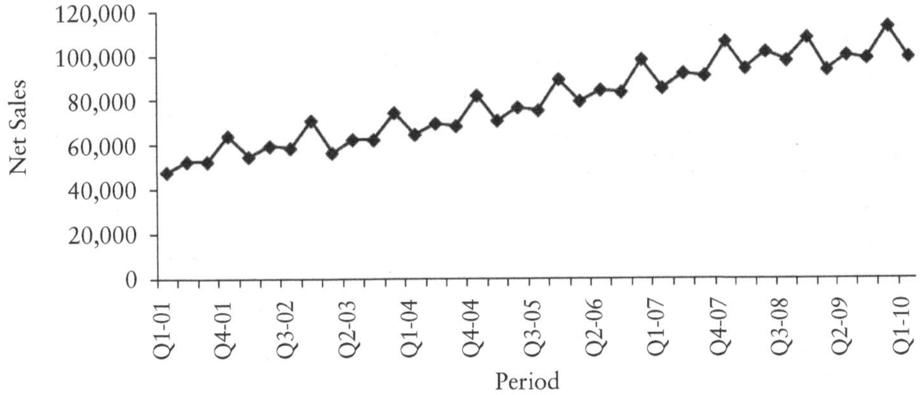

seasonal component of the model will be 1, that is, P=1 and Q=1. Since there is no spike, other than at a seasonal lag, the value of both AR and MA of the non-seasonal component of the model will be zero, that is, p=0 and q=0. The distribution of coefficients both of ACF and PACF are similar to the theoretical distributions given in Figures 24.3A and 24.3B, where each one has one spike, though the spikes in the theoretical distributions are positive, but, in our case, negative. Because of the first degree of differencing and seasonal differencing, the value of I in both non-seasonal and seasonal components of the model will be 1. Again, here s is 4. The model then becomes:

$$\text{ARIMA } (0, 1, 0)(1, 1, 1)^4$$

↙ ↘

(Non-Seasonal Component) (Seasonal Component)

After the model has been specified, we estimate the model, that is, we calculate the values of its parameters, which are given in Table 24.6. The next step is to evaluate the model to see how good it is. The parameters of the model are given in Table 24.6, and model fit statistics in Table 24.7. The regular R^2 is .989, which is excellent, but the stationary R^2 is .386, which is okay. MAPE is 1.436%, which is very good. However the t value of MA, given in Table 24.6, is not significant. Let us also look at the ACF and PACF of residuals, which are given in Figure 24.13. They appear to be excellent because all of them are well within limits. So, the model appears to be fairly good. Let us now make a forecast for the period, Q2-2010, which was held as a holdout period. The forecast of that period comes to \$106,248 million. Since the actual of this period was \$103,016 million, the error came to -3.1%.

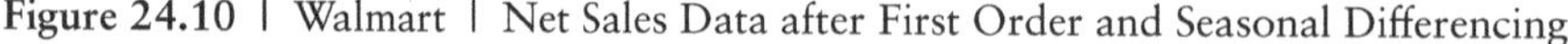

Figure 24.10 | Walmart | Net Sales Data after First Order and Seasonal Differencing

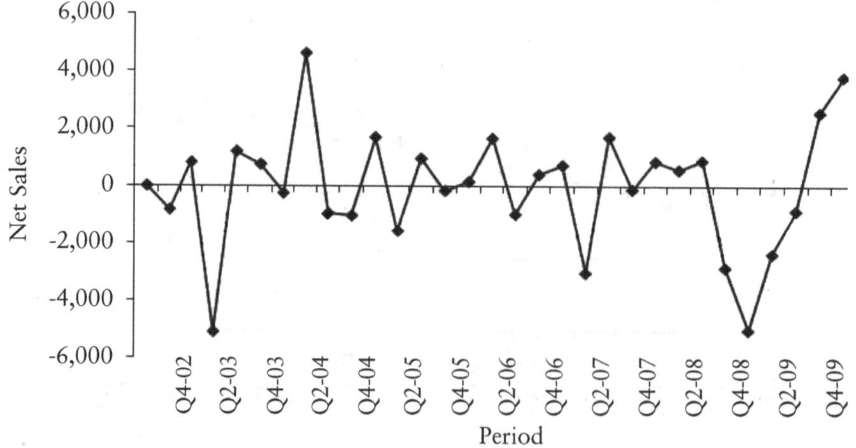

Table 24.5 | Walmart | Net Sales (Q1-2001– Q1-2010)

Period	Sales (Mil. of $)	Period	Sales (Mil. of $)
Q 1-2001	48,052	Q 4-2005	89,273
Q 2-2001	52,799	Q 1-2006	79,613
Q 3-2001	52,738	Q 2-2006	84,524
Q 4-2001	64,210	Q 3-2006	83,543
Q 1-2002	54,960	Q 4-2006	98,090
Q 2-2002	59,694	Q 1-2007	85,387
Q 3-2002	58,797	Q 2-2007	91,990
Q 4-2002	71,073	Q 3-2007	90,880
Q 1-2003	56,718	Q 4-2007	106,269
Q 2-2003	62,637	Q 1-2008	94,122
Q 3-2003	62,480	Q 2-2008	101,159
Q 4-2003	74,494	Q 3-2008	97,634
Q 1-2004	64,763	Q 4-2008	107,996
Q 2-2004	69,722	Q 1-2009	93,471
Q 3-2004	68,520	Q 2-2009	100,082
Q 4-2004	82,216	Q 3-2009	98,667
Q 1-2005	70,908	Q 4-2009	112,826
Q 2-2005	76,811	Q 1-2010	99,097
Q 3-2005	75,436		

Table 24.6 | Walmart | ARIMA Model Parameters (Q1-2001– Q1-2010)

		Estimate	t
Constant		-62.775	-.355
Difference		1	
AR, Seasonal	Lag 1	-.780	-4.246
Seasonal Difference		-.086	
MA, Seasonal	Lag 1	.337	-.299

Table 24.7 | Walmart | Model Fit Statistics (Q1-2001– Q1-2010)

Regular R-Squared	Stationary R-Squared	MAPE
.989	.386	1.436

Figure 24.11 | Walmart | Autocorrelations after First Order and Seasonal Differencing of Sales Data (Q1-2001– Q1-2010)

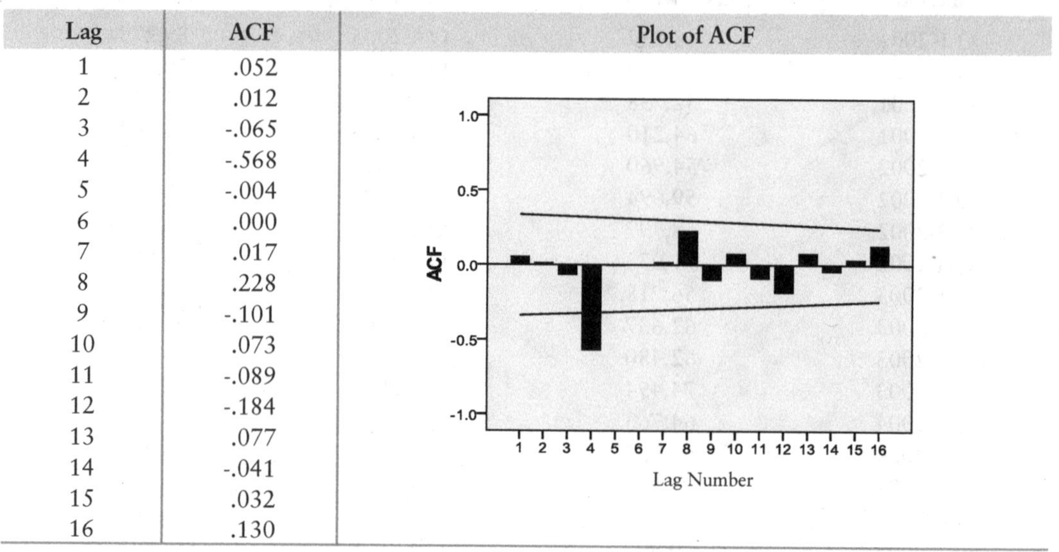

Lag	ACF
1	.052
2	.012
3	-.065
4	-.568
5	-.004
6	.000
7	.017
8	.228
9	-.101
10	.073
11	-.089
12	-.184
13	.077
14	-.041
15	.032
16	.130

Figure 24.12 | Walmart | Partial Autocorrelations after First Order and Seasonal Differencing of Sales Data (Q1-2001– Q1-2010)

Lag	PACF	Plot of PACF
1	.052	
2	.009	
3	-.066	
4	-.565	
5	.052	
6	.019	
7	-.063	
8	-.134	
9	-.118	
10	.128	
11	-.159	
12	-.197	
13	-.033	
14	.085	
15	-.156	
16	-.108	

1.0
0.5
0.0
-0.5
-1.0
Partial ACF
1 2 3 4 5 6 7 8 9 10 11 12 13 14 15 16
Lag Number

Figure 24.13 | Walmart | ACF and PACF of Residuals (Q1-2001– Q1-2010)

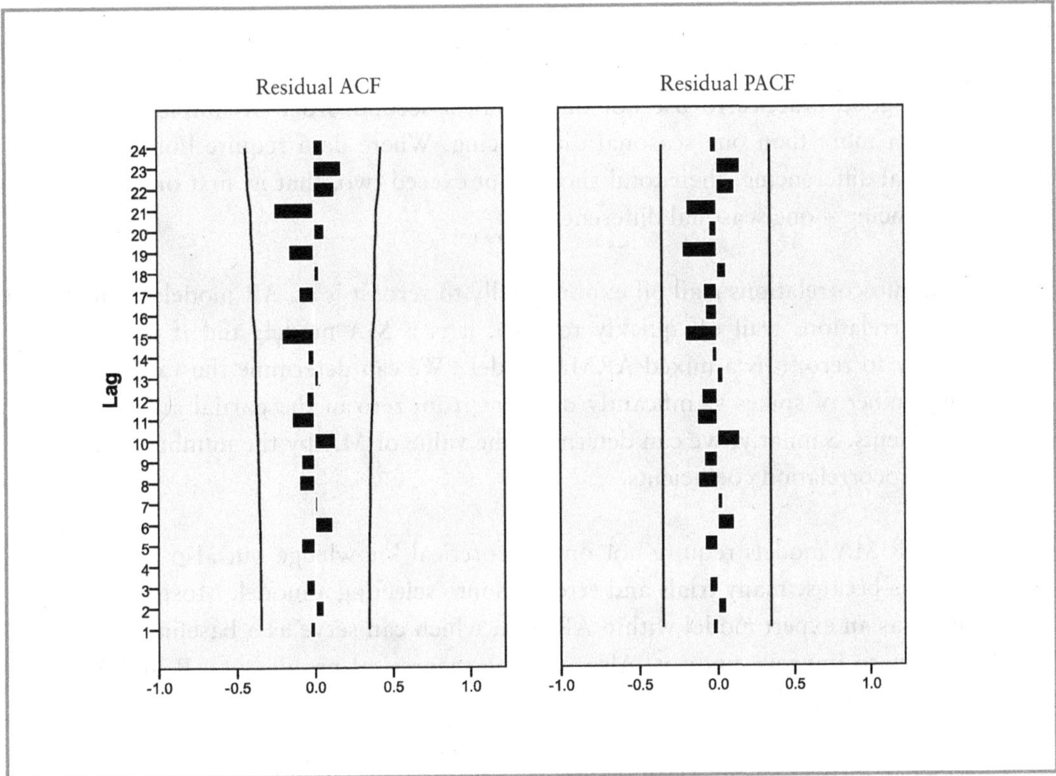

THINGS YOU SHOULD KNOW ABOUT ARIMA MODELING

There are certain things you should know about ARIMA modeling:

1. In ARIMA modeling, we need a relatively large number of observations particularly to accommodate data losses resulting from differencing. It is commonly believed that we should have at least 35 or more observations to use this model.

2. If both ACF and PACF drop near to zero quickly, it means that the data are stationary.

3. Most of business data series are non-stationary. Therefore, the data require transformation

of one kind or the other to make them stationary. Transformations include simple and seasonal differencing, and logarithmic transformation. Logarithmic transformation is used where there is exponential growth in the series.

4. It is a good practice to use not more than a second order of simple differencing, and not more than one seasonal differencing. Where data require both simple and seasonal differencing, their total should not exceed two, that is, first order of simple differencing + one seasonal differencing.

5. If the autocorrelations trail off exponentially to zero, it is an AR model; if the partial autocorrelations trail off quickly to zero, it is a MA model; and if both trail off quickly to zero, it is a mixed ARMA model. We can determine the value of AR by the number of spikes significantly different from zero in the partial autocorrelation coefficients. Similarly, we can determine the value of MA by the number of spikes in the autocorrelation coefficients.

6. The ARIMA models require not only theoretical knowledge but also experience in the area because many trials and errors go into selecting a model. Most software like SPSS has an expert model within ARIMA, which can serve as a baseline model, and then try to improve upon it. Also, use the theoretical profiles of AR and MA as a guide, not as a bible.

7. Although there are many diagnostic tools to evaluate an ARIMA model, what matters in the end is how well it forecasts. So try, among other things, a couple of ex posts forecasts (not just one) to finalize the selection of a model.

SUGGESTED READING

1. Wang, George C. S. "A Guide to Box-Jenkins Modeling." ***Journal of Business Forecasting.*** Spring 2008, pp. 19-28.
2. Wang, George C. S. and Chaman L. Jain. ***Regression Analysis: Modeling & Forecasting.*** New York: Graceway Publishing Company. 2003.
3. Wilson, J. Holton, Barry Keating, and John Galt Solutions, Inc. ***Business Forecasting.*** New York: McGraw Hill. 2007.

QUESTIONS FOR REVIEW

1. What are ACF and PACF, which are used in ARIMA modeling? What role do they play in selecting a model?
2. Why is it essential to have a large number of observations for using an ARIMA model? Explain.
3. What is the theory behind ARIMA modeling? Explain.
4. What are the different steps followed in generating a forecast with an ARIMA model; among them, which one is the most difficult and why?
5. Explain how AR and MA coefficients are used to determine their terms.
6. What are the ACF and PACF residuals, and what purpose do they serve? Explain.
7. Why is it necessary for the data to be stationary for using an ARIMA model? Explain.
8. Which ARIMA model would be appropriate if the autocorrelation coefficients have two negative spikes significantly different from zero, and the accompanying partial autocorrelation coefficients decrease exponentially to zero with alternating positive and negative values?
9. How do we determine in ARIMA modeling whether or not the data have seasonality? Explain.
10. Explain in brief:
    a. What are autoregressive models?
    b. What are moving average models?
    c. What do we mean by the stationary data?
    d. What is differencing, and why do we do it?

CHAPTER 25

NEURAL NETWORKS

George C. S. Wang, Ph.D.
Independent Consultant

An Artificial Neural Network (ANN) is another model in the tool-kit of causal models. It is basically a nonlinear regression model but is generally much more complicated than other models. The structure of an ANN model somewhat resembles the neural network of a human body, and the model is, therefore, called an Artificial Neural Network. The ANN name itself has caused some confusion in forecast modeling. The terminology employed in its modeling process is very confusing; even many sophisticated modelers find it difficult to work with.

For example, a simple ANN model has three layers like a neural network: An input layer, an output layer, and an in-between hidden layer with nodes. Layers, especially the hidden one along with its nodes, are unfamiliar in regression modeling. However, once the model is specified and the modeling terminology is understood, ANN modeling does not look as esoteric as it sounds.

The best way to learn about ANN modeling is to first understand its basic concepts and then go through its modeling procedure using familiar terms. This way ANN modeling becomes as straightforward as other types of forecast modeling.

BASIC CONCEPTS OF NEURAL NETWORK

ANN is said to simulate the nervous system of a human body. Let's see how the nervous system looks like and works:

1. The nervous system consists of a set of neurons or nodes; the neurons are hidden in the body for processing signals received from different outside sources. This is the hidden layer, or hidden layer activation functions.

2. Inputs are signals from sources outside the body. The signals feed into the neurons for processing. The signals are inputs in the input layer.

3. The processed signals are then sent to an output function, which is the overall response to the processed signals. The output function is also called output activation function or the output layer.

This is a simple description of the neural network, which has three layers, and the neurons (or nodes) are truly hidden in the hidden layer, which lies between the input and output layers. The hidden layer in an ANN model, however, is not as hidden as we often think; the hidden layer nodes are simply complicated nonlinear functions of independent variables.

THE HIDDEN LAYER OF AN ANN MODEL

A simple ANN model takes the following form:

$$y = B_0 + B_1H_1(x_1, x_2, x_3) + B_2H_2(x_1, x_2, x_3) + B_3H_3(x_1, x_2, x_3) + u \qquad ...(25.1)$$

Equation 25.1 looks like a regression model in terms of H_1, H_2, and H_3, where B_0 is the constant; B_1, B_2, and B_3 are the coefficients of three Hs. But what are x_1, x_2, and x_3, and why are they entered this way in the model? This is the first mystery in ANN modeling. In ANN terminology, H_1, H_2, and H_3 are nodes in the hidden layer, and x_1, x_2, and x_3 are inputs fed into the nodes. This may be somewhat confusing, but we will re-define them as we proceed to illustrate the modeling process.

ANN MODELING PROCEDURE

Normally forecast modeling involves four steps: (1) Model identification, (2) model estimation, (3) model evaluation, and (4) forecasting. Does ANN modeling also use these four steps? The answer is yes, but they are somewhat different from other types of modeling, especially step (1).

Model Identification: In linear regression modeling, we choose our independent variables for a model on the basis of their correlation with the dependent variable. Figure 25.1 shows four curves. Series 1 is a plot of the original data of certain quarterly sales, which is the dependent variable (y). Let x_1, x_2, and x_3 be three independent variables, which cause the sales to vary from quarter to quarter. All the variables here are time series, but for simplicity sake, we specify our model without the t-subscripts. The linear regression model is as follows:

$$y = c_0 + c_1x_1 + c_2x_2 + c_3x_3 + u \qquad \ldots(25.2)$$

Equation 25.2 is a familiar multiple regression equation. What can we do if x_1, x_2, and x_3 are not linearly related to y, but are related to y in a very complex way? One way to approach this problem is to select a nonlinear model, which is effective in recognizing the true pattern of a data set. The neural network like Equation 25.1 is such a model. But Equation 25.1 includes three H functions that are hidden from our view. Let's see how we can specify the H functions.

Economic data usually varies around its mean, and the variations around the mean can be

Figure 25.1 | Decomposition of Data

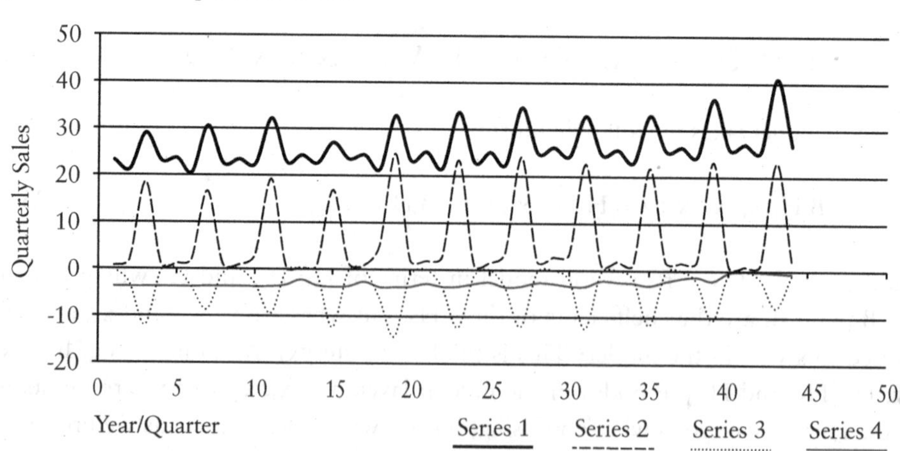

decomposed into several components. Figure 25.1 shows the plots of the original data Series 1, and its three components, series 2, 3, and 4. Series 2 is convex upwards, Series 3 is concave upwards, and Series 4 is a linear line. Notice that the curvatures of series 2, 3, and 4 were drawn on the basis of the author's experience in modeling the type of data represented by series 1. Other modelers may decompose the data into shapes other than those plotted in Figure 25.1. If we can find an equation that simulates the shapes of these three curves, we can use that equation as the three H nodes in Equation 25.1. The logistic curve, as shown in Figure 25.2, is one of the curves that possess these characteristics.

In Figure 25.2, along the x-axis, the curve concaves upwards from -4 to -1; it is roughly linear from -1 to +1; and it is convex upwards from +1 to +4. These three shapes are useful in pattern recognition. If we break these three sections apart and mix them with a different set of weights for each of the shapes, we can simulate a large number of curve patterns. The algebraic form of the logistic curve is as follows:

$$L = \frac{1}{1 + e^{-aX}}$$

Series 1 in Figure 25.1 was decomposed into three curves similar to three sections of the logistic curve. Since the three independent variables, x_1, x_2, and x_3, are responsible for the shapes of the curves, the L function becomes:

$$H = \frac{1}{1 + e^{-(a_0 + a_1x_1 + a_2x_2 + a_3x_3)}} \qquad \ldots(25.3)$$

Equation 25.3, therefore, can be used to model each of the three curve shapes shown in Figure 25.1 by assigning different values to the coefficients (a_0, a_1, a_2, and a_3). These coefficients are called connection weights in ANN terminology because they connect the x-inputs to the H-nodes. Therefore, H_1, H_2, and H_3 in the hidden layer can all be expressed in the form of Equation 25.3 except that their coefficients (a_0, a_1, a_2, and a_3) will have different values. With nodes expressed as in Equation 25.3, the hidden layer is no longer hidden. The nodes are simply complicated nonlinear functions of the x-variables, which in ANN terminology are called Hidden Layer Activation Functions.

We have just specified the H-nodes. The next task is to connect the three H-nodes into a model. In Equation 25.1, the coefficients B_0, B_1, B_2, and B_3 are the connection weights, connecting the three H-nodes together into an ANN model, which is called Output Activation Function in ANN terminology.

Figure 25.2 | Logistic Curve

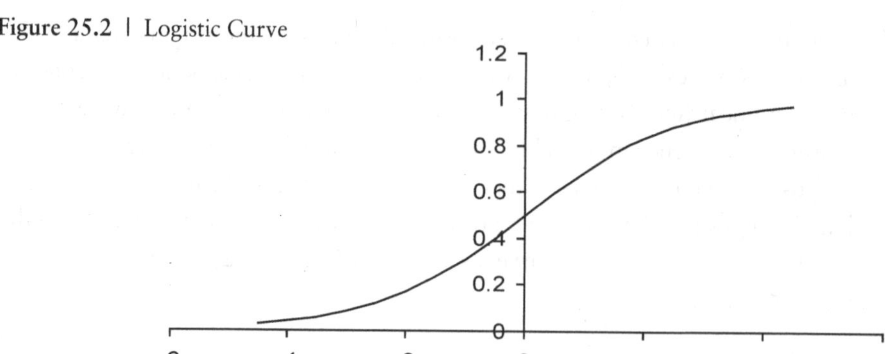

Notice that a regression model like Equation 25.2 has only one set of coefficients to be estimated (c_0, c_1, c_2, and c_3), but in an ANN model we have four sets of coefficients to be estimated: Three sets for the three nodes and one for the output activation function. Each set includes four coefficients; therefore, a total of 16 coefficients are to be estimated.

ANN Model Estimation: In Equation 25.1, nodes H_1, H_2, and H_3 are in the same algebraic form, meaning that they are perfectly correlated. That is, the model has multicollinearity. In regression modeling, the model cannot be estimated if its independent variables are highly correlated. But can we estimate the ANN model where H_1, H_2, and H_3 are perfectly correlated? Yes, we can by assigning a different set of coefficients to each node so that each node models a part of the curve.

Because of the unusual structure of the ANN, we cannot use the Ordinary Least Squares (OLS) method or the conventional nonlinear least squares procedure to estimate the model. We need a special estimation procedure and computer software to do the job. Several computing software packages are commercially available. Although the software packages for ANN modeling require modelers to select node functions and to set estimation criteria, they are generally user friendly. Once node functions are chosen and estimation criteria are set, estimation and forecasting become automatic. Usually the estimation procedure includes the following four steps:

1. Select a function for each node from the list of functions built into the software, of which the logistic function, Equation 25.3, is usually one of them. If the model includes three nodes as expressed in Equation 25.1, modelers may select one of the functions for all three nodes, or select a different function for each of the nodes.

2. Select an initial set of coefficients for each H function using random numbers. Given a

seed, the computer software automatically produces the required random numbers. In our example, we will require 16 random numbers; that is, four for each set of the four sets of coefficients. This is the starting point of the estimation algorithm. (A seed is an integer, say, from 1 to 99. Each time a different seed is given, a new group of required random numbers is generated, and a new starting point is set. Consequently, a new model is estimated.)

3. Set the convergence criteria. For convergence, the computing algorithm progresses from the starting point by iteratively adjusting the estimated coefficients so that the sum of squared errors of the model, Σu^2, converges to a minimal point in accordance with the pre-set criteria. Iteration stops when the sum of squared errors decreases less than a pre-set small number, say less than 0.01, or when the number of iterations reaches a desired number, say 200, whichever comes first.

4. Because of the complexity of ANN structure, it is virtually impossible for the sum of squared errors to converge to the global minimum (absolute minimum). Convergence usually occurs at one of the myriad local minima (low points, but they are not as low as the absolute minimum). If modelers are not satisfied with the model, it is easy to re-estimate a new one; all they need to do is to provide a new seed to start the computing algorithm again, as described in Step 2.

Notice that every time a new starting point is selected, a new model is produced, which will be different from the previous ones. This feature is called model training in ANN terminology.

Model Evaluation: The estimation procedure we have just described sounds like a trial-and-error approach, which actually is, but it is a good approach for ANN modeling. ANN is a good technique for pattern recognition; in other words, it is a good technique for complex curve fitting. However, because of the complexity of model structure and estimation procedure, the model residuals and estimated coefficients are unlikely to be normally distributed. Thus, hypothesis testing, such as F test, t test, etc., are no longer valid.

Even though hypothesis testing is no longer valid, R^2 and standard error, s, of the model are still good measures of the model's goodness of fit. The closer the value of R^2 is to 1, the higher is the correlation between the y dependent variable and the x independent variables. The smaller is the s value, the better the model fits the data. When several alternative models are compared, the one with highest value of R^2 and smallest value of s should be chosen.

Another measure of model accuracy is to generate ex post forecasts. For example, if the model is designed to forecast four quarters ahead, we will exclude the actual data of the last four quarters in the historic period from the model, and then use the developed model to make forecasts of these four quarters. The forecasts are then compared with actual data, and their forecast errors are computed. We can do this with various models, and then select the one that yields, on average, the lowest error.

Forecasting: Forecasting is here a straightforward operation. There is no need to make further explanations except that it does not make much sense to calculate the confidence intervals about the forecasts because the required normality assumptions for the residuals and estimated coefficients do not hold here.

ANN TERMINOLOGY

As we went through the modeling process, we have defined the ANN terminology along the way. For convenience, we have summarized all these terms in Table 25.1.

Table 25.1 | Teminologies | Regression vs. Artificial Neural Network

Regression	Artificial Neural Network
Linear or Nonlinear Equation	ANN with Layers and Nodes
Independent Variables, X	Network Inputs
Dependent Variable, Y	Network Output Target
Sample	Training Set
Coefficients	Network Connection Weights
Model Estimation/Updating	Training/Learning

CONCLUDING REMARKS

We have described the modeling procedure of a simple ANN model. Depending on the circumstances, the ANN model can be much more complicated than the one we have described here, but the basic concept and modeling procedure are the same for all ANN models.

The ANN is a very good technique for modeling complicated data patterns for short-term forecasting. For example, it is very difficult, if not impossible, to develop a regression model to forecast hourly electric load or hourly load of telephone calls at a call center, but the ANN model can.

Relative to other types of models, the ANN model is obviously not parsimonious, meaning that the ANN model is a great deal more complicated than other types of models. If a regular regression model or an ARIMA model yields results similar to an ANN model, use the simpler ones. But when circumstances call for an ANN application, we should not hesitate to try it, especially where we have massive amount of data with complex patterns; there the neural network model may be the best choice. ☐

SUGGESTED READING

1. McMenamin, J. Stuart. "A Primer on Neural Networks For Forecasting." *Journal of Business Forecasting.* Fall 1997, pp. 17-22.

QUESTIONS FOR REVIEW

1. Explain where ANN models are most appropriate for forecasting.
2. The Neural Network model works around three layers. Explain what these layers are and what role each one plays in modeling.
3. Are Neural Network models linear or non-linear? In what ways are they similar or different from regression models often used in forecasting?
4. Does multicollinearity pose a problem in ANN modeling? Why or why not?
5. Explain the steps that are usually taken to estimate an ANN model.
6. Explain how a model is evaluated for the goodness of fit in ANN modeling.
7. Explain how these ANN terms compare with those of regression:
   a. Network Inputs
   b. Training Set
   c. Network Connection Weights
   d. Training/Learning

PART VII

PERFORMANCE METRICS

INTRODUCTION

Metrics to measure performance are a must, because nothing improves unless it is measured. There are many different forecasting metrics available; each one looks at the performance from a different perspective. Here, we will discuss those that are mostly used in business. No matter what we do, there will be a certain amount of error. Therefore, the objective should be not how to eliminate the error, but how to minimize it; and not how to blame someone for the error, but how to cope with it. Above all, error is not terrible as long as it is within an acceptable range, we don't repeat the same error, we learn and take advantage of it, and we are not intimidated by it. If we have perfect knowledge, then there would be no error. But, this is not the case. In fact, business has become more dynamic and more complex. It is humanly impossible to avoid errors. To cope with them, we have to know how to measure them, what caused them, and how to minimize them, which is the objective of this part. Further, we will discuss how much progress we have made over the last decade in improving forecasts.

CHAPTER 26

PERFORMANCE METRICS

If something is not measured, it will never improve. To improve forecast performance we have to have metrics in place to measure and monitor them. With growing competition from home and abroad, it is becoming more important than ever to improve forecasts in an effort to cut costs and increase sales. The over-forecasting error increases the cost of inventory, transshipment, shrinkage, and obsolescence. The under-forecasting error increases production, procurement and transportation costs, as well as the loss of sales because of stock-outs. Further, if we can measure and recognize the error, we can do something about it. Plus, with the knowledge of the error, we will be in a better position to manage the risk associated with it.

FUNDAMENTALS OF FORECASTING ERRORS

There are some fundamentals of forecasting errors, which everyone should know. The more we know, the better it would be; not only for improving errors but also for coping with them. The most important ones are:

1. The error decreases as we forecast at a more and more aggregate level. (The opposite is true when we forecast at a more and more granular level.) The error is generally lower at an aggregate level than at a category level, and lower at a category level than at a SKU

level. The error decreases when forecasted at an aggregate level because some of the under-forecasting errors at a category level are offset by the over-forecasting errors. The same is true when forecasted at a category level; some of the under-forecasting errors of SKUs are offset by the over-forecasting errors. Figures 26.1, 26.2, and 26.3 show the forecasts errors of all the industries combined at three levels (SKU, category, and aggregate) and over four different forecast horizons (1-month ahead, 2-month ahead, 1-quarter ahead, and 1-year ahead) based on the Institute of Business Forecasting and Planning (IBF) survey of 2005-2009. The numbers shown are the averages over the five-year period.

The same applies to buckets in which we prepare forecasts. Forecasts prepared in monthly buckets would be more accurate than in weekly buckets, more accurate in quarterly buckets than in monthly buckets, and so on.

2. The error increases as we forecast further into the future. In other words, it is easier to forecast what would happen next month than next year. For that reason, operational forecasts are generally more accurate than strategic forecasts. This also is partly because further ahead in time we forecast, the less attention we pay to the quality of forecasts. It also can be observed in Figures 26.1, 26.2, and 26.3.

3. All products are not equally forecastable—some are more difficult than others. New products, highly promoted and volatile products, products with a short life cycle, and products with intermittent demand are generally more difficult to forecast than others. Also, forecasting errors vary from industry to industry.

4. The more competitive the market, the more volatile would be the demand, and thus more difficult to forecast.

Figure 26.1
% Forecast Errors at a SKU Level
All Industries Combined

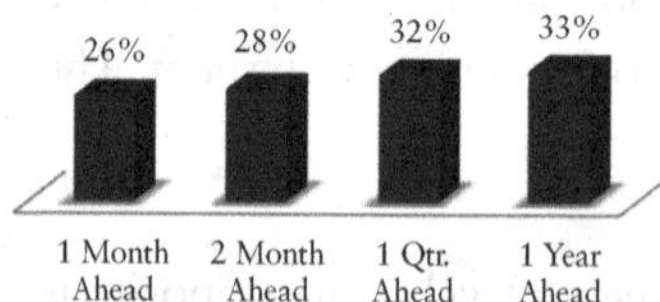

Figure 26.2
% Forecast Errors at a Category Level
All Industries Combined

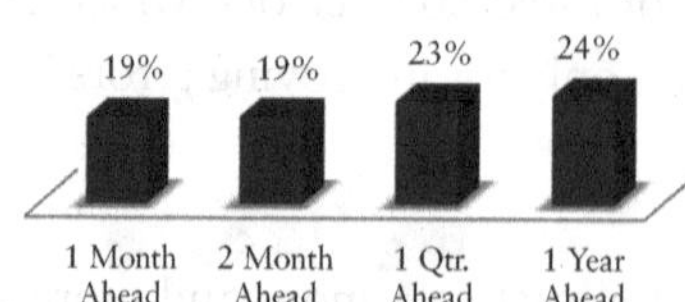

Figure 26.3
% Forecast Errors at an Aggregate Level
All Industries Combined

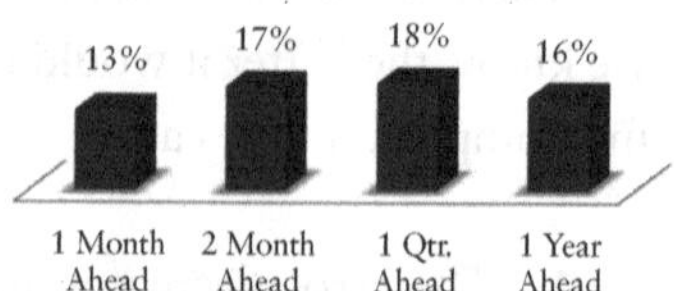

Source: Based on the IBF Surveys.
Note: The errors are averages of four years–2005-2009.

5. How much improvement in forecasting errors can be made depends, among other things, on the stage of development the forecasting function is in. In the initial stage, it is generally easier to improve them. But, as the function matures, further improvements become harder and more costly. Therefore, in our continuing efforts to improve forecasts, we should keep in mind the incremental cost and the incremental benefit.

6. There are two things that are certain in life—death and taxes. In forecasting, we can add the third one—the forecast error. So, we need not only to improve forecasts further but also how to cope with errors. Plus, forecast errors should be an "open book." The users of forecasts should know which product lines' and SKUs' forecasts are likely to be more accurate than others, and when their next update will be available. The longer the time span between forecast updates, the more important it is for a forecaster to communicate quickly the next update to users.

7. It is important to measure forecast performance at a SKU level as well as at a category/brand level. For manufacturing what matters most is the error at a SKU level because inventory decisions are made at that level. Plus, it is the SKU level error that affects the customer service. However, for Marketing and other functions, errors at a more aggregate level may be more important.

PERFORMANCE METRICS

To evaluate the performance of forecasts, we need to have metrics. Although there are number of metrics discussed in the forecasting literature, here we will discuss only five that are used or can be used effectively in business. These are:

1. Mean Percent Error (MPE)
2. Mean Absolute Percent Error (MAPE)
3. Weighted Mean Absolute Percent Error (WMAPE)
4. Forecast Bias
5. Range of Error

Mean Percent Error: The Mean Percent Error (MPE) is the average of percent errors. It is computed as follows:

Step 1: Compute the forecast error, which is the actual value minus forecast. Table 26.1 gives the data of one product with 10 SKUs. The forecast error is given in Column 4 of the same table.

Step 2: Convert the error into a percentage by dividing the error of each period by the actual of the same period, and then multiplying the quotient by 100. (We divide it by the actual because we want to know by how much the forecast deviated from the actual, and not the other way around.) The percentage error of the first period comes to 3.33% [(50 ÷ 1,500) × 100]; of the second period, -4.55% [(-4 ÷ 88) × 100]; and so on. All the percentage errors are given in Column 5.

Step 3: Compute the average percentage error. It is done by dividing the total of percentage errors by the number of observations, which are 10 in this case. It comes to -3.65% (-36.46 ÷ 10).

Note here we compute MPE of a product with 10 different SKUs. If we had a product with the error data of 10 different periods, we would have computed its MPE the same way.

The major flaw with this metric is that an error is an error whether it results from an over- or under-forecast. If it is positive, the error resulted from under-forecasting; if it is negative, it resulted from over-forecasting. But with MPE, over-forecasted (under-forecasted) errors are somewhat offset by under-forecasted (over-forecasted) errors, thereby giving a low error. The next metric, Mean Absolute Percent Error (MAPE), takes care of this problem. However, there is one virtue of MPE, which is, it gives good information about the overall direction of the error. If MPE is negative, which is the case here, it means that we, on average, over-forecasted. If it was positive, it would have meant that we, on average, under-forecasted.

Mean Absolute Percent Error: As mentioned earlier, an error is an error, whether we over- or under-forecast. To account for each type of error we compute the average of percentage errors with signs ignored, that is, average of absolute percentage errors, given in Column 6, Table 26.1. The MAPE here comes to 6.46% (64.55 ÷ 10).

Weighted Mean Absolute Percentage Error: There is also a flaw in MAPE, which is, it gives equal amount of weight to each error. In other words, the error of a small volume product gets the same weight as the error of a large volume. In Table 26.1, for example, the error (5%) of SKU 6, which has sales revenue of $5 million, gets the same amount of weight as the error (14.29%) of SKU 8, which has sales revenue of only $70,000. The WMAPE (Weighted Mean Absolute Percentage Error) overcomes this problem by giving a weight to each by the volume of sales of that product. Here we follow three additional steps:

Step 4: Multiply each absolute percentage error by the sales and put the product in Column 7 in Table 26.1. The product of first period, for example, comes to 5,000 (1,500 × 3.33).

Step 5: Add all the products of Column 7, which comes to 43,700.

Step 6: Compute the Weighted Mean Absolute Percentage Error by dividing the sum total of the product, shown in Column 7, by the total amount of weight, which comes to 5.13% (43,700 ÷ 8,518).

Forecast Bias: Before calculating the bias, it is important to define it, which may vary from one company to another. Technically, there is a bias in a forecast if the accuracy of a forecast is

Table 26.1 | Three Different Forecasting Error Metrics: MPE, MAPE, AND WMAPE

SKU (1)	Sales (thous. of $) (A) (2)	Forecast (thous. of $) (F) (3)	Error (A–F) (4)	% Error $(\frac{A-F}{A} \times 100)$ (5)	Abs.% Error $(\frac{\lvert A-F \rvert}{A} \times 100)$ (6)	Wt. × Abs.% Error (Col.2 × Col.6) (7)
1	1,500	1,450	50	3.33	3.33	5,000
2	88	92	-4	-4.55	4.55	400
3	240	250	-10	-4.17	4.17	1,000
4	450	480	-30	-6.67	6.67	3,000
5	700	750	-50	-7.14	7.14	5,000
6	5,000	5,250	-250	-5.00	5.00	25,000
7	100	95	5	5.00	5.00	500
8	70	80	-10	-14.29	14.29	1,000
9	140	132	8	5.71	5.71	800
10	230	250	-20	-8.70	8.70	2,000
SUM	**8,518**	**8,829**		**-36.46**	**64.55**	**43,700**

$$\text{MPE} = \frac{\Sigma \frac{(A-F)}{A} \times 100}{N} = \frac{-36.46}{10} = -3.65\%$$

$$\text{MAPE} = \frac{\Sigma \frac{\lvert (A-F) \rvert}{A} \times 100}{N} = \frac{64.55}{10} = 6.46\%$$

$$\text{WMAPE} = \frac{\Sigma \frac{\lvert (A-F) \rvert}{A} \times 100 \times A}{\Sigma A} = \frac{43{,}700}{8{,}518} = 5.13\%$$

less than 100%, which is often the case. Since we don't have perfect knowledge, a certain amount of inaccuracy is bound to exist in every forecast, no matter what we do. Therefore, the best way to define it is that there is a bias in a forecast if the accuracy falls below a certain threshold. The threshold can be the accuracy of your baseline forecast. Let's say the threshold of accuracy of a one-month-ahead SKU forecast of a certain product is 80%. This means that we regard the accuracy of 80% as the norm, and anything below that is the result of a bias. The bias can result from a certain individual, department, and/or model. Some forecasters are pessimistic, and others, optimistic, which is reflected in their forecasts. Some departments and individuals have their own agenda, which shows up in their overrides. Production people, for example, may have an over-forecasting bias if they are evaluated on the basis of customer service and production cost. Salespeople, on the other hand, may have an under-forecasting bias, particularly, if their quotas are based on them. Pharmaceutical companies often over-forecast because the loss of profit resulting from a stock-out is far greater than the cost of holding excess inventory. The model used in preparing a forecast may have a tendency to give accuracy much below the norm (or forecast generated by the expert system), which can also be labeled as bias.

Before taking any action, it is important to know how much the bias is and who is causing it? It can be estimated as follows: Prepare a baseline forecast with a statistical model often used by the company or by the expert system. Let's say the accuracy of a baseline forecast is 80%, which we can regard as our threshold. Then determine the accuracy of a forecast with an override of the Sales department, which comes to, say, 70%. This means that the Sales' override has caused a bias of 10 percentage points (80%-70%). If Finance's override resulted in accuracy of 60%, then it created a bias of 20 percentage points. If, on the other hand, Marketing's override gave the accuracy of 90%, then its override has a positive effect because it improved the forecast.

Some businesses consider one-directional consistent forecast error as a bias. In other words, there is a bias in a forecast if it is over-or under-forecasted, say, three periods in a row. Therefore, to improve forecasts, bias must be investigated, so that a proper action can be taken.

Range of Error: The range of error is the expected spread between the smallest and largest error. The range of error can be determined by calculating the standard deviation (SD) of % errors. The larger the SD, the more uncertainty is in a forecast. The SD of the % errors can be computed with Microsoft Excel. (See Appendix A for instructions) The SD of % errors given in Column 6, Table 26.1 comes to 3.17.

There are three ranges that are often used, each with a different probability of occurrence 68%, 95%, and 99%. One SD is associated with 68% level of confidence, two SD with

95% level of confidence, and three SD with 99% level of confidence. If we want to be right 68 times out of 100 (68% level of confidence), the range of % error will be MAPE ± 1 SD, that is, 6.46% ± 1 × 3.17%. This means that the % error can go as low as 3.29% and as high as 9.63%. If we want to be right 95 times out of 100 (95% level of confidence), then the range of % error will be MAPE ± 2 SD, that is, 6.46% ± 2 × 3.17%, as low as 0.12% and as high as 12.80%. Similarly, we can compute the range of % error at 99% level of confidence, which would be MAPE ± 3 SD. This means that the error can be as low as 0% and as high as 15.97%.

How much inventory we should hold depends, among other things, on the size of a forecast error. The higher the error, the more uncertainty is in a forecast, and thus a larger inventory will be required. But we cannot afford to hold large inventory for each and every SKU where forecast error is fairly high. The best strategy may be to hold inventory based on the upper limit of the forecast of a product that is high in profit margin, and lower limit for a product that is low in profit margin. For that reason, pharmaceutical companies often use the upper limit of their forecasts to determine inventory levels.

IMPROVING FORECASTS

To improve forecasts we have to approach them from two different angles: One, break up the institutional barriers that stand in the way. Two, make some procedural changes that are conducive to forecasting.

Institutional Roadblocks: Preparing forecasts is difficult enough, but improving them is even harder particularly where numerous institutional roadblocks stand in the way. Here are the key roadblocks that have to be removed:

1. *Lack of support from the senior management:* Without support from the senior management, it is difficult to get resources for preparing and improving forecasts, and equally difficult for getting cooperation from other functions. The cooperation of other functions is needed because no one has all the information to prepare forecasts. Based on the Institute of Business Forecasting and Planning (IBF) survey conducted in 2009, the senior management of only 49% of companies is fully committed to the forecasting function.

2. *Presence of silo structure:* The silo structure means that each function works as a separate entity within an organization, and there is little or no communication among them. Each one is for itself. Each function prepares forecasts for its own use. No one is watching the numbers of others. As such, there is no pressure to improve forecasts.

3. *Lack of forecasting process:* Forecasts improve when there is a process in place. Without that, there won't be any set procedure for gathering and analyzing data/information, deciding on a model, and preparing forecasts. After statistical forecasts are generated, there won't be any consensus process for overlaying judgment. Judgmental overlay often improves forecasts because it accounts for information that cannot be quantified as well as for the one that was not available at the time forecasts were created. Further, in the absence of a process, there won't be any procedure for monitoring and revising forecasts.

4. *Same amount of attention paid to each product family (SKU):* It is unlikely for forecasts to improve where the same amount of attention is paid to each SKU or brand/category because of limited resources often available for this function. The best strategy, therefore, should be to pay the most attention to products that are high in value and difficult to forecast, and least to those that are low in value and easy to forecast.

5. *Conflicting goals and incentives:* Forecasts are less likely to improve if goals and incentives of different functions are in conflict. In that case, there would be a tug of war; each function would be biasing forecasts in the direction favorable to its own cause. Salespeople would be biasing downward if quotas are based on them. Production people would be biasing upward if their performance is measured on the basis of customer service. The solution may very well be to have an incentive plan that is based on the overall performance of the company as a whole and not on the performance of a specific activity.

6. *Using forecasting software as a black box:* Forecasting software is great because it can automate the process, and prepare forecasts of hundreds and thousands of items in a matter of minutes. Further, it can use the most sophisticated algorithm, which is not possible if they are prepared manually. The problem arises, however, when its output is used at face value without having any understanding of what and why it occurred, the forecaster does not know how to interpret its output, and when there is a problem how to deal with it. The problem becomes even worse if forecasts are not monitored.

7. *No centralized data warehouse, and different data on different platforms:* It is not unusual to find where even the forecaster does not to know what different data exist within an organization and where; if known, they are available on different platforms, making it difficult to retrieve and use them. Without the access to the right data, it is difficult to improve forecasts.

8. *Political bias.* Political bias distorts the forecasts, which arises from the wishes/agendas of senior management and/or from the conflicting interest of different departments. After forecasts are developed, the senior management typically has to sign off, which, at times, becomes a problem. If forecasts are expected to go over the plan, they may be reluctant to approve. If they are expected to go below the plan, which is often the case, they may still be reluctant to accept. There are organizations where the budget is used as a forecast. Persistent bias, according to the late Dick Clark, owner of Demand Planning Global Process at P&G, is an on-going problem in many businesses, which erodes Demand Planning credibility with customers of forecasts.

   Conflicting agendas of different departments also cause a problem. In the case of one food manufacturing company, demand planners' forecast for one product was consistently higher than the actual, which continued for nine months. After three months, demand planners wanted to adjust downward their forecasts, but Marketing did not let them because of a fear of cutback in their promotional budget. Similar problems occur in the case of a new product. For the product manager who has spent a great deal of time in developing the product, it is difficult for him/her to accept that it would fail. At times, the product manager jacks up the forecast to make sure that the product meets the company's financial target for getting the approval.

Procedural Changes: Besides breaking the institutional roadblocks described above, there are a number of procedural changes that are needed to improve forecasts.

1. *Find the source of the problem.* If we know where the problem is, we may know what to do to correct it. An error can result from using wrong and dirty data, wrong assumptions, and/or wrong model. Make sure that the data used are clean and consistent. If we are forecasting shipments, make sure all the observations are of shipments; if we are forecasting orders, make sure all the observations are of orders; and so on. Also, make sure that all the assumptions hold. We planned to spend $20 million on promotion, make sure we do it; your customer planned to open 25 new stores, make sure it occurs; and so on. If any of the assumptions did not hold, neither would the forecasts. At times, some unusual things happen. We expected one large order from a customer, which was not realized; or, we got one large order, which we did not expect. Finally, make sure the model we used was the right one. If there was seasonality in the data, the model accounted for it; if there was a cause-and-effect relationship, the model captured it; and so on. Plus, data were properly analyzed and adjusted for such things as outliers, structural changes, and missing values before generating forecasts.

2. *Use right number of observations.* Make sure the right number of observations (12 months of data, 24 months of data, or any other number) is used for preparing forecasts, which may vary from industry to industry, and from company to company. This can be determined by preparing ex post forecasts. (For detail, see Chapter 13.)

3. *Test forecasts of two or more combined models.* In some cases, forecasts may improve if two (or more) models are combined, say, one from time series and another from regression, or two different models from the same type. The final forecast may be a simple or weighted average of these two forecasts. Again, this should be tested with ex post forecasts.

4. *Eliminate a SKU(s) with a different pattern.* In some cases, it may be necessary to take out one or more SKU(s) from a category/brand because they form a pattern contrary to the pattern of others. For example, regular oven cleaner and fume-free oven cleaner belong to the same category yet form a different pattern, because one cannibalizes the other. The same is true with sugar-free cake and regular cake. The elimination of such SKUs from the category/brand will improve the forecast.

5. *Track the impact of different touch points.* A typical forecasting process includes a number of touch points where various process participants (Sales, Marketing, etc.) override the statistical forecast based on their information. Track their overrides and determine which one is improving the forecast, and which one is not. Eliminate those overrides that are not adding any value.

6. *Seek collaboration from customers.* Collaboration with customers helps. They can provide not only their input about such things as business plans but also their forecasts. "If forecasts are available, use them as an input and not as final forecasts," says Charles Bonomo, former Vice President of Strategic Program at Arrow Electronics. Customers often have a tendency to inflate forecasts to ensure plenty of stock will be available to service their orders.

7. *Use POS data.* Where possible, use Point-of-Sale (POS) data instead of demand and shipment data. POS data are generally more stable, and thus give more accurate forecasts. From POS forecasts, demand and shipment forecasts can be derived, if needed.

8. *Forecast at a higher level of aggregation where necessary.* Products that are difficult to forecast should be forecasted at a more and more aggregate level. If you cannot forecast well at a SKU level, forecast it at a category/brand level. Forecasts improve when prepared

at a higher and higher level of aggregation.

9. *Use skilled people.* It is important the persons involved in forecasting are qualified professionals. The qualified professional here is the one that has self confidence, and knows how to work with cross-functional teams. Besides some statistical background, he or she also has inter-personal and communicative skills, as well as the knack of solving problems and improving processes. Above all, he or she knows the product and the market, and how to get things done.

10. *Make on-going improvements a motto.* The world we live in, market dynamics are continuously changing, and so have to be the models and processes. Therefore, it is important to audit models and processes regularly to find out where improvements are needed.

THINGS TO KEEP IN MIND

An error is an error. No one wants it, but it happens all the time. Here are few things to keep in mind while forecasting:

1. *Error is not bad as long as it is within the acceptable range.* The acceptable range is relative. There are two ways of looking at it. One is the adjustment capability of a company. The quicker a company can adjust to an error, the larger the error it can tolerate. Two, the cost of an error—the higher the cost of an error, the less the company can afford.

2. *Error is not bad as long as we learn from it and put it to a good use.* At times error turns out to be a blessing and opens up new opportunities. Agonizing over the past error does not help, but what can help us is the emotion-free analysis of the error. One direct-mail company that raised funds by mail tested a list that had a lot of duplications. The list did very well. On the next test of the same list, the marketing manager thought it could further improve the response if duplications were removed. Instead, the response went down sharply. That opened up the eyes of the manager—duplications don't hurt; they help. With that information, the company started going back to donors six weeks after they made the donation, acknowledged their donation, and at the same time asked for more. On the acknowledgment mailing, the company started getting a response close to 12%, something unheard of. As such, the error turned out to be a blessing for the company; it provided additional source of revenue. In addition, by investigating the error we may find the root cause; when corrected would improve forecasts.

3. *Error is not bad as long as we are not intimidated by it.* If we are afraid of making an error, we might be afraid of making a decision. In business, decisions have to be made whether right or wrong. If a certain decision turns out to be wrong, learn from it, and move forward.

4. *No credit for good forecasts.* Forecasters must recognize that they are less likely to get any credit for good forecasts, but surely be blamed for bad forecasts, which is part of the job. In other words, good forecasts are rarely remembered, but bad ones are never forgotten.

5. *Never accept forecasts at face value.* Always question the basis on which forecasts were generated. Each forecast is based on a set of assumptions about the economy, media spending, price, etc. If any of the assumptions is wrong, so would be the forecast. Also, statistics is generally the basis of forecasts. If it is misused, it can cause a disaster. Disraeli once said, "There are three kinds of lies: lies, damn lies, and statistics."

HOW MUCH PROGRESS HAVE WE MADE?

Over the last two decades or so, a number of developments have taken place; some helped to improve forecasts, and others made them worse. The advancement in computer technology has improved our computing power and enabled us to use even the most sophisticated algorithms, which previously was not possible. The development of enterprise data warehouse technology has enabled us not only to store all the data at one place but also made it easier to access. The process plays an important role in forecasting, which has progressed from Silo Forecasting (SF) to Consensus Forecasting (CF) to Sales And Operations Planning (S&OP) to Collaborative Planning, Forecasting and Replenishment (CPFR®) to Integrated Business Planning (IBP). The access to POS data provides the marketers a handle on the changing market dynamics quickly and pretty accurately about what products consumers are buying and not buying. The skill set of forecasters has greatly improved, and so has the perception about forecasting. Forecasting is no longer viewed as a voodoo science but an important tool for planning. All these helped to improve forecasts. At the same time, a number of other developments have taken place, which have made forecasting more difficult. Forecasting is now demand driven, not supply driven; consumers are less loyal and more demanding; the number of products have exploded; the number of channels of distribution have proliferated; the life cycles of products have shortened; and the competition has become more intense because of globalization.

What happened to the quality of forecasts over time is the net result of these two opposing forces. To determine whether or not we have made progress, we analyzed the survey data of forecast errors collected over the last 10 years (2000-2009). The surveys were conducted by the

Institute of Business Forecasting and Planning (IBF) at their forecasting conferences and tutorials, and the errors surveyed were MAPEs. We broke down the data into two groups, five years each, 2000-2004 and 2005-2009. We investigated the improvement at three levels: SKU, category, and aggregate, and at four different forecast horizons: one-month ahead, two-month ahead, one-quarter ahead, and one-year ahead. We compared the five-year average of each error of both groups, that is, of 2000-2004 against 2005-2009. The data show when all the industries are combined, forecast errors at all levels (SKU, category, and aggregate) and at all the four different forecast horizons (1-month ahead, 2-month ahead, 1-quarter ahead, and 1-year ahead) either stayed the same or went up, with one exception of category level forecast at 2-month ahead forecasts where it went down though slightly. (See Figures 26.4-26.6)

Further, we investigated two industries—Consumer Products and Food & Beverages—to see how much progress they made in forecasting errors. The data show that the Consumer Products industry did not make much progress. By and large, errors went up instead of going down (see Figures 26.7 through 26.9). However, the Food and Beverages industry made some progress. This may be because products produced by this industry are relatively more stable (see Figures 26.10 through 26.12).

Figure 26.4
% Forecast Errors at a SKU Level
■ 2000-2004 vs. ■ 2005-2009
All Industries Combined

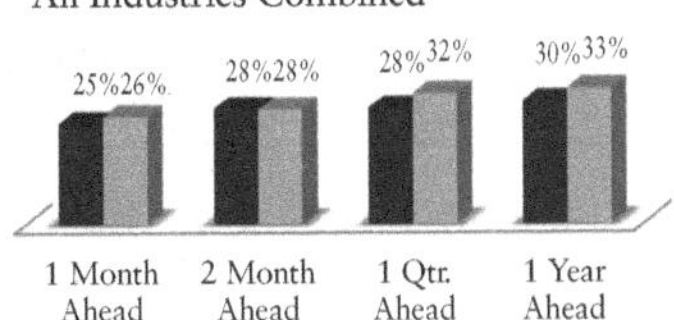

Figure 26.5
% Forecast Errors at a Category Level
■ 2000-2004 vs. ■ 2005-2009
All Industries Combined

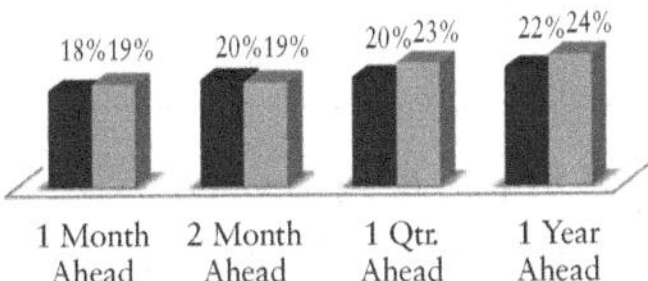

Figure 26.6
% Forecast Errors at an Aggregate Level
■ 2000-2004 vs. ■ 2005-2009
All Industries Combined

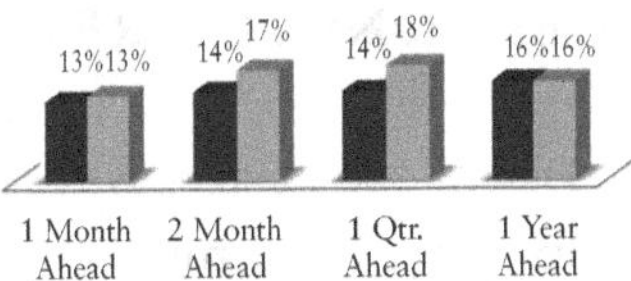

Figure 26.7
% Forecast Errors at a SKU Level
■ 2000-2004 vs. ■ 2005-2009
Consumer Products Industry

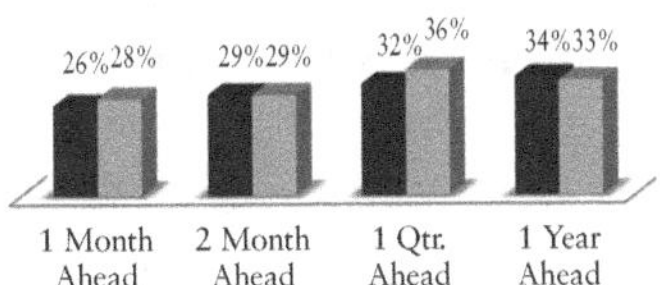

Figure 26.8
% Forecast Errors at a Category Level
■ 2000-2004 vs. ■ 2005-2009
Consumer Products Industry

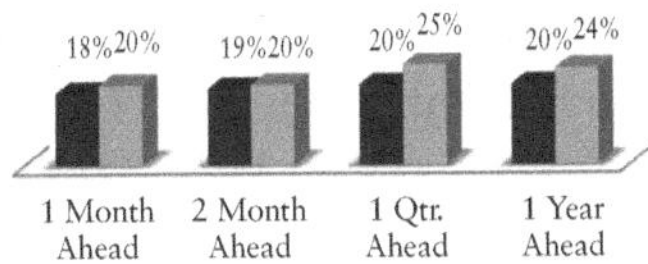

Figure 26.9
% Forecast Errors at an Aggregate Level
■ 2000-2004 vs. ■ 2005-2009
Consumer Products Industry

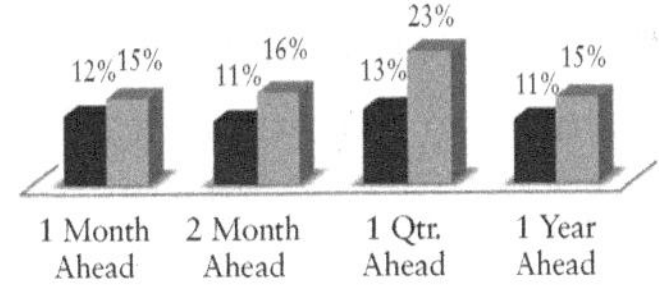

Source : Based on the IBF Surveys.
Note : The errors are averages of five years—2000-2004 & 2005-2009.

Figure 26.10
% Forecast Errors at a SKU Level
■ 2000-2004 vs. ■ 2005-2009
Food and Beverage Industry

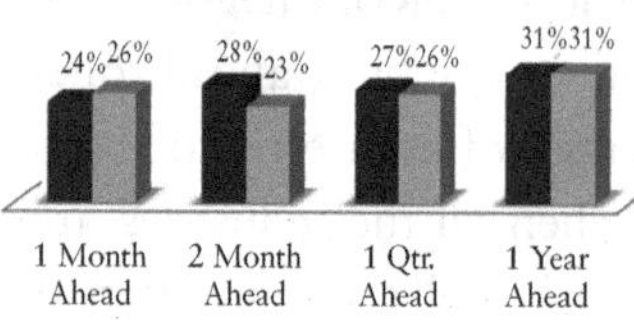

Figure 26.11
% Forecast Errors at a Category Level
■ 2000-2004 vs. ■ 2005-2009
Food and Beverage Industry

Figure 26.12
% Forecast Errors at an Aggregate Level
■ 2000-2004 vs. ■ 2005-2009
Food and Beverage Industry

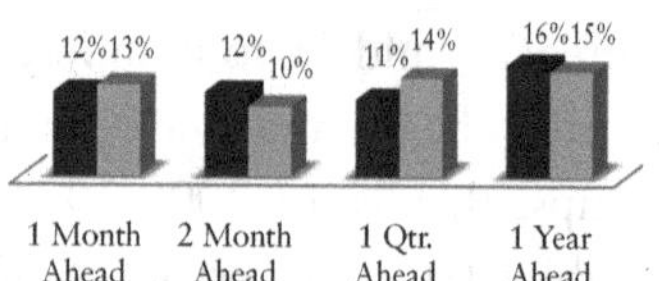

Source : Based on the IBF Surveys.
Note : The errors are averages of five years—2000-2004 & 2005-2009.

SUGGESTED READING

1. Bonomo, Charles. "Forecasting from the Center of the Supply Chain." *Journal of Business Forecasting*. Spring 2003, pp. 3-9.
2. Drum, William J. "Living With Forecast Error." *Journal of Business Forecasting*. Summer 1992, p. 23.
3. Gilliland, Michael. "Alternative Metrics for Forecasting Performance." *Journal of Business Forecasting*. Winter 2003-04, pp. 17-20.
4. Milliken. Alan. "Key Ingredients of Successful Performance Metrics in the Supply Chain." *Journal of Business Forecasting*. Summer 2001, pp. 23, 28.

QUESTIONS FOR REVIEW

1. Describe what steps we can take to improve forecasts.
2. Explain why customers provide over-forecasted numbers to their suppliers.
3. Explain in what way WMAPE, the error metric, improves over MAPE.
4. Describe four key fundamentals of forecasting errors.
5. Why does forecast error decrease as we forecast at a more and more aggregate level? Explain.
6. Explain why it is difficult to forecast in a highly competitive market.
7. Explain how incentives given to different functions stand in the way of improving forecasts.
8. "The longer the time span between forecast updates, the more important it is for a forecast function to communicate quickly the updates to users." Explain.

9. The table below gives sales and forecast data of China Shoe Company. From the data, compute:
   a. MAPE
   b. Range of errors at 68% level of confidence.

China Shoe Company		
SKU	Actual Sales (Mil. of $)	Forecast (Mil. of $)
1	2,400	2,350
2	70	74
3	300	288
4	551	560
5	825	820
6	6,500	6,450
7	150	160
8	60	51
9	241	248
10	260	271

Answers:
a. 4.36%
b. Low, 0.11% and high, 8.61%

10. From the table given in question 9, compute WMAPE.
Answer: 1.47%

PART VIII

COMMUNICATING FORECASTS

INTRODUCTION

No matter how good the forecasts are, if they are not accepted and used, they are useless. The job of a forecaster is not only to prepare forecasts but also sell them. This requires a special skill for reporting and presenting forecasts, as well as for building trust with customers. This part explains what kinds of problems, political or otherwise, a forecaster often encounters and how to deal with them. The road to success in forecasting is long and arduous. But with determination, hard work, and perseverance, a forecaster can make it.

CHAPTER 27

REPORTING, PRESENTING, AND SELLING FORECASTS

Accurate forecasts are important, but their value is greatly enhanced if they are properly reported and communicated. Forecasts have no value if they are neither accepted nor used. One forecasting director once remarked, "I would rather spend my time on refining and improving forecasts than on selling them, but business realities don't permit this." Therefore, it is important for a forecaster to learn not only how to prepare forecasts but also how to report, present, and sell them.

RULES FOR REPORTING, PRESENTING, AND SELLING FORECASTS

There are rules for reporting, presenting, and selling forecasts; if followed, they can greatly enhance the forecasts' value. Here we will describe rules for each one of these. However, there are some general rules that apply to all of these that we will discuss here.

General Rule No. 1
Know Your Customers

One of the key rules to successful reporting, presenting, and selling forecasts is to know your customers. Who are they, what do they want, and where and how do they use forecasts? Here customers are the forecast users. Different functions including Production, Logistics, Sales, Marketing, Planning, and Finance are the customers, and so is the senior management. It is easier for forecasts to be accepted and used if they get what they want. Therefore, before preparing forecasts, it is important to know their needs: (1) Which variables are to be forecasted—shipment, demand, cash flow, etc.? (2) In what form do they need forecasts—in dollars, units, and/or percent? (3) What level of detail do they want, that is, do they want forecasts at a SKU level, category/brand level, and/or aggregate level? On an entity level, do they want forecasts by sales division, distribution center, manufacturing location, broker, and/or account? On a channel level, of which trades/companies do they need forecasts? For a food channel, for example, they may need forecasts of the channel as well as of its key companies such as Pathmark, Shoprite, and Public; for a drug store channel, of its channel as well as of its key accounts such as Drug Emporium, Walgreens, and CVS; for a warehouse club channel, of its channel as well as of its key companies such as Costco and Sam; and/or of government units? (4) In what time buckets do they need forecasts—by day, week, quarter, year, and/or by any other time bucket? (5) How far ahead do they need them—one-month ahead, one-quarter ahead, one-year ahead, and/or by any other time period? (6) What is their acceptable forecasting error?

The senior management is also an important customer; it may need forecasts in both dollars and units, but at a more aggregate level. Further, it may need not only forecasts and their expected errors but also what drives the business, says, Charles Chase, Market Strategy Manager at SAS Institute, Inc. The management also wants to know how promotional activities, competitive actions, and price changes affect the business. It also wants to know which factors are controllable and which are not. Above all, it wants to know not only what can happen but also what can be done to change it.

General Rule No. 2
Involve Your Customers in the Process

The participation of forecast users in the process is important not only for knowing their needs, but also for getting their buy-in and improving forecasts. They can help the forecaster by providing input, establishing assumptions, determining most probable scenarios, and overlaying judgment over statistical forecasts. Forecasts are not prepared in isolation. The forecaster needs input from Sales and Marketing. From Sales, it needs market intelligence—what consumers/customers are buying and not buying, and why. From marketing, it needs promotional plans, products they plan to introduce and abandon, and markets they plan to enter and exit. Finance often controls the budget. Involvement of various functions in the process enables the forecaster to not only get their input but also to take care of their issues and concerns before they become snarling arguments. Maybe they are not getting forecasts on time; maybe they need forecasts by account and not by territory; and/or maybe they just don't trust the numbers. If users are involved in the process, it would be easier for a forecaster to know their issues and concerns, and then do something about them. Further, with their involvement, it would be easier to get their buy-in. It would also make it possible for a forecaster to circulate preliminary forecasts, and resolve most or all of the issues before the final presentation. If something is not resolved, the forecaster may know how to defend himself/herself in the meeting.

General Rule No. 3
Educate Forecast Users

In most presentations, the burden of effective communication is placed on the communicator. It is a heavy burden; not only must the communicator make complex issues easy to understand, but also present them in an entertaining way. Implicit in this view is that the listener has no responsibility; he/she needs only to lend an ear. Of course, there can be no communication in the absence of listening. But listeners cannot fully understand unless they have some working knowledge about the subject. While a thorough knowledge of advanced statistics is required to build a model, it does not follow that listeners need the same degree of knowledge to understand and make a judgment. What they need is the working knowledge. It would be sufficient if the managers know what kinds of assumptions are made in preparing forecasts, where Time Series models are appropriate, where Cause-and-Effect models are used, why forecasts cannot be 100% accurate, how to evaluate the forecast performance, and so on. Assumptions might be about the advertising budget, price, competitive action, and state of the economy. The forecast users must understand that forecasts are necessary for planning. The choice is to either make plans with informally generated numbers or with ones that are formally created. (If forecasts are formally prepared, they are more likely to improve over time.) They also have to understand that forecasts are neither a goal nor a plan; instead, they are based on a plan. We cannot just change the forecast numbers without changing the plan. Above all, they have to realize that forecasting is not entirely a science; a great deal of judgment goes into it. For effective communication, the burden of communication falls both on the forecaster and the listener.

Forecasts are often not accepted because of the perception that forecasters are just "quantitative techies" who don't understand what really goes on in the marketplace; they were burned out in the past; they don't fully understand how forecasts were developed; and/or they have a disagreement on the premises that were used in generating forecasts. To shed the image of "quantitative techies," forecasters have to prove themselves with good forecasts, which may be a long drawn-out process. Forecasters have to make the customers aware that all SKUs/categories are not equally forecastable; some are easier than the others. To resolve the issue of forecast premises, the forecaster should have an agreement on them before preparing forecasts.

The forecaster can play an important part in educating forecast users. The users can be educated by offering them a seminar on forecasting and/or explaining something about it at the organization's regularly scheduled meeting. Attending forecasting conferences and/or tutorials can also help. No matter how we educate them, keep in mind that managers want to learn, they don't want to be taught.

Forecasters themselves also need some learning. They need to change their perception about users. I have heard some forecasters saying:

> *I feel like I'm dealing with a bunch of idiots. They don't seem to grasp even the basic logic of what I'm trying to tell them. After running hundreds and hundreds of scenarios and thousands of simulations, I really want to tell them: Shut up. If you don't trust my numbers, then why ask?*

It appears there is a communication gap that has to be closed. The users are smart too. They don't want to accept anything at face value. It is the responsibility of forecasters to prove to them why they should be using their numbers. Therefore, to succeed in this function, forecasters have to educate the users. They have to build trust, which, of course, does not happen overnight.

REPORTING FORECASTS

Although it is very difficult to lay down rules for reporting, presenting, and selling forecasts specific to each activity because of some overlapping, we did the best we could. First we will describe the rules for reporting.

Reporting: Rule No. 1
Report Forecasts in Detail

The forecast report should be in as much detail as needed, because each function has its own need. The report should be such that it satisfies everyone. Production needs forecasts in units at a SKU level; Finance in dollars at an aggregate level; and Sales may need both in units and dollars at a category/brand level as well as by geographical territory and account. The senior management may need them only at a highly aggregated level. In some cases, particularly in a volatile economy, forecasts under different scenarios may be needed, for example, what would happen if the recession continues, or the economy grows just by 1%. Forecasts with multiple scenarios, particularly during volatile times, can increase confidence in decisions because a wide range of options have been evaluated. At times, range forecasts—"worst case" and "best case" scenarios—can alert decision makers that such possibilities exist.

Although detailed forecasts are needed for reporting, the presentation should be concise and brief because of limited time and because it is difficult to hold the attention of listeners for a longer period of time. If anyone is interested in more detail, he/she can always go to the report.

Reporting: Rule No. 2
Give Assumptions

Give all the assumptions made in preparing forecasts. Each forecast is based on some assumptions about the promotional plan, products to be introduced or abandoned, the state of the economy, competitive action, etc. The acceptance or rejection of forecasts depends very much on how well the users agree with the assumptions. Therefore, where possible, the forecaster should get an agreement on assumptions before preparing forecasts. The forecaster, for example, may prepare forecasts on the basis that a price increase will cause a significant forward purchase by the channel distributors by stockpiling the product at a lower price, but the users may disagree on the grounds that the cost of financing a large chunk of inventory would reduce their margin over time because of the high inventory carrying costs.

Reporting: Rule No. 3
If the Forecast Deviates from the Norm, Explain

If a forecast deviates significantly from the norm, give reasons. The forecast of a certain product may be high because one of the large customers plans to add a few more stores, one of the competitors has gone out of business, and/or the company expects to receive a large order from the government. By the same token, the forecaster may expect a significant decline in sales of a certain product because of the introduction of a new product by a competitor, recall of a certain product, and/or political changes in a country where it is exported. Explaining all these upfront helps the users to understand the numbers better, and creates trust as well.

Reporting: Rule No. 4
Make Sure Forecasts Are Internally Consistent

Make sure all the calculations are correct, all the forecasts are internally consistent, and each column adds up correctly. Forecast users often look upon forecasts with suspicion and distrust. If one thing is wrong, they will regard the whole thing wrong.

Reporting: Rule No. 5
Show Forecasts Along with Actuals

To build trust, it is important to show forecasts along with actuals so that they can see how good they were. Also, show current forecasts along with targets (plans) to see whether or not targets would be met. If there are gaps, explain why. Identify what options we have to close the gaps and their implications. Maybe we have to divert resources from one brand to another; restructure the product folio and bring some new products to the market a little earlier; and/or look for another market here and abroad. Whatever options there may be, bring each to their attention along with associated costs and likelihood of success. If there is a change in trend in any product, indicate that too. A brief narrative on these along with supporting documents is necessary to build trust, says Martin Joseph, Managing Director, Rivershill Consultancy, Ltd.

Reporting: Rule No. 6
Use a Standard Format

The use of a standard format for forecast reporting makes it easier for users to find forecasts. They will know right away where forecasts of their interests are listed. Also, use the same metrics every time forecasts are reported. This makes it easier to determine how good the forecasts are and how much progress has been made. Changing them may create a suspicion in the mind of users, thinking the forecaster did it so that he or she looked good. Changing forecasting techniques also can create a similar problem. But, when a change is necessary, explain why.

PRESENTING FORECASTS

How forecasts are communicated also makes a difference. A good presentation can turn even the skeptics into believers. Here are the key rules for presenting forecasts.

Presenting: Rule No. 1
Use Simple Language

Present forecasts in a plain and simple language, free of any jargon. Every business has its own culture, terminology, and language. Use the terms and the language they are accustomed to. With that, the forecaster is likely to get a more sympathetic ear from its audience. They will feel that you are one of their own, and not an outsider. Keep the presentation broad and concise. If they want more detail on any forecast, they can look at the report. Remember, you have a limited time to make the presentation.

Presenting: Rule No. 2
Use Graphs, Not Tables

In presenting forecasts, use graphs because it takes longer to process and understand the information when presented in a tabular format, particularly when a trend in the data has to be demonstrated. By plotting actuals against the forecasts, a forecaster can easily demonstrate how good the forecasts are. By overlaying forecasts over the plan, the forecaster can show how forecasts compare with the plan. Graphs also make the job of the forecaster easier where the cause-and-effect relationship has to be demonstrated. But if they are loaded with text, which the forecaster just reads in the meeting, they can create resentment. In that case, listeners might think they would have saved time and boredom if the forecaster just e-mailed the file.

Presenting: Rule No. 3
Let Them Know Products Easier/More Difficult to Forecast

The forecast users will be better judges of forecasts if they know which products are easier and more difficult to forecast, and why. It is important, therefore, for a forecaster to educate the users. The more they understand the problems, the more they will appreciate the forecasts.

Presenting: Rule No. 4
Be Diplomatic

For an effective presentation, forecasters have to be very diplomatic, and stay neutral wherever possible. At times, forecasters may have to show different options and their consequences, but the decision has to be theirs—the users. They have to decide themselves which option to take. Also, try to compromise and not to confront. At times, they may question a certain forecast(s)—it may be either too high or too low. If it is not too far away, compromise. A forecast is a forecast. The actual may turn out to be somewhat higher or lower than the projected number. If the proposed number is far away from the forecast, make a case. If that does not work, accept it, but document the numbers, yours and theirs. When the actual is in, everyone will know it.

Remember, the function of forecasters is to provide input and not to make decisions. They are not indispensable. Managers can make decisions even without their input.

Presenting: Rule No. 5.
Observe Your Audience Closely

While making a presentation, the forecaster should be conscious of how listeners are responding to the presentation, which can be observed by watching how attentive they are, their body language, and/or whether or not they are asking any questions and/or taking notes. If the observation is contrary to the expectations, stop right there and clean up your act.

SELLING FORECASTS

As mentioned earlier, forecasts have no value if they are not accepted and used. So, forecasters not only have to produce good forecasts but also know how to sell them. Here are a few rules that can be helpful.

Selling: Rule No. 1
Blessing of Top Management

Nothing will work if the top management does not see the value in forecasts and is not committed to the forecasting function. This requires education and understanding. Wherever possible, dollarize the benefits of improving forecasts. For example, how much money we would have saved if we had reduced the inventory by five days, and how much sales we would have increased if we had cut down the stock-out by 10%. Furthermore, the forecaster must appreciate the perspective of users. They may be sensitive to the organization's structure, limitations, and priorities. At times, the forecasters may find that a given project is not viable yet management decides to hold on to it because it cannot afford to lay off so many people at one time, or people from the top echelon have a special interest in the project, or are afraid of the adverse publicity that might come with the termination of the project. Terminating a project is not like deleting a line on a computer.

Selling forecasts may become a little easier if forecasters first sell forecasts to a senior manager (a person with a big clout) and then to the first line of subordinates in a meeting with the manager, and then to line subordinates. If forecasters have buy in from the big boss, the others are more likely to accept. Also, the reality is not just how accurate the forecasts are but how strong an alliance the forecasters have developed with people at the top and others. Most of the organizations now have a Consensus process in place. When forecasts are collectively finalized, it is easier to get their buy-in.

Selling: Rule No. 2
Discover New Uses

Discover new and better ways of using forecasts; this will encourage users to use more of them. When Adam Pilarksi, former Chief Economist of Douglas Aircraft Company, McDonnell Douglas Corporation, told his purchasing department how they could use forecasts of foreign exchange and inflation rates of different countries in negotiating contracts for purchasing parts from abroad, they were mighty pleased. Their forecasts helped them to negotiate better deals with foreign sub-contractors, enabling them to save millions of dollars.

Selling: Rule No. 3
Have Patience

To get buy-in, forecasters have to win the confidence of forecast users, which can be a long and frustrating battle, but it is attainable with determination, patience, and perseverance. The forecast users often question why the crystal ball of forecasters is better than their own. At Parke-Davis, it was an uphill task to sell forecasts to the marketing management, but with patience, determination, and the proper strategy they succeeded, says Debra M. Schramm, former Manager of Sales Forecasting. They followed their strategy in two steps: First, they took a hard look at the information they were generating and asked themselves whether it would stand up to the scrutiny from both within and outside the department. They tracked system-generated forecasts in relation to the management-generated numbers. They identified their confidence level for each forecast and were prepared to defend their position. After that, they started introducing their own forecasts into the management process. In the beginning, the management showed no interest whatsoever in their forecasts. Tactful persistence became a must. Each month, the forecast staff stressed those forecasts in which they had high confidence and documented how and why they were better than those generated by the management. They issued a report, which they thought would be helpful to them, and with that included their own forecasts. Eventually, those attending the meeting became accustomed to seeing the forecasts, and began to question why their numbers were different from their own. That was a turning point. Today, forecasts prepared by the forecasting staff are an integral part of the management process.

Selling: Rule No. 4
Give Credit Where Credit Is Due

It is important to give proper credit to those who contributed to the development of forecasts by providing inputs and commenting on preliminary forecasts, because this would give them the recognition to senior management, ensuring that management knows who participated in the process. Also, if participants realize that their contributions would be recognized, they are likely to be more supportive and more appreciative of forecasts.

Selling: Rule No. 5
Eliminate the Line That Separates

The worst thing forecasters can ever do is to brag about their forecasts; doing so may imply that they know more than the decision makers, and thus are superior to them. Braggarts forget the fact that forecasts can go sour any time. People tend to remember bad forecasts much longer than good forecasts. They also forget that they are not the boss; they simply provide the input used in making decisions. Equally bad is for forecasters to use the word "You" instead of "We" in presenting forecasts; that is, talking about what "You" should be doing instead of what "We" should be doing. By using "You," forecasters draw a line, separating themselves from the others— the forecasters are outsiders, not a part of the same team and the same problem/solution. Furthermore, with that perspective, a true dialog will never emerge. Forecasters will never be accepted and get the respect they deserve.

Very often, forecasters think that their relationship with the users is strictly business, tied to the data, technical skill, and professional expertise. They are afraid if they combine their personal relationship with the profession, they will lose objectivity and professionalism. They forget the fact that business is driven by people, who are the important part of the equation. Mastering the technical skill is not enough without the recognition of human values and how to deal with them. Forecasting is not an exclusively logical and rational process. It is an emotional duet between the forecasters and the users, which has to be played together. To succeed, forecasters have to learn not only how to recognize and deal with the duet role, but also how to respond to the emotions of users.

There are three key elements that play a part in decision making—substance (hard facts), process, and people. In a recent workshop of decision makers, there was a strong consensus that substance plays a very small role—only 10%. The element that plays a critical role is people—50%. (See Figure 27.1)

LEARNING FROM REAL LIFE EXPERIENCE

Hu Song and John Triantis have spent a number of years in presenting and selling forecasts in the pharmaceutical industry. Here we share their learning. For the sake of convenience, we will identify them by the name of David.

Don't challenge the assumptions of others but make them understand: David was once asked to create a sales forecast of a new formula. The brand team believed that the switching rate of patients from the current formula to the new one would be 80%, despite the fact that the new formula would not be available until six months after the existing formula's patent expires. David felt that the switching rate was overly optimistic, but was afraid to tell, thinking it might cause an opposite reaction. So, he thought it would be better if he could make the team itself recognize the reality of the market. So, David started asking these questions to the team:

1. Does the new formula have significant benefits over the old one?
2. Would the cost per course of therapy be different?
3. What would be the price of a generic?
4. How long would it take for a generic to replace the brand drug?
5. Would the company commit adequate resources to promote this new formula?

Figure 27.1 | What Percent of Descisions Are Based on Substance

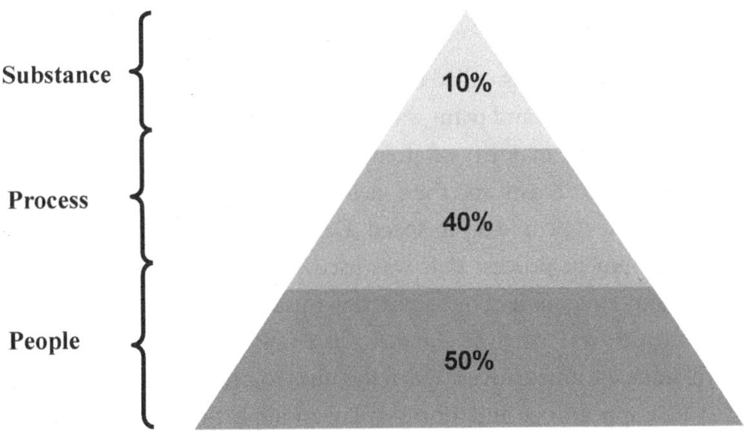

With that, the brand team became more aware of market realities, and started working with David to come up with a forecast that was more realistic and achievable without twisting anyone's arm.

What clients want the most is not necessarily the most precise forecast, but someone who can take away their worries and be on their side. Yet all too often, they encounter forecasters who add to their worries, threaten their pride, and create extra headaches, thereby forcing them to confront—something they really don't want to do. In the above assessment, David felt that the team was working hard to retain its sales and hold the market position. At the same time, it was fighting for having more internal resources. What was needed here was assurance as well as ways to rationalize their estimates and enhance their credibility in the eyes of the senior management. Challenging the 80% switching rate would have simply added salt to the team's wound. So, the first thing to do in that case was to move away from confrontation. If we want to influence a client, we must find ways to prove that we are there to help, not to criticize them or their work. Furthermore, we must demonstrate that we are not in any way superior to them. Therefore, to succeed in this function, forecasters must build an alliance with the users.

Earn your trust: Once David was assigned to work with one team. During the introductory meeting, the director looked at David and said that he had lots of experience in forecasting, but his key staff members were not well trained in the area. He wanted someone to train them. David volunteered for this job. By doing this, David won the trust and the team's respect. One of the team members commented: "David, you have turned the most painful task into an enjoyable learning experience." Providing training not only helped the director and his group, but also benefited David. It lowered the communication barriers, brought them closer, and gave them the opportunity to understand him better.

Rise to the occasion: One time David was called on to present an approved sales forecast in a pre-launch meeting. He noticed that the brand team was in a panic, because several very different sales estimates were floating around, the majority of attendees did not know each other, and were not aware of existing approved sales forecasts and their methodology. So, his first goal was not to present his forecasts but bring the new people up to speed. David spent most of the time walking them through the forecast development process that was used, the underlying logic, the market research findings, and the assumptions made. For forecasters to succeed, they should be both an introvert and extrovert. Be an introvert when it comes to listening to comments and criticism, which at times can be very blatant. Be an extrovert when it comes to presenting and talking to the team members and clients. Here appearance and attitude play an important role.

Know your client: Whoever the forecast users or clients are, forecasters should try to know them as much as possible—their job responsibility, professional background, personal interests, their concerns, and the issues that are very close to their heart. By knowing these, forecasters will know better how to deal with them.

A few years ago, David was assigned to work with a medical director. Six forecasters before him were fired or let go by this medical director. He had a worldwide reputation, but was very arrogant. Very few people wanted to work with him. It appeared that the director suffered from "attention deficit disorder." So, David arranged his first meeting with him not in his office, but in the company's cafeteria. Before the meeting, David went over all his publications. At the meeting, the conversation mostly centered on their college experiences and child health issues. David discovered that he and the medical director graduated from the same university. As such, they ended up having a great working relationship, co-authored publications, and the medical director even served as a job reference for him.

Dealing with different perspectives: Dealing with different perspectives requires that forecasters understand how others see things, make them recognize their biases, and try to argue from their perspective. David once had to review discrepancies between the forecast his forecasting group created and the forecast generated by one of the marketing companies, which was fairly aggressive. The forecast developed by the David's forecasting group had a modest goal. Based on the David's research, the forecast submitted by the marketing company was too high to achieve. This may be because the marketing company was under pressure to bring the forecast number close to the client's expectation. David chose not to challenge directly the marketing company's sales forecast. Instead, he used all the data provided by the marketing company to construct several scenarios. These scenarios indisputably showed that the marketing company's forecast was unrealistic because it exceeded the total number of patients potentially available for any kind of treatment. As a result, the marketing company withdrew its aggressive sales forecast.

Dealing with team dynamics: Often forecasters have to deal with multiple teams with people from different constituencies with different perspectives, and different personalities. On one occasion, David was asked to develop forecasts for three line-extension projects under a very short deadline. Three directors were assigned to work with him; each led a different line extension project. Based on David's previous experience working with them, he would get three different directions on the same issue from these three different directors. Not only that, they have a tendency to override each other's decision. So, David's approach was to set up a clear agenda by getting all the three together, and agreeing on the direction. Before starting the work, David asked all the three directors to make a commitment to work together. He also worked out guidelines, which they all had to sign on. With that, they were able to deliver reasonable estimates for all the three projects within budget and on time.

Not enough to be right: When David started his consulting career, he was once asked to conduct a secondary epidemiological assessment. The task was clear and the research was straightforward. A week later, the project was completed and mailed to the client. To David's surprise, he got a call from the client who did not like the report and was very angry. So, she sent the report back to him. David went back and checked and re-checked all the data, logic, tables, charts, and references. He could not see any problem in the report.

David had to re-establish the communication to find out why she felt the way she did. He put together a letter for the client and further explained the methodology, data, and findings. A brief message came back from the client indicating that David's assessment was not comprehensive. So, David went back to all the scientific publications, government reports, syndicated reports, and even looked at the congressional debate reports of the last 20 years. At the same time, one of the David's colleagues arranged a face-to-face meeting with the client, and found out that the client had a preconceived idea about the market. To support her preconceived notion, the client's company had already invested substantial amount of money and time in a clinical trial. Accepting a very different forecast would have harmed the client's reputation and, more importantly, brought changes in the strategic plan, jobs, and resource distribution.

Now David had to find a way to get the message to his client: "Your baby is not as pretty as you think." By then, three weeks had passed. All of the data and results had to be reviewed by an internal investigation team. By a stroke of luck, the chief epidemiologist of the client's company investigated the David's report and found his data and methodology highly acceptable. But David never got a chance to present his findings to the senior management of the client.

If David had done his homework to determine what his client really needed (in this case, what she needed was confirmation to take away her worries), he would not have spent all the time in checking and re-checking all the data. Instead, David's findings forced her to confront him. This happened also because David did not earn her trust before he offered his honest and objective advice.

The lesson that David learned is that it is not enough for a professional to be right; a forecaster's job is to be helpful. David had to earn the right to be critical. We forecasters need to develop a skill of telling clients that they are unrealistic in a way that they don't feel threatened, and are willing to study our report a little more seriously.

SUGGESTED READING

1. Song, Hu and John Triantis. "Building Alliance with Clients: Key to Success in Forecasting." *Journal of Business Forecasting.* Winter 2002-2003, pp. 2-8.
2. Migliaro, Al and Robert Brown. "The Yogi and Kommissar" in *Practical Guide to Business Forecasting.* New York: Graceway Publishing Company. 2005, pp. 438-443.
3. Cleghorn, J. Robert. "How to Prepare, Report, and Present Forecast: CLECO Power's Experience." *Journal of Business Forecasting.* Summer 2001, pp. 3-4, 22.
4. Chase Jr., Charles W. "Getting People to Use Your Forecasts." *Journal of Business Forecasting.* Spring 1998, pp. 2, 30, 40.
5. Schramm, Debra M. "How to Sell Forecasts to Management." *Journal of Business Forecasting.* Winter 1991-1992, p. 22.

QUESTIONS FOR REVIEW

1. In presenting forecasts, should we use the word "You" or "We," or does it matter? Explain.
2. In presenting forecasts to upper management, should the forecaster convey his or her message in technical or simple terms, and why? Explain.
3. What is the best strategy for a forecaster to follow—sell first to the boss and then to the first line of subordinates, or sell first to the first line of subordinates and then to the boss? Explain.
4. Should a forecast presentation to the upper management be concise or detailed, and why? Explain.
5. Is it appropriate to use a different format each time forecasts are reported? Why and why not?
6. Does management look for forecasts at a more granular level or at a more aggregate level, and why? Explain.
7. Should we give forecast training to those who prepare forecasts, to those who use forecasts, or to both? Explain.
8. Are most of the decisions made by decision makers based on emotions or hard facts? Explain.
9. Explain three key rules for reporting forecasts.
10. Explain two key rules for selling forecasts to forecast customers.

IX

WORST PRACTICES

INTRODUCTION

To take care of any problem, it is important that you recognize and acknowledge it. If you don't recognize it as a problem, you won't do anything about it. In this part, we will describe what practitioners of demand planning and forecasting are doing wrong, resulting primarily from a lack of understanding about the fundamentals, and improper uses of processes, data, models, performance metrics, and software/systems. The purpose here is to bring to light those practices so that practitioners can see and do something about them.

CHAPTER 28

WORST PRACTICES IN DEMAND PLANNING AND FORECASTING

The first step to improve demand planning and forecasting is to recognize the problems. If you don't recognize them, you won't do anything about them. In this chapter, we highlight the worst practices in demand planning and forecasting, and the problems they cause. The person who started with a mission to bring "Worst Practices" into the open was Michael Gilliland, Product Marketing Manager-Forecasting at SAS Institute.

MISUNDERSTANDING OF THE BASICS

There are practitioners who do not fully understand the basics of demand planning and forecasting, with the result they either don't use at all forecasts formally generated or they use them poorly. In this section, we describe worst practices resulting from such misunderstandings.

There is no difference between forecasts and business plans. There is a difference. A forecast is an unbiased projection about the future based on a set of assumptions underlying the business plans and market conditions. Business plans are simply what the company plans to do. It may call for how much money it plans to spend on promotion, how much price it plans to charge, how many new products it plans to introduce, and so on. In this respect, business plans drive the forecast. But the forecast can change the business plan. If the forecast is not giving what we want, we may have to change the plan (by spending more money on promotion, lowering price, etc.) so that we can hit the target. So, the forecast and business plans are not the same, though they are interrelated.

A demand plan is not a forecast. The final forecast, which drives the business plan, is different from a demand plan. A forecast is an estimate of the market demand, while a demand plan is what we decide to provide to the market. The difference, obviously, is that the demand plan takes into account production, backlogs, and distribution capacity, while a forecast does not. If the expected demand is greater than supply, the demand plan may call for increasing the capacity, increasing the price, and/or ways for allocating the limited supply. On the other hand, if the demand is expected to be less than the supply, the company may take some measures to increase the demand. As such, a forecast and a demand plan are not the same.

A forecast is not a budget. If the budget is the forecast, then there is no need to forecast. A budget may be wishful thinking or the management's commitment to what the company will sell. If the budget calls for producing and selling one million units of widgets next year, then one million units cannot be regarded as a forecast. A forecast is what we can realistically expect to sell. The budget is what top management has made a commitment to. Once prepared and approved, a budget often does not change. A forecast, however, changes when there is a change in the business plan as well as when there is a change in the market conditions. Further, the budget may be an aspirational target, which everyone in the organization strives to achieve. Its objective may very well be to provide motivation to meet and exceed targets.

We don't need forecasts because we are a small company. No matter how big or small a company is, forecasts are needed because every plan is based on some kind of estimate about the future. Even a small deli shop has to estimate how many loaves of bread it can sell next week before placing an order. There are even some large companies that don't believe in forecasting. The president of one of the Fortune 500 companies once said, "We don't forecast—we just respond to the customer!" The fact is that with good forecasts we can respond better to the customer demand (give them what they want, when they want, and where they want), and at the same time reduce our costs and increase our sales and profit.

Our demand is always greater than supply. If we know in advance that our demand would be greater than the supply, we may be able to increase our supply. With that, we would be able to increase our sales and, consequently, profit.

PROCESS USES

The forecasting process plays an important role in improving forecasts and making better decisions. Although the process has evolved from Silo to Consensus Forecasting to Sales and Operations Planning (S&OP) to Collaborative Planning, Forecasting and Replenishment (CPFR®), often they are not properly implemented. Among all the processes, the processes that are now widely talked about and used are S&OP and CPFR®. We will discuss worst practices only in these two processes.

Within S&OP: One way to recognize the worst practices within S&OP is to answer these questions:

1. Does senior leadership participate in the process? If not, it means that the top management does not see any value in it. Without the top management support, not only is it difficult to get cooperation from other functions but it is also challenging to get adequate resources to run this process efficiently and effectively.

2. How often is the S&OP review meeting held—weekly, monthly, quarterly, or annually? If held quarterly or annually, it means that the process exists only by name. In reality there is no process in place. To run it effectively, the meeting must be held, at least, once a month. Some companies even hold such a meeting weekly so they can respond quickly to the changing market dynamics.

3. Is there a champion for setting up the agenda, building a consensus, making sure meetings are held regularly ensuring that all the functions as well executives participate, and the agendas are strictly maintained? Without that person, the process won't work as efficiently as it should. The champion is a facilitator, educator, and consolidator of information. Ideally, the person assigned to this responsibility should not reside in any functional area. Otherwise, there may be skepticism and lack of trust of other functions.

4. Does the process focus on short-term issues, long-term issues, or both? If the focus is primarily on short-term issues, then it is only for putting out fires and not for achieving long-term goals. An effective S&OP process pays attention to both. Another way of saying this is check to see if the agenda of each meeting focuses on operational forecasts and plans, strategic forecasts and plans, or both. If the answer is operational forecasts and plans or strategic forecasts and plans, then there is a problem. The focus should be on both.

5. Who owns the process? If the process is owned by one specific department and/or individual, then the process would be biased and would focus only on what matters to that department or individual. For optimum results, the process must be such that optimizes results across all departments. Also, for best results, it should be jointly owned and everyone should be accountable.

6. Do we have single or multiple forecasts? If multiple forecasts exist, it means that each function is driving its own plans with its own forecasts, which are not in sync with others.

7. Are incentives function-specific or are they based on overall performance? Function-specific incentives often create conflicts because with them, each function will bias forecasts in the direction that maximizes its specific interest. Also, with function-specific incentives, we are likely to compete more with people across the hall than with our real competitors.

8. Does demand planning include both forecasting and demand management? This is important because both are the key drivers of S&OP.

9. Do you often have excess inventory or stock-outs and don't know why? Both are the result of poor forecasting and planning, which a good S&OP process tries to mitigate. Excessive inventory causes markdowns and obsolescence, whereas excessive stock-outs increase production and expediting costs and at the same time reduce sales.

10. Do you have performance metrics in place to measure and evaluate performance? If not, performance is neither measured nor evaluated. With that neither forecasts nor the process will improve. What gets measured gets improved.

11. Do you have a process in place for continuous improvement? To keep the process robust, it is important to continually look for problems and fix them. Market dynamics are constantly changing; to keep up with them, the process may have to be changed.

12. Are you paying the same amount of attention to each and every SKU/brand? If you are, you won't get the optimum results from your limited forecasting resources. For best results, use segmentation strategy so that you can allocate more resources to forecasting those products that yield the maximum return.

Within CPFR®: For a CPFR® to work effectively, we need the full cooperation from customers as well as from people within the organization, which often is lacking. To determine whether the CPFR® process is working effectively, answer these questions:

1. Do you have an access to the customer's business plans, marketing plans, inventory on hand, and forecasts, in addition to the POS data? All these are important for generating forecasts and driving production plans.

2. Do customers provide POS data daily, weekly, monthly, quarterly, or annually? If data are provided for any interval longer than one month, we are not receiving the market information fast enough to react.

3. Are the POS data provided via EDI or by some other way difficult to retrieve, format, and analyze? Data provided on a spreadsheet is generally very difficult to manage and analyze. The longer it takes to format and analyze the data, the less time we will have to react.

4. Do customers provide forecasts that are highly biased? Often forecasts provided by customers to vendors have an upward bias to assure products would be available when needed. If taken at face value, they will bloat the inventory of vendors.

5. Do customers trust vendors and vendors trust customers? If not, collaboration won't work.

6. Is there an agreement on the metrics to be used for evaluating performance? Without that, the performance will neither be evaluated nor be improved.

7. Are the roles and responsibilities of the customer and the supplier clearly defined? Are schedules of activities/transactions detailed, and rules of engagement (what to do when two parties are in disagreement) clearly described? Otherwise, you would be wasting lot of time in arguing who is responsible for what.

8. Is your S&OP process integrated with the CPFR® process? If not, you won't be able to reap the full benefits of CPFR®.

9. Does your CPFR® partner have a collaborative experience? In other words, does it have a Consensus Forecasting process, S&OP process, and/or VMI program, which are based on some kind of collaboration? Without any collaborative experience, you can expect nothing but problems.

10. Did you rollout the CPFR® program without testing it with one or two key SKUs or category? If not, you may be in for a suprise. You may find out that the senior management of your trading partner is not as committed as you thought. Different functions of the partner involved may not see any value in the program, and thus will not fully cooperate. Maybe the technology your trading partner has is not compatible with yours. Testing a program with one or two SKUs or categories can give you an idea whether it is worth the effort to work with that partner.

TYPES OF FORECASTS USED

Although the types of forecasts used have evolved from shipment to demand to POS, there are many companies that still use shipment forecasts for all their planning needs. We do need shipment forecasts for production, procurement, and logistics planning, as well as for determining the cash flow, but they don't give a clear picture about the consumer demand, which is our main concern. We run into the same problem with demand forecasts because they also don't give a clear idea about the consumer demand. What we need are POS forecasts, which provide a better handle on the consumer demand. Once we have POS forecasts, they can be converted into shipment and demand forecasts, and the forecasts based on them will be much more accurate. Many big box retailers provide their POS data to their vendors free of charge. The POS data obtained from customers can be supplemented with the data obtained from third party vendors such as AC Nielsen and Symphony IRI Group. There are many other stores that sell your products but don't provide their POS information. The third party data vendors for the most part fill that gap.

MODEL SELECTION

There are various misconceptions about forecasting models. Here are few examples:

1. There is a misconception that the more complex the model is, the better would be the forecasts. But, very often simple models give the best forecasts. In fact, among three types of models—Time Series, Cause-and-Effect, and Judgmental—the models that are used most are Time Series, which are, by and large, the easiest to understand and use. Within Time Series, the models that are used most are averages and trend, which again are very easy to understand and use.

2. The other misconception is that statistical forecasts are the best because they are unbiased. At times, judgmental fine tuning of statistical forecasts improves accuracy because it adjusts for elements that cannot be quantified but have a bearing on the forecasts, and/or for the information that was not available at the time forecasts were generated.

3. There is also a misconception the model that fits best to the historical data will always give the best results. If we have five observations like these—10, 14, 15, 32, and 35—the best-fit model won't work. Something happened in the last two periods, which drastically changed the sales pattern. Maybe sales rose because of the launch of a new product, one of the customers opened new stores during that time, the company acquired another company, or for any other reason. Thus, the best-fit model may not always be the best. Some adjustments in the statistical forecasts may be needed.

METRICS USED FOR PERFORMANCE MEASUREMENT

The performance measurement metrics are critical to ensure continuous improvement. In the area of forecasting, they may be Mean Percent Error (MPE), Mean Absolute Percent Error (MAPE), and Weighted Mean Absolute Percent Error (WMAPE). In the area of supply chain, they may be on-time-in-full shipments, delivering on-time to a commit date, delivering on-time to an original customer request date, and so on. Alan Milliken from BASF shares his experience about performance metrics used in business.

Most businesses do not fully know their performance. I recently worked with a business unit whose on-time shipping performance measurement was reported as 98% plus compliance. Performance reporting was done manually. It recently implemented an automated system based on the data entered via the order processing software. The first month's result was a dismal 88%. Management asked Customer Service how this could be. It was found that a postponement agreed to by the customer was not previously recorded as non-compliance.

The company uses too many performance measurement metrics. With too many metrics it is difficult to make any assessment. At the beginning of our performance evaluation, we always ask the business for a list of performance metrics they use. In most cases, the list quickly reaches 100 or so, making it difficult to make any assessment. To do it right, the number of performance metrics has to be restricted to the most important few that can be easily managed.

Performance metrics don't support the organization's primary objective. On a recent project, one manager was proud of many performance measures currently in place. When I asked if these were aligned with business strategies, he said he wasn't sure because he had not seen the strategies lately. For a good performance measurement, performance metrics must be aligned to the company's strategies which must be agreed on collectively by all the stakeholders.

There is no accountability. No matter how good the metrics are, nothing will happen unless we make someone accountable for the improvement.

Successful performance, according to Alan Milliken, is a journey, not a destination. Everyone wants to be considered "World-Class" or "Best-in-Class." This cannot happen overnight because performance improvement is a gradual process. Further, goals must be the ones that are realistic and achievable. By aiming too high and too suddenly, participants may lose confidence and refuse to lend support to the project.

The best metric for measuring forecast accuracy is the WMAPE, which gives weight to each error depending on the importance of the SKU or category. Most of the companies, however, use MAPE, which gives equal amount of weight to each. There are some companies that use MPE, which understates the forecasting errors because it negates the over-forecasting errors with the under-forecasting ones.

SELECTING AND USING FORECASTING SOFTWARE/SYSTEM

There are many worst practices in selecting and using forecasting software/systems. Many practitioners believe the moment they get a good software/system all their forecasting problems will go away. Forecasting software is a great tool for generating forecasts for thousands of products automatically and quickly with no human intervention. But if the data form an unusual pattern or are impacted by unusual circumstances, the software will go berserk and create forecasts that don't make sense. It is, therefore, important to have a process in place that calls for regularly monitoring and revising forecasts. Also, the forecaster must have some basic knowledge about models to evaluate their performance. In 2000, Nike learned the hard way when it used its newly purchased forecasting system, and lost $400 million by over-forecasting certain products and under-forecasting others. It appears that they used the software as a black box and accepted its forecasts at face value. If a monitoring and revising process had been in place and the forecaster had a basic understanding about models, the problem would have been detected much earlier, and something could have been done to correct it before it was too late.

It is not unusual for a company to buy a forecasting software/system and then try to align it with the forecasting process. It is like putting the cart before the horse. We first need to know our requirements—how many forecasts are required and at what level of detail, how far ahead are the forecasts to be prepared, are the forecasts required in units or dollars or both, and so on? After the requirements are defined and agreed on, we should structure the process. After that, we should look for technology that can support that process.

No matter how good a software/system is, it won't help if it is not used. In one instance, in a multi-million dollar company, a newly hired forecaster found to his surprise a forecasting CD that was purchased and licensed a long time back but was sitting in the drawer of a forecaster who left several months ago.

There are several companies who bought the forecasting software/system without involving the people who would be using it. If the users are not on board, they may not use it at all or use it half-heartedly. Further, a company may purchase software/system that has many more functionalities than it needs, thereby paying for every one of them without using them.

CASE STUDIES OF WORST PRACTICES AND THEIR SOLUTIONS

Lad A. Dilgard who has a long experience in forecasting and supply chain management shares his experience about worst practices in demand planning and forecasting.

The warehouse planner drives forecast for the entire organization. I was brought into a large multinational instruments company to develop and improve the logistics and procurement capability for its $400 million North American sales and service organization. There were many challenges, but one that prohibited improving customer service, delivery, warehouse operations, and marketing plan was the lack of collaboratively built forecasts, and using forecasts that were widely misunderstood. Per-item demand history and expected future sales were owned and managed by a warehouse planning manager, working in an entirely separate organization than the product managers. Marketing leaders, product managers, and I (the logistics leader for the marketing organization) had no input into demand planning, which drove procurement, shipment, and warehouse storage of expensive instruments and accompanying spare parts. Also, the warehouse planner has a different set of incentives than the marketing organization—his central purpose was to keep inventory down. Because of that we were getting complaints from marketing/sales leaders such as:

> *"We don't have enough stock to satisfy our customers!"*
> *"Our customers have to wait too long!"*
> *"We don't have any input into the expected demand!"*
> *"We can't incorporate market data into the forecast!"*
> *"The warehouse has no incentive to meet customer demand!"*

Furthermore, marketers did not like the way the warehouse manager calculated future demand.

He just pulled the historical demand from the ERP system, plugged it into a homemade database, extrapolated the historical demand by using moving averages to arrive at the future demand, and then where necessary made intuitive adjustments for known manufacturing capacity and for whatever knowledge he had about the product and market. The organization provided neither appropriate tools nor a collaborative process to add market data into the forecast. The warehouse manager was not apprised at all of such things as sales, discounts, and large upcoming customer contracts.

The company faced many other familiar forecasting challenges—no math, statistics, or tools deployed; no marketing input; no concentration of efforts on "A" items; no collaboration; no metrics for performance measurement; and no performance review process to drive improvement.

Due to budget constraints and lack of top management buy-in to invest in forecasting, my team built a minimal, short-term solution. The objective was, at the very least, to provide a vehicle for integrating marketing input into the forecast. We built an Excel-based tool with minimal mathematical capability (moving averages, seasonal adjustment calculations, and the like) and devoted efforts to items that mattered most—the top 80% of total sales. Every month, we pushed the tool, populated with demand history, to prepare rough forecasts (through the end of year plus one year), which we sent to product managers, asking them to make adjustments based on their market information. We also requested that they should document market information they used for future reference, and started tracking forecast errors. The forecasts so prepared were then pushed to factories in China. In this way, not only was the manufacturing planning greatly improved, but also rancor associated with lack of forecast collaboration was reduced.

Interestingly, once product managers were involved in the process, our team prodded them to provide input. They were concerned that their input would be used to alter their warehouse buying plan or the plant production plan. They did not want to see their efforts go to waste. Even after proving the actual benefit of their input, obtaining input from product managers was still sometimes difficult because providing good forecasts was not part of their job description or incentive plan. They also did not understand how better forecasts could be translated into more available inventory for their customers. Both were huge obstacles to forecast improvement, a problem I have witnessed also at many other organizations.

Part requirement from the Bill of Material (BOM) blowout was considered a "forecast." As a divisional logistics executive at a Fortune 500 diversified manufacturer, I was charged with the responsibility of improving inventory and materials management at five distinctly separate companies. Each had different systems, culture of people, products, processes, and locations. But one thing was consistent: There was a complete lack of forecasting initiative at virtually all levels.

One company in my division was engaged in the "fire drill" method of pleasing customers. Rather than analyzing the historical data and deploying forecasting techniques for new products or large customers, it decided that its products could not be forecasted. By leaning heavily on suppliers, managers, and employees, it scrambled to meet customer demand as it arrived, and lived every day in an emergency mode.

When I began inquiring about planning and forecasting processes, I quickly learned why there was no forecasting capability. It was because the division's CFO was very hostile to the idea of forecasting and resisted every effort to have a formal forecasting process. Although he was a competent accountant he was the one who was entrusted, among other things, with the responsibility for managing IT. I explained to him how improved forecasting could help meet customer demand and reduce excess and obsolete inventory. His response was:

> *"How can you say we don't forecast?! We have a great forecasting capability in our ERP system! We simply plug in the product we need to build, and it blows out each item we need to buy or build, and even lead times."*

When the VP of Procurement pointed out that the CFO had identified a plan, not a forecast, there was a sense of a sinking feeling in the room—this was an educational challenge of great proportion. The CFO and most other members of the leadership team did not understand the difference between a forecast and a plan.

The presidents of three other companies in the division stated that their company's products simply could not be forecasted or planned for, and thus trying to forecast or plan was an exercise in futility. Therefore, the best they could do was to respond to customer orders. It is true there were many customer orders that were difficult to forecast, but to completely ignore analyzing the historical demand was startling and self-defeating.

Sales target developed by top executives is a forecast. It is this forecast that is often pushed wdown to managers to make it work. At one company, a very famous and large fashion retailer, forecasting had two major difficulties:

1. The "forecast" was actually an aggregate-level sales revenue target, created by management to drive sales growth across the company. It sounded like this:

> *"Our sales target for 2012 is $2 billion. Every department and all sales divisions need to figure out how they can do their part to achieve it."*

2. The actual forecasting was done at a micro level by home office analysts, simply for replenishing store inventory at a store / SKU level. No forecast existed except a simple moving average with minor qualitative intervention.

This was their budgeting and forecasting process. All the organizational functions were doing their own forecasting to build a plan to meet the top management's sales target. The problem with that was middle managers lacked item-level historical demand or collaborative forecasts to build a case on how they could meet their "forecasts." A budgetary sales target without any hard facts generally results in missed opportunities, poorly understood results, and mysteriously built inventory. Companies are then stunned why their sales targets are not met, and why their inventory is so high. Forecasts in the company described above were continually "adjusted" throughout the year, and there was little or no information available as to what was changed and why.

Most companies have only anecdotes, stories, and assumptions to rely on. Wins and misses are found too late, and adjustments are made too slowly to redeploy or reduce inventory investment. Heads sometimes roll, but most companies live with mistakes, pain (inventory), or missed opportunities. If there is a robust forecasting function in place, it can quickly recognize hits and misses, and give a ready-made plan to address them.

SUGGESTED READING

1. Dilgard, Lad A. "Worst Forecasting Practices in Corporate America and Their Solutions—Case Studies." *Journal of Business Forecasting*. Summer 2009, pp. 4-13.
2. Milliken, Alan. "Key Ingredients of Successful Performance Metrics in the Supply Chain." *Journal of Business Forecasting*. Summer 2001, pp. 23-28.
3. Neil, MacLeod. "SO&P." Blog. October 27, 2008.

QUESTIONS FOR REVIEW

1. Are plans and forecasts the same? If they differ, in what ways? Explain.
2. Explain three key worst practices in running an S&OP program.
3. Explain how forecasts can be used to hit the desired target.
4. Explain three key worst practices in running a CPFR® program.
5. Why is it important to study worst practices? Explain.
6. Explain worst practices that are often observed in forecast modeling.
7. Describe worst practices in measuring and improving forecasting performance.

8. Which are the best data to use for forecasting demand, and why? Explain.
9. Why is it important to set up a process before buying a forecasting system? Explain.
10. Explain in brief the following:
    a. Demand plan vs. forecast
    b. Forecast vs. budget
    c. Demand data vs. POS data
    d. S&OP vs. CPFR®

PART X

FORECASTING SOFTWARE PACKAGES AND SYSTEMS

INTRODUCTION

The forecasting package is a stand-alone forecasting engine for preparing forecasts. The forecasting system, on the other hand, does much more than forecasting. It also links forecasts with the production module to generate a production plan, with the logistics module to generate a logistic plan, with the financial module to generate a financial plan, and so on. The main issue with both—the forecasting package and the forecasting system—is how to select the one that fits in with your forecasting needs. This section describes in detail how to go about selecting the right forecasting package and/or forecasting system. It also discusses which forecasting packages and forecasting systems are available and their market share, as well as what lessons the users have learned.

CHAPTER 29

FORECASTING SOFTWARE PACKAGES

Given the demands on professional forecasters with regard to the number of items to be forecasted and the continual quest for improvements, it is virtually impossible to do a good job without the aid of a proper forecasting package. Today's forecasters must prepare forecasts covering thousands of SKUs, broken down by regions, distribution centers, marketing channels such as food and drug stores, and customers. The increasing globalization of markets has further added to the responsibility of a forecaster. In some cases, the forecaster is required to prepare forecasts for both domestic and foreign markets. In recent years, a large number of forecasting packages have emerged, enabling forecasters to do their job effectively and efficiently. Still, a pertinent question surfaces: Which is the right forecasting package for me? In this chapter we will discuss how to go about selecting a forecasting package, given the unique needs and requirements of an organization.

The forecasting package is a stand-alone forecasting engine. It not only prepares forecasts but also has the capability to look for problems in the data such as missing values, outliers, and structural changes, and then takes care of them. Furthermore, where needed, it can slice and dice the data—slicing the category level forecast into SKUs, for example.

Before proceeding further, it is important to know the difference between a forecasting package and a statistical package. Although forecasting packages are based on statistical models, they are not the same. There are two main differences between them. One, statistical packages just estimate the predictive equation, but don't give the forecast. Two, some of the statistical models were not developed for forecasting, and thus cannot be used as they are. They have to be modified. For example, moving averages and exponential smoothing were developed to smooth the data, not to prepare forecasts. For a forecasting use, they have to be modified.

FORECASTING PACKAGES: A TOOL

Although forecasting packages play an important role in forecasting, they are nothing more than a tool in the hands of a forecaster. To be the best in the field, you have to know the craft, that is, you have to know the fundamentals of forecasting, what data/information you need, how to analyze and treat data, how much data to use, which model to apply and when, how to evaluate forecasts, when and how to incorporate judgment into a forecast, and so on. With the right knowledge of the forecasting craft and the right software, you can get the best results. Furthermore, armed with the depth of forecasting knowledge, you will be in control of the package, and not the package in control of you. Every step of the way, you will need to know what is happening and why. You need to know when to accept forecasts at the face value, when to reject them outright, and when to make adjustments. So, the forecasting package should be used as an aid to forecasting, and not as a black box. You should always question forecasts.

SELECTING A FORECASTING PACKAGE

There are a large number of forecasting packages available in the market, but to select the right one is not easy. It requires a great deal of homework to determine what you really need and what is available. But the job does not end there. You have to make sure it is used and used effectively; updated when new functionalities become available, provided they make the task more efficient; and/or modified or replaced if your needs change. Therefore, it is important to first determine what kind of package you need; and after it is purchased, how it would be implemented and used.

Before starting the search, it is important to spell out the requirements in as much detail as possible. Without that, we won't know what to look for. The requirements should cover not only the current needs but also what might be needed in the future. For best results, the selection of a package should be driven by the company's needs, and not what the vendor has to offer. The requirements may include:

1. Types of forecasts required
2. Data analysis and data treatment capability
3. Capability to aggregate and disaggregate the data and forecasts
4. Scalability
5. Required models
6. Overriding capability
7. Expert system
8. Diagnostics tools
9. Reporting capability
10. Hardware in existence
11. Budget available
12. Ease of use
13. Vendor support

Types of forecasts required: The first thing is to determine what kinds of forecasts are required. You may need forecasts of shipments, demand, and/or POS. Regarding the level of detail, you may need them at a SKU level, category level, and/or company level. With respect to form, you may need them in dollars, units, or both. In terms of the forecast horizon, you may need them one-month ahead, one-quarter ahead, and/or one-year ahead. Forecasts may be required by distribution channel hierarchy such as food and drug stores, by geographical hierarchy such as by region and state, by customer hierarchy such as by mass merchandisers and others, and by customer-store hierarchy. The approach used—top-down, bottom-up, or middle-out—also matters. Whatever they may be, spell them out in as much in detail as possible.

Data analysis and data treatment capability: Data analysis refers to spotting problems in the data, which may be missing values, outliers, and structural changes. Once problems are discovered they have to be treated. Data analysis can also determine the characteristics of the data, that is, whether the data have seasonality, trend, and/or cause-and-effect relationships, which can help in deciding about the model. Therefore, the package you choose must have not only the capability for analyzing the data but also treating problems. It is also important to know how many observations and variables will be used in preparing forecasts, and whether or not the package you are considering can handle them.

Capability to aggregate and disaggregate the data and forecasts: Depending on the need of forecast users, at times, actual and forecast data may have to be aggregated or disaggregated. The disaggregated data may have to be aggregated; for example, SKUs into categories and categories into a company level. On the other hand, daily data may have to be aggregated into weeks, weekly data into months, monthly data into quarters, and so on. After the forecasts are prepared, they may have to be disaggregated depending on the needs. Also, forecasts may have to be generated both in dollars and units. The production people, for example, need forecasts not only in units but also at a SKU level; whereas Finance needs them at a somewhat higher level of aggregation, and in dollars. Forecasts are generally more accurate when prepared at a higher level of aggregation. Furthermore, to determine performance, actual data and forecasts may have to be compared at different levels of aggregation. If a package has such a capability, it will reduce the workload of a forecaster significantly.

Scalability: Scalability is another feature that plays a big role in selecting a forecasting package. Many retailers and manufacturers now want to forecast at SKU/store level across hundreds and thousands of stores. Not only that, they may want them to be prepared within a desired timeline, that is, daily, weekly, etc. The number of forecasts to be prepared determines the scalability. If you have 10 customer groupings, 1,000 items, and 100 locations across 12 periods, the package has to generate 1,200,000 forecasts. Also, it is important to make sure that the package can handle both current and future needs.

Required models: As mentioned earlier, there are three types of models: (1) Time Series, (2) Cause and Effect, and (3) Judgmental. Make sure that the package has the models you use or want to use. Within each type, there are a number of sub-models; for example, Time Series has sub-models such as moving averages, exponential smoothing, and classical decomposition. Make sure that the package you are considering has all or most of them. If you launch many new products every year, you will also need models of new product forecasting.

Overriding capability: As mentioned earlier, forecasting is partly an art and partly a science. At times, forecasts have to be manually adjusted. Therefore, it is important that the package has the capability that allows overriding by those who have the authority.

Expert system: Where hundreds and thousands of forecasts have to be prepared every month or every quarter, it is difficult for a forecaster to identify the best model for each and every product, and/or for each and every category. There you will need an expert system that automatically selects the best model, and then prepares forecasts. Here it is important to know from which models the expert system makes the selection and the criteria it uses for selecting it. It may use MAPE (Means Absolute Percent Error) or some other error metric to select the best model.

Most software selects the best model on the basis of the average error computed from the same data as used in developing a model. However, the forecaster can get a better idea about the model by using holdout periods. Here the forecaster builds different models by using all the data except of the last three to four periods (called holdout periods), prepares their forecasts with each model, and then compares them with the actual sales data. The model that, on average, gives the least amount of error is the one that is considered the best. This feature helps not only in selecting the best model but also gives the error that is likely to occur in the future.

To determine the quality of an expert system, you can ask the vendor to prepare forecasts of certain products of the next three to four periods, the data of which were not provided, and then compare their forecasts with the actual numbers. This will give some confidence in the package. The data given to the vendor for a test drive should be of normal products, not of unique and extremely difficult products. Otherwise, it would defeat the purpose because most of the products you would be forecasting won't fall in that category.

The number of forecasts a package can prepare automatically at a time also matters because each package has its limits.

Diagnostic tools: These are used to determine the quality of a model. In the case of Time Series models, we may need MAPE and standard deviation of errors, whereas in a regression-based model we may need test statistics such as R-square, t-test, F-test, and Durbin-Watson statistic. While statistical diagnostic tools are important, it is equally important if it can provide a comparison among different time periods, that is, how current forecast errors compare with those of last year.

Reporting capability: The reporting capability is another feature to be looked into. Since each user has a different need, the package should be such that meets the needs of all. Some may want forecasts in units and the others in dollars. Some may want them by category/brand and the others by SKUs. Also, forecasts may have to be broken down by customer, channel of distribution, region, and country.

Every forecast is based on some assumptions, which may be internal, such as the price to be charged and the amount of money to be spent on advertising, and/or external, such as state of the economy and competitive action. The package should be such that it reports the assumptions. Also, it has the capability to flag exceptions such as a given forecast is extremely high or low, and/or is far below the target.

Hardware in existence: Before buying a package, it is also important to know what kind of hardware, connect-ware, and data warehouse are in place. The package to be purchased has to be compatible with the existing infrastructure, unless you are willing to change it to accommodate it.

Budget available: The forecasting package can easily cost from a few thousand dollars to hundreds of thousands of dollars. So, it is important to have some idea about the budget available for purchasing a package before starting the search.

Ease of use: It makes a difference how easy or difficult it is to use a forecasting package for downloading and uploading, cleansing and massaging the data when necessary, and preparing forecasts. It is not unusual to find a company that spent a large sum of money on a package, but it was either not used at all or was used only a fraction of it. Maybe it was very difficult to run, or a large portion of the functionalities in the package was not applicable to the company's needs. Also, it makes a difference whether the forecaster and users were consulted before purchasing it. If not, their heart won't be in it, and the package will either remain unused or will be used only half-heartedly .

Vendor support: No matter how well the manual is written, at times the forecaster will need the help of the vendor. Therefore, it is important to know the support system the vendor has, because any delay in response may cost a great deal of money. This kind of information can be obtained by talking to various current users of the package. They can also provide information how satisfied/dissatisfied they are with the package.

LESSONS LEARNED

Here are few lessons that can be learned from those who have bought and used a forecasting package:

1. Keep in mind that the forecasting package is just a tool and not a substitute for human judgment. So, don't use it as black box.

2. The forecasting package does not replace the forecasting process, which you will need to make the most out of it.

3. To use a forecasting package effectively, you will need to have some basic knowledge about statistics as well as about the products you would be dealing with.

4. Before buying a package, make sure that you have the approval of those who will be using it. If they are not enthusiastic about it, the package may not be used at all or used only halfheartedly.

MARKET SHARE OF FORECASTING SOFTWARE PACKAGES

Although in principle there is a distinct difference between a forecasting software package and a forecasting system, in practice, it is difficult to identify which one is which. So, we used our best judgment in identifying them. Based on the 2009 survey of the Institute of Business Forecasting and Planning, the key players in the forecasting software market are John Galt Solutions, SAS, Forecast Pro, and Smart Software.

There are several companies that use a spreadsheet package as a tool for forecasting. According to the survey, 41% of the companies use spreadsheet packages either wholly or in combination with forecasting software.

SUGGESTED READING

1. Reilly, David P. "How to Select a Dedicated Forecasting Software." *Journal of Business Forecasting*. Summer 2007, pp. 10-15.
2. Lapide, Larry. New Developments in Business Forecasting." *Journal of Business Forecasting*. Spring 1999, pp. 12-14.

QUESTIONS FOR REVIEW

1. What is the difference between statistical packages and forecasting packages? Explain.
2. Why is it important to have an overriding capability in a forecasting package? Explain.
3. How does a forecasting package help the forecasters? Once an organization buys a forecasting package, does it solve all its forecasting problems? Why or why not?
4. Explain why many of these packages are not fully utilized.
5. Explain how and where does the slicing and dicing feature of a forecasting package help?
6. Explain this statement. "We should be in control of a forecasting package, and not the package in control of us."
7. What kind of reporting capability should a forecasting package have? Explain.
8. How would you test an expert system? Explain.
9. How would you determine whether a vendor is likely to give a good support to the customer? Explain.

10. Explain in brief the following:
    a. Three lessons learned from those who bought and used a forecasting package
    b. Scalability
    c. Holdout period
    d. Diagnostic tools

CHAPTER 30

FORECASTING SYSTEMS

Before discussing forecasting systems, it is important to know the difference between the system and the package. The forecasting package is a stand-alone package that generates forecasts either by using a model selected by a forecaster or by using an automatic feature (expert system) embedded into the software package. The forecasting system, on the other hand, does more than forecasting. After forecasts are finalized, it links them to various modules, for example, to the production module for preparing production plans, to the procurement module for making plans for purchasing raw materials, and to the logistic module for making plans for transportation. Depending on the system, it may also link forecasts to the financial module to generate a financial plan, to the sales module to generate a sales plan, and to the marketing module to generate a marketing plan. To select the right system, here again we have to first determine our requirements, and then look for the one that meets them. Since the forecasting package is part of the forecasting system, most of the requirements of a package described in the previous chapter are applicable to a system as well. Here we discuss only those that are unique to a system.

A SYSTEM IS NOT A PROCESS

When designing, developing, and implementing a demand forecasting system, or any system for that matter, one must realize that the system itself is not a process. It is a tool that facilitates the process. For best results, your system must be built around the forecasting process, and not the other way around. Unfortunately, most systems, particularly the off-the-shelf ones, assume that your process will be designed around the system. Therefore, companies that purchase such a system have to either re-engineer the process to fit the system or redesign the system to accommodate the process. In most cases, the company ends up doing both, which can cost thousands of dollars in additional resources and consulting fees. In fact, there is no integrated off-the-shelf solution that can meet all the needs of every customer. Some customizations will always be needed; of course, the less the better.

BEFORE YOU START LOOKING FOR A SYSTEM

Before you start looking for a forecasting system, be aware of two important things: One, you need the support from the top management because systems don't come cheap. They can easily run into thousands and millions of dollars plus annual maintenance fees. And, of course, management has to be convinced about its value and the benefits that would come with it in ways of improved efficiency and increased sales and profit. Equally important is the approval of stakeholders—ultimate users of the system. They should be on board. Otherwise, the system may be in place, but it is not used at all or is used only half-heartedly. In one case, management decided to implement SAP-APO without consulting the forecasting group. The management did so because the SAP system was already used for other purposes; it felt it would be appropriate to add APO to the existing SAP platform. Since the forecasting group was not consulted, it deeply resented the SAP-APO. Instead of using it, the group bought another forecasting software package to do the forecasting.

SELECTING A FORECASTING SYSTEM

Like a forecasting package, before you start looking for a forecasting system, first determine what you would like to have, based on your requirements, and what is available. As mentioned earlier, some customization will always be needed. If you already have a system in place and you want to upgrade or replace it, then you should think in terms of what is lacking. Here we describe what kind of system architecture you should be looking for and why. Here is the list of some key features:

1. Open and object oriented
2. Multi-dimensional
3. Flexibility
4. Inter-operability
5. Knowledge base
6. Querying capability

Open and object oriented: The system should have an open and object-oriented architecture. The open architecture means that it can run multiple off-the-shelf software packages including forecasting and spreadsheet packages to create an integrated solution. The object oriented architecture, on the other hand, implies that each object can be modified without disrupting other functions. For example, if a user requests a certain enhancement to the current object, it can be done simply by editing that particular object without shutting down the entire system.

Multi-dimensional: This means that a system has built-in Time Series, Cause-and-Effect, and Life-Cycle models that can be used at the touch of a button. In the Life-Cycle models, forecasts are prepared by identifying the life cycle of a product and the phase the product is currently in. The life cycle of a product generally varies anywhere from three months to a lifetime. Forecasting products with a short life cycle require the use of special techniques. The software can save you a great deal of time if it can forecast by the phase of the cycle the product is in.

Furthermore, in some cases, forecasts prepared by different functions have to be reconciled and consolidated. In other cases, strategic and tactical forecasts have to be aligned. It would be great if the system has the capability to facilitate the consolidation/alignment of these forecasts.

Flexibility: The system should be flexible enough to aggregate and disaggregate the data/forecasts at any level of granularity, as well as letting you update the information easily and quickly. Businesses often operate along three hierarchies—customer (small and large customers, customers by the channel of distribution, etc.), geography (region, distribution centers, etc.), and product (SKU and category, promoted and non-promoted, seasonal and non-seasonal, etc.). The system should let you aggregate and disaggregate at all these levels.

The ability to update information also helps. It not only saves time and resources but also makes it possible to react to the market dynamics quickly and wisely. If you lost a customer, you can easily delete it from the system. If you have a new customer, it lets you easily add it. Not only that, it lets you add or remove products and territories that correspond to a customer that you want to add or drop. Without this kind of flexibility, you may wind up spending a good deal of time and resources in adding products, removing customers, and realigning territories and sales reps; but with a flexible system, it will be a snap.

Inter-operability: The system chosen must be inter-operable so that it can be easily integrated with the existing infrastructure, because the prior investment in the infrastructure cannot be easily scrapped. Although a number of companies have set standards for technology purchases, that is, what types of machines they can or cannot buy, there are many that don't have standards. It is not unusual to find a company with disparate systems—for example, the historical data in SYBASE, syndicated data in Red Brick, financial information in Oracle, and so on. In terms of application, Marketing may use Windows; Finance, Macintoshes; and Salespeople, laptops with remote access. Furthermore, a company may have technology standards, but if they are department-specific, you will still have a problem for one department communicating with another. Therefore, the system should be such that it has an interface, which supports an automated link with other system databases both internal and external—internal for retrieving customer orders, shipment history, etc., from other departments, and external for retrieving POS data, warehouse withdrawals, outstanding inventory, etc., from customers. With CPFR® and VMI arrangements, the link with external databases is a must.

Also, the system should be such that lets you interact with your trading partners both within and outside the organization. You may want the input of various departments within the organization as well as of your customers in preparing forecasts. After forecasts are generated, you may want them to review and comment on them. The interaction among them will be possible only if the system is inter-operable. At times, senior management may also like to interact with different departments about forecasts or for any other issue.

Knowledge base: The system should also have a knowledge base for storing key learning, which would help in further improving forecasts and making decisions. The information may be why the forecast error at certain times of a year is unusually high, what lift a given promotion provides, how price changes affect the demand, how seasonality of different regions varies, how much time after a product launch is required to determine whether a new product is likely to succeed or fail, and so on.

Querying capability: The querying capability lets you to do the ad hoc analyses, such as determining which customers are doing well or poorly, and why; which territories are doing better than others; which SKUs/categories are moving fast or slowly; how a new product is performing; how a certain promotion is working; and so on. It also lets you view actual numbers against the forecasts.

IMPORTANCE OF CORPORATE DATA WAREHOUSE

The forecasting system will be highly successful if there is a Corporate Data Warehouse (CDW) where all the data reside at one place and the system provides all the necessary information to make decisions. The information may be about seasonal patterns, trends, market changes, and effectiveness of trade promotion. Most companies have all the necessary information but often the data reside in different databases, making it difficult to analyze as well as to interact with one another. Data queries made through the Management Information Systems (MIS) department often take weeks or even months to get the answers, thereby forcing decision makers to make critical decisions with gut feelings. It is, therefore, important to have a corporate data warehouse that has the capability to untangle and consolidate the maze of sales, marketing, financial, and external information to generate the necessary information needed for making decisions.

The CDW must have a relational database to store and manage data because it links disparate data tables through common references, such as product codes, customer names, and UPC (unique product code) numbers. When any of the information is needed it can be obtained at the click of a button.

Very often data at the source change, which may require data at the CDW to be updated. For example, a market research firm has published a new report, a competitor has announced a new promotion on its website, or the Department of Commerce has put out new and revised data. All of these events call for an update of your database. You can easily do it if the CDW has a separate link with each data source to retrieve and display the latest information. Not only that, we may like to retrieve all the information on a single spreadsheet to make it easier to view and manipulate the data. Walmart, with its data warehouse, has successfully turned data into actionable information, enabling it to determine, among other things, what its customers want—which item and when, at which store, and at what price.

The growth in data will continue. By the end of the decade, it will not be unreasonable for data warehouses to have terabytes or pentabytes of data. Those working in the area of multi-media applications are concerned that even the speed of light may not be fast enough to distribute this quantity of data across current network technology.

HOW TO IMPLEMENT A SYSTEM

Like any other system implementation, the upfront planning, the understanding of the process by the development team, and, most of all, the support of senior management is vital for a successful implementation of a forecasting system. Those planning to implement a system must recognize that for many people it may be a cultural shock. The main shock may come when the data analysis tasks are shifted from the management information systems staff to forecast preparers and users. The wall that separates one function from the other has to be broken. Different functions, instead of working independently, have to start working together as one team. Also, getting started does not mean that we will start out with a perfect system, but it will improve over time. Plus, the system will grow and expand as our needs and capabilities grow.

The collaboration among forecast preparers and users is essential. If we leave someone out of the loop, he or she is less likely to cooperate in providing the input, and will have less respect for your forecast numbers. There is no single right way to collaborate. Here are a few things that can help:

1. The system enables one to send and receive e-mails from those who are involved in forecasting either as a user or as a preparer.

2. If it is not possible to meet frequently with all the participants in person, a meeting online can bridge the gap. The system should be such that allows you to do that.

3. The system allows each one to view information in a way that is helpful to him or her. For example, if one wants to see sales in dollars, it lets him or her have it in that format.

4. The system enables the user to attach a picture, a comment, or a link to a document of the forecast in a way that gives a better understanding about the numbers. If, for example, one decides not to change the forecast of October, the system lets its partner know why. It may be because a certain event would occur in that month that would significantly increase the sales, and/or a special order is expected from the government. Whatever it may be, the system allows attaching comments with the forecast.

5. If different functions come up with different forecasts for the same market, the system facilitates the reconciling process.

AFTER IMPLEMENTATION

Following the implementation, there will be a continuing need to fine tune the forecasting system as well as the forecasting process. Watch closely what is working and what is not, and where changes are needed. Maybe we need a system that flags exceptions, that is, flags brands/SKUs that are performing above and below the average, brands/SKUs that are out of stock, forecasts that don't make sense (either too high or too low), and so on. To enhance the system, it is important to review the system periodically—reporting of forecasts and data, interfaces with end-users, and overall integration of the system with the process. The roles and responsibilities of each participant must be fully understood and agreed upon. Above all, the system response and timelines must be analyzed on a continuing basis. Companies' needs evolve over time, and so does the technology. Also, as the forecasting process matures, business requirements change and the technology advances, the system has to change too. Many changes may be significant and costly. Before making any change, be sure to look at both the incremental costs and benefits.

LESSONS LEARNED

Whether you are starting a forecasting system from a scratch or trying to enhance the existing one, either way lessons learned by others can be helpful. Systems are very costly to implement and maintain. If done correctly, rewards can be enormous. Here we share the lessons learned by Jeriad Zoghby, Director of Enterprise Strategy at Merkel, Inc., and by others in implementing and maintaining a system. There are many companies where the system is in place but not used at all or used very poorly either because they don't have any idea what can be accomplished with it or don't know how. It is not unusual to find a company where a large sum of money was invested in the system, but forecasts are still prepared by an outside package, and then brought back into the system for planning.

Lesson No. 1
Buy an Industry-Specific Forecasting System

It is difficult to find an industry-specific system, if you do, this may be the best bet for you because each industry has its own requirements. But in reality, no such system exists, no matter what the vendors say. You have to invest time and effort in customizing it. Of course, the less time and effort you put into it, the better it would be. Keep in mind that vendors who develop an industry-specific system limit their profit opportunities. Because of that, systems are created to serve a diverse group of companies and industries. If the system is flexible enough, you can easily customize it to meet your needs as well as of your trading partners. The flexibility in a system can also help in meeting your future needs.

Lesson No. 2
Consultants Are Not Necessarily the Experts

There is a very good chance that the consultant you have hired to guide you does not have much experience—neither in your industry nor in the system you have selected. Although consultants are paid exorbitantly, their background is seldom checked. They are often hired not on the basis of their background and experience but on the basis of the company they are affiliated with. Therefore, it is important to check the reference of a consultant who would be working on your project.

Lesson No. 3
Have an In-House Expert

Besides using outside consultants, you must have an in-house expert. This is because when the implementation is finished, someone has to take over. The in-house expert you select must understand the business jargon and statistics necessary to converse with consultants and customer support people. Also, if the in-house expert is in charge of the system, he or she will take the ownership, and guarantee its continuation and success. This does not in any way imply that you should not use consultants. They are needed, because with their expertise and insight into the project, they often shorten the learning curve and speed up the implementation process. After the project is completed, the in-house expert can take over.

Lesson No. 4
Do Your Homework

It is important to do your homework before starting a project. Define what your requirements are and whether or not the system you are considering will be able to meet them. Good preparation avoids unnecessary additional consulting fees as well as helps to complete the project on time and within budget. This again implies that we should have an in-house expert on board before initiating a project.

Lesson No. 5
Robust Solutions with Automatic Tasks and Room for Future Enhancements

Whatever system you put in, make sure it offers robust solutions, automates various tasks, and is flexible enough to allow you make necessary enhancements in the future. The most-often heard complaint of any system is that it takes too long to complete even a small request. This happens because the developer at the time of designing and implementing the system did not fully understand your needs. If all the solutions are robust, you should be able to make many of the changes easily and effortlessly. It is easier said than done, but many of the problems can be avoided if proper attention was given at the time of designing and implementing a system. Automating different processes in a system is quite tricky. To fully understand what is to be automated and how, one has to do first all the processes manually.

Another important consideration in implementing a system is the plan for the future. One has to foresee what would be needed when the company grows. Make sure that the system has the capability to meet most of those needs. It is difficult to foresee the future clearly, but with proper preparations, one can avoid many of the problems.

Lesson No. 6
Don't Implement Too Many Modules at the Same Time

It is important not to implement too many modules (modules for financial planning, sales planning, production planning, etc.) at the same time. The best thing is to implement one or two modules at a time. Otherwise, they may create chaos and disruptions. Even with one or two modules you may experience numerous bugs that have to be taken care of. At the same time, there may be a strong resistance from the users. It is also important not to do the implementation during the busiest time.

Lesson No. 7
Canned Models May Not Be Adequate

One of the most important components in the success of a forecasting system is accurate forecasts. The canned models embedded in a system may not be adequate to give you the accuracy you need. In this case, you may have to add your own models, which is possible only if the system is flexible enough and the in-house expert is well versed with the models as well as with the system.

Lesson No. 8
No System Will Work Without Collaboration

Don't treat a forecasting system as an isolated system. You need input from various users to design and implement it, as well as to run it. Nobody can tell better what your needs are other than those who would be using it. Scrutinize their needs as closely as possible. You may find some of the needs currently pursued are no longer needed. Also, make sure the software, hardware, and forecasting process you plan to use or make changes in are reviewed together and final decisions are collectively agreed on. This way everyone will be on board. This will help not only in bringing everyone on the same page but also in building confidence in the system.

Lesson No. 9
Train the Forecast Preparers and Users

To make sure that the system runs smoothly and the forecasts are effectively used, both preparers and users of forecasts should be trained. Otherwise, forecasts prepared will not be up to par nor will they be properly used. According to the 2009 survey of the Institute of Business Forecasting and Planning, only 51% of the capability of a software package/system is currently utilized. Also, training is a continuous process. With time, market dynamics change; so do the needs and technology. Regular training will help to keep everyone up to the speed.

Lesson No. 10
Continuous Improvement

As mentioned earlier, needs change over time and so does the process and technology. So, it is important to review regularly the needs, process, technology, and skill set of preparers and users of forecasts. Where there is a gap, try to close it. In this respect, it will also be helpful to develop contacts with outside professionals, as well as with those using the same or similar system. Attending forecasting conferences can help in making such contacts.

In addition, it is also important to look into what other enhancements the vendor you are considering is planning, how big and active its user group is, and how responsive it is to the needs of users. Also, while purchasing a system, keep in mind that people who sell it are merely salespeople. They don't have any experience in implementing and customizing a system. Neither do they have any experience in customer service. So, make sure whatever they promise is given in writing.

Companies will continue to implement a forecasting and planning system because accurate forecasts are important in planning. But the road to system implementation is difficult and costly. The lessons described above will help not only in protecting your investment but also in maximizing the return.

MARKET SHARE OF FORECASTING SYSTEMS

Although there are plenty of vendors of forecasting systems, the one that leads the pack, according to the 2009 survey of IBF, is JDA Software with a market share of 30%, followed by SAP with a share of 27%. The other key vendors are Oracle, IBM, Logility, and Demand Solution. (See Figure 30.1)

Figure 30.1 | Marketing Share of Different Forcasting Systems (All Industries Combined)

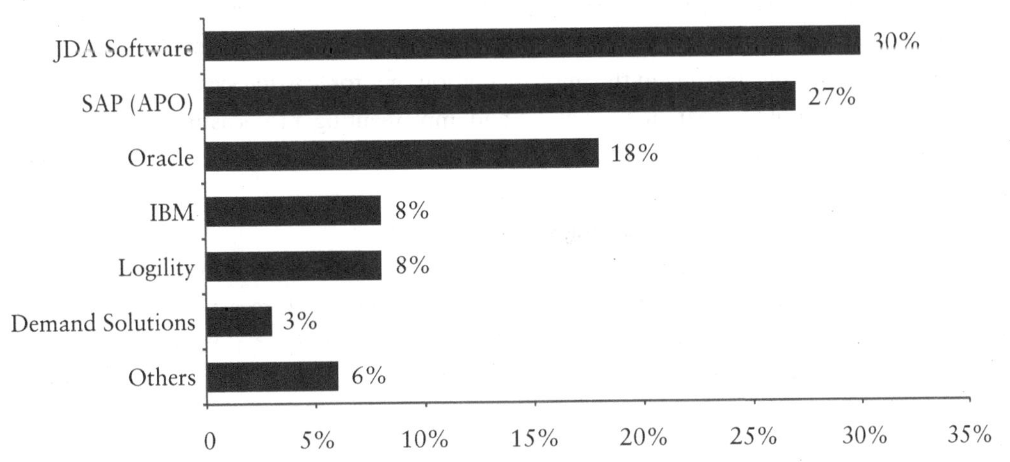

Source: 2009 study of IBF.
Notes: 1. JDA Software includes Manugistics and i2 Technologies.
2. IBM includes Cognos, Adaytum, and Applix.
3. Oracle includes PeopleSoft, JD Edwards, Hyperion, and Demantra.

SUGGESTED READING

1. Chase, Jr., Charles W. "What You Need to Know When Building a Sales Forecasting System." *Journal of Business Forecasting.* Fall 1996, pp. 2 & 23.
2. Lapide, Larry. "New Developments in Business Forecasting." *Journal of Business Forecasting.* Spring 1999, pp. 12-14.
3. LeVee, Gary S. "The Key to Understanding the Forecasting System." *Journal of Business Forecasting.* Winter 1992, pp. 3-4.
4. Powers, Anthony M. "Architecture of the Enterprise Forecasting System." *Journal of Business Forecasting.* Volume 14. Summer 1995, pp. 6-9.
5. Power, Anthony M. "How to Create an Enterprise Forecasting System." *Journal of Business Forecasting.* Fall 1994, pp. 3-6.
6. Safavi, Alex. "Choosing the Right Forecasting Software and System." *Journal of Business Forecasting.* Fall 2000, pp. 6-11 and 14.
7. Shahbaz Alibaig and Bryan Lilly. "Updating Your Forecasting System: Wisconsin Tissue's Experience." *Journal of Business Forecasting.* Fall 1999, pp.13-18.
8. Zoghby, Jeriad. "Lessons Learned from Implementing Forecasting and Planning System." *Journal of Business Forecasting.* Spring 2002, pp. 17-18.

QUESTIONS FOR REVIEW

1. What is the difference between a forecasting package and a forecasting system? Explain.
2. What are the key lessons learned in the implementation of a forecasting system? Explain.
3. Explain how one should prepare for designing and implementing a forecasting system.
4. Explain what we have to do after the implementation of a forecasting system to ensure that the system remains robust.
5. Who are the key players in the forecasting system market?
6. Is it necessary to have consultants for implementing a forecasting system? Why and why not?
7. Why is it important to have an in-house expert in implementing a forecasting system?
8. Why do we need a corporate data warehouse? What role does it play in the implementation of a robust forecasting system?
9. Building a successful forecasting system is a collaborative effort. Explain.
10. Explain in brief the following:
    a. Multi-dimensional architecture
    b. Relational database
    c. Inter-operable architecture
    d. Open architecture

PART XI

THE FUTURE

INTRODUCTION

Demand planning and forecasting are the keys to the success of any business, because without these, demand cannot be managed effectively and efficiently. Like most disciplines, the field of demand planning and forecasting will grow. We will see development in technology for storing, retrieving, analyzing, and communicating data and information. More and more companies will use POS data in their demand planning. Forecasting software will advance to the next level. Not only will they use more advanced algorithms but also they will provide "what-if" analysis and more efficient capability for data mining and flagging exceptions. We will have more collaboration within organizations as well as among suppliers and customers. We will also see more collaboration and transparency between suppliers and suppliers' suppliers. In addition, the collaboration among global trading partners will grow further, though not without challenges because of the differences in their cultural background.

CHAPTER 31

THE FUTURE OF DEMAND PLANNING AND FORECASTING

Over the last three decades or so, the field of demand planning and forecasting has grown by leaps and bounds, and the growth is expected to continue in the future. Most of the future progress will come from developments that already have taken root, including awareness about the need for demand planning and forecasting, collaboration both within and outside the enterprise, modeling, data mining, and technology. Among them, collaboration will lead the way—both within and outside an organization. However, the road ahead won't be smooth and easy. Businesses will experience numerous hurdles along the way arising from changing market dynamics as well as from working with people with different nationalities and cultural backgrounds.

THE INCREASING ROLE OF COLLABORATION

Although collaboration has evolved from Silo to Consensus Forecasting to Sales and Operations Planning (S&OP) to Collaborative Planning, Forecasting and Replenishment (CPFR®), there is still a long way to go. Although a number of companies now use S&OP and CPFR® processes, they are still in a rudimentary stage: All the functions don't participate; meetings are held, though not regularly and periodically; and management's support is lukewarm at best. All this will change. Many companies that have collaboration with customers still don't make full use of POS data, partly because of incompatibility of technology of the suppliers and customers, and partly because customers are still reluctant to share fully their data/information.

More and more companies with an international presence will globalize their collaborative processes, though again not without a challenge. It is difficult enough to create collaboration within a country, but to do it globally would be even harder because of the differences in their cultural backgrounds. Although many companies have a domestic S&OP process in place, its global aspect is still either non-existent or in a rudimentary stage. It is not well established whether or not the global S&OP should be centralized; and if it were to be centralized, it is unclear at what level—regional or global. But pretty soon we will have the answer.

Further, the name of the game in forecasting is visibility of products—how much is sitting in the customers' and distributors' warehouses, and how much has been sold to ultimate consumers. The difference in culture and marketing practices in emerging markets has made this visibility very obscure. In China, for example, a large percentage of consumer goods are sold to distributors who then sell to sub-distributors and then to sub-sub-distributors, making it difficult to determine how much inventory each one is holding. However, with time, more and more big-box retailers like Walmart are likely to emerge, which will make it easier for suppliers to access the information they need.

With time, we will also see collaboration not only among different functions within an organization and between customers and suppliers, but also between suppliers and second- and third-tier suppliers. We will also see collaboration among suppliers in the area of logistics to reduce the shipping costs. Instead of sending a truck that is less than full, they may start filling the unused space in a truck with products of other suppliers, provided they are going to the same customer and are complementary . This is like shipping together Clorox Bleach of The Clorox Company and Tide Laundry Detergent of P&G to the same customer, say, Walmart.

ADVANCES IN TECHNOLOGY

Significant progress has been made in technology, particularly in the areas of automation, scalability, data warehousing, and the incorporation of structured judgment into forecasts, which is expected to continue. More and more companies will centralize their warehouses. Radio Frequency Identification (RFID) and voice recognition will improve the supply response to demand. We expect to see a lot of developments in the Enterprise Resource Planning (ERP) systems, which are currently deployed mostly to minimize costs and inventory. They assume that good forecasts are available, which is generally not the case. The future ERP systems are expected to have forecasting capability. They will also be able to cope much more efficiently with numerous forecast updates resulting from changing market dynamics.

The future forecasting software may be able to track the source of an error, that is, whether the error is coming from data, model, assumptions, or the bias of an individual. Once we know the source, we may know how to correct it. We also expect further advancements in the data mining technology, which would further enhance the market intelligence and, consequently, the marketing strategy.

Exceptions play an important role in demand planning, that is, what to do when demand is expected to be much more or much less than the norm, the error of a specific product or product line is expected to be exceptionally high, and inventory level of a certain product is expected to be extremely high or low. The future forecasting system will alert the suppliers ahead of time so that demand planners can take an appropriate action.

Expert systems will improve. At present, most of the expert systems use only Time Series models. The future systems will also use regression models. Further, it will use many more models than a handful of models that are currently used.

We also see the emergence of more advanced "what-if" simulation software, which will not only speed up the decisions but also improve them. This kind of functionality will be extremely helpful in the Executive S&OP meeting when deciding on the best course of action; for example, whether to reduce the price or increase the promotional budget, and by how much, to hit the target.

There will also emerge on-demand software, where the customer will pay only for what he or she uses rather than paying the upfront signing cost along with the monthly maintenance fee. (As mentioned before, only 51% of the capability of a forecasting software/system is currently utilized.) This will increase competition among software companies resulting in lower prices and better services. With that, a customer won't be locked into any one vendor. It can easily switch, depending on which one provides better price and service. Some companies such as Oracle and SAP have already started using this marketing approach on some of their products.

MORE STATISTICAL ANALYSIS AND LESS JUDGMENT

As technology advances and statistical models get better, the use of quantitative modeling will increase and the role of judgment will decrease, though at no point statistical models are expected to completely replace the judgment. Although many academicians and practitioners have worked on forecasting for many years, they still have not found a magic formula that can guarantee good forecasts. Probably, this will never happen. However, the increasing computing power will allow us to select the best model not from a handful of models but from a large number of them. It will also help to use models that are highly complex. At present, most of the companies use Time Series models. But, over time, the use of Cause-and-Effect models will increase.

As collaboration among suppliers and customers further strengthens, the use of POS data in demand planning and forecasting will increase, which will help suppliers to respond quickly to market changes.

Forecasts improve if we can determine the source of the problems. Wrong assumptions are one of them. In the future, we are going to see more and more documentation of assumptions, making it easier to determine what happened to the forecasts and why.

USE OF ONLINE DATA

The use of data in forecasting has evolved from shipment to demand to POS. But in the future, we may also see the use of online retailers' data such as of Amazon.com and Barnes & Noble. Their sites allow customers to pre-order a product, that is, order it before the launch date. On a number of sites, customers can now pre-order products such as books, movies, music, and video games. These orders provide valuable information to marketers about their future demand. Further, in the United States, it is a common practice for marrying couples and expecting mothers to create an online registry, which contains a list of items they would like to have. Such registries tell not only what is going to be purchased, but also provide a fairly good idea of when they would be purchased. If they did not get a certain item as a gift, they most likely would buy it themselves. Some retailers also let people create a wish list—the products they would like to have for their birthday, anniversary, or for any other occasion—that they may e-mail to their friends and family. Such lists can provide a good insight as to what consumers are likely to buy in the future. Retailers who have access to such data may very well start syndicating it like AC Nielsen and Symphony IRI Group do with POS.

In short, with advances in computer technology, software, and statistical methods as well as with the use of consumption data, demand planning and forecasting will improve. However, there would be some countervailing forces, which would work against them. Those forces will emanate from rising competition because of globalization, an explosion in the number of new products and channels of distribution, and shorter and shorter life cycles of products.

SUGGESTED READING

1. Keifer, Steve. "Why Amazon.Com Has the Best Demand Forecasting Data." *Blog*. December 11, 2009.

QUESTIONS FOR REVIEW

1. What kinds of developments do we expect to see in the future in the area of collaboration that will improve demand planning and forecasting? Explain.
2. What kinds of developments do we expect to see in the future in the area of technology that will improve demand planning and forecasting? Explain.
3. What improvements do we expect to see in the future in expert systems? Explain.
4. What is an Enterprise Resource Planning (ERP) system? What developments in the future can we expect to see in this system?
5. Can we hope to find a model in the future that will work well with every dataset? Describe.
6. What forces are we likely to encounter in the future that would make it harder to improve forecasts? Explain.
7. How do you see the role of judgment in forecasting in the future? Would it increase or decrease, and why? Explain.
8. What kinds of problems would globalization, increasing number of new launches, and shorter life cycles of products present in forecasting? Explain.
9. What is the best data to use in operational forecasting? Do you see any change in the type of data to be used?
10. Explain in brief the following:
    a. Expert system
    b. Enterprise Resource Planning
    c. Wish list
    d. Benefits of using online pre-order data in demand planning

GLOSSARY

A

ABC Classification: Classifying products or customers by sales volume. Classification A may represent products or customers that generate, let us say, 70% of the total revenue; classification B, 20% of the total revenue; and the Classification C, the balance. These percentages are arbitrary. The idea here is to align inventory management, customer service policies, and cost controls with the value of the product or customer. The other way of looking at it is to pay the most attention to high revenue generating products and customers, and less to others. Some companies use the 80%/20% rule, where 80% of the sales come from 20% of products or customers—this is usually the case.

ABCxyz Analysis: Here we first classify products by using ABC analysis, that is, the most valuable products are A, less valuable products are B, and the least valuable products are C. Then, within each classification, we further categorize them by xyz, that is, products within "A" classification are categorized by "x" (products with very little variation), "y" (products that have some variation), and "z" (products that have most variation). The more variation there is in the sales data of a product, the more difficult it is to forecast.

Account Based Forecasting (ABF): Forecasting products at an account (customer) level.

Actual Demand: It represents what was actually ordered or desired, without any adjustment for availability. It is also called unconstrained demand.

Additive Composition Model: Decomposition models are of two types: (1) Additive and (2) Multiplicative. In the Additive model, we add various components such as seasonality, trend, and business cycle to arrive at a forecast; whereas in the Multiplicative model, we multiply them.

Adjusted R^2: It shows how well independent variables explain the variations in the dependent variable. Here R^2 is adjusted for the number of independent variables as well as for the number of observations. It varies between 0 and 1. The higher the value, the better the model is.

Advanced Planning and Scheduling (APS): It is a manufacturing management process that analyzes and plans logistics and manufacturing resources during short, intermediate, and long-term periods. APS software uses advanced math and heuristics to perform simulations and optimizations for such things as finite capacity scheduling, demand planning, sales and operations planning, logistics resource planning, etc. The process considers constraints and business objectives to provide decision support and recommended solutions.

Aggregate Forecast: This is a sales forecast for a group of products or customers. It may be a forecast of all products within a family, all customers in a given region for the sales and operations planning process, or total forecast for the year or budgetary period. It is often used to compare the current plan with the annual operating plan and budget so that appropriate actions can be taken.

Algorithm: Any detailed operation or set of rules used to solve a problem, or express an outcome using a finite number of steps.

Analog Model: This is a judgmental model of forecasting. In this model, we look for an analog of a variable to be forecasted, and then use it as a basis for forecast. For example, when the television first came on the market, forecasters used the sales of radios as an analog to prepare a forecast for television sales. Analog provides confidence in the projection in the sense that if it happened before, it can happen again. To use such a model wisely, the forecaster must select an analog objectively, and not to support a desired outcome.

ARIMA (Autoregressive, Integrated, Moving Average) Model: See Box-Jenkins Model.

Artificial Volatility in Demand: This is variation in demand resulting from the organizational policies and practices. For example, the cigarette industry in the past created fluctuations in demand by telling customers that they would be raising prices by the end of a quarter. If a customer bought by the deadline or before, it would be getting them at old prices. This caused a surge in demand before the end of the quarter and, after that, the demand sharply declined. This type of volatility in demand is artificially created.

Assemble to Order (ATO): In an ATO business (e.g., in personal computers and customized cars), the product or service is assembled on receipt of the sales order. Key components are planned or stocked in anticipation of a sales order.

Assortment Planning: It is used to determine the quantity of each product to be purchased that would fit not only into the overall merchandise plan but also would help in optimizing sales and profit. The assortment includes specifying in detail color, size, brand, materials, etc.

Assumption Error: The error resulting from an assumption(a) made at the time the forecast was generated. For example, the model assumed that the GDP would increase by 3%, but it actually increased by only 2%.

Autocorrelation: It refers to correlation between values of the same time series at different time intervals, that is, how the value of the t period is related to the value of t-1 period, how the value of t-1 period is related to the value of t-2 period, and so on. In regression modeling, a model is believed to be robust if there is no autocorrelation among residuals (difference between actual value and fitted value), meaning residuals are not correlated with each other. It is also called serial correlation.

Autocorrelation Function (ACF): The pattern of autocorrelations at different time intervals is called autocorrelation function. In ARIMA modeling, it is used, among other things, to determine the appropriate model.

Autoregressive (AR) Model: It is a part of an ARIMA model and assumes that the sales of the current period depend on the sales of the past values of the same series at different time lags. In other words, it assumes that sales of the current period depend on the sales of one period before (lag of one period), two periods before (lag of two periods), and so on.

Autoregressive-Moving Average (ARMA) Model: It is a combination of autoregressive (AR) and moving average (MA) models. See also Autoregressive (AR) and Moving Average (MA) models.

Available to Promise (ATP): It consists of the uncommitted portion of a company's inventory and planned production. The ATP quantity is used to support customer order promising.

Average Inventory:

$$\text{Average Inventory} = \frac{\text{Order Quantity}}{2} + \text{Safety Stock Quantity}$$

Average Period Inventory: It is often measured as:

$$\text{Average Period Inventory} = \frac{\text{Beginning Inventory} + \text{Ending Inventory}}{2}$$

Average Value: This measures the central tendency of a data series. It is calculated by taking the sum of the observations in a data series and dividing the result by the number of observations in the data series. (This is also called the arithmetic mean.)

B

Base Demand: The demand of a company that results from existing customers devoid of any promotional effects. This type of demand is pretty much known and recurring.

Baseline-Demand Forecast: It is a statistically generated demand forecast where the data were adjusted for all the problems including outliers, structural change, and missing values. The impact of promotion and unusual events was removed from the forecast.

Batch Forecasting: Automatically generated forecasts for a large number of products based on set rules for analyzing and treating data as well as for selecting a model.

Batch Size or Quantity: The number of units that will be produced after a machine has been set up.

Benchmarking: It is a process of comparing a firm's business processes and performance metrics to practices in the industry (industry averages). Benchmarking performance metrics include cost per unit and forecast error, and at the business process level, best practices in implementing S&OP and using forecasting models.

"Best-in-Class" Forecast Errors: The average forecasting errors of "best-in-class" companies, which may be the average of top 25 or 30 performing companies.

Bias: In forecasting, bias occurs when there is a consistent difference between actual sales and the forecast, which may be of over- or under-forecasting. Companies often measure it with Mean Percentage Error (MPE). If it is positive, bias is downward, meaning company has a tendency to under-forecast. If it is negative, company has a tendency to over-forecast. It often results from the management's desire to meet previously developed business plans or from a poorly developed reward system. For example, if sales performance is measured by meeting the sales quotas, salespeople will be more inclined to under-forecast.

Big Data: The massive volume of data in existence today, both structured and unstructured, which cannot be stored, processed or analyzed with traditional techniques and software. Unstructured data originate from non-traditional sources such as sensors, smart devices, social media, text, web data, tweets, audio, video, click streams, log files, and more.

Bill of Material (BOM): A list of parts or components that are required to build a product.

Bottom-Up Forecasting: Forecasts that originate from the bottom; for example, aggregating detailed forecast (e.g., SKU level by Product/Package/Location) to a higher level (e.g., by Product/Package or Product). However, in practice, Marketing, Sales, and Management first review and adjust aggregate forecasts, which are then forced down to a detail level, using an apportionment method.

Box-Jenkins Model: A time series model that has been named after the developers of this model. It is a part of the time series models that assume that the sales of a company depend on previous values of the same series. For example, the sales of a company depend on the sales of one period before (lag of one period), two periods before (lag of two periods), and so on. It is also called ARIMA model.

Bullwhip Effect: A small change in the downstream demand near the end consumers causes a significant change in the upstream demand closer to the manufacturer. In other words, a small change in consumer demand causes a much greater change in the inventory of each participant in the supply chain, and the change becomes bigger and bigger as we move upstream, say, from inventory of finished goods to inventory of raw material. The bullwhip effect is the result of lack of visibility in consumer demand, unusual changes in consumers' buying patterns, and poor forecasts. Increased collaboration and visibility across the chain are used to mitigate the bullwhip effect.

Business Cycle: Business cycle refers to long-term fluctuations that occur regularly, but not periodically. The length of a cycle is always more than one year. Each business cycle goes through phases of revival, prosperity, peak, recession, depression, and trough. This is a continuous process. Here, fluctuations occur regularly but not at a set time interval.

Business Forecasting: The practice of making predictions about business related issues such as sales, shipments and cash flow based on assumptions such as price, advertising spend, number of new products, competitor behavior, state of the economy, etc.

Business Intelligence: The practice of employing data analysis techniques to support business decision-making processes. It uses architectures, databases, analytical tools, strategies, applications, and methodologies to gain insight from data. This insight can be used to make business decisions about which products to launch, when and how to launch them, and whether to raise the price, etc.

Business Plan: A plan that outlines the roadmap for a business to achieve specific goals that are believed to be attainable. The business plan may be tactical or strategic. The tactical plan may include promotional and a special event plan to achieve a certain sales target. The strategic plan, on the other hand, may include new product launches, opening and closing of stores, entering new markets and channels of distribution, SKU reduction, store format changes, warehouse expansion, and capacity planning to achieve certain long-term goals.

C

Capable to Promise: An advanced order promising technique used to determine when a new, unscheduled customer order can be delivered. The process uses finite scheduling techniques, as well as such things as material and capacity constraints across multiple nodes in the supply chain. For example, computer firms that sell personal computers on an assemble-to-order basis use Capable-to-Promise functionality to determine delivery-date promises.

Cash Conversion Cycle (CCC): It is a metric used to measure the effectiveness of a company's management and, consequently, its overall health. The calculation shows how fast a company can convert cash on hand into inventory and accounts payable, through sales and accounts receivable, and then back into cash. Its formula is:

CCC = DIO + DSO - DPO

Where:
DIO (Days Inventory Outstanding) = Avg. Inventory/COGS per Day;
DSO (Days Sales Outstanding) = Avg. Accounts Receivable/Ending Account Receivable)/2
DPO (Days Payable Outstanding) = (Beginning Accounts Payable + Ending Account Payable)/2;

Causal Model: A model based on the cause-and-effect relationship. If, for example, sales (effect) depend on price (cause), the regression model, which is one of the cause-and-effect models, will statistically calculate the relationship between them, and then use that relationship to prepare a forecast for the next period.

Census X-11: This is an advanced form of a Classical Decomposition model. It decomposes the data into seasonal, trend, cyclical, and random (irregular) components, and then uses them to generate a forecast for the next period. (Also, see Classical Decomposition Model.)

Classical Decomposition Model: The model that decomposes a time series into different components to generate a forecast. The time series is decomposed into trend, seasonal, cyclical, and irregular (random) components.

Click-Stream Data: Such data include series of page visits and associated clicks executed by website visitors while navigating through the site. Analysis of click-stream data can help a company to understand which products, website content, or screens are of most interest to customers.

Cloud Computing: Used to store, process, compute and access data using a network of remote servers, rather than a personal computer or local server. It works through an Internet connection and is maintained and controlled by a provider such as Google, Amazon or Microsoft. It allows businesses to access their data from any internet-connected device, anytime and anywhere.

Co-Managed Inventory (CMI): It is a continuous replenishment process where the manufacturer is responsible for replenishing products in consultation with its customer.

Cochrane-Orcutt Procedure: An iterative estimation procedure for handling the first order autocorrelation problem.

Coefficient of Determination (R^2): A measure of goodness of fit in a regression model. It shows how well the variations in the dependent variable are explained by the independent variables. Its value varies between 0 and 1. The higher the value, the better the model is.

Coefficient of Variation (COV): It measures the percentage of variation around the arithmetic mean of a series, and is calculated as follows:

$$\text{Coefficient of Variation} = \frac{\text{Standard Deviation}}{\text{Mean}}$$

It is commonly used as a measure of volatility in demand to assess the predictability of a demand pattern, that is, how well it can be forecasted. If COV >1.0, it can be said that variations in demand are high, and thus, statistical techniques should not be applied without further review.

Collaborative Planning, Forecasting and Replenishment (CPFR®): It is a process that enables companies to work together with their trading partners in an effort to improve forecasts, reduce inventory and production costs, and increase sales and profit.

Collinearity: Also called multicollinearity, this exists when two or more independent variables are highly correlated. The presence of collinearity in a regression model weakens the predictability of a model.

Confidence Level: It is a concept of probability distribution used in hypothesis testing, as well as in range forecasting. For example, in range forecasting, if we want to be right 95 times out of 100 (95% level of confidence), the forecast error will range between the mean error ± 2 standard deviations.

Consensus Forecast: A forecast that is jointly agreed upon across different functions of an organization.

Constrained Demand: The adjusted demand plan or forecast after applying constraints, such as production capacity or material shortages. In other words, constrained demand is equal to orders received minus orders that won't be fulfilled for one reason or other. The implication is that more can be sold if there are no constraints.

Consumer Demand Driven: The demand driven by end-consumers, such as demand reflected in the Point-of-Sale (POS) data.

Consumer Promotions: Sales and marketing tactics that are used to encourage consumers to purchase their products, such as a buy-one-get-one-free special.

Continuous Replenishment Program (CRP): A technique whereby the customer provides access to almost real-time inventory data, which are used by the supplier to continuously replenish the customer's stock. The customer and supplier jointly establish safety stock levels and order points. The primary difference between CRP and Vendor Managed Inventory (VMI) is that CRP is performed continuously, while VMI, periodically.

Correlation Coefficient: A standard measure of the relationship between a dependent and independent variable. Its value varies between -1 and 1. Zero means there is no correlation between them, and one means a perfect correlation. Positive value means that the relationship is positive, that is, when one goes up, the other also goes up. Negative value means they are negatively related.

Correlation Matrix: The correlation coefficients are often presented in the form of a matrix, which is called a correlation matrix. It shows how X_1 is related to Y; X_2 is related to Y; X_1 is related to X_2; and so on.

Correlogram: A graphic representation of autocorrelation and partial autocorrelation coefficients. (For more detail, see Autocorrelation and Partial Correlation Coefficient.)

Cost of Error: The monetary cost of forecast error to a company. Another way of looking at it is how much money the company can save by reducing error. The savings may be in terms of reducing inventory, cost of production, stock-outs, etc.

Cross-Sectional Data: The data drawn across regions, age groups, or income levels in a given period.

Cycle Stock: The average amount of inventory a business needs to meet customer demand between the times it orders more inventory from suppliers. A company goes through its cycle stock inventory as it sells products and restocks inventory.

$$\text{Cycle Stock} = \frac{\text{Economic Order quantity (EOQ)}}{2}$$

Here EOQ is the optimal amount of inventory business buys each time it restocks.

D

Dashboard: Provides instant snapshots of such things as designated key performance indicators (KPIs) and real-time trends and reports for making business decisions. With a drill-down capability, one can move from a summary level to greater detail; for example, how our KPIs compare with industry benchmarks or how the actual of this compares with the forecast. (See also Workbench)

Data Mart: It is a subset of data warehouse, usually geared toward a specific business line or team.

Data Mining: The collection, exploration, pattern identification and deployment of data for the purposes of gaining insights and extracting useful information. For example, identifying which products consumers buy together, when they buy them, etc.

Data Repository: A logical partitioning of data where multiple databases, which apply to specific applications or sets of applications, reside. For example, several databases of revenues and expenses that support financial applications may reside in a single financial Data Repository.

Data Warehouse: It is where data are stored after they are cleaned, transformed, and cataloged, and then made available for analysis, data mining, market research, and decision support.

Database: Usually a large collection of typically quantitative information organized especially for rapid search and retrieval (normally by a computer). Within the forecasting realm, models and forecasts are based on databases that contain sales information that has dimensions such as product, geography, period, customer, and measure.

Days of Supply (DOS): It measures how long the inventory on hand will last. If, for example, a manufacturer consumes 100 units a day of a certain component in manufacturing and has 800 units on hand, it has an eight-day supply.

Decomposition Model: (See Classical Decomposition Model)

Degrees of Freedom: The number of data points available for producing useful information. In regression modeling, for each additional independent variable added to a model, we lose one degree of freedom.

Delphi Model: It is a structured group technique where the coordinator receives unbiased input from a wide range of experts, both within and outside the company, to create a forecast. The process requires several rounds of feedback and, with each subsequent round, forecast gets better. The model is commonly used for new products where there is a high degree of uncertainty.

Demand: It represents the amount of sales or orders received. It may be constrained or unconstrained. The unconstrained demand is total demand, irrespective of whether or not it can be fulfilled, whereas constrained demand is what can be fulfilled.

Demand Collaborator System: It is used to capture, assemble, and process the market intelligence obtained from a variety of sources including field sales and marketing personnel and downstream customers to prepare forecasts.

Demand-Driven Supply Chain or Network: Building supply chains in response to demand signals. The main driver is customers' demand, not supply as used in the traditional "supply-driven" or "demand-push" model.

Demand Forecasts: They represent expected orders, irrespective of whether or not they will be fulfilled. They are also called unconstrained demand forecasts.

Demand Management: The process of identifying and managing demands for goods and services. It involves prioritizing demands, gaining input on demands from all key stakeholders, reaching cross-functional agreement on the demand plans, executing and monitoring plans, and taking action as required. The overall goal is to maximize sales and profit.

Demand Plan: A course of action a company plans to take to maximize sales and revenue, based on a forecast and insights gained from data. The plan may include products it plans to launch, prices it would charge, products to be promoted and/or discontinued, volume to be produced, inventory held, etc.

Demand Planner: A role responsible for facilitating the demand planning process. They help to establish and maintain the process with key functions, providing metrics and performing diagnostics to improve business performance. The demand planner must be proficient in math and statistics and have the ability to influence and reconcile differences, as well as the ability to communicate effectively across the organization.

Demand Planning System: In addition to preparing forecasts, it helps in generating optimal production, procurement, logistics, financial, sales, and/or marketing plans.

Demand Pull: How much end-consumers are pulling. Replenishment of material or finished good is pulled downstream based on actual consumption data. In consumer goods, replenishment is driven by Point-of-Sale (POS) data. In lean operations, the movement of goods from the supplying node to those who consume them is based on the real-time demand.

Demand Push: When suppliers push sales to customers by giving incentives such as special price discounts and rebates.

Demand Sensing: It is sensing and evaluating demand signals, and then predicting demand. Demand signals include consumption (POS) and order data.

Demand Shaping: It is influencing the demand of a product to achieve a desired goal. If the demand of a product is expected to be greater than supply, the supplier/customer may shape (more appropriately re-shape) the demand by increasing its price and/or by cutting down the promotion. It may also try to drive down its demand by promoting substitutes. If, on the other hand, the demand is expected to be less than supply, supplier/customer may shape the demand by lowering its price and/or by promoting it more heavily.

Demand Signals: Information about demand that can be obtained by analyzing usually downstream data, such as consumption (POS) and order data.

Dependent Variable: A variable that we wish to forecast. In regression modeling, the variable to be predicted is called the dependent variable. For example, if the model states that the sale (effect) of a product depends on its price (cause), then sale is the dependent variable.

Diagnostic Checking: The model evaluation step used in the ARIMA modeling.

Differencing: It refers to the difference between two values of different time periods of the same time series. It is often used in ARIMA modeling to make the data stationary.

Diffusion Models: They are mostly used in new product forecasting. In this context, a set of mathematical equations or formulas are used to estimate sales revenue in different phases of product life cycle from introduction to growth, to maturity, and to a declining phase. Examples of diffusion models are Logistic, Gompertz, Rodgers, and Bass.

Direct-to-Store Delivery (DSD): A method used by a manufacturer to sell and distribute goods directly to point of sales (POS) or point of consumptions (POC).

Disaggregate Forecast: An aggregate forecast broken down into a granular level. For example, in top-down forecasting, a company-level sales forecast broken down into a category level, or a category-level forecast broken down into a SKU level.

Distribution: The percentage of stores a product or group of products is being sold.

Distribution Centers (DC): A warehouse that receives merchandise from different suppliers, and then distributes them to multiple customers.

Distribution Channels: The pathways that companies use to sell their products. The company may sell its products by mail and/or through dealers, distributors, and retailers. The term "Channels" is also used to describe different types of retailers like Grocery, Mass Merchandiser, Drug Store, Convenience Store, and Warehouse Club.

Distribution Requirements Planning (DRP): It determines the inventory required for warehouses to meet the anticipated demand over time to maintain a given level of customer service.

Distribution Resource Planning (DRP II): In addition to DRP, this does the planning for non-inventory resources such as labor, storage space, and trucks.

Double Exponential Smoothing: See Exponential Smoothing Models and Holt's Exponential Smoothing Model.

Double Moving Average: The moving average computed twice; in other words, computing the moving average of the moving average.

Downstream Data: Information obtained from a supply chain partner that is closer to the consumer/end user. For a manufacturer, sales data from its customers who may be distributors, wholesalers, or retailers are examples of downstream data. (See also POS Data)

Dummy Variables: The variables that are used in regression modeling to account for the impact of qualitative elements such as a strike, a terrorist attack, or a snowstorm. It is also used to determine the impact of seasonality. The dummy variables take the value of 0 and 1.

Durbin-Watson (DW) Test: It is a diagnostic tool used to test a regression model. It measures the presence of autocorrelation in residuals. Its value varies between 0 and 4. The model is regarded as the best if its value is 2. Normally, a value between 1.5 and 2.5 is acceptable.

Dynamic Regression: A regression model that includes lagged values of independent variables, dependent variable, or both. For example, if certain promotional activities affect the sales only after one or two months, the model will become more efficient if the promotional spending is lagged.

E

Eache: It represents a consumer unit of purchase, e.g., a 12 oz. bottle of soda or one box of cereal.

Econometric Model: In this type of modeling, a set of equations are used to incorporate the interrelationship between internal and external variables. Furthermore, in this type of modeling, time series and judgmental models may be used in addition to regression.

Economic Indicator: It provides an indication as to the direction of the economy, that is, whether the economy is likely to go up or down. The indicator can be coincident, leading and lagging.

Economic Order Quantity (EOQ): The order quantity that minimizes the total holding and ordering costs. Manufacturers strive to balance and optimize the units so as to minimize the total cost associated with the purchase, delivery, and storage of products.

Economic Profit: It is the difference between the revenue generated from sales of products or services and the opportunity cost of inputs used. This is not the same as accounting profit.

EDI (Electronic Data Interchange): It is used for transmitting documents such as invoices, orders, status of order, and Point-of-Sale data to another party.

Efficient Consumer Response (ECR): It is an approach in which retailers, distributors, and suppliers work together to make the supply chain more efficient in an effort to reduce inventory, eliminate paper transactions, and provide products and services that consumers want.

Elasticity: It measures how sensitive demand is with respect to such things as price, income, and wealth. For price elasticity, it measures the percentage change in demand of a product with a one-percentage change in price. Here it is assumed that price affects demand. For example, if price elasticity is -5, it means a one-percentage decline in price will increase sales by 5%.

End Cap: It is shelf spaces at the end of aisles in a retail store, which is often given to a manufacturer on a rotating basis. Products placed at the end cap provide a significant lift to the sales.

End User: It is the ultimate consumer of a product or service. It is the very last link in the supply chain.

Endogenous Variable: A variable that is under the control of a company, e.g., price of a product and the amount to be spent on promotion. The company can change these variables any way it wants. It is also called an internal variable.

E-Procurement: An initiative to reduce the cost of purchasing goods as well as the related administrative costs by using consolidated procurement and web-enabled systems. It also speeds up the purchasing process.

ERP (Enterprise Resource Planning): It provides an integrated real-time view of core business processes, using common databases maintained by a database management system. It tracks business resources such as cash, raw materials, and production capacity, and the status of business commitments such as orders, purchase orders, and payroll. In other words, it provides totally integrated suites of software that support all functions within the organization including Finance, HR, Supply Chain Planning, and Procurement. With ERP, information flows smoothly among all business functions, and helps to manage connections with outside stakeholders. Its overall goal is to effectively plan and control resources to create a sustainable competitive advantage.

Error Metrics. They are mostly used to measure an error in a forecast.

Error Term: The difference between the actual and the forecasted value.

Estimated Model: It is a model with estimated values (coefficients) of all parameters. In forecasting, an estimated model is a predictive model from which a forecast can be generated.

Event Modeling: It allows determining the impact of one or more special events, such as an irregular promotion or a natural disaster, and then enabling to incorporate it into a forecast.

Ex Ante Forecast: Forecast of a period for which the actual value is not known; for example, a forecast of next month or next year.

Exogenous Variable: A variable over which the company has no control, e.g., competitive price and state of the economy. The modeler has to accept it as is, because it cannot be changed. It is also called external variable.

Expert System: A software system that determines an optimum solution based on pre-determined rules. The solution may be finding an optimum production schedule, most desirable demand plan, or best forecast. For a forecast, for example, the expert system first automatically selects the best model for a given dataset based on models embedded in the system and the criteria established for determining the best model, and then uses it to prepare a forecast.

Explanatory Variable: Also called an Independent Variable, it affects the dependent variable we wish to forecast. Let's say that the sales depend on price. Then price is the explanatory variable.

Exponential Smoothing Models: A class of time series models where the assigned weight for each previous period decreases exponentially as we go back. In other words, in these models more weight is given to recent observations and less to others. This contrasts with simple moving average models where each observation is weighted equally.

Ex Post Forecast: Forecast of a period for which the actual is known. It is used to test how well a model forecasts.

External Variable: See Exogenous Variable.

Extrapolative Approach: An approach where forecast is prepared by extrapolating the past data using one model or the other. For example, if the sales are increasing on the average by 5% from one period to the next, then the sales of the next period will be the sales of the current period plus 5%. Time series models are basically extrapolative models.

F

Face Validity: It refers to whether or not the forecasting model appears to be reasonable. For example, a linear regression model that uses the rain in Spain as an independent variable for sales in the U.S. makes no sense.

Fill Rate: It measures delivery performance and is expressed in percentage. Typically it is the percentage of orders, or line items shipped on time, complete, and without substitution.

Finite Scheduling: The objective of finite scheduling is to set a schedule, within the constraints of capacity and other resources, that maximizes output and ensures work will proceed at an even and efficient pace throughout the plant.

Fitted Forecasts: Statistical forecasts of past periods (ex post forecasts), derived by using the historical data and a selected statistical model. The purpose here is to compare fitted forecasts with actuals to see how well a given model performs.

Fitted Values: Same as fitted forecasts.

F-Statistic: In a regression model, it is used to determine the overall performance of a model. The higher the value, the better the model is.

Forecast Accuracy: How accurate the forecast is. It is computed as follows:

$$\text{Forecast Accuracy} = 1 - \left(\frac{\text{Actual} - \text{Forecast}}{\text{Actual}} \times 100\right)$$

Forecast Attainment: How much of the forecast we have actually attained. It is computed as follows:

$$\text{Forecast Attainment} = \left(\frac{\text{Actual}}{\text{Forecast}}\right) \times 100$$

Forecast Error: The difference between the actual value and forecast value.

Forecast Horizon: How far ahead a forecast has to be prepared. If we prepare a forecast two months ahead, then two months is the forecast horizon.

Forecast Value Added (FVA): FVA is a metric for evaluating the performance of each step and each participant in the forecasting process to determine which one adds value and which one does not, so that the one that does not can be eliminated. For example, each forecast may have many touch points; some of them add value to the forecast and others make it worse. The objective of FVA analysis is to determine which touch points (activities) help and which don't, so that one can eliminate those that don't help. The override of one person may improve the forecast; while of others makes it worse. The metric-to-measure performance may be Mean Absolute Percent Error (MAPE), bias, or any other.

Forecasting Package (Software): It is a stand-alone software package designed specifically for preparing forecasts.

Forecasting Process: The process that lays out key steps in the generation and review of forecasts, including what kind of information is needed to prepare forecasts; who has that information; how that information would be collected and then transmitted to a forecaster; where the forecasting function would reside; which forecasting philosophy would be followed—one number or multiple numbers; which forecasting approach would be used; who would participate in the process; and after forecasts are prepared, how their performance would be evaluated for future improvement.

Forecasting System: A system that includes a forecasting function and feeds forecasts to various modules for planning. In addition to preparing forecasts, it passes forecast data to other planning systems for such things as production, procurement, distribution, and sales planning.

Forward Buy: This occurs when an account buys extra quantity during the deal period to be used or sold after the deal has ended.

G

Goodness of Fit: How well the estimated (forecasted) values fit the historical data. There are several statistical tools for determining the goodness of fit, but for business forecasting practitioners, it may be the MAPE (Mean Absolute Percent Error). The lower the MAPE, the better the fit is.

Gross Margin Return on Inventory Investment (GMROI): This is calculated as follows:

$$\text{GMROI} = \frac{\text{Gross Margin}}{\text{Average Inventory Cost}}$$

H

Hadoop: An open source (free) software for processing huge data sets.

Heteroscedasticity: This condition occurs when residuals (errors) do not have a constant variance across the entire range of values. It is used in regression modeling to determine whether or not the model is robust. The model is robust if, among other things, there is no heteroscedasticity in the residuals.

Heuristic Approach: Where rules used for solving problems are based on business practices, experience, and/or expert intuition rather than on the quantitative optimization.

Hit Rate: The percentage of forecasts within a pre-determined accuracy tolerance. For example, if the goal for accuracy is set at 70% or above at the SKU level, it is the percent of items forecasted that meet this goal.

Hold-and Roll: It is assumed here that misses in a plan will be rolled into future periods. If you miss 20% of sales in January, it will be captured in February. So, it is added to the forecast of February.

Holdout Period: The period for which data are held for testing a model. Let's say we prepare a forecast of January 2017 by using the monthly data of January 2014 through December 2016. We have the data of January 2017, but we don't include it because we want to use it to test the model. By comparing the actual of that period with the forecast, we can determine how good the model is. The January 2017 period in this case is the holdout period.

Holt's Exponential Smoothing Model: It is an extension of Single Exponential Smoothing Model. It has two smoothing parameters: one adjusts for level and the other for trend in the data. It is used where there is a trend in the data. It is also called the Double Exponential Smoothing Model.

Holt-Winters' Exponential Smoothing Model: It is also an extension of Single Exponential Smoothing Model. It uses three parameters: one for level, one for trend, and one for seasonality. It is used where there is trend and seasonality in the data.

Homoscedasticity: This is a condition where residuals have a constant variance across the entire range of values. It is opposite of heteroscedasticity. In regression modeling, a model is robust if, among other things, there is homoscedasticity in the residuals.

Hypothesis Testing: A probabilistic method for testing the significance of a coefficient of a specified model on the basis of estimated statistics.

I

Identification: In regression modeling, it is a process of identifying, at least tentatively, an appropriate model for forecasting. After a model is identified, the next steps are estimation and validation.

In Store Merchandising: Sales and marketing efforts that are designed to facilitate consumer purchasing for their products via such means as displays and features. Displays include displaying products at a special price in various locations around the store. Feature, on the other hand, is referred to in the store circular.

Independent Variable: It is a variable that affects the variable we wish to predict. Let's say that sales depend on price. Then, price is the independent variable that affects the sales. An independent variable is also called explanatory variable, predictor variable, and driver. Independent variables are of two types: external and internal. External variables are those over which we have no control, and thus cannot be manipulated. The state of the economy, the unemployment rate, and competitive prices are a few examples of external variables. Internal variables, on the other hand, are those over which we have control, and thus can be manipulated to meet a certain goal. They are also called manipulated and controlled variables. Price, media spending, and the number of new launches are a few examples of internal variables.

Inherent Volatility in Demand: This volatility comprises the variations in demand due to the nature of the data, and not caused by artificial means such as promotions. The variations in demand, for example, stemming from seasonality and an intermittent nature of demand, are natural and not caused by any artificial means.

Integrated Business Planning (IBP): See also Sales and Operations Planning (S&OP). The term todayis highly debated between two groups of practitioners: one defines it as the planning process that includes demand review, supply review, product management review, management business review, financial reconciliation, and business strategy. Some view IBP as a broader version of S&OP, which also emphasizes the role of strategic planning. It continues to evolve.

Intercept: In regression, it explains what the forecast value would be if all the Xs (independent variables) have a zero value. It is also called a constant.

Intermittent Demand: This term is used for demand that is not continuous, rather it exists in some periods and not in others. In other words, in one month we have a demand, and then for a number of months there is no demand. The data exhibit no pattern. It is also called sporadic or lumpy demand.

Internal Variable: See Endogenous Variable.

Intervention Analysis: It is used to determine the effect unusual changes in the independent variables have on a forecast. An unusual change may result from a new advertising campaign, strike, or change in import/export tariffs.

Inventory Quality Ratio (IQR): A measure to track the quality of inventory value. It is measured as:

$$\text{IQR} = \frac{\text{Active Inventory}}{\text{Total Inventory}}$$

Here active inventory equals total inventory minus slow-moving and obsolete inventory.

Inventory Turnover: It is a measure of the number of times inventory is sold or used in a time period, such as in a year. It is often measured as:

$$\text{Inventory Turnover} = \frac{\text{Total Cost of Goods Sold}}{\text{Average Inventory}}$$

J

Judgmental Adjustment: A judgmental adjustment over statistical forecasts (baseline forecasts) for the elements that cannot be quantified or were not known at the time the forecast was generated. For example, the recall of a certain product has an effect on the forecast of a competitor, but it was not known at the time it was generated.

Judgmental Forecasting: Forecasts based on judgmental models such as Delphi and Survey. This type of forecasting is done where historical data are not available; if available, they are not applicable.

Just In Time (JIT): It is an inventory strategy to increase efficiency and decrease waste by receiving goods only as they are needed in the production process, thereby reducing inventory costs. For this strategy to work, a high degree of forecast accuracy is needed.

K

Key Performance Indicators (KPIs): The metrics used to monitor and control process performance. In forecasting, key metrics used are MAPE, WMAPE, FVA (fair value added), and bias; in the supply chain, they are customer service level, cost performance, and inventory performance such as inventory turns.

L

Lagged Dependent Variable: A dependent variable that is lagged in time. For example, if Y_t is the dependent variable, then Y_{t-1} will be a lagged dependent variable with a lag of one period. Lagged values are used in Dynamic Regression modeling. They are also used in ARIMA modeling where it is assumed that the forecast of the next period depends on past values of the same series.

Lead Time: The interval between the initiation and the execution of a process. In supply chain order fulfillment, lead time is the time needed to deliver the goods after the receipt of the orders; in replenishment lead time, it is the time needed for a product to be available for delivery.

Lean Forecasting: Improving forecasts with least amount of sources.

Least Squares Estimation: An estimation method that minimizes the sum of squared residuals of a model to arrive at a model.

Level of Significance: The level of risk for accepting/rejecting a null hypothesis; for example, we may reject a null hypothesis at the 95% level of confidence. (Also see Confidence Level.)

Life Cycle: A new product life cycle usually goes through four phases: Phase 1 where sales increase though slightly (introductory phase); Phase 2 where sales first increase at an increasing rate and then at a decreasing rate (growth phase); Phase 3 where sales flatten (maturing phase); and Phase 4 where sales start falling off (declining phase). In recent years, the life cycle of certain products has dramatically changed. For products like iPhone, a significant amount of sales come in first few weeks, and then taper off.

Line Extension: In a line extension, the number of product variations within a line expands. For example, a company adds a new flavor, color, or size to an existing product line.

Linear Model: In a linear model, the relationship between the dependent variable (e.g., sales) and independent variable (e.g., advertising expenditures) is considered linear. If the relationship between sales and advertising expenditures is 1:5, it assumes that it will remain the same for every level of advertising expenditures. That is, when advertising expenditures increase by one dollar, sales will increase by 5 units, if it increases by two dollars, sales will increase by 10 units, and so on.

Logarithmic Transformation: Statistical procedure used in modeling where the original data series is transformed through a logarithm function. Usually one does this when the data are non-linear, but could be transformed to a linear series through the use of a logarithm.

Logistic Curve: It forms an S-shaped curve and is used in new product forecasting where the life cycle of a product is expected to take this shape. Here, the percentage change in sales becomes smaller and smaller over time, and ultimately becomes negative.

Lumpy Demand: See Intermittent Demand.

M

Machine Learning: An algorithm or technique that enables systems to be "trained" in terms of learning patterns and associations from inputs that recalibrate from experience without being explicitly programmed. Machine learning is a subset or application of artificial intelligence.

Macro Data: Country specific data such as Gross Domestic Product (GDP) and Disposable Income.

Macro-Forecast: Forecast of an economy as a whole; for instance, forecasts of unemployment and GDP.

MAD (Mean Absolute Deviation): See Mean Absolute Deviation.

Make-to-Order: In this environment, products are manufactured after the receipt of a customer order.

Make-to-Stock: An approach to production where a firm first estimates demand and then makes products in advance to meet that demand. Here customer orders are fulfilled from the existing stock.

Managing Exceptions: It simply implies how to deal with exceptions if and when they occur. Exceptions may include a forecast that is significantly higher or lower than the norm, inventory that is significantly above or below a certain threshold, dealing with a product that has been recalled, and so on.

MAPE (Mean Absolute Percentage Error): It is a simple average of absolute percentage errors. It is calculated as follows:

$$MAPE = \frac{\sum \frac{|A-F|}{A} \times 100}{N}$$

Here A= Actual, F= Forecast, N= Number of observations, and the vertical bars stand for absolute values.

Marginal Cost: The incremental cost for producing one more unit.

Marginal Profit: Profit derived by selling an additional unit.

Marginal Revenue: Revenue derived from an additional unit.

Market Extension: Here, the market of a product is expanded either within the existing market by re-positioning the product (e.g., positioning diapers not for convenience but for comfort), by going into a new channel of distribution (e.g., selling it on a cable network), or by entering into new markets (e.g., going into emerging markets).

Market Response Model: It is used to understand how consumers individually and collectively respond to marketing activities, and how competitors interact.

Material Requirement Planning (MRP): A time-phased planning technique that uses bills-of-material, inventory status, and planning factors (lead time, safety stock, lot size, etc.) to convert demand for finished products into requirements for raw materials and intermediates or sub-assemblies. The outputs of the process include the quantity required and the date when each component of the finished product is needed.

Matured Products: Products that have passed their growth phase, and sales have flattened.

Maverick Buying: Purchasing materials from suppliers that are not under procurement contracts. This source usually increases the cost of products, but adds flexibility within the supply chain.

Maximum Likelihood Estimation: A method of estimating parameters of an equation that maximizes the probability so that the estimated model best represents the population.

Mean Absolute Deviation (MAD): It is an average of absolute forecast errors.

Mean Absolute Percentage Error: See MAPE.

MSE (Mean Squared Error): This is another measure of error. Here, errors are squared before the average is computed. Its formula is:

$$\text{MSE} = \frac{\Sigma\ (\text{Actual - Forecast})^2}{\text{Number of Observations}}$$

Metadata: It is information about data. It describes how, when, and by whom a particular set of data was collected, and how it was formatted. This helps in understanding the data stored in a data warehouse.

Micro Forecast: Forecast generated at a company level; sales forecast, for example.

Middle-Out Forecasting: In contrast to top-down and bottom-up forecasting, forecasts of middle-out originate from somewhere in the middle of a planning hierarchy; for example, from a specific product line or category.

Model: In forecasting, a model is a quantitative method, an algorithm, or an equation, used in preparing a forecast.

Model Error: Forecast error resulting from a model.

Model Identification: It means specifying a model, that is to say, which variables should be considered in a model.

Moving Average (MA) Model: Described in the context of two different time series models—(1) Traditional and (2) Box-Jenkins. In the traditional context, the MA model averages sales of certain periods to make a forecast for the next period. If, for example, we use a two-period moving average, then the average value of the last two periods becomes the forecast of the next period; if we use a three-period moving average, the average value of the last three periods becomes the forecast of the next period; and so on. How many periods of average to use depends on how far back the data seem to affect the sales of the forecast period. If you believe that the next period sales will be affected only by the last three periods, and then use the moving average of last three periods, and so on.

Multi-Tier Forecasting: Arriving at a forecast using this method involves using data of multiple levels or tiers of downstream supply chain trading partners, such as POS data, inventory level of retailers, distributors and wholesalers, and promotional activities of customers.

In the context of Box-Jenkins, the MA model assumes that Y_t (dependent variable) depends on the past errors (residuals). (See also Box-Jenkins Model)

Multicollinearity: This is another name for collinearity. (See Collinearity)

Multiple Correlation Coefficient (R): It measures the strength of association between the independent (explanatory) variables and the dependent variable (the variable we wish to forecast). Its value varies between 0 and 1; the higher value, the stronger the association.

Multiple Regression Model: A regression model where two or more independent (explanatory) variables are used to arrive at a predictive value.

Multiplicative Model: The Classical Decomposition model can be multiplicative or additive. In the multiplicative model, we multiply all the four components (trend, seasonal, cyclical, and random components) to arrive at a forecast, and in the additive, we add them.

Multivariate Model: A model that uses two or more independent variables. (Time series models use only one variable and are hence called univariate models.)

N

Naïve Model: A model in which minimum amounts of effort and manipulation of data are used to prepare a forecast. Most often naïve models used are random walk (current value as a forecast of the next period) and seasonal random walk (value from the same period of prior year as a forecast for the same period of forecasted year.)

Noise: The random component in a series is called noise.

Non-Stationary Data: Time series data are non-stationary if their mean, variance, and co-variance don't remain constant over time.

Normal Distribution: This is where data form a bell shape curve, that is, 50% of the distribution is above the mean and another 50% is below it. Also, in a normal distribution, the median is equal to the mean. Many statistical forecasting techniques assume that the historical data are normally distributed about the mean, and will yield poor results if this is not the case.

Normalized Variable: It is a transformed variable. It is computed by subtracting the mean from the value and then dividing it by the standard deviation.

O

Object Oriented Architecture: The object oriented architecture in a forecasting system implies that each object can be modified without disrupting other functions. For example, if a user requests a certain enhancement in the current object, it can be achieved by simply editing that object without shutting down the entire system.

Observations: Number of data points in a series.

Open Architecture: The open architecture in a forecasting system means that it can run multiple, off-the-shelf software. It can easily communicate with other systems via different devices. It allows the use of an MS Excel spreadsheet within the system's forecast engine.

Operational Forecasts: They are short-term forecasts at a detailed level (e.g., SKU) used to drive production scheduling, transfer of goods in the distribution network, procurement of materials required to meet schedules, etc. The planning horizon used for operational forecasting varies with the lead time required to execute supply planning.

Order Fulfillment: It includes the complete process from customer inquiry to the delivery of a product to the customer and payment of the invoice. Order-fulfillment lead time varies greatly, depending on the fulfillment approach (e.g., Make-to-Stock, Make-to-Order, and Assemble-to-Order), and the manufacturing lead time.

Ordinary Least Squares (OLS): An estimation method that minimizes the sum of squared residuals to arrive at the best model. It is most often used in regression because of its statistical properties.

Outliers: Observations or values that are out of the norm, either too large or too small.

Out of Sample MAPE: The MAPE (Mean Absolute Percentage Error) of the ex post forecast errors of a holdout sample. Also see MAPE.

P

Parameters: These are characteristics of a population, and not of a sample taken from it. For example, mean and standard deviation of a population are parameters.

Parsimony: It simply implies that the model should be kept as simple as possible. In regression modeling, it is suggested that we should use as few independent variables as possible.

Partial Correlation Coefficient: The partial autocorrelation describes the correlation between the current value of a variable and the earlier value of the same variable when the effects of all intervening time lags are held constant. In other words, if we calculate the partial autocorrelation between Y_t and Y_{t-2}, we keep the effect of the intervening value Y_{t-1} constant.

Perfect Order: A discrete measurement defined as the percentage of orders delivered to the right place, with the right product, at the right time, and in the right quantity with the right documentation to the right customer. It is an important metric for measuring supply chain performance.

Plan-O-Gram: It refers to how products are displayed and stacked on the retail floor.

Pooled Data: They are when time series and cross-sectional data are pooled together for building a model.

Pooled Regression: This is a regression model in which both time series and cross-sectional data are pooled together.

POS Data: They are the scanning data, generated when a cashier at the counter prepares a sales bill. They are also called consumption data.

Predictive Analytics: A process and strategy that uses a variety of advanced statistical algorithms to detect patterns and conditions that may occur in the future.

Price Elasticity: How sensitive the product/service is with respect to price. It is highly elastic if a small change in price leads to a large change in demand. It is highly inelastic if a large change in price leads to a small change in demand.

Procurement Lead Time: The time required from the point of recognizing the need for an item to receiving it.

Product Life Cycle: See Life Cycle.

Production Planning: The process of establishing overall manufacturing output levels required to meet demand and achieve business objectives. The tactical level production plan is a key output of the sales and operations planning process.

Proxy Variable: The variable that is substituted for an unobserved explanatory variable in a model. It is often used when it is infeasible or too expensive to use a more relevant variable. (For example, to use income as a measure of ability to purchase, even though it does not fully represent it, because the ability to purchase depends also on wealth, unreported income, gifts, etc.).

P-Value: Like t in t-test, it is often used to determine whether a given explanatory variable is significant or not. Often, a variable is considered significant if the P-value is less than 0.05, though this threshold is arbitrary.

Q

Qualitative Data: Data that are descriptive but not numeric. Such data are typically the result of opinion or description.

Qualitative Forecasting: Refers to the use of opinion or subjective judgment in developing forecasts. It is used for mid- to long-term forecasting when no data exist, as in the case of new products. The qualitative models of forecasting include Delphi, Historical Analogy, and Market Research.

Quantitative Forecasting: Used to develop a future forecast using past data. Math and statistics are applied to the historical data to generate forecasts. Models used in such forecasting are time series (such as moving averages and exponential smoothing) and causal (such as regression and econometrics).

Quick Response (QR): A system that links retailer Point-of-Sale data with production and distribution planning to improve efficiency in manufacturing and supply chain process. One of its key objectives is to reduce lead times across the chain.

R

R^2: See Coefficient of Determination.

Radio Frequency ID (RFID): The use of wireless technology to transfer data to identify and track tagged objects automatically. The tags (chips) contain electronically stored data, which can be transmitted via the use of scanners or battery-powered chips. Tags are used to identify the location of products and people, as well as to transmit status information.

Random Walk Model: A model that regards the current period value as the forecast of the next period. For example, the forecast of 2017 is the same as the sales of 2016. This is also called naive model.

Reconciling Forecasts: This refers to reconciling forecasts prepared by two or more different models or approaches to arrive at one set of numbers. For example, one set of forecasts might have been prepared with the bottom-up approach, and the other, with the top-down approach. The reconciliation process converts two or more sets of forecasts into one.

Reference Forecast: A forecast originated from outside of the forecast model, but used for retention, comparison, and possible consideration in the creation of a final consensus forecast. For example, a judgmental forecast of Sales, Management, or another Demand Planner.

Regression: A class of cause-and-effect models, where the first relationship between cause (independent variable) and effect (dependent variable) is determined, which then is used to prepare a forecast. If the model states that sales are a function of advertising, then the model will first compute the relationship between sales and advertisements, using the historical data, and then use that relationship to arrive at a forecast.

Regression Coefficient: Each independent variable in a regression model has a regression coefficient, which is often denoted by "b." Each "b" value (regression coefficient) measures the average relationship between the dependent variable and independent variable when all other things are kept constant. If the regression coefficient of media spending is 2, it means, on the average, one unit of change in media spending will cause a change in sales by 2.

Regressor: An explanatory (independent) variable.

Relational Database: It is the database that links disparate data tables through common references, such as product codes, customer name, UPC (unique product code) numbers, and geographical locations. It makes it easier to pull the sales information by any selection criteria.

Replenishment Lead Time: The time between when the need of a product is determined and the time it becomes available for use or sale.

Residual: It is the difference between the actual value and the fitted (estimated) value.

Return on Investment (ROI): It is a financial measure of return, and is computed by dividing the income realized from the investment by the amount invested.

Revenue Management (RM): It deals with how to maximize the revenue by selling the right product, at the right time, and at the right price.

Rough-Cut Capacity Planning (RCCP): The process of translating the master production schedule into requirements for key resources (such as labor, machines, and space) and then comparing them to available resources to ensure the master schedule is achievable.

Round Robin Tournament Approach: The approach that tests different models with the same data to find out the one that gives the least amount of error.

Run Rate: Estimating from current or known performance to predict future performance. If a machine, on average, produces 10 defective parts a month, this means that it would produce 120 defective parts a year. Then the run rate is 10.

S

Safety Lead Time: An element of time added to normal lead time to protect against fluctuations in lead time.

Safety Stock: A quantity of stock used to buffer for variation in demand and supply during lead time. Safety stock for finished goods items can be calculated using historical demand variance or forecast error. Techniques for computing can be quantitative (statistical) or qualitative (judgmental).

Sales and Operations Planning (S&OP): A structured business process that aligns all functional areas to integrate demand, supply and financial planning into one game plan. It is used to balance supply and demand, links strategic plans to operational plans, and develops the most desirable product portfolio and product mix to maximize sales and profit.

Sales, Inventory, and Operations Planning (SIOP): Another name for S&OP.

Sales Ratio Model: A forecasting model where ratios of monthly or quarterly sales to annual sales are computed from the historical data, and then used to make an annual forecast based on results to date.

Sampling Error: It is often called standard error of the estimate. It is an error that results from using a sample, as opposed to using all the observations of a population.

Saturation Level: Also known as maturity level, it is a sales level achieved after the growth phase and before the declining phase of the life cycle of a product.

Scenario Forecasting: It is a judgmental method of forecasting where an intuitively determined scenario (assumption) is used to prepare a forecast. For example, what would happen to sales if the Olympic Games were held in this country?

Seasonal Adjustment: Removing seasonality from the data.

Seasonal Index: It shows how a given period, say, January, affects the sales. It is based on the average of 100. If a given month has an index of higher than 100, it means that month's sales perform better than the average. Let's say that the index of February is 126. It means that February sales, on the average, perform 26% better than the average.

Seasonal Inventory: Building inventory in anticipation of a seasonal demand; for example, building inventory of candy for Halloween.

Seasonal Variations: See Seasonality.

Seasonality (or Seasonal Variations): It refers to fluctuations that occur regularly and periodically. The length of a seasonal cycle is always less than one year. Seasonal fluctuations can be quarterly, monthly, weekly, or daily. For example, the sales in department stores are the highest in the month of December because of Christmas. This happens every year and at the same time.

Segmentation: The process of defining and sub-dividing a large data set into clearly identifiable segments having similar or dissimilar characteristics.

Sell-In Forecast: Forecast of sales of a manufacturer to distributors or retailers.

Sell-Through Forecast: Forecast of sales to end users, that is, consumers.

Serial Correlation: Another name for autocorrelation. (See Autocorrelation)

Shipping Data: Data of merchandise shipped.

Shocks: Disturbances that occur once in a while and are unpredictable. For example, the incident of terrorist attacks on September 11, 2001, was a shock to business.

Simple Regression Model: A regression model with only one independent variable.

Single (Simple) Exponential Smoothing Model: It is a time series model of forecasting that gives more weight to a most recent value and less to others. Further, the weight assigned to a value decreases exponentially as we go back in time.

SKU (Stock Keeping Unit): It refers to a specific item and location combination or the lowest level of planning of any attribute. For example, a shirt with a 15-inch neck, half sleeves, and a white color is one SKU, and a shirt with a 15-inch neck, half sleeves, and a blue color is another SKU.

Slope: The rate of change (incline or decline) in a line. In regression, the coefficient of a variable is the slope of that variable. It shows how much Y (dependent variable) will change with one unit of change in X (independent variable).

Smoothing: In the forecasting context, it is referred to as smoothing the data. Data are often smoothed to get a better idea about the data pattern. Smoothing is done by methods such as moving averages and exponential smoothing.

Special Events: Events that occur irregularly and cause a temporary change in demand. For example, there may be a sharp increase in sales because the Olympic Games are in town.

Specification Error: The error caused by the omission of an important variable(s) or by the inclusion of irrelevant variable(s) in a model.

Structured Query Language (SQL): Computer language designed for managing data in relational databases to query, insert, update, and delete data.

Standard Deviation: A measure of variations within a series, that is, how much the data of a product vary over time.

Standard Error of Estimate: In a regression model, it is a measure of error estimate, and provides a crude measure of how much the actual values are likely to deviate from the forecasted values.

Standard Error of Regression: The standard deviation of the model residuals.

Standardized Values: The standardized values are computed by subtracting the mean from each value and then dividing it by the standard deviation. (It is the same as normalized values.)

Stationary Data: Time series data are stationary if their mean, variance, and co-variance do not change over time.

Stepwise Regression: It is a procedure for selecting independent variables for a model from a large number of available variables. It is done two ways: forward estimation and backward estimation. In the forward estimation, one independent variable is added at a time to the regression equation on the basis of its partial correlation coefficient. That is, first include the variable with the highest partial correlation coefficient, then the one with the second highest partial coefficient, and so on. After each variable is added, the partial F-test on the last entered variable is performed. The process is stopped as soon as the partial F-test indicates that the last entered variable is insignificant. In the backward estimation, all the independents are included in the equation. Then the insignificant ones are dropped from the model, one at a time.

Stock-Out: When inventory isn't available to meet orders in a timely manner.

Strategic Forecasts: Long-term forecasts, usually for several years into the future. Strategic plans usually have a 3-5 year horizon, or longer in some industries such as utilities.

Structural Change: A permanent change in the data pattern resulting from such things as acquisition of another company and introduction of a new product that revolutionized the market.

Structured Data: Structured data is well organized and easy to enter, store, query and analyze. It resides in a fixed field within a record, or in a file where it is stored in relational databases and spreadsheets. Further, it can be stored in numeric, currency and alphabetic format, as well as by name, date and address. Examples include point-of-sales (POS) data, customer order data, shipment data, financial data and website data.

Supply Chain Management: The design, planning, execution, control, and monitoring of supply chain activities with the objective of creating net value, building a competitive infrastructure, leveraging worldwide logistics, synchronizing supply with demand, and measuring performance globally.

Supply Chain Planning: It includes processes and systems to manage most efficiently the flow of goods and inventory. The processes include demand planning, production and procurement planning to complete orders and/or replenish stocks, transportation planning, load planning, warehouse planning, and scheduling shipments.

Supply Collaborator System: It helps to gather information from various sources such as suppliers of raw material and contract manufacturers to determine the supply.

Supply Signals: Information that can be obtained from analyzing usually upstream data, such as which suppliers have and plan to have materials, components, and products needed to support future demand and manufacturing needs.

Survey Error: It is the difference between a population parameter (such as the mean, total, or proportion) and the estimate of that parameter based on the sample survey.

Survey Model: This is a judgmental model in which data are derived from a survey conducted by mail, telephone, or e-mail, which then become the basis of a forecast.

Syndicated Data: Point-of-Sale scanned data, purchased from retailers by companies such as AC Nielson and Information Resources, Inc. These companies syndicate the data after combining data of all stores, channels, geographies, as well as competitors. The data are scrubbed and standardized for ease of use for demand planning and forecasting efforts.

T

t-test: It is used in regression to determine whether a given independent variable's coefficient is significant or not. If not, remove that variable from the model. As a rule of thumb, the variable is considered significant if its value is 2 or higher.

Tactical Forecasts: Short- and mid-term forecasts used to drive production planning in the sales and operations planning process. They are usually developed at an aggregate (e.g., product group) level for a period of 12-18 months.

Take Away: It is referred to as sales to consumers.

Throughput: Productivity of a machine, procedure, or system over a fixed time; for example, output per hour.

Time Fence: Borderlines between different periods in the planning horizon, separating windows of time where planning restrictions may be employed to minimize costly disruptions in the supply chain. Some S&OP organizations' policies block forecast changes inside of some planning time fences, until supply feasibility has been considered.

Time Series Data: A collection of values observed sequentially over time. Sales data of a company over time are time series data.

Time Series Models: In these models, it is assumed that the past data pattern will continue in the future. Here, one needs only the data of a series to be forecasted. There are numerous time series models, including averages, exponential smoothing, and classical decomposition.

Top-Down Forecasting: Here, the forecast is first prepared at a higher level of aggregation and then disaggregated into lower levels of aggregation (e.g., categories and SKUs).

Tracking Signal: It is used to measure whether or not the basic pattern in the data has changed; if yes, the model has to be changed.

Transformation: Transforming the data from one form to another. It is often used in regression to improve a model. There are several ways to transform data, such as converting current dollars into constant dollars, calculating second order polynomial (X^2), and converting data into logarithms.

Trees: A method of analyzing data by splitting the data into different groups.

Trend: It is statistically computed, which shows, despite the ups and downs, sales on the average are moving upward or downward. It is also called secular trend.

U

Unconstrained Demand: Total amount of orders received irrespective of whether or not they could be be fulfilled. They are also called true demand.

Uniform Code Council (UCC): A non-profit organization that establishes and promotes standards for product identification manufactured by different companies and industries.

Univariate Models: This is where a forecaster needs only the data of a series to be forecasted. If we want to forecast sales, we will need only the data of sales. All time series models are univariate models.

Unstructured Data: Unstructured data is not well organized. Its files often include text in different languages and multimedia content such as e-mail messages, videos, photos, audio files, cell phone conversations, sensors, GPS signals and webpages. It is typically text-heavy, but may include dates, numbers and facts. It is difficult to store in traditional databases, or in a format that a computer can understand, process or analyze.

UPC (Universal Product Code): It is the standardized bar code used to identify a product at the cash register.

V

Validation: Used to determine whether a model is valid or not. There are different diagnostic tests available such as R^2, t-test, F-test, and ex post forecasts to make that determination.

Variable: An attribute or factor that can be observed. It can be an independent or dependent variable. For example, advertising affects sales. Here, sales are the dependent variable, and advertising is the independent variable.

Variance: It is a measure of variations from the mean in the data. It is the average of squared deviations from the mean, which is difficult to interpret; for that, standard deviation is often used as a measure of variations.

Vendor Managed Inventory Program (VMI): Under this program, it is the vendor or supplier who manages the inventory of a customer based on a set of rules, jointly agreed upon. The rules may be that the customer will not have inventory above a certain level, the vendor will maintain a certain fill rate, and so on.

Voluntary Inter-Industry Commerce Standards (VICS): A non-profit organization that focuses on improving product and information flow throughout the supply chain. It is responsible for establishing rules and guidelines for Collaborative Planning, Forecasting and Replenishment (CPFR®), when customer and supplier decide to work together.

W

Weighted Mean Absolute Percentage Error (WMAPE): It is a MAPE where errors are weighted by the sales volume. Its formula is:

$$\text{WMAPE} = \frac{\sum \frac{|A-F|}{A} \times 100 \times A}{\sum A}$$

Here: A = Actual, F = Forecast

Workbench: The workbench allows decision makers to access databases linked to a variety of analysis and modeling tools all within an interactive interface without having an issue of file format compatibility. It supports two types of information to be shared during S&OP meetings. One, the workbench generates dashboards that portray the planned supply versus "unconstrained" demand, as well as supply-side metrics (such as expected plant utilizations, production capacity shortages, and critical component shortages/surpluses) and demand-side metrics (such as expected unfulfilled customer demand and customer order backlogs). The dashboard functionality also allows S&OP participants to quickly conduct what-if analyses of potential changes in the supply and/or in the demand plans. Two, it provides information that is needed in the S&OP process to determine how well it is working. The workbench generates scorecards of Key Performance Indicators (KPIs) that reflect how well the S&OP process has worked over time.

Note: A number of people have contributed to this glossary to whom I am highly grateful, particularly, Mark Covas, Demand Planning Director at Johnson & Johnson, Consumer Products Division; Todd Dunn, Director of Supply Chain at Accucaps Industries Limited; Barry Keating, Professor of Economics and Business Analytics, Department of Finance, Notre Dame University; Larry Lapide, Lecturer at the University of Massachusetts, Boston and an MIT Research Affiliate; Mark Lawless, independent consultant; Alan Milliken, Senior Manager, GSB/SC Supply Chain Capability Development, BASF; Sara Park, Vice President, Planning and Logistics, Coca-Cola Refreshments; Andrew Schneider, Demand and S&OP Manager, Medtronic; Randy Willip, Leader of Global Commercial Forecasting; Merck & Co., Inc.; and Eric Wilson, Director of Demand Planning, Berry Plastics.

REFERENCES

1. Business and Economic Research Group, Executive Offices, 6275 Neil Road, Reno, Nevada 89511.
2. Consumer Goods Technology SourceBook 2001. **Glossary.**
3. Markrdakis, Spyros, Steven C. Wheelwright, and Rob J. Hyndman. *Forecasting Methods and Applications*. New York: John Wiley & Sons, 1998.
4. Vitasek, Kate. **Logistics Terms and Glossary.** Bellevue, Washington: Supply Chain Visions. Council of Logistic Management's Website.
5. Wilson, J. Holton, Barry Keating, and John Galt Solution. *Business Forecasting*. New York: McGraw Hill, 2007.

SUGGESTED READING FOR IBF CERTIFICATION

Suggested Reading for Certified Professional Forecaster (CPF)

CERTIFIED PROFESSIONAL FORECASTER (CPF) EXAMS 1, 2 & 3

EXAM 1

Chapter 1	Forecasting: What and Why
Chapter 2	Evolution in Forecasting
Chapter 3	Fundamentals of Demand Forecasting and Supply Planning
Chapter 4	Demand Planning
Chapter 5	Point-of-Sale-Based Demand Planning
Chapter 6	The Process
Chapter 7	Silo to Consensus Forecasting
Chapter 8	The Sales and Operations Planning Process
Chapter 9	Collaborative Planning, Forecasting and Replenishment
Chapter 10	Building Collaboration

EXAM 2

Chapter 11	What You Need to Know About Data
Chapter 12	Data Analysis and Treatment
Chapter 13	How Much Data to Use in Forecasting
Chapter 14	Fundamentals of Models and Modeling
Chapter 15	Averages
Chapter 16	Moving Averages
Chapter 17	Exponential Smoothing
Chapter 18	Trend Line
Chapter 19	Classical Decomposition
Chapter 20	Sales Ratios
Chapter 21	Family Member Forecasting
Chapter 26	Performance Metrics

EXAM 3

Chapter 27	Reporting, Presenting, and Selling Forecasts

Suggested Reading for Advanced Certified Professional Forecaster (ACPF)

ADVANCED CERTIFIED PROFESSIONAL FORECASTER (ACPF) EXAMS 4 & 5

EXAM 4

Chapter 22 Simple Regression Models
Chapter 23 Multiple Regression Models
Chapter 24 Box-Jenkins

EXAM 5

Chapter 28 Worst Practices in Demand Planning and Forecasting
Chapter 29 Forecasting Software Packages
Chapter 30 Forecasting Systems

EXAM 6 *Coming Soon!*

The Role of Artificial Intelligence in Demand Planning & Forecasting

APPENDICES

APPENDIX A

HOW TO COMPUTE COEFFICIENT OF CORRELATION AND STANDARD DEVIATION WITH MICROSOFT EXCEL 2007

To compute any statistical function, one needs "Data Analysis" as a selection in the Data Menu. If it is not there, follow these steps:

1. Click "Office" Button.
2. Click "Excel" Options.
3. Click "Add in."
4. Check "Analysis ToolPak."
5. Click "OK."

This will place "Data Analysis" as a selection in the Data menu.

COEFFICIENT OF CORRELATION

Once the "Data Analysis" menu is incorporated, follow these steps:

1. Click "Data" on the menu bar.
2. Click "Data Analysis."
3. Click Correlation.
4. In this menu you have to indicate the data you wish to use.
   i. In the "Input Range" indicate from where the X and Y values start and end.
   ii. In the "Output Range" indicate where you want the output to be written.
   iii. Click "OK."

STANDARD DEVIATION

Again, once the "Data Analysis" menu is incorporated, follow these steps:

1. Click "Data" on the menu bar.
2. Click "Data Analysis."
3. Click "Descriptive Statistics."
4. In the input range, plug in the data of which standard deviation has to be computed.
5. Indicate in the output range where output should appear.
6. Click "Summary Statistics."
7. Click "OK."

APPENDIX B

HOW TO COMPUTE A REGRESSION MODEL WITH MICROSOFT EXCEL 2007

We need a menu of "Data Analysis" to run regression. (To see how to create this menu, go to Appendix A.) Once the "Data Analysis" menu is incorporated, follow these steps:

1. Click "Data" on the menu bar.
2. Click "Data Analysis."
3. Click "Regression."
4. In this menu you have to indicate the data you wish to use.
    i. In the "Input Y Range," indicate from where the Y value starts and ends. (Here Y is the dependent variable.)
    ii. In the "Input X Range," indicate from where X value starts and ends. (Here X is the independent variable.)
    iii. In the "Output Range," indicate where you want the output to be written.
    iv. If you need any of the following information, click its box:
        a. Residual
        b. Standardized Residuals
        c. Residual Plot
        d. Line Fit Plot

APPENDIX C STUDENT'S t DISTRIBUTION

v \ P	.10	.05	.025	.01	.005
1	3.078	6.314	12.706	31.821	63.657
2	1.886	2.920	4.303	6.965	9.925
3	1.638	2.353	3.182	4.541	5.841
4	1.533	2.132	2.776	3.747	4.604
5	1.476	2.015	2.571	3.365	4.032
6	1.440	1.943	2.447	3.143	3.707
7	1.415	1.895	2.365	2.998	3.499
8	1.397	1.860	2.306	2.896	3.355
9	1.383	1.833	2.262	2.821	3.250
10	1.372	1.812	2.228	2.764	3.169
11	1.363	1.796	2.201	2.718	3.106
12	1.356	1.782	2.179	2.681	3.055
13	1.350	1.771	2.160	2.650	3.012
14	1.345	1.761	2.145	2.624	2.977
15	1.341	1.753	2.131	2.602	2.947
16	1.337	1.746	2.120	2.583	2.921
17	1.333	1.740	2.110	2.567	2.898
18	1.330	1.734	2.101	2.552	2.878
19	1.328	1.729	2.093	2.539	2.861
20	1.325	1.725	2.086	2.528	2.845
21	1.323	1.721	2.080	2.518	2.831
22	1.321	1.717	2.074	2.508	2.819
23	1.319	1.714	2.069	2.500	2.807
24	1.318	1.711	2.064	2.492	2.797
25	1.316	1.708	2.060	2.485	2.787
26	1.315	1.706	2.056	2.479	2.779
27	1.314	1.703	2.052	2.473	2.771
28	1.313	1.701	2.048	2.467	2.763
29	1.311	1.699	2.045	2.462	2.756
30	1.310	1.697	2.042	2.457	2.750
40	1.303	1.684	2.021	2.423	2.704
60	1.296	1.671	2.000	2.390	2.660
120	1.289	1.658	1.980	2.358	2.617
∞	1.282	1.645	1.960	2.326	2.576

Note: The first column lists the number of degrees of freedom (p). The headings of the other columns give probabilities (P) for t to exceed the entry value. Use symmetry for negative t values.

Source: Reprinted with permission from the publisher of P. B. Hoel, **Introduction to Mathematical Statistic**, 4th ed., New York, John Wiley & Sons, 1971, p. 393.

APPENDIX D F DISTRIBUTION FOR F TEST (5% Points for the Distribution of F)

Degree of Freedom for Denominator (v_2)	Degree of Free								
	1	2	3	4	5	6	7	8	9
1	161.4	199.50	215.70	224.60	230.20	234.00	236.80	238.90	240.
2	18.51	19.00	19.16	19.25	19.30	19.33	19.35	19.37	19.3
3	10.13	9.55	9.28	9.12	9.01	8.94	8.89	8.85	8.81
4	7.71	6.94	6.59	6.39	6.26	6.16	6.09	6.04	6.0
5	6.61	5.79	5.41	5.19	5.05	4.95	4.88	4.82	4.7
6	5.99	5.14	4.76	4.53	4.39	4.28	4.21	4.15	4.1
7	5.59	4.74	4.35	4.12	3.97	3.87	3.79	3.73	3.6
8	5.32	4.46	4.07	3.84	3.69	3.58	3.50	3.44	3.3
9	5.12	4.26	3.86	3.63	3.48	3.37	3.29	3.23	3.1
10	4.96	4.10	3.71	3.48	3.33	3.22	3.14	3.07	3.0
11	4.84	3.98	3.59	3.36	3.20	3.09	3.01	2.95	2.9
12	4.75	3.89	3.49	3.26	3.11	3.00	2.91	2.85	2.8
13	4.67	3.81	3.41	3.18	3.03	2.92	2.83	2.77	2.7
14	4.60	3.74	3.34	3.11	2.96	2.85	2.76	2.70	2.6
15	4.54	3.68	3.29	3.06	2.90	2.79	2.71	2.64	2.5
16	4.49	3.63	3.24	3.01	2.85	2.74	2.66	2.59	2.5
17	4.45	3.59	3.20	2.96	2.81	2.70	2.61	2.55	2.4
18	4.41	3.55	3.16	2.93	2.77	2.66	2.58	2.51	2.4
19	4.38	3.52	3.13	2.90	2.74	2.63	2.54	2.48	2.4
20	4.35	3.49	3.10	2.87	2.71	2.60	2.51	2.45	2.3
21	4.32	3.47	3.07	2.84	2.68	2.57	2.49	2.42	2.3
22	4.30	3.44	3.05	2.82	2.66	2.55	2.46	2.40	2.3
23	4.28	3.42	3.03	2.80	2.64	2.53	2.44	2.37	2.3
24	4.26	3.40	3.01	2.78	2.62	2.51	2.42	2.36	2.3
25	4.24	3.39	2.99	2.76	2.60	2.49	2.40	2.34	2.2
26	4.23	3.37	2.98	2.74	2.59	2.47	2.39	2.32	2.2
27	4.21	3.35	2.96	2.73	2.57	2.46	2.37	2.31	2.2
29	4.20	3.34	2.95	2.71	2.56	2.45	2.36	2.29	2.2
29	4.18	3.33	2.93	2.70	2.55	2.43	2.35	2.28	2.2
30	4.17	3.32	2.92	2.69	2.53	2.42	2.33	2.27	2.2
40	4.08	3.23	2.84	2.61	2.45	2.34	2.25	2.18	2.1
60	4.00	3.15	2.76	2.53	2.37	2.25	2.17	2.10	2.0
120	3.92	3.07	2.68	2.45	2.29	2.18	2.09	2.02	1.9
∞	3.84	3.00	2.60	2.37	2.21	2.10	2.01	1.94	1.8

Source: Printed with permission from the Biometrika Trustees, publisher of E.S. Pearson and H. O. Hartley. Tables for Statisticians. **Biometrika Tables For Statisticians.** Vol. 1, 3rd Edition. 1966, pp. 169-175.

Numerator (v_1)									
10	12	15	20	24	30	40	60	120	∞
41.90	243.90	245.90	248.0	249.10	250.10	251.10	252.20	253.30	254.30
19.40	19.41	19.43	19.45	19.45	19.46	19.47	19.48	19.49	19.50
8.79	8.74	8.70	8.66	8.64	8.62	8.59	8.57	8.55	8.53
5.96	5.91	5.86	5.80	5.77	5.75	5.72	5.69	5.66	5.63
4.74	4.68	4.62	4.56	4.53	4.50	4.46	4.43	4.40	4.37
4.06	4.00	3.94	3.87	3.84	3.81	3.77	3.74	3.70	3.67
3.64	3.57	3.51	3.44	3.41	3.38	3.34	3.30	3.27	3.23
3.35	3.28	3.22	3.15	3.12	3.08	3.04	3.01	2.97	2.93
3.14	3.07	3.01	2.94	2.90	2.86	2.83	2.79	2.75	2.71
2.98	2.91	2.85	2.77	2.74	2.70	2.66	2.62	2.58	2.54
2.85	2.79	2.72	2.65	2.61	2.57	2.53	2.49	2.45	2.40
2.75	2.69	2.62	2.54	2.51	2.47	2.43	2.38	2.34	2.30
2.67	2.60	2.53	2.46	2.42	2.38	2.34	2.30	2.25	2.21
2.60	2.53	2.46	2.39	2.35	2.31	2.27	2.22	2.18	2.13
2.54	2.48	2.40	2.33	2.29	2.25	2.20	2.16	2.11	2.07
2.49	2.42	2.35	2.28	2.24	2.19	2.15	2.11	2.06	2.01
2.45	2.38	2.31	2.23	2.19	2.15	2.10	2.06	2.01	1.96
2.41	2.34	2.27	2.19	2.15	2.11	2.06	2.02	1.97	1.92
2.38	2.31	2.23	2.16	2.11	2.07	2.03	1.98	1.93	1.88
2.35	2.28	2.20	2.12	2.08	2.04	1.99	1.95	1.90	1.84
2.32	2.25	2.18	2.10	2.05	2.01	1.96	1.92	1.87	1.81
2.30	2.23	2.15	2.07	2.03	1.98	1.94	1.89	1.84	1.78
2.27	2.20	2.13	2.05	2.01	1.96	1.91	1.86	1.81	1.76
2.25	2.18	2.11	2.03	1.98	1.94	1.89	1.84	1.79	1.73
2.24	2.16	2.09	2.01	1.96	1.92	1.87	1.82	1.77	1.71
2.22	2.15	2.07	1.99	1.95	1.90	1.85	1.80	1.75	1.69
2.20	2.13	2.06	1.97	1.93	1.88	1.84	1.79	1.73	1.67
2.19	2.12	2.04	1.96	1.91	1.87	1.82	1.77	1.71	1.65
2.18	2.10	2.03	1.94	1.90	1.85	1.81	1.75	1.70	1.64
2.16	2.09	2.01	1.93	1.89	1.84	1.79	1.74	1.68	1.62
2.08	2.00	1.92	1.84	1.79	1.74	1.69	1.64	1.58	1.51
1.99	1.92	1.84	1.75	1.70	1.65	1.59	1.53	1.47	1.39
1.91	1.83	1.75	1.66	1.61	1.55	1.50	1.43	1.35	1.25
1.83	1.75	1.67	1.57	1.52	1.46	1.39	1.32	1.22	1.00

INDEX